Exploring maths

Class Book

4

PEARSON
Longman

**Anita Straker, Tony Fisher, Rosalyn Hyde,
Sue Jennings and Jonathan Longstaffe**

Published and distributed by Pearson Education Limited, Edinburgh Gate, Harlow, Essex, CM20 2JE, England
www.longman.co.uk

First published 2008
Third impression 2008
ISBN-13 978-1-405-84414-7
Cover illustration by M.C. Escher

Freelance development editor: Sue Glover

Typeset by Tech-Set, Gateshead

Printed in China GCC/03

The publisher's policy is to use paper manufactured from sustainable forests.

Picture Credits
The publisher would like to thank the following for their kind permission to reproduce their photographs:
(Key: b-bottom; c-centre; l-left; r-right; t-top)

Alamy Images: Ace Stock Ltd 232; Bubbles Photolibrary 254b, 254t; Chris Stock Photography 121; Doug Houghton 140br; David J. Green 162; Jim Lane 44; Jeff Morgan education 126; Nick Hanna 140bc; North Wind Picture Archives 58l; Paul Gapper xi; stockfolio 157; thislife pictures 158; Rob Walls 278b; Tony Watson viit; **Ancient Art & Architecture:** 286; Ronald Sheridan 239t; **Bridgeman Art Library Ltd:** Bibliotheque de l'Institut de France, Paris, France, Alinari 238; Musee d'Art ed d'Histoire, Narbonne, France, Lauros/Giraudon 58r; **British Museum:** (c)The Trustees of the British Museum 288; **Corbis:** Don Mason 123t; Envision 211t; Gabe Palmer viiibl; Jeremy Horner 30l; Lawrence Manning viiibr; Patrick Robert/Sygma 239b; Serge Kozak/Zefa 228b; Stapleton Collection 146; **DK Images:** Andy Crawford 253; De Agostini Editore Picture Library 48; Gary Ombler viibl, viibr; Geoff Brightling 118t; Kim Sayer 123c; Nick Hewetson 219, 290; Paul Bricknell 118b; Tim Ridley 61; Steve Gorton 45, 101, 169b; xt; **Mary Evans Picture Library:** 177b; **Getty Images:** Bob Thomas/Stone 88t; Mason Morfit/Taxi 248; StockFood Creative/ Lew Robertson xb; **IOC Museums Collection © IOC :** 241; **iStockphoto:** vi, ixt, ixb, 35, 47, 52, 53, 57b, 57t, 81, 91, 102, 108, 109, 110, 119, 120, 122, 140bl, 142, 145, 166, 171, 176b, 176t, 177t, 203, 211b, 230, 231, 247b, 257, 258, 277, 278t, 280b, 330; David Chadwick xii; Jason Stitt xiiit; **Jupiter Unlimited:** BananaStock 169t; Brand X xiiib; **NASA:** 90; **Pearson Education Ltd:** 135, 140tc, 140tl, 140tr, 247tl, 247tr; Courtesy Dr. Michael Hadfield, Department of Zoology, University of Hawaii/Photo by Frank LaBua 30r; EMG Education Management Group 37, 280t; Pearson Learning Studio 7; Prentice Hall School Division 79; **PunchStock:** ImageSource 84; Stockbyte 123b; **Science Photo Library Ltd:** 11; Science Source 21; **The M.C Escher Company-Holland:** M.C Escher's Symmetry Drawing E55(c)2007 The M.C Escher Company-Holland. All rights reserved. www.mcescher.com 189; **www.statistics. gov.uk:** Crown Copyright material is reproduced with the permission of the Controller Office of Public Sector Information(OPSI) 224

Front Cover: The M.C Escher Company-Holland: M.C Escher's Symmetry Drawing E55(c)27 The M.C Escher Company-Holland. All rights reserved. www.mcescher.com

All other images © Pearson Education

Picture Research by: Louise Edgeworth

Every effort has been made to trace the copyright holders and we apologise in advance for any unintentional omissions. We would be pleased to insert the appropriate acknowledgement in any subsequent edition of this publication.

Contents

Tier
4

Functional Skills Activities

for any time of the year

Functional skills 1

Tiling patterns

This group activity will help you to:

- recognise that a situation can be represented using mathematics;
- choose how to model the situation;
- examine patterns and relationships;
- communicate results and solutions.

Background

Tiles can be cut to fit awkward corners. A tiler has to work out how best to lay tiles so that there is as little waste as possible.

For example, carpet tiles have to be cut to fit the shape of the floor. Wall tiles have to be cut to fit the size and shape of the wall, and paving stones have to be cut to fit the shape of the patio.

Problem 1

Paving a patio

Paving tiles are 30 cm square.

You have to tile a rectangular patio that measures 3.6 m by 4.8 m.

You have decided to buy tiles in two colours and to design a pattern.

a Create four different patterns for the patio.

For each pattern, work out how many of each tile you need to buy.

b The tiles are sold only in packs of 9 tiles. Which of your patterns is the cheapest?

Problem 2

Carpet tiles

You are having a makeover of your bedroom.

You are having new carpet tiles for the floor. They are a plain colour.

The carpet tiles are 30 cm square.

The floor is a rectangle measuring 400 cm by 200 cm.

Some of the tiles will have to be cut to fit.

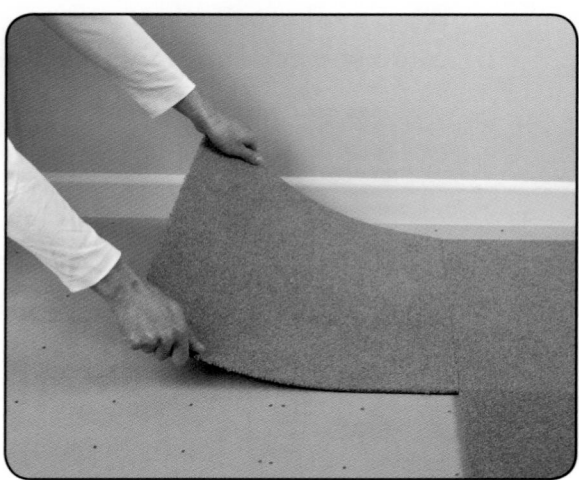

How many tiles will you need to buy so that there is as little waste as possible?

Be prepared to justify your conclusions to other groups.

Functional skills 2

Where is the mathematics?

This group activity will help you to:

- identify the mathematics in a situation;
- identify mathematical questions to ask;
- choose appropriate language and forms of presentation to communicate conclusions.

Background

Mathematics is all around us.

Looking for the maths in a situation or in information will help you to understand how widely maths is used.

Problem 1

What mathematical questions could you ask about this picture?

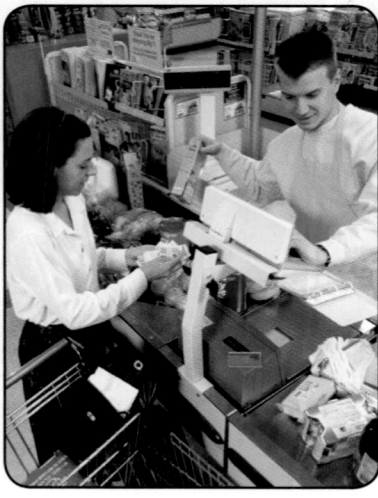

What answers would you give?

Problem 2

What mathematical questions could you ask about this picture?

What answers would you give?

Problem 3

What mathematical questions could you ask about this picture?

What answers to your questions would you give?

Problem 4

What mathematical questions could you ask about this picture?

What answers to your questions would you give?

Be prepared to discuss your questions and answers with other groups.

Functional skills 3

Making fudge

This group activity will help you to:

- make an initial model of a situation using suitable forms of representation;
- change values to see the effects on answers in the model;
- decide on the methods, operations and tools to use, including ICT;
- consider how appropriate and accurate your results and conclusions are.

Background information

Fudge is easy to make (though you have to take care with the hot mixture).

Here are the ingredients for making nine 250 g packs of fudge.

3 cans	*condensed milk*
350 g	*butter*
1.4 kg	*soft brown sugar*
450 ml	*fresh milk*

Say you make fudge to sell at a school fair or to take to a bring and buy sale.

If you are going to do this, you will want to make a profit.

This is what it might cost you to buy items in a supermarket.

397 g can condensed milk	£1.20
250 g butter	90p
1 kg soft brown sugar	£1.68
568 ml fresh milk	42p

The cost of making fudge

(1) Assume you make 9 packs of fudge.

    a What do you pay in total in the supermarket to buy enough of all the ingredients?

    b What do you pay to make 1 pack of fudge?

    c You can buy sugar only in an exact number of kilograms.
How much extra do you pay for the sugar you don't use?

(2) If you don't want to waste any sugar, how many packs of fudge would you need to make?

(3) Assume you make 72 packs of fudge.

    a How many cans of condensed milk do you need to buy?

    b How many 250 g packs of butter do you need to buy?

    c How many 1 kg bags of sugar do you need to buy?

    d How many 568 ml bottles of milk do you need to buy?

    e What do you pay in total in the supermarket to buy enough of all the ingredients?

    f What do you pay to make 1 pack of fudge?

    g Why is this answer different to the answer to 1b?

Making a profit

(1) A supermarket charges 99p for 221 g of its own brand of fudge.
Do you think that this is a fair price?
Give your reasons.

(2) Assume you want to sell fudge
at the school fair.

    a How many packs of fudge will you make?
What will you charge for 1 pack?

    b Given the cost of supermarket fudge,
do you think people will buy all your fudge?
Why?

    c How much profit will you make if you
sell all your fudge?

What other questions could you ask about making fudge?

Be prepared to present your arguments to other groups.

Functional skills 4

Choosing a mobile phone contract

This group activity will help you to:

- model a situation and change values to see the effects on answers;
- select the information, methods and tools to use, including ICT;
- interpret results and draw conclusions.

Background information

Most mobile phone networks have a vast range of tariffs, or plans. Spending time investigating the sort of deals you can get can save a fortune.

You need to know how much you use your mobile phone before you can choose the best plan for you.

Mobo Phone Company has two plans.

Plan A

The monthly charge for a mobile phone on **Plan A** is £15. This includes 75 minutes of free calls and 75 texts.

After that there is a charge of 12p per minute and 10p per text.

Plan B

The monthly charge for **Plan B** is £20. This includes 100 minutes of free calls and 300 texts.

After that there is a charge of 12p per minute and 10p per text.

Problems

Comparing the costs

1. Compare the costs of using Plan A and Plan B for 200 minutes talk and 100 texts in one month.

    Don't forget to include the contract cost.

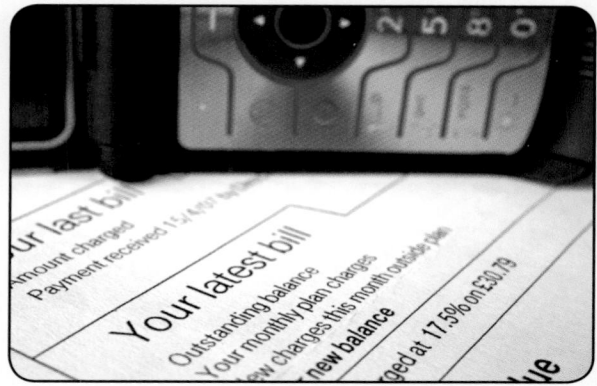

Choosing a contract

2. This chart shows Lucy's mobile phone usage over 4 months.

Month	Minutes of talk time	Number of texts
January	100	90
February	90	140
March	88	120
April	100	150

    Would Plan A or Plan B be better value for money for Lucy? Explain why.

Pay as you go

3. PAYG Plan Z costs 15p a minute for calls and 15p for texts.

    There is no monthly charge.

    Would Lucy be better off or worse off if she used PAYG Plan Z for January to March?

    By how much?

4. If you had to use one of Plan A, Plan B or PAYG Plan Z, which would you choose.

    Why?

Be prepared to present your findings and conclusions to other groups.

Properties of numbers

This unit will help you to:

- use the order of operations and brackets;
- add, subtract, multiply and divide positive and negative numbers;
- work with small positive powers, square roots and cube roots;
- recognise multiples, factors and primes;
- write a number as the product of its prime factors;
- use the function keys of a calculator for sign-change, brackets, powers and roots;
- solve problems involving properties of numbers.

1 Order of operations

This lesson will help you to calculate in the right order, including with a calculator.

We use a set of rules to tell us which operations to do first so that everyone gets the same answer.

- If brackets appear, work out the value of the expression in the brackets first.
- If there are no brackets, do multiplication and division before addition and subtraction, no matter where they come in an expression.

Example 1

$8 \times 2^2 - 10 \div 5$

First work out the square:	$8 \times 4 - 10 \div 5$
Then the division:	$8 \times 4 - 2$
Then the multiplication:	$32 - 2$
Then the subtraction:	30

Example 2

$(3 + 2)^2 \times 8 \div 5$

First work out the bracket:	$5^2 \times 8 \div 5$
Then the square:	$25 \times 8 \div 5$
Then the multiplication:	$200 \div 5$
Then the division:	40

Example 3

$27 \div [12 - (6 + 3)]$

First work out the inside bracket:	$27 \div [12 - 9]$
Then the outside bracket:	$27 \div 3$
Then the division:	9

Example 4

$30 - [24 \div (12 \div 3)]$

First work out the inside bracket:	$30 - [24 \div 4]$
Then the outside bracket:	$30 - 6$
Then the subtraction:	24

Exercise 1

1. Work out each of these calculations **in your head**.

   a $32 \div 4 + 4^2$

   b $32 \div (4 + 4)^2$

   c $2 \times 3 + 2^2$

   d $2 \times (3 + 2)^2$

   e $\sqrt{13^2 - 5^2}$

   f $150 \div [20 - (7 - 2)]$

   g $\dfrac{100}{2 \times 4}$

   h $\dfrac{90 - 30}{3 \times 5}$

   i $\dfrac{(20 - 15)^2}{4 \times 5}$

2. Put brackets in each expression to make it true.

   a $2 \times 9 - 1 = 16$

   b $5 + 3 \times 2 = 16$

   c $2 + 3 \times 1 + 4 = 25$

   d $3 + 7 \times 4 - 1 = 24$

   e $10 - 6 \times 3 \div 2 = 1$

   f $90 \div 20 - 13 - 2 = 10$

   g $5 \times 6 - 3 - 2 = 13$

   h $9 - 8 - 1 \times 8 = 16$

You can find the value of $(3 + 4) \times 2$ with these calculator key presses:

$$(\quad 3 \quad + \quad 4 \quad) \quad \times \quad 2 \quad =$$

---

3. Do these calculations **using your calculator**.

   a $5.6 - (4.89 - 3.7)$

   b $1.44 \div (0.6 - 0.48)$

   c $(9.5 + 3.17) \times 3.3$

   d $(20.5 - 4.16) \div 2$

   e $(8.3 + 4.05) \div (1.2 - 0.7)$

   f $(88.6 + 23.4) \div 3.5 + 10.2$

   g $(25.6 + 4.9) \times (6.25 - 3.75)$

4. Each red circle represents a missing operation ($+$, $-$, $\times$ or $\div$).
   Copy and complete these equations. **Use your calculator** to help you.

   a $(37 \bullet 21) \bullet 223 = 1000$

   b $(756 \bullet 18) \bullet 29 = 1218$

   c $27 \bullet (36 \bullet 18) = 675$

   d $31 \bullet (87 \bullet 19) = 2108$

   e $(486 \bullet 18) \bullet 15 = 12$

   f $(56 \bullet 63) \bullet 49 = 72$

   g $837 \bullet (46 \bullet 12) = 285$

   h $52 \bullet (96 \bullet 16) = 5824$

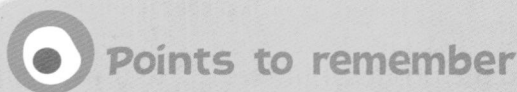

Points to remember

⊙ Deal with brackets first. When there are no brackets, multiply and
divide before you add and subtract.

2 Adding and subtracting directed numbers

This lesson will help you to add and subtract positive and negative numbers.

 Did you know that...?

The Indian mathematician
Brahmagupta (598–668) was
the first to extend arithmetic
to negative numbers and zero.
He described rules for addition
and subtraction.

A **directed number** is a number together with a + or a − sign. Examples are:

$$+5 \qquad -9 \qquad +6.2 \qquad -230$$

Directed numbers can also be shown on a number line.

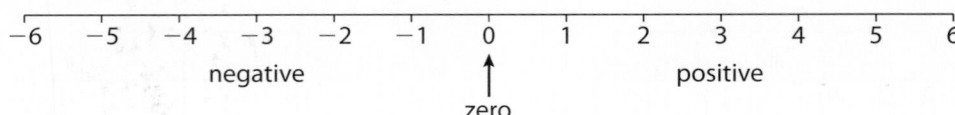

Numbers to the right of 0 are called **positive numbers**.
Numbers to the left of 0 are called **negative numbers**.

When you add or subtract directed numbers, it is useful to put them in brackets but they can
also be written without.

Addition

The sum $(-3) + (+2)$ means add the positive number $+2$ to the negative number -3, or 'start at -3', followed by 'move right 2'. The answer is -1.

The sum $(-4) + (-6)$ means 'start at -4' followed by 'move left 6'. The answer is -10.

Subtraction

Subtracting any number from itself always gives the answer 0.

So: $(+5) - (+5) = 0$

Compare this with the addition: $(+5) + (-5) = 0$

So subtracting $(+5)$ is the same as adding (-5).

Also subtracting -5 from itself gives 0: $(-5) - (-5) = 0$

Compare this with the addition: $(-5) + (+5) = 0$

So subtracting (-5) is the same as adding $(+5)$.

Example 1

Work out $(-6) + (-5)$.

Start at -6 and move left 5. You finish on -11.

Example 2

Work out $(+5) - (-7)$.

Subtracting -7 is the same as adding $+7$.

So $(+5) - (-7) = (+5) + (+7)$

Start at $+5$ and move right 7. You finish on 12.

Exercise 2

1. As you go up the pyramid, subtract the number on the right from the number on the left to get the number immediately above.

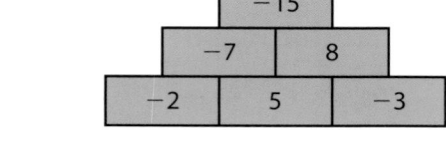

Copy and complete these pyramids.

a

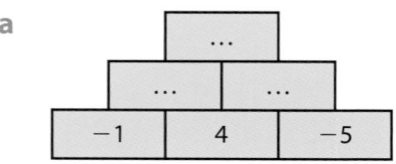

b

c

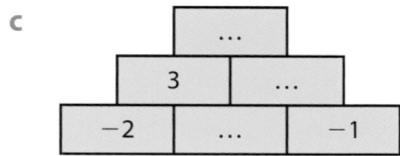

d

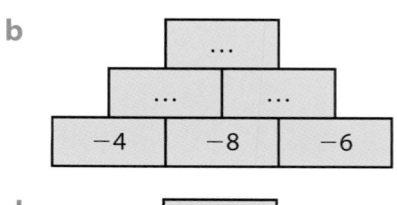

2 In a magic square, the numbers in any row, column or diagonal add up to the same total.
Copy and complete each of these magic squares.

a

−5		0
3		
−4		

b

−4	−3	−8
−2		

c

3			−9
−7		−4	
	1	−3	
0		−1	−6

3 Choose numbers to go in the boxes from the set of numbers on the cards.
Copy and complete each equation.

a $2 + (−5) + \square = 4$

b $(−3) − \square − 8 = −3$

c $7 − \square + (−8) = 1$

d $\square + 6 − (−3) = 4$

e $\square + 7 + \square = 0$

f $12 − \square − \square = 0$

g $3 + \square + \square = 2$

h $\square − \square + \square = −1$

3	0	−5	9
2	−8	7	−2

Choose the number to give the **lowest** possible answer.

i $(−2) + \square = \ldots$

j $(−2) − \square = \ldots$

Choose the number to give the **highest** possible answer.

k $(−1) − \square = \ldots$

l $\square − 4 = \ldots$

Extension problem

4 The letters A to I stand for these numbers, but not in this order:

$$−5, \ −4, \ −2, \ −1, \ 0, \ 1, \ 2, \ 5, \ 7$$

The sum of the three numbers in each circle is zero.

Which letter stands for which number?

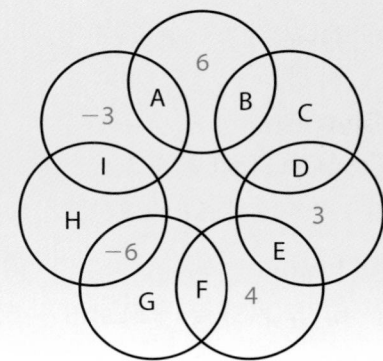

Points to remember

⊙ When you are adding or subtracting positive and negative numbers, two signs together can be regarded as one sign:
+ + is **+**   **+ −** is **−**   **− +** is **−**   **− −** is **+**
Two signs that are the same can be regarded as **+**.
Two signs that are different can be regarded as **−**.
Examples: $5 + (−3) = 2$ $9 − (−4) = 13$ $6 − (+2) = 4$

3 Multiplying and dividing directed numbers

This lesson will help you to multiply and divide positive and negative numbers.

Multiplication

You know that $2 + 2 + 2 = 2 \times 3 = 6$.
Similarly, $(-2) + (-2) + (-2) = (-2) \times 3 = -6$.
You can also write this as $3 \times (-2) = 6$.

Look at the patterns in the table on the right.
The left-hand column is decreasing by 1 and
the right-hand column is increasing by 2.

$$(+3) \times (-2) = -6$$
$$(+2) \times (-2) = -4$$
$$(+1) \times (-2) = -2$$
$$(0) \times (-2) = 0$$

Use the patterns to continue the table.

$$(-1) \times (-2) = +2$$
$$(-2) \times (-2) = +4$$
$$(-3) \times (-2) = +6$$

From the patterns you can see that:
positive $\times$ positive $=$ positive
positive $\times$ negative $=$ negative
negative $\times$ positive $=$ negative
negative $\times$ negative $=$ positive

Division

From the fact $3 \times 2 = 6$, write down two related facts:
$6 \div 3 = 2$ and $6 \div 2 = 3$

So from the fact $(+3) \times (-2) = (-6)$, write down two related facts:
$(-6) \div (+3) = (-2)$ and $(-6) \div (-2) = (+3)$

And from the fact $(-3) \times (-2) = (+6)$, write down two related facts:
$(+6) \div (-3) = (-2)$ and $(+6) \div (-2) = (-3)$
From the patterns you can see that:
positive $\div$ positive $=$ positive
positive $\div$ negative $=$ negative
negative $\div$ positive $=$ negative
negative $\div$ negative $=$ positive

When you multiply or divide two directed numbers, remember that:
☺ if the signs are the **same**, the answer is **positive**;
☺ if the signs are **different**, the answer is **negative**.

Example 1
Work out $(+5) \times (-3)$.
The signs are different so the answer is negative, so $(+5) \times (-3) = -15$.

Example 2
Work out $(-18) \div (-2)$.
The signs are the same so the answer is positive, so $(-18) \div (-2) = 9$.

Exercise 3

1 Copy and complete this table.

A	B
3	−6
−15	−3
−8	−2
...	...

A + B	A − B	A × B	A ÷ B
...	...	...	...
...	...	...	...
...	...	...	...
−1	−5	...	...

2 Work out the answer to each of these.

a $72 \div (-3)$ b $(-25) \div (-5)$ c $(-22) \div 11$

d $(-36) \div (-3)$ e $48 \div (-4)$ f $(-5) \div 2$

g $(-12) \times (-3) \times (-2)$ h $(-10) \times 4 \times (-5)$ i $(-12) \times (-3) \div (-6)$

3 In a history quiz, the contestants win
3 points for a right answer.
They lose 2 points for a wrong answer.
What is the final score for these answers?

a   12 right and 8 wrong answers
b   7 right and 12 wrong answers
c   4 right and 14 wrong answers

Three contestants scored 14 points.
d   Ruth gave 5 wrong answers. How many questions did she answer correctly?
e   Nasreen gave 10 right answers. How many questions did she get wrong?
f   James got the same number of right and wrong answers.
How many questions did he answer?

4 Put brackets in each of these expressions to make them true.

a $2 \times (-5) + 4 = -2$ b $(-2) + (-6) \times 3 = -24$

c $9 - 7 - 4 = 6$ d $(-3) \times (-4) - 6 = 6$

e $8 - (-2) \div (-5) = -2$ f $14 - 6 - 7 = 15$

⑤ Emily's grandfather prefers to use the Fahrenheit scale for temperatures.
Emily knows a formula to change degrees Celsius (C) to degrees Fahrenheit (F):
$F = 1.8 \times C + 32$
Use Emily's formula to change these temperatures to Fahrenheit (°F).

a $-10°C$ b $-2°C$ c $20°C$ d $-5°C$ c $-40°C$

Extension problem

⑥ Work out the answer to each of these.

a $32 \div (-8) + (-4)^2$ b $(-27) \div [(-7) + 4]^2$ c $15 + 2 \times (-3)$

d $7 \times [(-9) + 4]^2$ e $22 - (-5)^2$ f $[(-4) + 6]^2 \times -2$

g $\dfrac{-100}{(-2) \times (-5)}$ h $\dfrac{(-90) + 30}{3 \times (-5)}$ i $\dfrac{[(-15) + 7]^2}{(3 - 5) \times (-4)^2}$

⦿ Points to remember

⦿ For addition or subtraction of directed numbers, two signs
together can be regarded as one sign:

$+ +$ is $+$ $+ -$ is $-$ $- +$ is $-$ $- -$ is $+$

⦿ For multiplication or division of directed numbers, two signs that
are the same result in $+$ and two signs that are different result in
$-$.

$+ \times +$ is $+$ $+ \times -$ is $-$ $- \times +$ is $-$ $- \times -$ is $+$

4 Powers and roots

This lesson will help you to work with powers, square roots and cube roots and solve problems
involving properties of numbers.

The square of a number n is n^2 or $n \times n$.

Examples: $9^2 = 9 \times 9 = 81, (-9)^2 = -9 \times -9 = 81$

You can find the value of 5^2 by pressing these calculator keys: $\boxed{5}\,\boxed{x^2}\,\boxed{=}$. Answer: 25.

The **square root** of n is $\sqrt{n}$. There are two square roots, one positive and one negative.

Example: $\sqrt{81} = \pm 9$

You usually find the square root of 81 by pressing these calculator keys: $\boxed{\sqrt{}}\,\boxed{8}\,\boxed{1}\,\boxed{=}$.

On some calculators you press the square root key last like this: $\boxed{8}\,\boxed{1}\,\boxed{\sqrt{}}$.

The **cube** of a number n is n^3 or $n \times n \times n$.

Example: $5^3 = 5 \times 5 \times 5 = 125, (-5)^3 = -5 \times -5 \times -5 = -125$

The **cube root** of n is $\sqrt[3]{n}$.

Example: $\sqrt[3]{125} = 5$

Some calculators have a cube root key $\boxed{\sqrt[3]{}}$, which works like the square root key.

The short way to write $2 \times 2 \times 2 \times 2 \times 2$ is as 2^5. The small number 5 is a **power**.

The calculator key to find powers of numbers is usually like this: $\boxed{x^y}$ or $\boxed{y^x}$ or $\boxed{\wedge}$.

Example: To find the value of 6^4, key in $\boxed{6}\,\boxed{y^x}\,\boxed{4}$. Answer: 1296

Calculator keys for finding roots vary. Find out how to use your calculator to find a root.

Exercise 4

1. **Without using your calculator**, work out:

   a 13^2 b 4^4 c 2^7 d 11^3

You may **use your calculator** for the rest of this exercise.
Where appropriate, give your answer correct to one decimal place.

2. Work these out.

   a 6^4 b 7^6 c 9^4 d 3^{11}

   e $(-2)^{12}$ f 1.7^6 g 24.2^3 h $2.78^4 + 9.76^4$

3. Work these out.

   a $\sqrt[2]{3136}$ b $\sqrt[4]{6561}$ c $\sqrt[5]{59\,049}$ d $\sqrt[3]{6859}$

   e $\sqrt[3]{13\,824}$ f $\sqrt[8]{256}$ g $\sqrt[4]{5643}$ h $\sqrt[3]{76}$

4. Some numbers can be written as the sum of two square numbers, e.g.

   $$34 = 3^2 + 5^2$$

   Write each of these numbers as the sum of two squares.

   a 80   b 61   c 104   d 145

(5) Write each of these numbers as the difference of two squares.

   a 16   b 40   c 144   d 77

(6) Solve these puzzles.

   a I am a two-digit square number.
      I am 17 more than the previous square number. Who am I?

   b I am a two-digit multiple of 11.
      The product of my two digits is both a cube and a square. Who am I?

   c I am a two-digit cube number.
      When you exchange my digits the number formed is the product of a cube and a square.
      Who am I?

   d I am a three-digit cube number.
      When you rearrange my digits you get a smaller cube number. Who am I?

   e I am a three-digit cube number that is also a square. Who am I?

Extension problem

(7) Copy and complete this cross-number puzzle.

Across	Down
2 $2^4 \times 3^2$	1 7 times 7 across
4 A multiple of 7	2 $\sqrt{121}$
5 5 times 2 down	3 5 across minus 10
7 $3^2 + (-5)^2 + 2^3$	6 Double 1 down
9 $4^3 - 6^2$	8 $7^2 - 5^2$
10 One quarter of 6 down	9 3^3

◉ Points to remember

⊙ When a negative number is raised to an even power, the result
is positive.

⊙ When a negative number is raised to an odd power, the result
is negative.

5 Multiples, factors and primes

This lesson will help you to write a number as the product of its prime factors and to solve problems involving multiples, factors and primes.

 Did you know that...?

Euclid (c. 325–265 BCE) was a Greek mathematician who taught in Alexandria in Egypt about 300 BCE.

Euclid proved that there are infinitely many prime numbers.

He also proved what is called the Fundamental Theorem of Arithmetic. This showed that every integer can be written as a product of prime factors.

You can use a **division method** to find the prime factors of a number.
The prime factors of 75 are $5 \times 5 \times 3 = 5^2 \times 3$.

$$
\begin{array}{r} 3)\overline{75} \\ 5)\overline{25} \\ 5)\overline{5} \\ 1 \end{array}
\qquad
\begin{array}{r} 3)\overline{24} \\ 2)\overline{8} \\ 2)\overline{4} \\ 2)\overline{2} \\ 1 \end{array}
$$

The prime factors of 24 are $3 \times 2 \times 2 \times 2 = 3 \times 2^3$.

You can use a **tree method** to find the prime factors of a number.
The prime factors of 48 are $2 \times 2 \times 2 \times 2 \times 3 = 2^4 \times 3$.

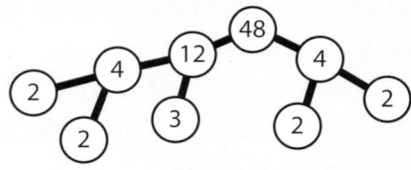

The prime factors of 200 are $5 \times 5 \times 2 \times 2 \times 2 = 5^2 \times 2^3$.

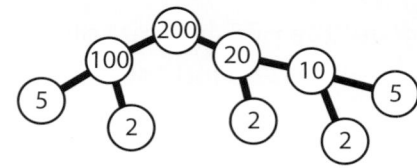

You can use prime factors to find the highest common factor (HCF) and the lowest common multiple (LCM) of two numbers.

Example

Find the HCF and LCM of 60 and 72.

The prime factors of 72 are $2 \times 2 \times 2 \times 2 \times 3$.
The prime factors of 60 are $5 \times 3 \times 2 \times 2$.
Put these on a Venn diagram.
The overlapping or common prime factors give the HCF
($2 \times 2 \times 3 = 2^2 \times 3 = 12$).
All the prime factors give the LCM ($2 \times 2 \times 2 \times 3 \times 3 \times 5 = 2^3 \times 3^2 \times 5 = 180$).

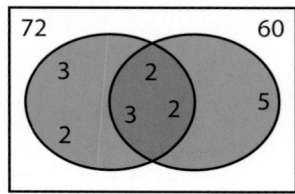

Exercise 5

1 Use a division method to find the prime factors of:
   a 36   **b** 140   **c** 128
   d 250   **e** 480   **f** 408

2 Use a tree method to find the prime factors of:
   a 28   **b** 72   **c** 180
   d 264   **e** 735   **f** 1656

3 Using the diagrams below, work out the HCF and LCM of:
   a 40 and 90   **b** 48 and 42

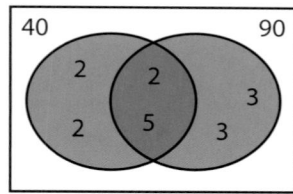   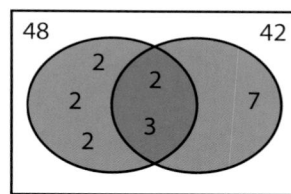

4 **a** The prime factors of 60 are 2, 2, 3, 5. The prime factors of 150 are 2, 3, 5, 5.
      Put these numbers into a Venn diagram.
      Use the diagram to work out the HCF and LCM of 60 and 150.
   b The prime factors of 126 are 2, 3, 3, 7. The prime factors of 210 are 2, 3, 5, 7.
      Put these numbers into a Venn diagram.
      Use the diagram to work out the HCF and LCM of 126 and 210.

5 Use prime factors to work out the HCF and LCM of:
   a 175 and 200   **b** 112 and 140   **c** 42 and 105

6 **a** Find two consecutive numbers with a product of 5700.
   b Find three prime numbers with a product of 7511.
   c Find three consecutive odd numbers with a product of 29 667.

Extension problems

 How many zeros are there at the end of the product of the numbers 1 to 10?

$$1 \times 2 \times 3 \times 4 \times 5 \times 6 \times 7 \times 8 \times 9 \times 10$$

How many zeros are there at the end of the product of the numbers 1 to 20?

$$1 \times 2 \times 3 \times 4 \times 5 \times 6 \times \ldots \times 17 \times 18 \times 19 \times 20$$

Explain why.

 Write 1 000 000 as the product of two factors, neither of which ends in a zero.

 Points to remember

⊙ Writing a number as the product of its prime factors is called the **prime factor decomposition** of the number.
Example: $24 = 2 \times 2 \times 2 \times 3$ or $2^3 \times 3$.

⊙ To find the **highest common factor (HCF)** of a pair of numbers, find the product of all the prime factors common to both numbers.
Example: 8 has prime factors $2 \times 2 \times 2$ and 12 has prime factors $2 \times 2 \times 3$. The highest common factor is 2×2.

⊙ To find the **lowest common multiple (LCM)** of a pair of numbers, find the smallest number that is a multiple of each of the numbers.

Example: 8 has prime factors $2 \times 2 \times 2$ and 12 has prime factors $2 \times 2 \times 3$.
The lowest common multiple of 8 and 12 is $2 \times 2 \times 2 \times 3 = 24$.

How well are you doing?

Properties of numbers (no calculator)

1. Here is a list of numbers:

$$-8 \quad -5 \quad -2 \quad -1 \quad 1 \quad 3 \quad 6$$

   a Choose two numbers from the list that have a total of 1.
   b Choose two numbers from the list that have a difference of -6.
   c Choose two numbers from the list that have a product of 5.
   d Choose two numbers from the list that have a quotient of -3.

2. Write two square numbers with a sum of 100.

3. What is the last digit of 24^3?

4. The three numbers missing from the boxes are all prime numbers bigger than 3.

$$\square \times \square \times \square = 455$$

   What are the missing prime numbers?

5. This three-digit number has 9 and 5 as factors:

$$495$$

   Write another number between 400 and 500 that has 9 and 5 as factors.

Angles and shapes

This unit will help you to:

- ◉ use diagrams and correct notation to solve geometrical problems;
- ◉ decide what information will help to solve a problem;
- ◉ work logically to explain why a statement is true;
- ◉ identify equal angles formed by parallel lines and a transversal;
- ◉ understand and use a proof that the angle sum of a triangle is 180°;
- ◉ understand congruence;
- ◉ recognise the properties of quadrilaterals.

1 Corresponding angles

This lesson will help you to solve problems involving corresponding angles formed by a pair of parallel straight lines and a transversal.

The marked angles are called **corresponding angles**.

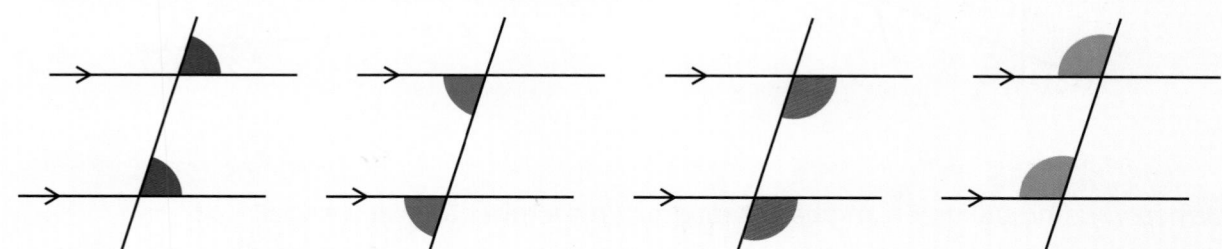

Corresponding angles are formed when a transversal cuts a pair of parallel straight lines. Corresponding angles are equal.

Corresponding angles can be used to solve problems.

Example

The diagram shows a pair of parallel straight lines cut by a transversal. Find the size of angles a and b.

Angle $a = 35°$ (corresponding angles)

Angle $b = 145°$ (angles on a straight line)

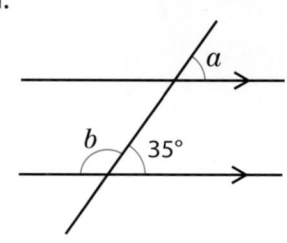

Exercise 1

1 In each diagram, a pair of parallel straight lines is cut by a transversal.
Find the size of each angle marked by a letter. Give your reasons.

a

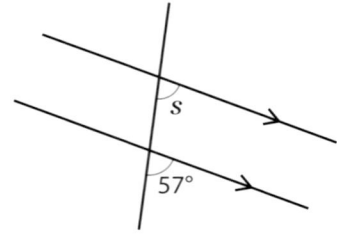

b

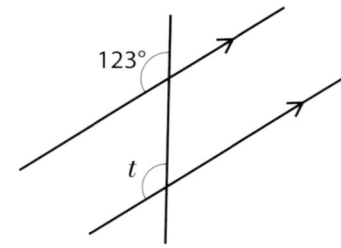

c

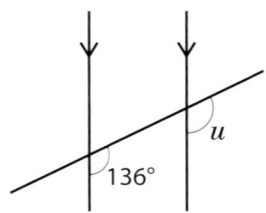

d

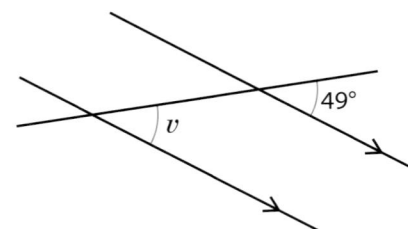

2 In each diagram, a pair of parallel straight lines is cut by two transversals.
Calculate the size of each angle marked by a letter. Give your reasons.

a

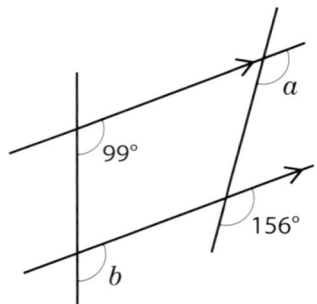

b

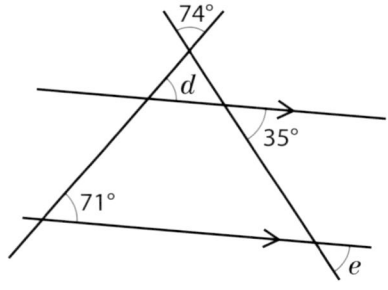

When you find unknown angles in a diagram, remember to give your reasons.

Example

In this diagram, a pair of parallel straight lines is cut by a transversal.
Find the sizes of all the other angles, giving your reasons.

$a = 45°$ (vertically opposite angles)

$b = 135°$ (angles on a straight line)

$c = 135°$ (angles on a straight line)

$d = 45°$ (corresponding angles)

$e = 45°$ (vertically opposite angles)

$f = 135°$ (angles on a straight line)

$g = 135°$ (angles on a straight line)

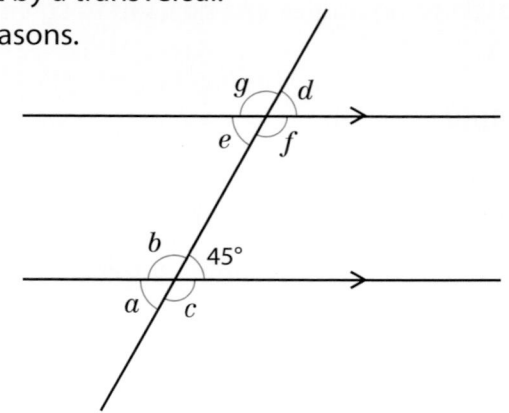

③ Each diagram shows a pair of parallel straight lines cut by a transversal.
Find the value of each letter. Give your reasons.

a

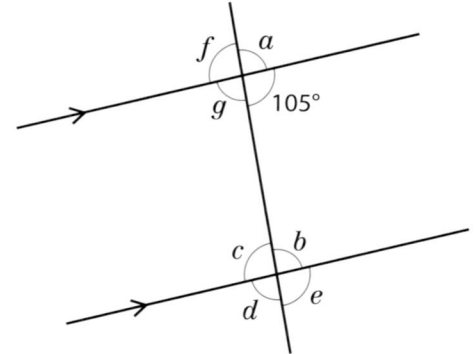

b

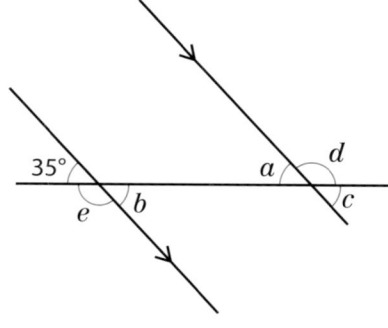

④ The diagram shows two pairs of intersecting parallel straight lines.
Write down which angles are equal.
Give your reasons.

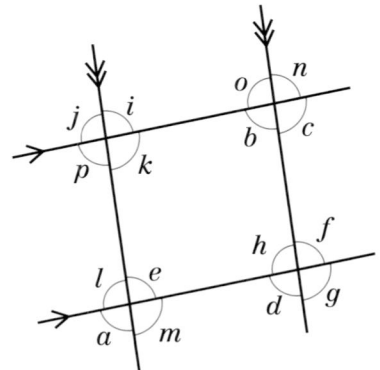

⑤ The diagram shows a pair of parallel straight lines cut by two transversals.
Find the size of each angle marked by a letter.
Give your reasons.

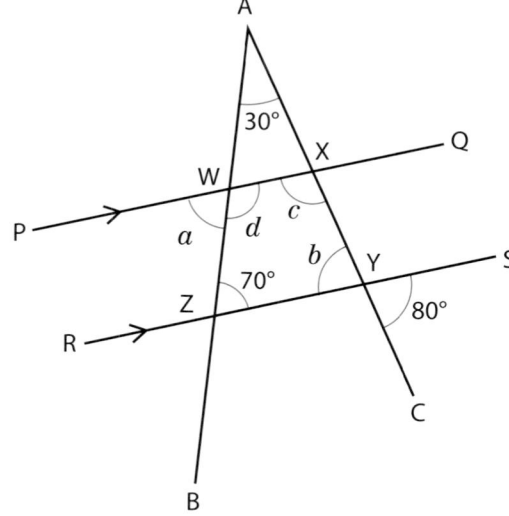

2 Alternate angles

This lesson will help you to solve problems involving alternate angles formed by a pair of parallel straight lines and a transversal.

The marked angles are called **alternate angles**.

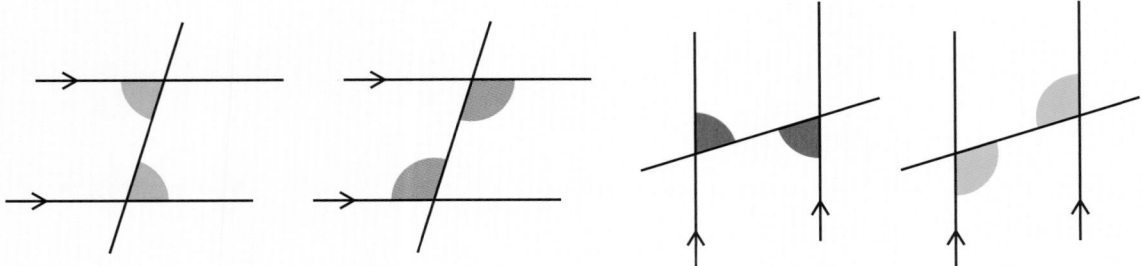

Alternate angles are formed when a transversal cuts a pair of parallel straight lines.
Alternate angles are equal.

Alternate angles can be used to solve problems.

Example

Each diagram shows a pair of parallel straight lines cut by a transversal.

a Find the value of a and b.

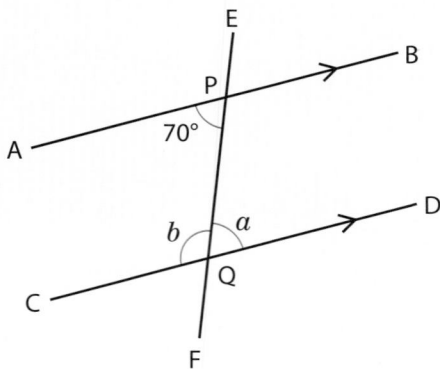

$a = 70°$ (alternate angles)
$b = 180° - 70° = 110°$
    (angles on a line add to 180°)

b Find the value of c, d and e.

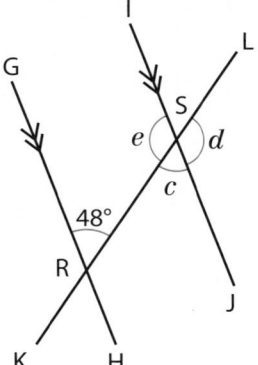

$c = 48°$ (alternate angles)
$d = 180° - 48° = 132°$
    (angles on a line add to 180°)
$e = 132°$ (vertically opposite angles)

Exercise 2

1 Find the size of the angle marked by each letter.

a

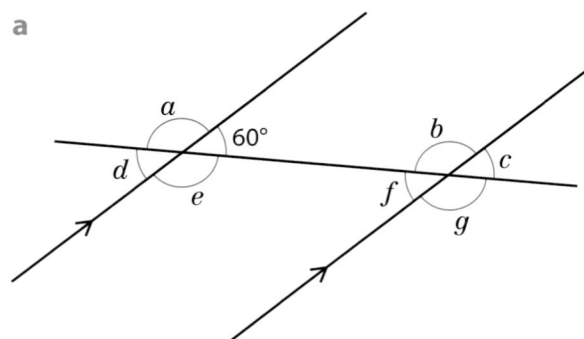

b

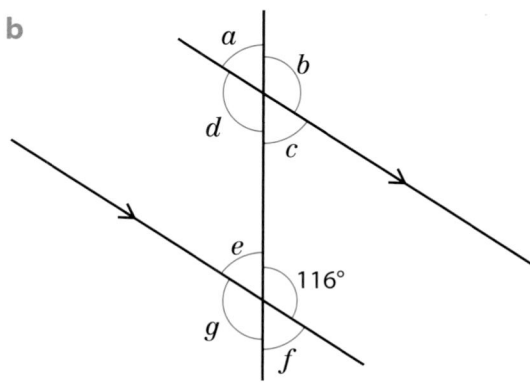

2 The diagram shows a pair of parallel straight lines cut by a transversal. State which angles are equal.

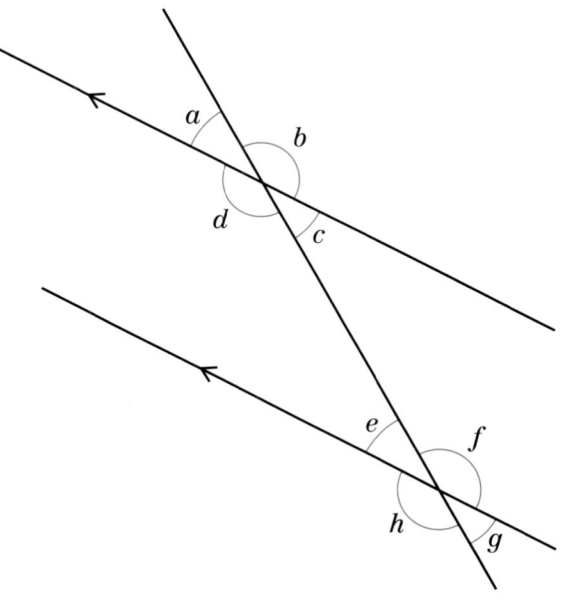

3 In the diagram, two pairs of parallel straight lines are cut by the same transversal. Find the value of each letter.

Give your reasons, choosing from:
angles on a straight line
angles at a point
vertically opposite angles
alternate angles.

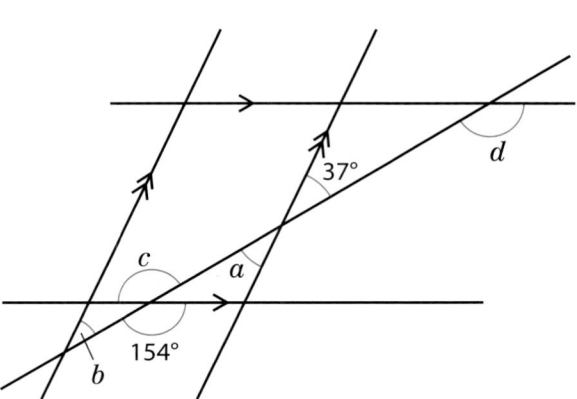

4 Each diagram shows a pair of parallel straight lines cut by a transversal. Find the size of the angle marked by each letter. Give your reasons.

a

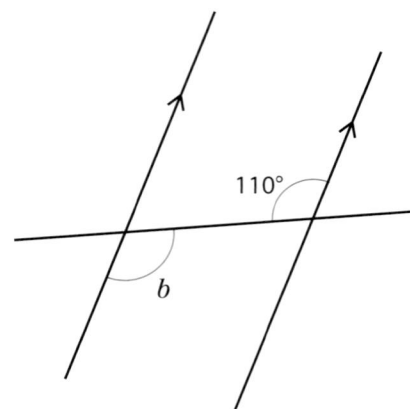

110°

b

b

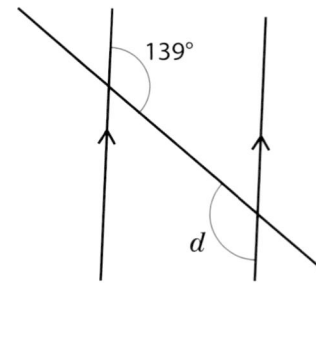

139°

d

5 In each diagram, a pair of parallel straight lines is cut by a transversal. Find the size of the angle marked by each letter. Give your reasons.

a

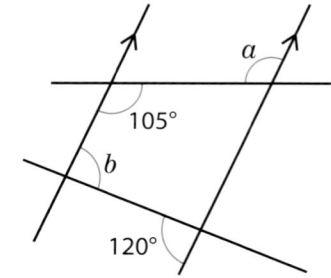

a

105°

b

120°

b

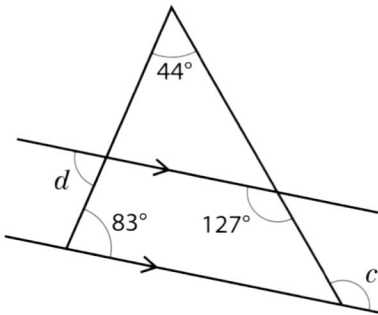

44°

d

83°   127°

c

6 Are lines AB and CD parallel? Explain your answer.

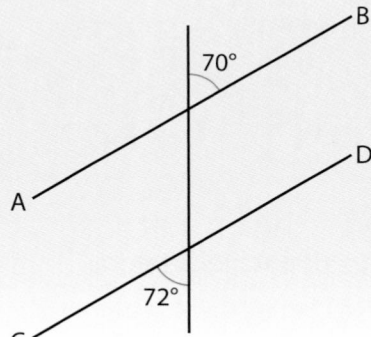

B

70°

D

A

72°

C

⊙ Points to remember

- ⊙ **Alternate angles** are formed when a transversal cuts a pair of parallel straight lines. Alternate angles are equal.
- ⊙ When you calculate angles, always include your reasons.
- ⊙ You may need to work out other angles along the way.
- ⊙ Draw diagrams neatly.

3 Angles in a triangle and a quadrilateral

This lesson will help you to solve problems involving angles in a triangle and in a quadrilateral.

 Did you know that...?

The Greek mathematician **Euclid (c. 325–265 BCE)**, mentioned in Unit N4.1 for his work on prime numbers, is also famous for his work on geometry. He developed his work in a series of 13 books called *Elements of geometry*.

In the *Elements*, Euclid defined the meaning of a *point*, a *straight line* and a *plane*. He also wrote about five ideas around which all Euclidean geometry is based.

Here is an example of a problem in Euclidean geometry.

Example

The diagram shows two pairs of parallel straight lines.
A transversal cuts one pair of the parallel lines.
Calculate angles MOP, MNP and AKE.

Angle MOP = 75° (alternate angles)
Angle KLG = 120° (angles on a straight line)
Angle MNP = 120° (corresponding angles)
Angle AKE = 120° (corresponding angles)

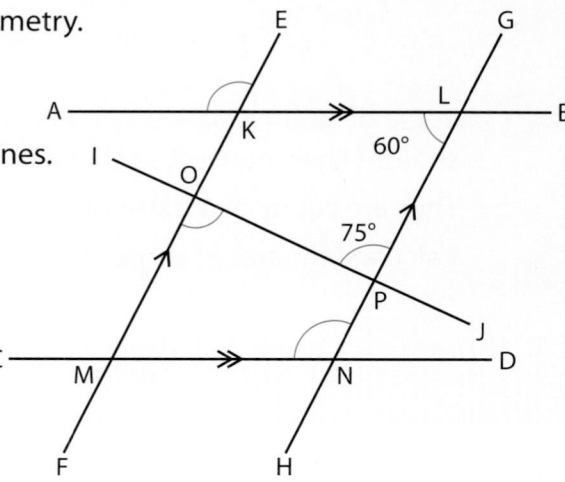

Exercise 3

Copy each diagram and work out the sizes of the unknown angles.
Remember to give your reasons.

1. In the diagram, ABCD is a rectangle.
   Find the size of angle *f*.

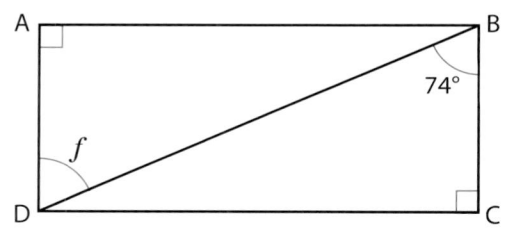

2 The diagram shows two pairs of parallel straight lines intersecting at right angles.

There are two transversals.

Find the sizes of angles a and b.

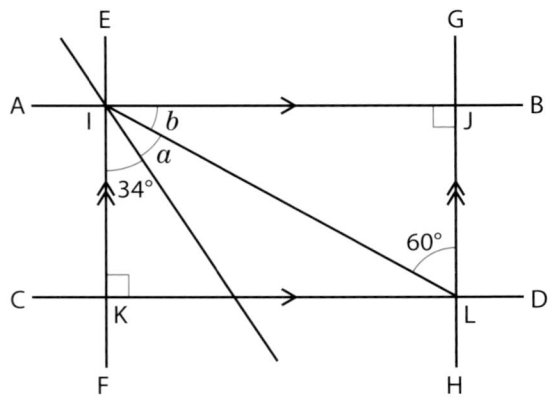

3 The diagram shows a pair of parallel straight lines cut by two transversals.

Find the sizes of angles m and n.

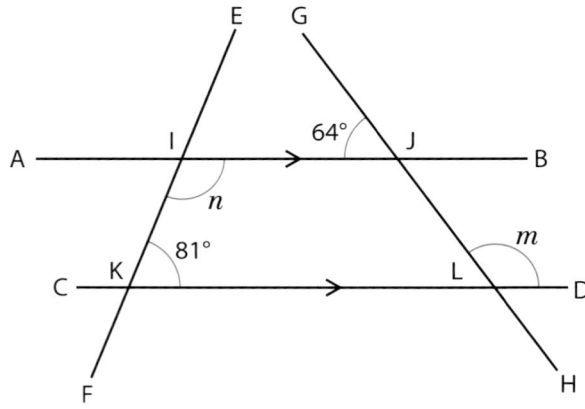

4 In the diagram, two sets of parallel straight lines intersect as shown.

They are cut by two transversals.

Calculate the size of angle PQR.

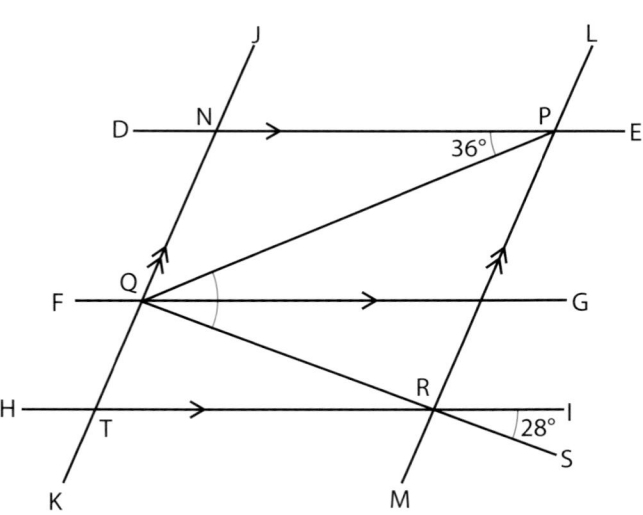

5 Calculate the size of angle z.

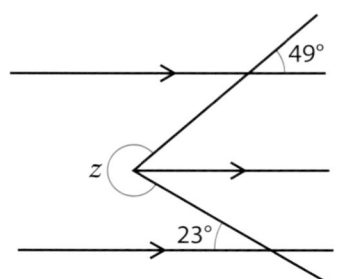

Extension problem

6 Angle a is 5 times the size of angle b.
Find the size of angle c.

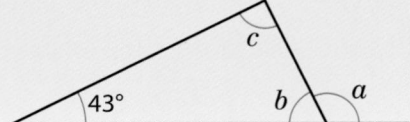

4 Understanding congruence

This lesson will help you to understand congruence and recognise the properties of quadrilaterals.

Shapes are called **congruent** if they are exactly the same shape and size.

In 2D congruent shapes, corresponding angles are equal and corresponding sides are equal.

Congruent shapes can be in different positions or orientations, or may be mirror images of each other.

Congruent rectangles

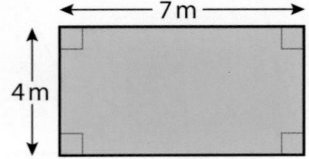
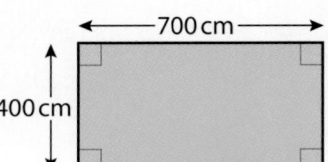

Congruent triangles

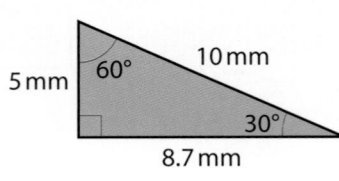
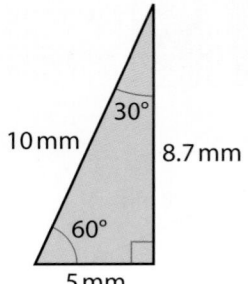

Shapes that are the same shape but a different size are called **similar**.

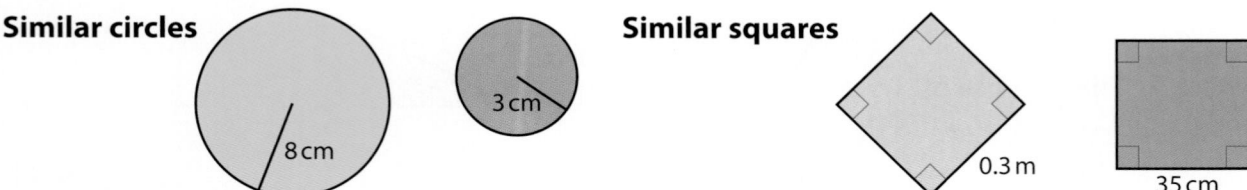

Similar circles   8 cm   3 cm   **Similar squares**   0.3 m   35 cm

Example

Look at the shapes in each pair and say whether they are congruent.

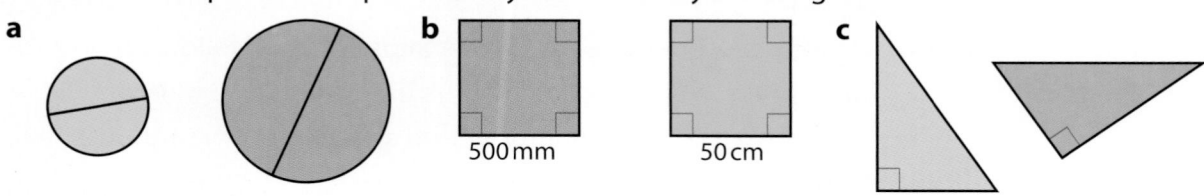

a   **b** 500 mm 50 cm   **c**

a   No, the circles are not congruent because they have different diameters.
b   Yes, the squares are congruent since 500 mm = 50 cm, so the sides of the squares are the same lengths.
c   Yes, the triangles are congruent. One triangle is the mirror image of the other.
   Use your ruler and a protractor to check that corresponding sides and angles are equal.

Exercise 4

You will need some squared paper for questions 2, 3 and 4 in this exercise.

1   Look at these shapes. Write down pairs that are congruent.

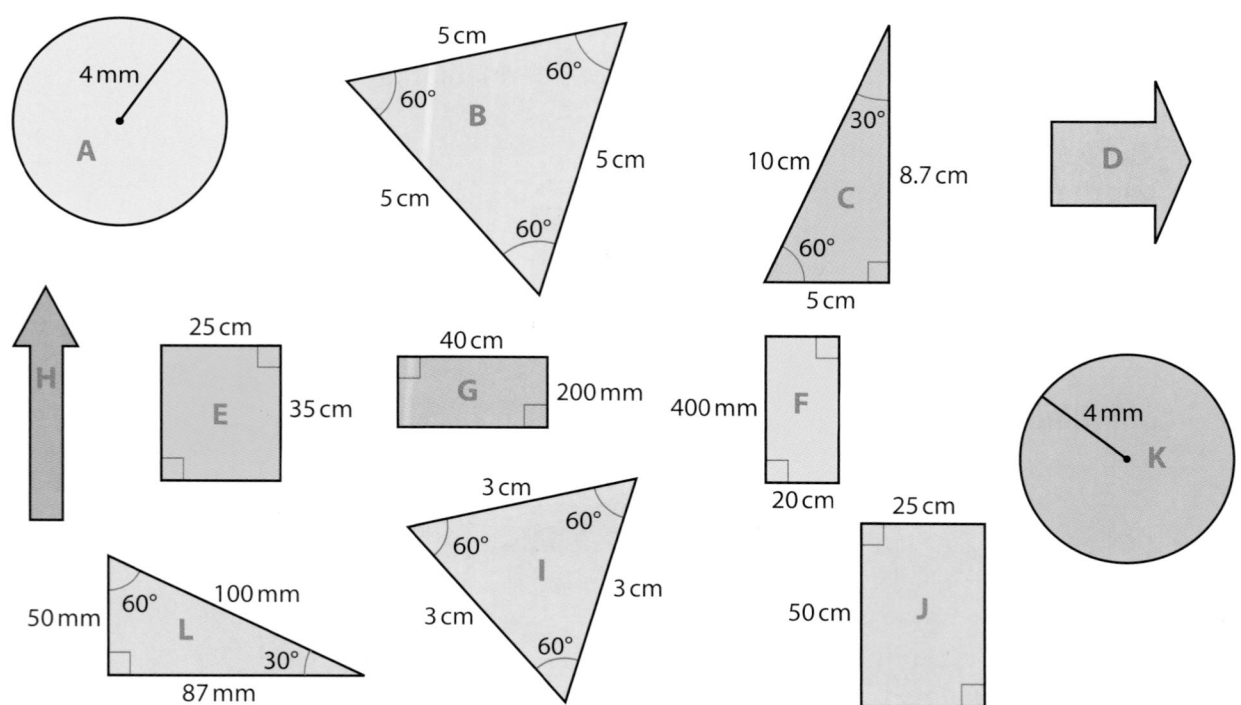

(2) On squared paper, draw:
  a two rectangles that are similar but not congruent
  b two rhombuses that are similar but not congruent

(3) You need some squared paper.

This 4 by 4 grid is divided into two congruent halves along the sides of the small squares.

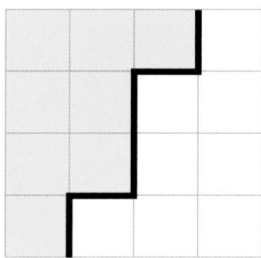

Investigate other ways in which you can divide a 4 by 4 grid into two congruent halves along the sides of the small squares.

How many different ways can you find?

Extension problem

 A 5 by 5 grid has its centre square cut out. Investigate different ways in which you can divide the grid with its centre square cut out into two congruent parts by cutting along the grid lines.

How many different ways are there?

Points to remember

⊙ **Congruent shapes** are exactly the same shape and size.
⊙ In congruent shapes, corresponding angles are equal and corresponding sides are equal.

5 Properties of quadrilaterals

This lesson will help you to recognise the properties of quadrilaterals.

Exercise 5

Work in a group of four.
  ⊙ Make two identical cut-outs of one of these triangles:
    scalene triangle
    right-angled triangle
    equilateral triangle
    isosceles triangle

- ⊙ Investigate the shapes that you can make by joining equal sides of your two triangles.
- ⊙ Do you always make a quadrilateral? If not, explain why.

Be prepared to explain your group's findings to the rest of the class.

 Points to remember

- ⊙ Rectangles, squares, parallelograms, rhombuses, kites and arrowheads are made up from pairs of congruent triangles.

6 Solving geometrical problems

This lesson will help you to:
- ◎ use correct notation and appropriate diagrams to solve geometrical problems;
- ◎ decide what information will help to solve a problem;
- ◎ work logically to show that a statement is true and explain your reasoning.

When you solve these problems, always draw a diagram.
Use a ruler and sharp pencil, and mark the key points.
Your diagram does not need to be drawn accurately.

Example

ABCD is a trapezium, with AB parallel to DC. AD = AC and angle D = 70°.
Find the size of angle DAB.

The diagram should look like this.
All the information in the question is marked on the diagram.

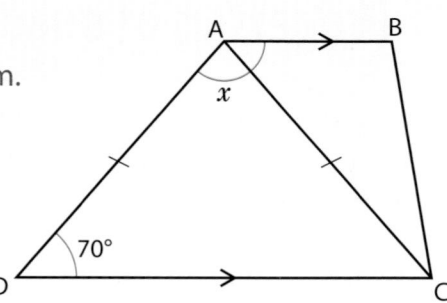

The angle to be found, angle DAB, is marked with an x.

You can see that if you work out the sizes of angles DAC and CAB you can add them together to find angle DAB.

Angle DCA = 70° (base angles of isosceles triangle ACD)

Angle CAB = 70° (alternate angles with AB // DC)

Angle DAC = 180 – (70 + 70) = 40° (angles in a triangle)

So angle DAB = angle CAB + angle DAC = 70 + 40 = 110°

You will need a sharp pencil and a ruler for this exercise.
For each question, start by drawing a diagram. Your diagrams need not be drawn accurately.
Remember to include reasons in your solutions.

1. Parallel lines AB and CD are cut by the line EF.
   EF meets AB at G and CD at F. Angle AGE is 36°.

   Find angle GHD.

2. WXYZ is a parallelogram.
   The line AB cuts WX and YZ at C and D respectively.
   Angle ZDC is 64°.

   Find angle WCD.

3. In isosceles triangle JKL, angle JKL is 55° and angle KLJ is 55°.
   Line MN is drawn parallel to side JL, to cut sides JK at P and KL at Q.
   a Find angle KQP.
   b What sort of triangle is triangle PKQ?
   c Find angle NPJ.

4. In rectangle PQRS, diagonal PR makes an angle of 33° with RS.
   Find angles SPR, QPR and PRQ.

   Write down what you know about triangle QPR and triangle SRP.

5. Two congruent triangles ABC and BCD are joined together along side BC
   such that angle BAC equals angle BDC and angle DCB equals angle CBA.
   What quadrilateral do the two congruent triangles make?

   Angle BAC is 73° and angle CBD is 41°.
   Find angle ACD.

6. In quadrilateral CDEF, CD is parallel to EF and DE is parallel to FC.
   Prove that angle FCD = angle DEF.

7. In quadrilateral WXYZ, XY = XZ and WY = WZ.
   Angle ZXY is 30° and angle XYW is 155°.
   Find angle YWZ.

8. AB and CD intersect at point E.
   AC is parallel to DB.
   Angle DEB is 35° and angle CAE is 70°.

   Find angle EDB.

Points to remember

- When you solve geometrical problems, draw a neat diagram.
- Mark on the diagram all the information in the question.
- Include reasons for the statements that you make.

How well are you doing?

Angles and parallel lines

1 *2007 level 6*

The diagram shows three straight lines.

Work out the sizes of angles a, b and c.
Give reasons for your answers.

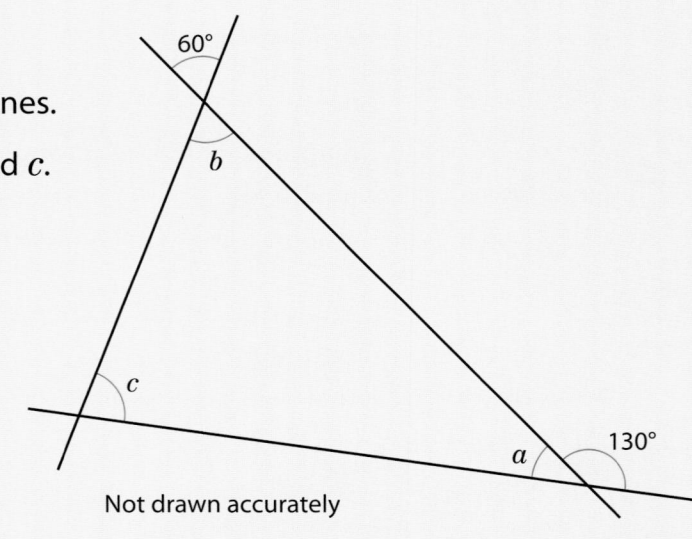

Not drawn accurately

2 *level 6*

The diagram shows a rectangle.

Work out the size of angle a.
Show your working.

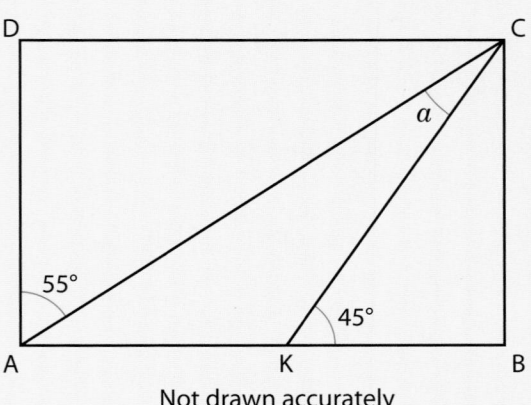

Not drawn accurately

Properties of shapes

3 Which of these shapes are congruent?

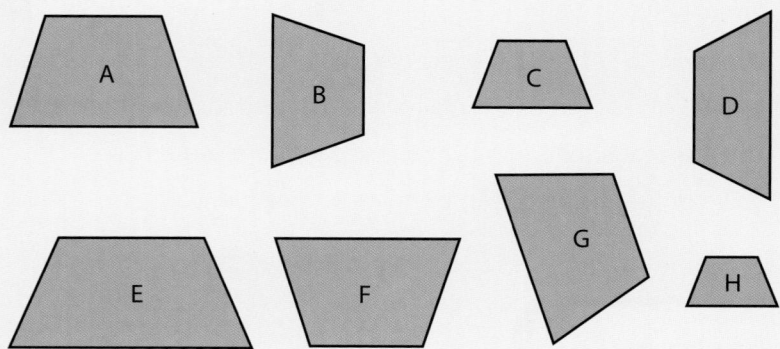

4 These two quadrilaterals are congruent.
Find the lengths of JK, KL, LM and MJ.

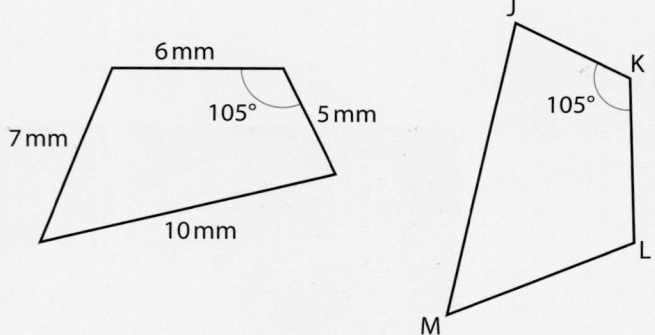

5 GH cuts a pair of parallel lines CD and EF at J and K respectively.
Angle CJG is 49°.
Find angle JKF.

6 In rectangle ABCD, angle BAC is 21°.
Find angle ACD.

Linear sequences

This unit will help you to:

- know what is meant by a 'sequence' and a 'term';
- use term-to-term rules and position-to-term rules to generate sequences;
- know how to find a formula for the nth term of a sequence;
- use a spreadsheet on a computer to explore sequences;
- solve problems involving patterns and sequences.

1 Term-to-term rules

This lesson will help you to use rules to generate sequences.

Did you know that...?

You can see patterns everywhere in the environment, particularly in nature, art and architecture.

Patterns also occur in algebra.

A **sequence** of numbers follows a rule.

Example

This is a sequence of numbers: 1, 5, 9, 13, 17, …

The difference between consecutive terms is 4.

The term-to-term rule of this sequence is 'add 4'.

The 1st term of the sequences is 1. The 2nd term is 5. The 3rd term is 9.

The next term of the sequence is 21.

The sequence is increasing.

The sequence is infinite.

Exercise 1

1. Look at this sequence of numbers:

50, 43, 36, 29, 22, …

   a What is the 1st term?
   b What is the 3rd term?
   c What is the difference between the 1st term and the 2nd term?
   d What is the difference between the 2nd term and the 3rd term?
   e What is the difference between consecutive terms?
   f Is the sequence increasing or decreasing?
   g What is the term-to-term rule?
   h Write the next five terms.

2. Write the term-to-term rule and the next five terms for each of these sequences.

   a 1, 7, 13, 19, …
   b 220, 195, 170, 145, …
   c −9, 10, 29, 48, …
   d 0, −5, −10, −15, …
   e $\frac{1}{5}, \frac{2}{5}, \frac{3}{5}, \frac{4}{5}, \dots$
   f $\frac{18}{19}, \frac{16}{19}, \frac{14}{19}, \frac{12}{19}, \dots$
   g 1, 4, 16, 64, …
   h 729, 243, 81, 27, …

3. Write whether each of these sequences is ascending or descending.

   a 2, 4, 6, 8, 10, 12, …
   b 500, 600, 700, 800, 900, …
   c $\frac{11}{7}, \frac{10}{7}, \frac{9}{7}, \frac{8}{7}, \frac{7}{7}, \dots$
   d $\frac{1}{8}, \frac{1}{4}, \frac{3}{8}, \frac{1}{2}, \frac{5}{8}, \dots$
   e 1.78, 1.76, 1.74, 1.72, …
   f 0, −10, −20, −30, −40, −50, …

4. Write down the first five terms of each of these sequences.

	1st term	Term-to-term rule
a	0	add 15
b	1000	subtract 22
c	0	subtract 2
d	−42	add 7
e	4096	divide by 4
f	1	multiply by 5
g	0	double and add 7
h	2	multiply by 3 and subtract 1
i	−1	multiply by 5 and add 2

5. Copy each sequence. Replace each box with the term of the sequence.

   a 5, □, □, 20, 25, □, □, …
   b □, □, □, 29, 37, 45, □, …
   c □, □, □, 0, 9, □, 27, …
   d 230, □, □, □, 186, □, …
   e □, □, 15, □, 10, □, 5, …
   f 1.5, □, □, 2.7, □, □, 3.9, …
   g □, □, □, $\frac{10}{5}, \frac{13}{5}$, □, $\frac{19}{5}$, …
   h $\frac{100}{25}$, □, □, □, $\frac{72}{25}$, □, $\frac{58}{25}$, …
   i □, −6, □, □, □, −30, …
   j −60, □, □, □, □, 15, …

⦿ Points to remember

⊙ A **sequence** of numbers follows a rule.
⊙ You can work out the next term in a sequence if you know the
term-to-term rule.

2 Position-to-term rules

This lesson will help you to use position-to-term rules to generate sequences
and find a formula for the nth term of a sequence.

Example 1

Look at this number sequence:

3, 6, 9, 12, 15, …

The numbers in the sequence are all multiples of 3.

The 1st term of the sequence is $3 \times 1 = 3$.
The 5th term of the sequence is $3 \times 5 = 15$.
The 10th term of the sequence is $3 \times 10 = 30$.
The nth term of the sequence is $3 \times n = 3n$.

Example 2

Look at these two number sequences:

3, 6, 9, 12, 15, …
5, 8, 11, 14, 17, …

The numbers in the second sequence are always 2 more than
the numbers in the first sequence.

The nth term of the first sequence is $3n$.
The nth term of the second sequence is $3n + 2$.

Example 3

If the formula for the nth term is $3n + 2$, then the 1st term is $3 \times 1 + 2 = 5$, the 2nd term is $3 \times 2 + 2 = 8$ and the 3rd term is $3 \times 3 + 2 = 11$.

Example 4

The differences between consecutive terms will help you to find the nth term.

9, 14, 19, 24, 29, …

The difference between consecutive terms is always 5.
The nth term is $5n + 4$.

Exercise 2

① Look at this number sequence:

5, 10, 15, 20, 25, 30, …

   a Describe the number sequence.

   b What is the 4th term of the sequence?

   c What would be the 10th term of the sequence?

   d What would be the 17th term of the sequence?

   e Explain how you would work out the 35th term of the sequence.

   f Write down the formula for the nth term of the sequence.

② Write down the nth terms of these number sequences.

   a 2, 4, 6, 8, 10, 12, …   b 7, 14, 21, 28, 35, 42, …

   c 10, 20, 30, 40, 50, 60, …   d 13, 26, 39, 52, 65, 78, …

   e 8, 16, 24, 32, 40, 48, …   f 25, 50, 75, 100, 125, 150, …

③ Find the nth terms for each pair of number sequences.

   a 4, 8, 12, 16, 20, 24, …   b 11, 22, 33, 44, 55, 66, …
       7, 11, 15, 19, 23, 27, …   5, 16, 27, 38, 49, 60, …

   c 9, 18, 27, 36, 45, 54, …   d 20, 40, 60, 80, 100, 120, …
       4, 13, 22, 31, 40, 49, …   11, 31, 51, 71, 91, 111, …

   e 6, 12, 18, 24, 30, 36, …   f 15, 30, 45, 60, 75, 90, …
       7, 13, 19, 25, 31, 37, …   23, 38, 53, 68, 83, 98, …

4 Use the formula for the nth term to generate the next five terms for each number sequence.

nth term	Sequence
a $7n$	7, 14, …
b $3n + 1$	4, 7, …
c $5n - 3$	2, 7, …
d $9n + 7$	16, 25, …
e $12n - 6$	6, 18, …
f $0.25n + 0.05$	0.30, 0.55, …
g $4n - 10$	$-6, -2, …$
h $\frac{1}{2}n + \frac{1}{4}$	$\frac{3}{4}, 1\frac{1}{4}, …$

5 Use the formula for the nth term of a sequence to work out the given term.

nth term	Find this term
a $2n + 4$	50th term
b $6n + 9$	100th term
c $8n - 5$	75th term
d $10n - 8$	400th term
e $3n + 2$	340th term
f $0.6n + 10$	150th term
g $0.5n - 0.1$	256th term
h $-2n - 1$	12th term

6 Find the formula for the nth term for each of these sequences.

a 8, 11, 14, 17, 20, …

b 9, 11, 13, 15, 17, 19, …

c 2, 7, 12, 17, 22, 27, …

d 5, 11, 17, 23, 29, 35, …

e 11, 20, 29, 38, 47, 56, …

f 9, 21, 33, 45, 57, 69, …

g 5, 12, 19, 26, 33, 40, …

h 14, 27, 40, 53, 66, 79, …

⊙ Points to remember

⊙ You can work out any term in a sequence if you know the formula for the **nth term**.

⊙ The difference between consecutive terms will help you find the nth term.

3 Using a spreadsheet to generate sequences

This lesson will help you to use a spreadsheet on a computer to explore sequences.

You can use a spreadsheet on a computer to help you explore number sequences.

Each cell on a spreadsheet is given a name using the column and row headings.

Cell A6 is in column A and row 6.

Exercise 3

Work with a partner. You will need a computer with spreadsheet software for this exercise.

1. a Use a computer spreadsheet to generate this sequence.

    b The first term of the sequence is in cell A2.
       In what cell will be the 100th term?

    c Use the spreadsheet to find the 100th term.

	A
1	**Sequence of numbers**
2	5
3	8
4	11
5	14
6	17
7	20
8	23
9	26
10	29
11	32

2. a Use a computer spreadsheet to generate this sequence.

    b Use the spreadsheet to find the 175th term.

	A
1	**Sequence of numbers**
2	256
3	247
4	238
5	229
6	220
7	211
8	202
9	193

3 **a** Work out the *n*th term for this number sequence.

Use the *n*th term to generate the sequence on a computer spreadsheet.

b Use the spreadsheet to work out the 365th term.

c Draw the graph showing the relationship between the position and the term.

	A	B	C
1	**Position**	**Term**	**Difference**
2	1	9	
3	2	13	
4	3	17	
5	4	21	
6	5	25	
7	6	29	
8	7	33	
9	8	37	
10	9	41	
11	10	45	
12	…	…	
13	n	?	

4 **a** Work out the *n*th term for this number sequence.

Use the *n*th term to generate the sequence on a computer spreadsheet.

b Use the spreadsheet to work out the 342nd term.

c Draw the graph showing the relationship between the position and the term.

	A	B	C
1	**Position**	**Term**	**Difference**
2	1	3	
3	2	12	
4	3	21	
5	4	30	
6	5	39	
7	6	48	
8	7	57	
9	8	66	
10	9	75	
11	10	84	
12	11	93	
13	12	102	
14	…	…	
15	n	?	

Extension problem

5 **a** Draw a table with columns for 'Position' and 'Term'.

Use it to record the coordinates of the points on this graph.

b Use the table to work out the *n*th term of the sequence.

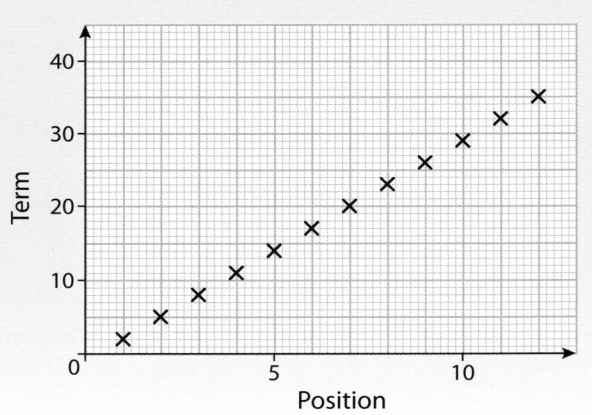

Points to remember

⊙ You can use a spreadsheet to explore sequences.

⊙ Each cell in a spreadsheet is given a name using the column heading and the row heading. For example, the first cell is called A1.

4 Exploring patterns

This lesson will help you to solve problems involving patterns and sequences.

Exercise 4

Patterns of tiles in a Mexican dairy

1. Square tiles are used to make border patterns in a bathroom.
   Draw the next two patterns for each of these designs.
   Work out the formula for the *n*th term of the sequence.

   a

   b

   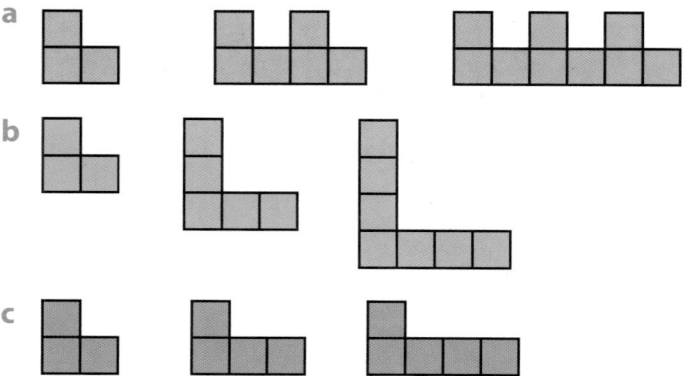

   c

2. Square paving slabs are used to surround different-sized rectangular swimming pools.

   a Find a formula for the number of slabs needed for different lengths of pools.
      Draw a graph to represent the relationship between the length of the pool and
      the number of slabs.

   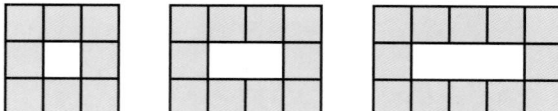

   b Investigate for pools of different widths.

3   a   Peter draws a pattern using equilateral triangles.
        Draw the next two shapes in his pattern.

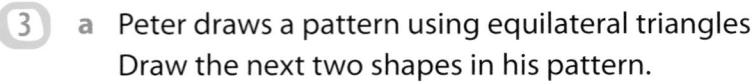

    b   Work out a formula for the number of triangles needed for any shape in Peter's pattern.
    c   Design your own pattern using equilateral triangles.
        Work out a formula for the number of triangles needed for any shape in your pattern.

4   Sarah notices that when there are three people altogether, including herself,
    she can throw a ball to two others.
    When there are four people, she can throw a ball to three others.
    When there are five people, she can throw a ball to four others.

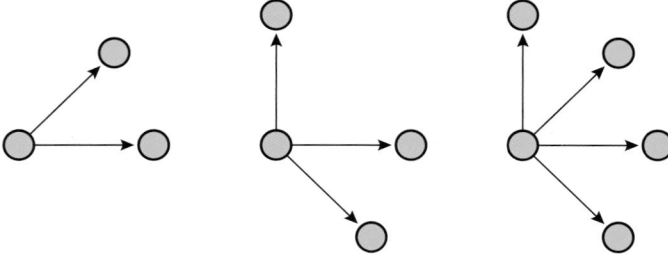

    Work out a formula for the number of other people she can throw the ball to
    when there are n people.

Extension problem

5   Chris noticed that a hexagon can be divided into four triangles.
    He used this to work out the sum of the angles of the hexagon.

    Work out how many triangles there are in different polygons.
    Find a formula for the sum of angles of an n-sided polygon.

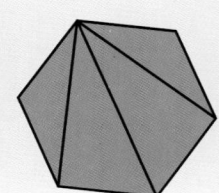

⊙ Points to remember

- ⊙ Always read the problem carefully.
- ⊙ Break down the problem into smaller chunks.
- ⊙ Look for patterns and make a conjecture.
- ⊙ Predict a new result and test it.
- ⊙ Make a generalisation.
- ⊙ Justify or prove your solution.

How well are you doing?

Can you:

- use term-to-term rules and position-to-term rules to generate sequences?
- find a formula for the nth term of a sequence?
- use a spreadsheet on a computer to explore sequences?
- solve problems involving patterns and sequences?

Linear sequences (no calculator)

1. Find the next five terms of this sequence.

   2, 9, 16, 23, ...

2. Work out the term-to-term rule for this sequence.

   84, 73, 62, 51, ...

3. Find the missing numbers in this sequence.

   103, 98, ☐, ☐, 83, 78, ☐

4. Generate the first five terms of the sequence using the formula
   $3n - 1$ for the nth term.

5. *2006 level 6*

   Look at these pairs of number sequences.
   The second sequence is formed from the first sequence by adding a number or
   multiplying by a number. Work out the missing nth terms.

   | a | 5, | 9, | 13, | 17, | ... | nth term is $4n + 1$ |
   | | 6, | 10, | 14, | 18, | ... | nth term is ? |

   | b | 12, | 18, | 24, | 30, | ... | nth term is $6n + 6$ |
   | | 6, | 9, | 12, | 15, | ... | nth term is ? |

   | c | 2, | 7, | 12, | 17, | ... | nth term is $5n - 3$ |
   | | 4, | 14, | 24, | 34, | ... | nth term is ? |

6. Draw the fourth shape in this pattern.
   Find the formula for the number of tiles in the nth shape.

Whole numbers, decimals and fractions

This unit will help you to:

- understand and use place value;
- multiply and divide whole numbers;
- find equivalent fractions and decimals;
- add and subtract fractions and decimals;
- find fractions of quantities;
- use a calculator, including the fraction key;
- investigate and solve number problems and compare solutions.

1 Place value

This lesson will help you to understand place value and round whole numbers and decimals.

The position of a digit in a number affects its value.
Each place after the decimal point has a value one tenth of the value of the place to its left.

In the number 4.763, the value of the digit 4 is four,
the value of the digit 7 is seven tenths,
the value of the digit 6 is six hundredths, and
the value of the digit 3 is three thousandths.

We can write:

$$4.763 = 4 + 0.7 + 0.06 + 0.03 = 4 + \frac{7}{10} + \frac{6}{100} + \frac{3}{1000}$$

When you round whole numbers, look at the first unwanted digit.
If it is 5, 6, 7, 8 or 9, add 1 to the last digit that you keep, otherwise make no changes.
Then replace all the unwanted digits by zeros.

Examples

45 6**2**1	to the nearest 100 is 45 600
963 2**7**5	to the nearest 10 is 963 280
429 **9**00	to the nearest 1000 is 430 000

When you round decimals, look at the first unwanted digit.
If it is 5, 6, 7, 8 or 9, add 1 to the last digit that you keep, otherwise make no changes.
Then leave off all the unwanted digits.

Examples   12.34**6**   correct to two decimal places is 12.35
                54.344**27** correct to three decimal places is 54.344
                39.9**95**   correct to one decimal place is 40.0

Exercise 1

1 Write in figures:
   a fourteen thousand and nine   b sixty thousand, six hundred
   c nine hundred thousand and fifty   d two million, forty thousand and twenty

2 Write in words:
   a 90 108   b 60 010
   c 7 060 800   d 403 040

3 Write the value of each red digit in words.
   a 1.02**5**   b 12.**3**07   c 7.8**2**   d 4.6**8**3
   e 2 4**3**2 500   f 2 **9**13 427   g 16 2**2**1 409 h 7.0**5**0

4 Write the number that is exactly halfway between each pair of numbers.
   a 1.7 and 2.5   b 4.2 and 9.2   c 3.25 and 4.25
   d 0.35 and 1.85   e 8.75 and 9.75   f 7.5 and 10
   g 1.33 and 1.34   h 4.99 and 5   i 6.77 and 7.78

5 Round these numbers to the nearest 10.
   a 706   b 10 495   c 2 500 998

6 Round these numbers to the nearest 100.
   a 4320   b 504 768   c 9995

7 Round these numbers to the nearest 1000.
   a 5503   b 59 900   c 7 329 500

8 Round these numbers to one decimal place.
   a 706.628   b 59.99   c 1.056 73

9 Round these numbers to two decimal places.
   a 12.128   b 3.462 5   c 0.038 76

10 Round these numbers to three decimal places.
    a 0.019 637   b 10.000 23   c 4.999 99

(11) Use only these calculator keys.

(1)(2)(+)(−)(·)

Make each of these numbers. Press as few keys as possible.

a 3.4　　　　　b 3.32　　　　　c 110　　　　　d 2.42　　　　　e 96

Record the key presses that you make on squared paper.

Points to remember

⊙ $0.3 = \frac{3}{10}$　　　$0.09 = \frac{9}{100}$　　　$0.004 = \frac{4}{1000}$

⊙ When you round decimals, look at the first unwanted digit.
If it is 5, 6, 7, 8 or 9, add 1 to the last digit that you keep.
Then leave off all the unwanted digits.

⊙ Round up 'halfway' numbers.
Examples: 42.5 rounds up to 43; 8750 rounds up to 8800.

⊙ 7.96 rounded to one decimal place is 8.0, not 8.

---

2 Ordering, adding and subtracting decimals

This lesson will help you to order, add and subtract decimals.

For column addition and subtraction of decimals:

⊙ line up the decimal points and write tenths under tenths, hundredths under hundredths, …;
⊙ fill gaps at the end of the decimal places with zeros if you wish;
⊙ show your 'carry' figures clearly;
⊙ change any units of measurement to the same unit.

Example 1

Find the total of 6.452 km, 2.78 km and 600 m.
First change 600 m to 0.6 km.

```
   6.452
   2.780
 + 0.600
   9.832
   1 1
```

Answer: 9.832 km

Example 2

Subtract 413 ml from 3.73 litres.
First change 413 ml to 0.413 litres.

```
   3. 7²3¹0
 − 0. 4 1 3
   3. 3 1 7
```

Answer: 3.317 litres

① In these sequences, the same number is added each time.
Copy each sequence and write the next three terms.

a 3.94   3.96   3.98   …   …   …

b 4.05   4.07   4.09   …   …   …

c 2.93   2.96   2.99   …   …   …

d 6.93   6.97   7.01   …   …   …

e 2.89   2.94   2.99   …   …   …

f 5.995   5.997   5.999   …   …   …

② Write down five different calculations.

◉ Take any number from column A.

◉ Add or subtract a number from column B.

◉ Find the answer in column C.

You may use each number only once.

A	B	C
14.31	3.776	3.262
1.097	4.109	16.394
12.618	9.77	11.771
15.88	11.048	10.867
0.847	0.514	0.333

Exercise 2B

When you compare two decimals, compare the sizes of digits in equivalent places.

Example

Which number is larger, 4.615 or 4.67?

4.615 or 4.67	In the units place, the digits are the same.
4.615 or 4.67	In the tenths place, the digits are the same.
4.615 or 4.67	In the hundredths place, the digit 7 is greater than the digit 1.

So 4.67 is larger than 4.615.

① Put these sets of numbers in order of size, starting with the largest.

a 2.60, 2.06, 2.162, 2.602

b 1.234, 2.34, 1.324, 1.43

② These were the lengths of the throws in a javelin competition.

Write down the names of the competitors who came first, second and third.

Name	Throw
Green	46.215 m
Black	46.059 m
White	45.671 m
Grey	46.519 m
Brown	45.716 m

(3) A factory makes matches that are 3.55 cm long.
If the matches made by a machine are 0.15 cm longer or shorter than 3.55 cm, they are rejected.

Here are the lengths of some matches. Which of them will be rejected?

3.695 cm   3.715 cm   3.485 cm   3.39 cm   3.7 cm   3.605 cm

(4) Work in pairs on this investigation.
Use a calculator to help you.

Two teams, Reds and Blacks, ran
a 4 by 100 metre relay race.
The times in seconds for the runners
are shown below.

Reds	
Chloe	13.41
Meena	12.37
Jessica	11.95
Sophie	14.08

Blacks	
Megan	12.56
Charlotte	13.60
Lauren	12.75
Olivia	14.12

a   Which team won? By how many seconds?

b   Rearrange the teams to make the fastest possible team.
What would their time be?

c   Rearrange the teams so that the relay race would be a dead heat.
What would the time be?

d   Find the team that would take 53.50 seconds.

◉ Points to remember

- ⊙ When you compare two decimals, compare the sizes of digits in equivalent places.
- ⊙ For column addition and subtraction of decimals:
  - line up the decimal points, write tenths under tenths, hundredths under hundredths, and so on;
  - if you wish, fill gaps at the end of the decimal places with zeros;
  - show any 'carry' figures clearly;
  - change units of measurement (e.g. pounds and pence, centimetres and metres) to the same unit.

3 Multiplication and division calculations

This lesson will help you to use written methods to multiply and divide whole numbers.

When you use written methods to multiply and divide, line up the numbers in columns.

Example 1   476 × 57

Estimate the answer as 500 × 60 = 30 000.

Answer: 476 × 57 = 27 132

$$
\begin{array}{r}
476 \\
\times\ 57 \\
\hline
23800 \quad (476 \times 50) \\
+\ 3332 \quad (476 \times 7) \\
\hline
27132 \\
\hline
{\scriptstyle 1\ 1}
\end{array}
$$

Example 2   846 ÷ 36

Estimate the answer as 800 ÷ 40 = 20.

In this calculation, you need to put in a decimal point and an extra zero in the tenths place.

Answer: 846 ÷ 36 = 23.5

$$
\begin{array}{r}
23.5 \\
36\overline{)846.0} \\
-\ 720 \quad (36 \times 20) \\
\hline
126 \\
-\ 108 \quad (36 \times 3) \\
\hline
18.0 \\
18.0 \quad (36 \times 0.5) \\
\hline
0
\end{array}
$$

Exercise 3

Work out the answers to these questions
without using a calculator.
Show your working clearly.

1. There are 45 drawing pins in a box.
    How many full boxes can you make
    with 750 drawing pins?

2. There are 132 postage stamps on a
    sheet of stamps.
    How many stamps are there on 48 sheets?

3. A school has collected £972 for theatre tickets from 72 pupils.
    What is the cost of one theatre ticket?

4. A large refrigerator costs £374.
    A superstore buys 25 of the refrigerators to sell on the Internet.
    How much does the store pay for the refrigerators?

5. Copy and complete the calculations below.
Choose from these numbers to go in the boxes.
Do not use a calculator.

29   58   42   65   91   32   82

a ☐ × ☐ = 2378   b ☐ × ☐ = 3770

c ☐ × ☐ = 2639   d ☐ × ☐ = 2730

e ☐ × ☐ = 3444   f ☐ × ☐ = 4756

g 928 ÷ ☐ = ☐   h ☐ × ☐ ÷ ☐ = 21

6. This is a multiplication table.
Each number is the product of the number at the beginning of the row and the number at the top of the column.

×	2	3	4
15	30	45	60
16	32	48	64

For example, 30 is the product of 2 × 15.
64 is the product of 4 × 16.

Without using a calculator, copy and complete this multiplication table.

×	6		8
			96
19		171	
	66		
	84		

Extension problem

7. The red 'ink blots' cover missing digits.
Without using a calculator, work out what the digits are.
Copy, complete and check each calculation. Show your working.

a ●3 × ● = 424   b 3● × ● = 315

c ●4 × ● = ●44   d 1● × ●3 = 731

e 93 × ●● = 70●8   f ●3 × ●7 = 41●●

Points to remember

⊙ For written methods of multiplication and division in columns:
 — estimate the answer first;
 — line up units under units, tens under tens, and so on;
 — when dividing, add zeros after the decimal point if necessary;
 — show 'carry' figures clearly;
 — use the estimate to make sure that the answer is about the right size and that any decimal point is in the correct place.

⊙ You can also check answers by using inverse operations.

4 Using a calculator

This lesson will help you to use a calculator to solve problems.

The memory of a calculator can help you to do calculations with several steps. The memory keys vary according to the type of calculator you are using. You may need to modify the instructions below to suit your calculator.

M+ This key adds the contents of the display to the contents of the memory.

M− This key subtracts the contents of the display from the contents of the memory. This is SHIFT M+ on some calculators.

MR This key recalls the contents of the memory and puts it in the display. The contents of the display will disappear but may still be involved in the calculation. This is RCL on some calculators.

Min This key puts the value in the display into the memory and any existing contents of the memory are lost. This is STO on some calculators.

Ask your teacher if your calculator works differently.

Exercise 4

Use your calculator for this exercise.

1 a The cost of a roundabout ride is £1.35.
      270 people had a ride on Friday.
      How much money is that altogether?

   b The roundabout took £810 in ride money.
      How many people had a ride?

2 How many lengths of wood 17 cm long
   can be cut from a piece of wood 4.5 m long?
   How many centimetres of wood will be left over?

3 How many bottles holding 375 ml can be filled
   with 5 litres of orange juice?
   How many millilitres of orange juice will be left?

4 A snack from a snack machine costs 65p.
The table shows the coins that were put
in the machine one day.
How many snacks were sold?

Coins	Number of coins
50p	28
20p	32
10p	45
5p	139

Did you know that...?

Gateway of India, Mumbai's famous landmark

The Indian mathematician
D. R. Kaprekar was born in 1905 near
Mumbai, in India. He worked
for most of his life as a teacher.

In 1955, he discovered something
interesting about four-digit numbers.

Follow the instructions in question 5 to
find out what he discovered.

5 Choose any four different digits, except 0. Using all four digits, make the largest and
smallest numbers possible. Find their difference.

For example, with 3, 6, 8 and 2 you would do this:

$$
\begin{array}{r}
8632 \\
- \ 2368 \\
\hline
6264
\end{array}
$$

Use the four digits of the answer to make the largest and smallest possible numbers.

$$
\begin{array}{r}
6642 \\
- \ 2466 \\
\hline
4176
\end{array}
$$

Keep repeating the process, always using the four digits of the answer
as the new starting point. What happens?

Investigate other sets of four digits. What do you notice?

What is the longest chain of subtractions you can find?

6 Find a partner and play **Target**. You need one calculator between you.
Take turns to go first. The aim is to get as close as possible to a target number.

Rules

- ⬤ The first player chooses a starting number between 1 and 100 (say 17).

- ⬤ The second player chooses a target number between 100 and 200 (say 157).

- ⬤ In turn, each player says what they will multiply the starting number by to get the target number.

- ⬤ Work out each of the calculations on the calculator.

- ⬤ The player who gets closest to the target number scores one point.

- ⬤ The winner is the first to get 10 points.

Example

Jack chooses 17 as a starting number. Alice chooses 157 as a target number.

Jack says he will multiply 17 by 8.3. Alice says she will multiply 17 by 9.5.

$17 \times 8.3 = 141.1$

$17 \times 9.5 = 161.5$

Alice is nearer to 157 than Jack. She gets one point.

Extension problem

7 Investigate these problems. Each ⬡ represents a missing operation ($+$, $-$, $\times$ or $\div$).
Copy and complete the calculations. Use your calculator to help you.

a (56 ⬡ 38) ⬡ 62 = 1116   b (2030 ⬡ 35) ⬡ 97 = 155

c 650 ⬡ (48 ⬡ 35) = 50   d 27 ⬡ (13 ⬡ 15) = 5265

 Points to remember

When you use a calculator:

- ⊙ estimate the result of a calculation;

- ⊙ use the CLEAR-ALL key before each new calculation;

- ⊙ use the CLEAR key to clear the last entry;

- ⊙ use the memory to store answers to parts of a calculation or to keep a total;

- ⊙ think carefully about the meaning of the numbers in the final display;

- ⊙ round the answer to a sensible number, depending on the context;

- ⊙ check the answer against the estimate.

5 Equivalent fractions and fractions of quantities

This lesson will help you to find equivalent fractions and work out fractions of quantities, including the use of a calculator.

- You can convert a fraction into an equivalent fraction by multiplying or dividing the numerator and the denominator by the same number.

- You can use your calculator to find equivalent fractions.

  The fraction key often looks like $\boxed{a^{b}/_{c}}$ or $\boxed{\frac{\square}{\square}}$.

  Enter $\boxed{4}$ $\boxed{a^{b}/_{c}}$ $\boxed{6}$. The display represents the fraction $\frac{4}{6}$ and will look something like:

  $$\boxed{4\_6}$$

  If you now press $\boxed{=}$ the fraction will be simplified to $\frac{2}{3}$.

- You can also use your calculator to change an improper fraction to a mixed number.

  Enter $\boxed{1}$ $\boxed{7}$ $\boxed{a^{b}/_{c}}$ $\boxed{5}$.

  If you now press $\boxed{=}$ the display will show:

  $$\boxed{3\_2\_5}$$

  which represents the fraction $3\frac{2}{5}$.

Ask your teacher if your calculator works differently.

Exercise 5A

1. **Without using a calculator**, cancel each of these fractions to its simplest form.

   a $\frac{14}{56}$
   b $\frac{35}{50}$
   c $\frac{36}{81}$

   d $\frac{24}{72}$
   e $\frac{110}{22}$
   f $\frac{96}{30}$

2. Copy and complete these equivalent fractions.

   a $\frac{2}{3} = \frac{\square}{72}$
   b $\frac{3}{8} = \frac{\square}{96}$
   c $\frac{5}{9} = \frac{35}{\square}$

   d $\frac{9}{5} = \frac{108}{\square}$
   e $\frac{13}{24} = \frac{\square}{96}$
   f $\frac{12}{11} = \frac{144}{\square}$

3 **Using a calculator**, write each of these fractions in its simplest form.

a $\frac{115}{161}$

b $\frac{68}{153}$

c $\frac{74}{111}$

d $\frac{104}{143}$

e $\frac{138}{299}$

f $\frac{154}{187}$

4 What fraction is the first quantity of the second?

a 24 centimetres; 3 metres

b 350 grams; 2 kilograms

c £1.50; £7

d 25 millimetres; 6 centimetres

e 8 days; 2 weeks

f 40 minutes; 4 hours

Exercise 5B

Find a fraction of a number by using multiplication and division.

Example   Find $\frac{5}{8}$ of 27.

$27 \div 8 = 3.375$ divide 27 by 8 to find one eighth

$3.375 \times 5 = 16.875$ then multiply by 5 to find five eighths

With a calculator, you can work it out in one sequence: ⟨2⟩⟨7⟩⟨÷⟩⟨8⟩⟨×⟩⟨5⟩⟨=⟩

The display will show | 16.875 | .

You can also work it out using the fraction key ⟨ $a^b/_c$ ⟩.

Enter the fraction and multiply by 27: ⟨5⟩⟨ $a^b/_c$ ⟩⟨8⟩⟨×⟩⟨2⟩⟨7⟩

The display will show | 16⌐7⌐8 | , which means $16\frac{7}{8}$.

1 Write the answers to these calculations. You may use a calculator.

a $\frac{13}{20}$ of 230

b $\frac{6}{25}$ of £1440

c $\frac{5}{32}$ of 80 kg

d $\frac{17}{40}$ of 70 m

e $\frac{7}{8}$ of 300 m²

f $\frac{15}{22}$ of 550 litres

g $\frac{3}{16}$ of 280 km

h $\frac{7}{24}$ of 3 hours

(2) Play **Fractions** with a partner. You need two dice.

Rules

- Play with a partner. Take turns.
- Roll the two dice. If the two numbers are the same, roll again.
- If the two numbers are different, write down a fraction. For example, if you roll 4 and 5 you can make $\frac{4}{5}$ or $\frac{5}{4}$.
- Find that fraction of 120. Write down the answer.
- The winner is the first player to get eight different answers.

Extension problems

(3) Hannah used her calculator to change a fraction with numerator 1 into a decimal. The display showed:

$$0.020408163$$

What was the fraction?

(4) **a** I am a fraction.
   If you add 1 to my numerator, my value is one third.
   If you add 1 to my denominator, my value is one quarter.
   Who am I?

   b I am a whole number less than 20.
   Two less than half of me is more than one third of me.
   Who am I?

(5) Parveen and Afzal are teenagers.
   The difference between one sixth of Parveen's age and one seventh of Afzal's age is one year.
   How old is Parveen? How old is Afzal?

◉ Points to remember

- ◉ Convert a fraction into an equivalent fraction by multiplying or dividing the numerator and the denominator by the same number.
- ◉ Find a fraction of a number by using multiplication and division.

6 Calculations with fractions

This lesson will help you to solve problems by calculating with fractions.

Given a fractional part, find the whole by using division, then multiplication.

Example

Four fifths of a bottle of water is 300 ml. How much water is there in a full bottle?

Four fifths is 300 ml.
One fifth is 300 ÷ 4 = 75 ml
Five fifths is 75 × 5 = 375 ml

Exercise 6A

(1) Two thirds of a length of rope is 8 metres. How long is the rope?

(2) Three fifths of the distance from Emma's home to the shops is 600 metres. How far is it from Emma's home to the shops?

(3) Emma spent three eighths of her savings on a new jacket.
The jacket cost £27.
How much did Emma have in savings?

(4) Four fifths of the sugar on some scales is 500 grams.
How much sugar is on the scales?

(5) A cake in an oven has cooked for three quarters of its baking time.
It has 14 minutes left to bake.
For how long has the cake been cooking?

(6) An advert of area 300 cm² takes up two ninths of a page of a newspaper.
What is the area of the whole page?

⑦ Lucy has used three eighths of her bottle of olive oil. She has 200 ml of olive oil left. How much olive oil was in the full bottle?

⑧ Harry spent five sevenths of his shopping bill on fruit and vegetables. The whole bill came to £9.80. What did Harry spend on other goods?

Exercise 6B

Add or subtract fractions with different denominators by first changing them to equivalent fractions with a common denominator.

Example 1 $\frac{5}{8} + \frac{7}{12}$

$\frac{5}{8} + \frac{7}{12} = \frac{15}{24} + \frac{14}{24}$ change the fractions to a common denominator

$= \frac{29}{24}$ add the fractions

$= 1\frac{5}{24}$ change the improper fractions to a mixed number

Example 2 $\frac{11}{12} - \frac{3}{4}$

$\frac{11}{12} - \frac{3}{4} = \frac{11}{12} - \frac{9}{12}$ change the fractions to a common denominator

$= \frac{2}{12}$ subtract the factions

$= \frac{1}{6}$ simplify the fraction by cancelling

When you add or subtract mixed numbers, deal with whole numbers first.

Example 3 $2\frac{5}{8} + 3\frac{7}{12}$

$2\frac{5}{8} + 3\frac{7}{12} = 5\frac{5}{8} + \frac{7}{12}$ first add the whole numbers

$= 5\frac{15}{24} + \frac{14}{24}$ change the fractions to a common denominator

$= 5\frac{29}{24}$ add the two fractions – if the result is an improper fraction,

$= 6\frac{5}{24}$ change the improper fraction to a mixed number

Example 4 $4\frac{5}{12} - 2\frac{3}{4}$

$4\frac{5}{12} - 2\frac{3}{4} = 2\frac{5}{12} - \frac{3}{4}$ first subtract the whole numbers

$= 2\frac{5}{12} - \frac{9}{12}$ change the fractions to a common denominator

$= 1\frac{17}{12} - \frac{9}{12}$ as you can't take 9 from 5, change 1 whole to 12 twelfths

$= 1\frac{8}{12}$ subtract the fractions

$= 1\frac{2}{3}$ simplify the fraction by cancelling

Make sure that you know how to use your calculator to add and subtract fractions.

1. Each number in this addition square is the sum of the two fractions at the top of the column and the left of the row.

+	$\frac{2}{3}$	$\frac{1}{4}$
$\frac{1}{3}$	1	$\frac{7}{12}$
$\frac{1}{2}$	$1\frac{1}{6}$	$\frac{3}{4}$

Copy and complete these addition squares.

a

+	$\frac{3}{4}$	$\frac{1}{5}$
$\frac{1}{2}$		
$\frac{1}{3}$		

b

+		$\frac{2}{3}$
	$\frac{13}{20}$	$\frac{11}{12}$
$\frac{1}{2}$		

c

+		
$\frac{1}{6}$	$\frac{23}{30}$	$\frac{2}{3}$
	1	

2. Choose from these fractions.

Copy and complete these calculations.

a   ◯ + ◯ = $6\frac{1}{4}$

b   ◯ − ◯ = $\frac{1}{6}$

c   ◯ + ◯ = $4\frac{7}{15}$

d   ◯ − ◯ = $1\frac{1}{12}$

e   ◯ + ◯ = $3\frac{1}{2}$

f   ◯ − ◯ = $\frac{29}{30}$

Extension problem

 You can travel through this maze to the right, to the left or down, but not up. Cells can be visited only once. As you pass through a fraction, add it to your score.

Investigate different paths through the maze.

a   Which is the least score for a path?

b   Which path gives a score of $2\frac{3}{8}$?

c   How many different paths through the maze are there?

d   What is the greatest score for a path?

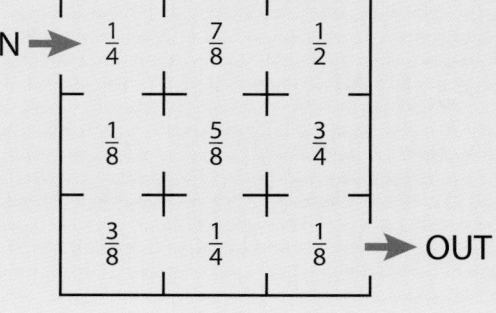

Points to remember

⊙ Given a fractional part, find the whole by using division then multiplication.

⊙ Add or subtract fractions with different denominators by first changing them to equivalent fractions with a common denominator. Deal with whole numbers first.

How well are you doing?

Whole numbers, fractions and decimals (no calculator)

1 **a** Which of these decimals is equal to three fifths?

0.3   0.4   0.5   0.6   0.7   0.8   0.9

b Two of these fractions are equal to $\frac{2}{3}$. Which are they?

$\frac{4}{5}$ $\frac{10}{15}$ $\frac{2}{6}$ $\frac{3}{2}$ $\frac{6}{9}$ $\frac{4}{12}$

2 **a** Which is the smallest number?

0.35   0.305   3.05   0.035   3.5

b Which two of these have a sum of 1?

0.1   0.65   0.99   0.45   0.35

3 *2007 level 6*

Copy and complete these fraction sums.

a $\frac{1}{4} + \frac{\square}{8} = 1$

b $\frac{1}{3} + \frac{8}{\square} = 1$

4 Without using a calculator, calculate:

a 273×46

b $32.5 - 7.831$

c $988 \div 38$

Whole numbers, fractions and decimals (calculator allowed)

5 Use a calculator to work out what number goes in each box.

   a $67.5 ÷ (4.07 − 0.32) = \Box$

   b $48.3 − (23.65 + 14.8) = \Box$

   c $\Box × 36.18 = 705.51$

6 A box and its contents of 220 matches weighs 45 grams.
The empty box weighs 12 grams.
Calculate the weight of one match.

7 **a** A paper clip is made from 9 cm wire.
How much wire is needed to make
1500 paper clips?
Give your answer in metres.

   b What is the greatest number of
paper clips that can be made from
20 metres of wire?

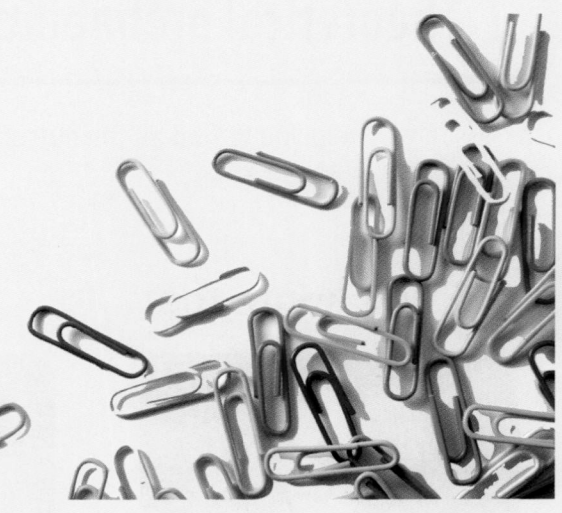

Probability

This unit will help you to:

- use the language of probability;
- find all the possible outcomes of events;
- work out theoretical probabilities;
- work out the probability of an event not happening;
- record results of experiments and use them to estimate experimental probabilities;
- compare experimental and theoretical probability.

1 Theoretical probability

This lesson will help you to find all the outcomes of a single event and work out its probability.

Did you know that...?

Blaise Pascal (1623–1662)

Pierre de Fermat (1601–1665)

In the 17th century **Blaise Pascal** and **Pierre de Fermat**, two French mathematicians, did a lot of work on probability.

One of the problems they discussed was how many times you needed to throw a pair of dice before you get a double six.

What do you think the probability is of throwing double six?

An **event** is something that can have different **outcomes**.
Outcomes are **equally likely** if an experiment is fair or unbiased.
With equally likely outcomes, the **theoretical probability** of a particular outcome is:

$$\frac{\text{number of favourable outcomes}}{\text{total number of possible outcomes}}$$

Example

When you roll a fair dice, there are 6 equally likely outcomes:

    1 2 3 4 5 6

There is 1 outcome favourable to 'rolling a 3':

    1 2 **3** 4 5 6

The theoretical probability of rolling a 3 is $\frac{1}{6}$.

There are 2 favourable outcomes for 'rolling a number less than 3':

    1 2 3 4 5 6

The theoretical probability of rolling a number less than 3 is $\frac{2}{6} = \frac{1}{3}$.

Exercise 1

1. A 1 to 6 fair dice is rolled. List all the possible outcomes for:

   a rolling a square number
   b rolling an even number
   c rolling a 5
   d rolling an odd prime number

   What is the probability of each of the events a, b, c and d?

2. Mohinder picks a card at random from this pack of cards.

1	2	3	1	2	4	3	5	4	5

   a What is the probability of these events?
      i picking a red
      ii picking a 2
     iii picking a red 2
     iv picking a red 2 or a blue 3
      v picking a blue 6
     vi picking a red or a blue card
    vii picking an even blue
    viii picking a factor of 10

   b Why is picking an even-numbered card less likely than picking an odd-numbered card?

3. Georgia makes a necklace from red beads and white beads.
   She chooses her beads at random from a box of 25 red and 75 white beads.

   Katie also makes a necklace from red beads and white beads.
   She chooses her beads at random from a box of 75 red and 150 white beads.

   Both necklaces have the same number of beads.

   Whose necklace is likely to have more white beads? Explain your answer.

Example

A box contains 3 red and 2 blue counters.

Tom picks a counter from the box at random and records its colour.

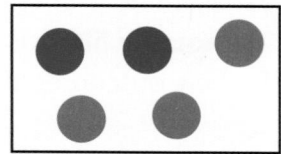

There are 5 equally likely possible outcomes (**R** stands for 'red' and **B** for 'blue'):

R R R B B

There are 3 equally likely outcomes of picking a red counter: R R R **B B**
The theoretical probability of picking a red counter is $\frac{3}{5}$.

There are 2 equally likely outcomes of picking a blue counter: **R R R** B B
The theoretical probability of picking a blue counter is $\frac{2}{5}$.

---

4 Boxes P, Q, R and S contain some coloured counters.

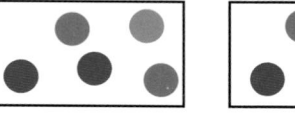 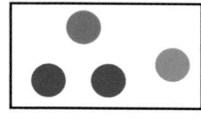 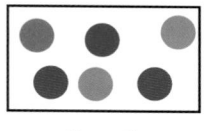 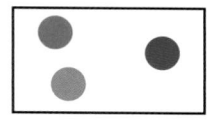

Box P   Box Q   Box R   Box S

a Josh wants to pick a green counter.
 Which box gives the best chance of this? Why?

b Amy wants to pick a blue counter.
 Why should she pick from either box Q or box R?

c Luke doesn't want to pick a red counter.
 Why should he pick from box R?

d Ryan says:
 'There are three colours in each box, so the probability of picking a red counter is $\frac{1}{3}$.'
 Explain why Ryan is wrong.

5 Ellie spins the arrow on spinner A.
 George spins the arrow on spinner B.
 Both spinners are fair.
 Ellie and George each record the score that their arrow lands on.

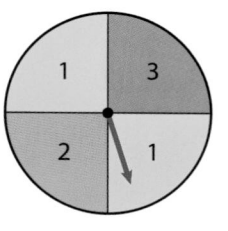 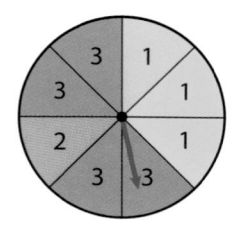

Spinner A   Spinner B

a Write down all the equally likely outcomes for spinner A.
 Write down all the equally likely outcomes for spinner B.

b Who is more likely to score 1? Why?

c Who is more likely to score 2? Why?

d Who is most likely to obtain the highest score? Explain your answer.

(6) Work out the probability that a month selected at random:

a has 31 days   b has 30 days

c contains 3 letters   d contains 4 or 5 letters

e begins with the letter J   f begins with a vowel

> *Thirty days has September,*
> *April, June and November.*
> *All the rest have thirty-one*
> *Excepting February alone,*
> *Which has but twenty-eight days clear,*
> *And twenty-nine each leap year.*

⊙ Points to remember

⊙ Probabilities range from 0 (impossible) to 1 (certain).
  They are written as fractions, decimals or percentages.
⊙ An event can have different **outcomes**.
⊙ **Equally likely outcomes** occur in fair trials.
⊙ If the outcomes are equally likely, the **theoretical probability** of a particular event is:

$$\frac{\text{number of favourable outcomes}}{\text{total number of possible outcomes}}$$

2 Events not happening

This lesson will help you to work out the probability of an event not happening.

A card is picked at random from a standard pack of 52 playing cards.
There are 52 equally likely outcomes.

Example 1

The 6 possible outcomes for picking a black picture card are:

K♣ Q♣ J♣ K♠ Q♠ J♠

The probability of picking a black picture card is $\frac{6}{52} = \frac{3}{26}$.

There are $52 - 6 = 46$ possible outcomes for **not** picking a black picture card.

The probability of not picking a black picture card is $\frac{46}{52} = \frac{23}{26}$.

Example 2

The 2 possible outcomes for picking a red king are:

K♦   K♥

The probability of picking a red king is $\frac{2}{52} = \frac{1}{26}$.

The probability of **not** picking a red king is $\frac{50}{52} = \frac{25}{26}$.

Exercise 2

① A whole number from 1 to 15 is picked at random.

  a The 7 equally likely outcomes for picking an even number are circled.

1 ② 3 ④ 5
 ⑥ 7 ⑧ 9 ⑩
11 ⑫ 13 ⑭ 15

What is the theoretical probability of picking an even number?

What is the theoretical probability of not picking an even number?

Repeat **a** for each of these:

  b picking a multiple of 3   **c** picking a multiple of 5

  d picking a square number   **e** picking a cube number

② Adam puts 4 red counters, 2 blue counters and 1 pink counter in a box.
He picks one of the counters at random.

Work out the probability that the counter is:

  a red   **b** **not** red   **c** blue   **d** **not** blue

  e green   **f** **not** pink   **g** red, blue or pink   **h** **not** red, blue or pink

③ Grace shuffles a pack of playing cards and then picks one at random.

  a Write down the number of equally likely outcomes for each of these events:

    i picking a black 7   **ii** **not** picking a black 7

    iii picking either a heart or a king   **iv** **not** picking either a heart or a king

    v picking a picture card   **vi** **not** picking a picture card

  b Write down the probability of each event in part **a**.

  c Calculate the probability that the card is:

    i **not** a diamond   **ii** **not** a diamond or an ace

    iii **not** a red card or a club   **iv** an even-numbered heart

    v an odd-numbered heart   **vi** **not** an even-numbered heart

    vii **not** an odd-numbered heart

4 A counter is taken at random from each of these boxes.

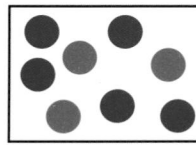   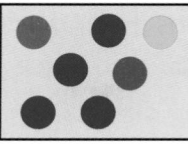   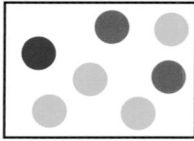   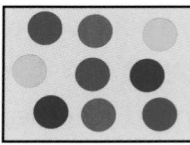

| Box P | Box Q | Box R | Box S |

a For each box, work out the probability that the counter taken from the box is:

   i blue   **ii** **not** blue

b What do you notice about the pair of probabilities you worked out in part **a**?

> ⊙ **Points to remember**
>
> ⊙ The probability of an event not happening is
>   1 minus the probability of the event happening.

3 The probability of two events

This lesson will help you to work out the probability of two events.

In some situations, you can calculate the probability of two events occurring.
These events can occur either at the same time or one after the other.

Example

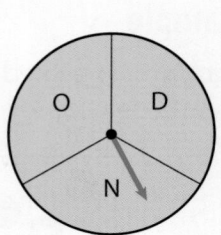

The arrow on this fair spinner is spun twice.
The letters that the arrow points to are recorded in order.
The complete set of nine equally likely **possible outcomes** is:

OO   OD   ON   DO   DD   DN   NO   ND   NN

The **red** letter shows the outcome of the first spin.
The **blue** letter shows the outcome of the second spin.

There are three equally likely outcomes that make a word

                ON   DO   NO

So the probability of making a word is $\frac{3}{9} = \frac{1}{3}$.
The probability of **not** making a word is $\frac{6}{9} = \frac{2}{3}$.

1 When a coin is thrown, it lands either heads (H) or tails (T).
In an experiment, Mohammed throws a fair coin twice.

   a Write down the four equally likely outcomes.

   b i What is the probability of throwing two heads?
   ii What is the probability of **not** throwing two heads?

2 Abigail spins this fair spinner twice.
She adds the numbers she gets.

   a Write a list of all the possible totals.

   b What is the probability that Abigail gets:
   i a total of 5?   ii a total that is different from 5?

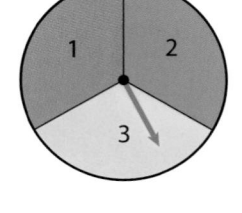

3 The primary colours of paint are blue, red and yellow.
Mixing two different primary colours makes a new colour.

   Oliver has a pot of blue paint and a pot of red paint.
   Molly has a pot of red paint and a pot of yellow paint.

   Oliver picks one of his pots at random.
   Molly picks one of her pots at random.
   They mix the colours they have picked.

   What is the probability that Oliver and Molly make a new colour?

Exercise 3B

You can use a **two-way table** to show the possible outcomes for two events.

Example

A counter is picked at random from box P.
Another counter is picked at random from box Q.

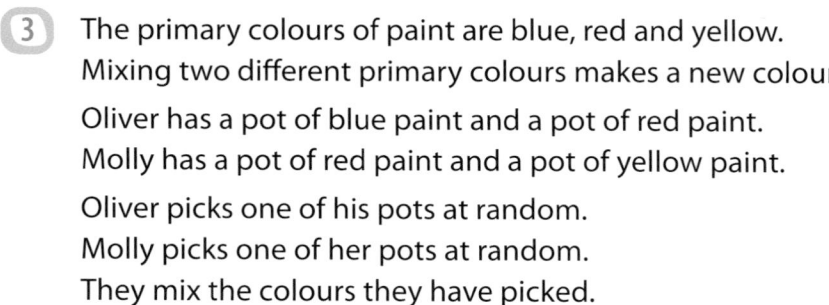

Box P   Box Q

Possible outcomes:

		Box Q		
		B	**R**	**R**
Box P	**B**	B B	R B	R B
	B	B B	R B	R B
	R	B R	R R	R R

The table shows all 9 possible outcomes.
Four of them are for two counters of the same colour.

The probability of picking two counters with the
same colour is $\frac{4}{9}$.
The probability of picking two counters with a
different colour is $\frac{5}{9}$.

You will need a copy of **S4.1 Resource sheet 3.1** to use in question 3.

1 Box 1 contains 3 red counters and 1 blue counter.
Box 2 contains 1 red counter and 1 blue counter.

A counter is taken at random from each box.

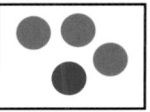 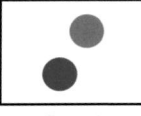

Box 1   Box 2

a Jordan makes this list of outcomes.
Is Jordan's list a complete list of equally likely outcomes?
Explain your answer.

Box 1	Box 2
R	R
R	B
B	R
B	B

b Jake uses a table to make a list of outcomes.
Is Jake's list a complete list of equally likely outcomes?
Explain your answer.

		Box 1			
		R	**R**	**R**	**B**
Box 2	**R**	R R	R R	R R	B R
	B	R B	R B	R B	B B

c What is the probability that the two counters are the same colour?
d Is picking two red counters more likely than picking two blue?
Explain your answer.

2 A red counter is taken out of box 1 and put in box 2.
A counter is then taken at random from each box.

a Make a two-way table to show all the possible outcomes.
b What is the probability that the two counters are a different colour?
c What is the probability that the two counters are the same colour?

3 A fair red dice and a fair blue dice are rolled. The scores are added.
a Complete the table on **S4.1 Resource sheet 3.1**.
b Connor said: 'I am lucky. I always roll a lot of double sixes.'
Comment on what Connor said.

c Why is a score of 7 more likely than a score of 12?

d Work out the probability of each of these:
  i scoring a total of 4
  ii scoring a total of 2
  iii scoring more than 8
  iv scoring the same number on both dice

Extension problem

 4 Chris and Ben play a game with two dice.

They take turns to roll the dice and add the scores.

On Chris's turn:

Chris wins if his total score is exactly 9.

Ben wins if Chris's total score is more than 9.

If Chris scores less than 9, it is Ben's turn.

On Ben's turn:

Ben wins if his total score is exactly 5.

Chris wins if Ben's total score is less than 5.

If Ben scores more than 5, it is Chris's turn.

Is this a fair game? Explain your answer.

Points to remember

⊙ When two events occur at the same time or one after the other, you can use a list or table to record all the possible equally likely outcomes.

⊙ Use the list or table to work out a probability from:

$$\frac{\text{number of favourable outcomes}}{\text{total number of possible outcomes}}$$

4 Experimental probability

This lesson will help you to:

⊙ understand the difference between theoretical and experimental probability;

⊙ use results of an experiment to estimate experimental probability.

You cannot calculate theoretical probability when outcomes are **not** equally likely.

But you can estimate probability from the results of trials in an experiment.

This is the **experimental probability**:

$$\frac{\text{number of successful trials}}{\text{total number of trials}}$$

Example 1

In an experiment 50 people were asked if they were left-handed or right-handed.
The results are shown in the table.

Outcome	Tally	Frequency
Left-handed	卌 ‖	7
Right-handed	卌 卌 卌 卌 卌 卌 卌 卌 ‖‖	43

The experimental probability of a person being left-handed is $\frac{7}{50}$.

Example 2

Cameron and Nathan do an experiment
using this spinner.

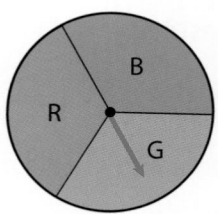

Cameron spins the arrow for 20 trials.
Here are Cameron's results.

Colour	Frequency
Red	9
Blue	7
Green	4

Nathan spins the arrow for 200 trials.
Here are Nathan's results.

Colour	Frequency
Red	74
Blue	88
Green	38

The experimental probabilities are:

Colour	Cameron's experiment	Nathan's experiment
Red	$\frac{9}{20} = 45\%$	$\frac{74}{200} = 37\%$
Blue	$\frac{7}{20} = 35\%$	$\frac{88}{200} = 44\%$
Green	$\frac{4}{20} = 25\%$	$\frac{38}{200} = 19\%$

The experiments show that experimental probabilities are not always the same.
Nathan's experiment gives a better estimate of the probability because there are more
trials.

Exercise 4

You will need a copy of **S4.1 Resource sheet 4.1** for questions 2 and 3.

This exercise consists of experiments and games.
Complete them in pairs or small groups.

When you have finished the experiments, your teacher will help you to compare your
results with those of other groups.

① You will need two coins.
Matthew throws two coins 40 times.
He records his results in a table.

Outcome	Tally	Frequency
HH	IIII III	8
HT	IIII IIII I	11
TH	IIII III	8
TT	IIII IIII III	13

a Work out the experimental probability of Matthew throwing:

  i   two heads;

  ii two heads **or** two tails;

  iii a head and a tail **or** a tail and a head.

b Repeat Matthew's experiment.
Do you get the same results?
Explain your answer.

② You will need two dice and a copy of **S4.1 Resource sheet 4.1**.
Ella rolls two dice and adds the scores.
She records the results in a table like this.

Score	Tally	Frequency
2		1
3		1
4		2
5		4
6		8
7		10
8		6
9		8
10		0
11		5
12		1

a The score of 7 appears more often.
Is this what you would expect? Explain your answer.

b Use your calculator to work out the experimental probability of a score of 7 correct to two decimal places.

c Repeat Ella's experiment.
Record the results in the first table on **S4.1 Resource sheet 4.1**.

d Use your calculator to work out your experimental probability of a score of 7 correct to two decimal places.

③ You will need four different coloured cubes in a bag or an envelope.
You will also need a copy of **S4.1 Resource sheet 4.1**.

⊙ Take a cube from the bag without looking.
Before you do this, ask your partner to guess its colour.

⊙ If the guess is correct, put a ✓ in the 1st column of the table on the sheet.
If the guess is wrong, put a ✗.

⊙ Put the cube on the table.

⊙ Repeat with another cube.
Carry on until all four cubes are taken from the bag.

a   Lena repeats the experiment for 10 trials. Her results are shown in this table.

Trial number	Guesses			
	1st	2nd	3rd	4th
1	✓	✗	✓	✓
2	✗	✓	✓	✓
3	✗	✗	✗	✓
4	✗	✓	✗	✓
5	✗	✓	✗	✓
6	✓	✗	✓	✓
7	✗	✗	✗	✓
8	✗	✓	✓	✓
9	✗	✓	✓	✓
10	✗	✗	✓	✓
Experimental probability				

Work out the experimental probability of each guess being correct.

b   Why is the experimental probability of the 4th guess 1?

c   Repeat Lena's experiment two more times.
Record your results in the tables on **S4.1 Resource sheet 4.1**.
Do you get the same results? Explain your answer.

Points to remember

⊙ The **experimental probability** of an event is $\dfrac{\text{number of successful trials}}{\text{total number of trials}}$.

⊙ Different experiments can give different values of experimental probability.

⊙ Experimental probability gives a better estimate of probability as the number of trials increases.

5 Are you lucky?

This lesson will help you to record results of experiments and use them to estimate experimental probabilities.

Exercise 5

In many games, particularly those involving dice or cards, chance plays a large part.
You can use probability to investigate the best strategies for winning games like this.

1. Play **Noughts and Crosses** with a partner.
   - Play 10 games, taking turns to go first.
   - Record who wins each game in a copy of this table.

Outcome	Tally	Frequency
Player 1 wins		
Player 2 wins		
Draw		

O	O	X
X	O	O
O	X	X

Game drawn

   a Work out the experimental probability of each of the outcomes.

   b What is the most likely result?

   c Would you expect the same results if you played against someone else?

   d How much chance is involved in this game? How much skill?

   e Is this a fair game?

The Game of Pig is a dice game for two to five players

Rules

- Take turns.
- The first player keeps rolling the dice and adding the scores, e.g. 2, 3, 5 scores 10.
- The player can decide when to stick.
- A player who rolls **1** before sticking scores zero for that turn.
- It is then the next player's turn.
- The winner is the first player to reach a score of 100.

70 | S4.1 *Probability*

Work in a group of two or three.

You will need a dice and **S4.1 Resource sheet 5.1**.

(2) Kieran and Leah played **The Game of Pig**. Here are the results. Leah won.

Turn	Kieran			Leah		
	Dice rolls	Score	Total	Dice rolls	Score	Total
1	3 3 2 6 4 4 **stick**	22	22	1	0	0
2	2 5 3 2 1	0	22	1	0	0
3	3 1	0	22	6 3 6 2 **stick**	17	17
4	2 4 3 5 3 5 **stick**	22	44	4 6 2 6 **stick**	18	35
5	3 5 4 6 6 **stick**	24	68	5 4 5 4 6 **stick**	24	59
6	6 5 1	0	68	5 3 3 1	0	59
7	1	0	68	3 6 3 5 2 **stick**	19	78
8	1	0	68	1	0	78
9	2 2 1	0	68	5 5 3 5 2 5 **stick**	25	103

a Kieran had 9 turns. He scored zero 6 times.
The experimental probability of Kieran scoring zero is $\frac{6}{9}$ or $\frac{2}{3}$.
What is the experimental probability of Leah scoring zero?

b Kieran rolled the dice a total of 32 times. He rolled 4 four times.
The experimental probability of Kieran rolling 4 is $\frac{4}{32}$ or $\frac{1}{8}$.
What is the experimental probability of Leah rolling 4?

(3) Play **The Game of Pig** in your group. Record your scores using
S4.1 Resource sheet 5.1.
a Work out your experimental probability of scoring zero.
b Work out your experimental probability of rolling 4.

(4) Discuss the game. What do you think is the best strategy for winning?

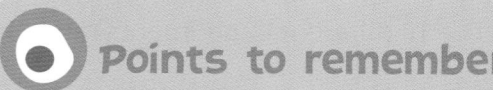

Points to remember

⊙ Some games involve chance. Some involve skill.
Some involve a mixture of both.

⊙ Using ideas of probability can give you the best chance of winning
a game.

6 Theory and experiment

This lesson will help you to compare experimental and theoretical probabilities.

When a probability experiment is repeated, the results may be different.

If a trial is fair, and the number of trials is large, the experimental probability is close to the theoretical probability.

Example

The theoretical probability of tossing a coin and getting a head is 0.5.

Ten pupils throw a coin 20 times each.
The table shows their results.

Pupil	Number of heads	Experimental probability of a head
Bill	11	$\frac{11}{20} = 0.55$
Sue	5	$\frac{5}{20} = 0.25$
Hamed	10	$\frac{10}{20} = 0.5$
Lucy	10	$\frac{10}{20} = 0.5$
Tim	12	$\frac{12}{20} = 0.6$
Derek	11	$\frac{11}{20} = 0.55$
Anna	10	$\frac{10}{20} = 0.5$
Tom	10	$\frac{10}{20} = 0.5$
Sadiq	12	$\frac{12}{20} = 0.6$
Emmie	8	$\frac{8}{20} = 0.4$
Total	**99**	$\frac{99}{200} = 0.495$

The experimental probabilities in the 10 different experiments range from 0.25 to 0.6.

All the results are combined.
The experimental probability is now 0.495, which is very close to the theoretical probability of 0.5.

It is likely that the coin is a fair coin.

Investigate spinning this spinner twice.

Work in pairs or threes.
You need **S4.1 Resource sheet 6.1** to help you.

Read these instructions before you begin.

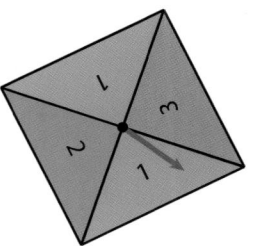

- Complete the table on the resource sheet to show all the possible outcomes for spinning the spinner twice.

- Do 40 trials.

  If you don't have a real spinner, you could use a computer simulation of the spinner.

  Or you could pick cards at random from four identical number cards shuffled face down, replacing the card after you draw each one.

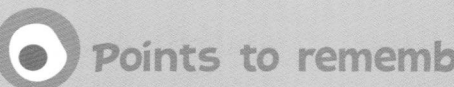

- When you have finished your experiment your teacher will help you combine your results with those of other pairs.

- Work out experimental and theoretical probabilities as decimals so that you can compare them easily.

● Points to remember

- ⊙ When a probability experiment is repeated, the results may be different.
- ⊙ If a trial is fair, and the number of trials is large, the experimental probability is close to the theoretical probability.

How well are you doing?

Can you:
- work out the theoretical probability of an event?
- work out the probability of an event not happening?
- use results to estimate the probability of an event?

Probability

1 *2007 level 6*

A computer is going to choose a letter at random from an English book.

The table shows the probabilities of the computer choosing each vowel.

Vowel	A	E	I	O	U
Probability	0.08	0.13	0.07	0.08	0.03

What is the probability that it will not choose a vowel?

2 *2005 level 6*

A spinner has the numbers 1 to 4 on it.

> The probability of spinning a number 4 is 0.1
>
> The probability of spinning a number 1 is 0.6
>
> The probability of spinning a number 2 is the same as the probability of spinning a number 3

Calculate the probability of spinning a number 3.

3 The colours of cars entering a school car park are shown in this table.

Colour	Silver	Red	White	Black	Blue	Other
Frequency	12	7	10	3	6	2

What is the experimental probability of each of these?

   a The colour of the next car to enter the car park is silver.

   b The colour of the next car to enter the car park is red or blue.

   c The colour of the next car that leaves the car park is not white.

4 *1999 level 5*

A coin has two sides, heads and tails.

a Sion is going to toss two coins.
Copy and complete the table to show the different results he could get.

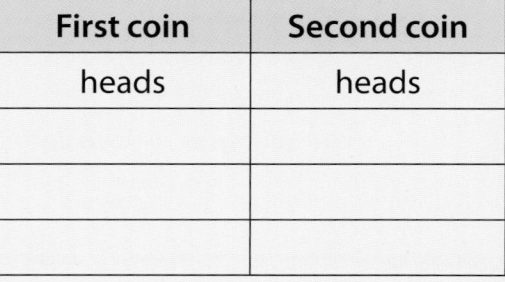

heads   tails

First coin	Second coin
heads	heads

b Sion is going to toss two coins.
What is the probability that he will get tails with both his coins?
Write your answer as a fraction.

c Dianne tossed one coin. She got tails.

Dianne is going to toss another coin.

What is the probability that she will get tails again with her next coin?
Write your answer as a fraction.

5 *1997 level 5*

Karen and Huw each have three cards, numbered 2, 3 and 4.
They each take any one of their own cards.
They add the numbers on the two cards.
The table shows all the possible answers.

a What is the probability that their answer is an even number?

b What is the probability that their answer is a number greater than 6?

Karen

+	2	3	4
2	4	5	6
3	5	6	7
4	6	7	8

Huw

c Karen and Huw each take any one of their own cards.

This time they multiply the numbers on the two cards.

Draw a table to show all possible answers.

d Copy and complete this sentence:
The probability that their answer is a number that is less than .... is $\frac{8}{9}$.

A 4.2

Expressions and formulae

This unit will help you to:

- know what is meant by a 'term', 'like terms' and 'algebraic expression';
- simplify expressions by collecting like terms;
- evaluate formulae by substituting numbers for letters;
- work with expressions and formulae involving powers.

1 Simplifying expressions

This lesson will help you to simplify algebraic expressions by collecting like terms.

The word **term** is used in algebra to describe one or more numbers and/or letters that are combined by multiplication or division. 6, $4x$, $3mn$, $6pqr$ are all terms.

Like terms have the same combination of letters. $3n$, $6n$ and n are all like terms.

You can **simplify** an expression by collecting like terms, like this:
$n + 2n + 3m + 5m = 3n + 8m$

You can use a grid to help you to multiply numbers.

Example 1   Multiply 8×73.

$\times$	70	+	3
8	560	+	24

Answer: $8 \times 73 = 584$

In the same way, you can use a grid to help you multiply out brackets.

Example 2   Multiply out $4(3x + 2)$.

$\times$	$3x$	+	2
4	$12x$	+	8

Answer: $4(3x + 2) = 12x + 8$

Exercise 1

1 Copy the expressions and underline the terms.

   a $2x + 3xy - 5y - 7xyz$

   b $5mn + 6mst - nst + ms - 4$

   c $9pq - 4p + 3q - 2r + pqr$

   d $13 + 2w - 3x - y + 2xy$

2 Copy the expressions.
   Underline like terms using different colours.
   Then simplify the expressions.

   a $x + x + x + x + x + x$

   b $y + y + 2y + 6y + 3y$

   c $2p + 2p + 5p + 7p$

   d $5 + 2q + 6 + 4q + 7$

   e $x + 2x + 3x + 7x + 8y + 2y$

   f $3 + 2n + 5 + 7n$

   g $2x + 3y + x + 6y$

   h $5p + 4p - p + 7$

   i $5t + 3s - 2t - s$

   j $4x - 2y - x + 7y$

   k $2w + 4l - 2 + 3w - 2l + 6$

   l $3ab + a - b + 4ab - b$

3 Use a grid to work out the products.

   a 4×53

   b 3×67

   c 7×62

   d 8×54

   e 9×98

   f 9×71

4 Multiply out the brackets.

   a $3(4 + x)$

   b $5(y + 7)$

   c $6(x + y)$

   d $2(x + y + 3)$

   e $3(2x + 4)$

   f $5(4a + 3b)$

   g $7(3 - 2t)$

   h $4(3x - 5)$

   i $6(2a + 3b - 5c)$

   j $9(4p - 3q + r)$

5 Multiply out the brackets and simplify the expressions.

   a $2(x + 3) + 3(x + 5)$

   b $4(y + 1) + 7(y + 6)$

   c $9(s + 4) + 5(s + 7)$

   d $6(p + 9) + 8(p + 1)$

   e $10(2a + 1) + 2(a - 4)$

   f $3(4x - 2) + 11(3x + 4)$

   g $8(4t - 7) + 7(2t - 9)$

   h $5(6b + 1) + 4(7b - 1)$

   i $6(8x - 2) + 9(5x + 8)$

   j $7(10y - 2) + 10(7y - 9)$

(6) Find the matching pairs.

$2(x + 4) + 6(x + 5)$

$9(x + 2) - (x + 7)$

$8x + 19$

$8x + 36$

$8x + 21$

$6(x + 7) + 2(x - 3)$

$8x + 11$

$3(2x + 1) + 2(x + 9)$

$7(2x + 1) - 3(2x - 4)$

$8x + 38$

(7) The expression in each cell is the result of adding the expressions in the two cells beneath it. Copy the diagrams and fill in the missing expressions.

a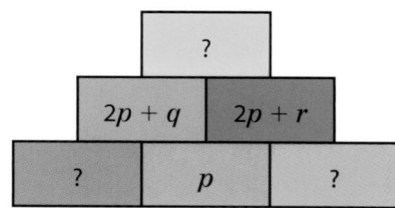

b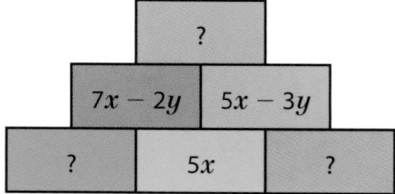

(8) In a magic square the sum of the expressions in each row, column and diagonal is the same.
Copy and complete this magic square.

$a - b$		$a + c$
	a	
$a - c$	$a - b$ $+ c$	

Extension problems

(9) Multiply out the brackets and simplify the expressions.

a $4(t + 7) - 2(t + 3)$

b $7(x + 4) - 5(x + 2)$

c $8(m + 7) - 2(m + 5)$

d $9(w + 1) - 3(w + 2)$

e $10(3x + 2) - 2(2x - 7)$

f $6(5q - 1) - (13q + 2)$

g $9(2r - 3) - 4(3r - 7)$

h $7(4s + 3) + 5(6s - 2)$

i $11(9x - 5) - 2(3x + 10)$

j $4(8y - 5) - 2(11y - 1)$

10 Factorise the expressions.

a $6x + 42$ b $8x + 36$
c $12x + 21$ d $15x + 25$
e $24x + 33$ f $26x - 39$
g $48x - 60$ h $30x + 55$
i $38x - 95$ j $34x - 119$

Points to remember

⊙ A **term** is one or more numbers and/or letters combined by multiplication or division.

⊙ **Like terms** have the same combination of letters. $2x$, $5x$ and x are all like terms.

⊙ An **expression** is one or more terms combined by addition or subtraction.

2 Using formulae

This lesson will help you to use formulae.

A **formula** is a concise expression where the letters represent a particular quantity.

You have already used formulae in geometry lessons.

For example, the formula for the area of a rectangle is lw, where l is the length and w the width of the rectangle.

Exercise 2

1 Let l be the length.
Let w be the width.

Perimeter $P = 2l + 2w$
Area $\quad\quad A = lw$

Copy and complete the table.

	Length l	Width w	Perimeter P	Area A
a	12 cm	5 cm		
b	17 cm	4 cm		
c	40 cm	7 cm		
d	8 cm	3 cm		
e	50 cm	30 cm		

2 Let b be the base.
Let h be the height.
The area of the triangle is $\frac{1}{2}bh$.

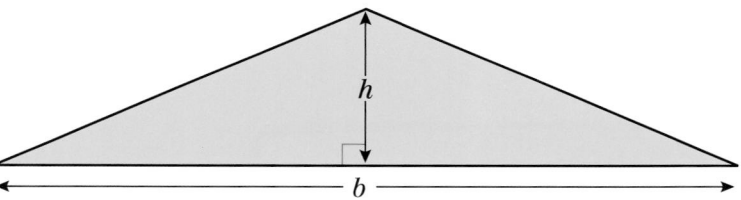

Copy and complete the table.

	Base b	Height h	Area A
a	8 cm	6 cm	
b	9 cm	5 cm	
c	12 cm	7 cm	
d	20 cm	14 cm	
e	15 cm	10 cm	
f	7 cm	4 cm	
g	2 cm	0.5 cm	

(3) Let x be the length in centimetres of each side of a regular hexagon. The perimeter of the hexagon is $6x$.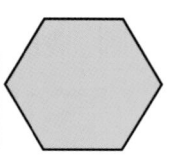

Calculate the perimeter of the hexagon when

a $x = 4$ cm b $x = 2.4$ cm c $x = 7.3$ cm d $x = 25$ cm

e $x = 1.5$ cm f $x = 14.6$ cm g $x = 19$ cm h $x = 0.75$ cm

(4) a The area of a rectangle is 42 cm². Its width is 6 cm. What is the length?

b The perimeter of a square is 11.2 cm. What is length of each side?

c The perimeter of a regular octagon is 28.8 cm. What is the length of each side?

d The perimeter of a rectangle is 28 cm and its length is 10 cm. What is its width?

e The area of a triangle is 30 cm² and its base is 12 cm. What is its height?

f The area of a triangle is 10.5 cm² and its height is 3 cm. What is its base?

(5) Let n be the number of emails that Jamie receives in a week. Work out an expression using n for each of these.

a Charlie receives four times as many emails as Jamie.

b Caitlin receives 20 more emails than Jamie.

c Holly receives a quarter as many emails as Jamie.

d Bradley receives six fewer emails than Charlie.

e Aaron receives twice as many emails as Caitlin.

f Laura receives half as many emails as Holly.

g Max receives seven times as many emails as Charlie.

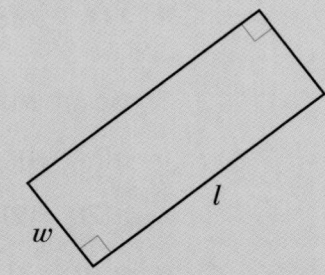

Extension problem

(6) a The nth term T_n of a number sequence is $T_n = 5n + 3$. What is the 220th term?

b Draw the graph of $T_n = 5n + 3$.

c Describe the graph.

⊙ Points to remember

⊙ A **formula** is shorthand for a general rule.

For example, the formula for the area of a rectangle is lw, where l is the length and w the width.
Substitute values for l and w to work out the area.

3 Simplifying expressions with powers

This lesson will help you to simplify expressions containing powers.

$3 \times 3 \times 3 \times 3 \times 3$ can be written in index form as 3^5.
We say this as 'three raised to the power of five'.
The number 5 is the **index** or **power**.
The value of 3^5 is 243.

Remember that $3^1 = 3$ and $3^0 = 1$.

You can simplify an expression by writing numbers that are multiplied by themselves in index form.

Example $2 \times 2 \times 2 \times 3 = 2^3 \times 3$

Exercise 3

1. Work out the value of the numbers written in index form.

    a 8^2 b 2^6 c 3^3 d 5^4

    e 4^7 f 6^3 g 7^5 h 9^4

2. Numbers can be written as the product of prime numbers.
    Simplify the expressions by using index form.

    a $360 = 2 \times 2 \times 2 \times 3 \times 3 \times 5$ b $2700 = 2 \times 2 \times 3 \times 3 \times 3 \times 5 \times 5$

    c $8575 = 5 \times 5 \times 7 \times 7 \times 7$ d $1134 = 2 \times 3 \times 3 \times 3 \times 3 \times 7$

    e $5775 = 3 \times 5 \times 5 \times 7 \times 11$ f $5040 = 2 \times 2 \times 2 \times 2 \times 3 \times 3 \times 5 \times 7$

3. Write the algebraic terms in index form.

    a $x \times x \times x \times x \times x$ b $y \times y \times y \times y \times y \times y \times y$

    c $p \times p \times p \times q \times q$ d $m \times m \times m \times m \times n \times n \times n$

    e $x \times y \times y \times z \times z \times z$ f $3 \times p \times q \times q \times r \times r$

4. These are nth terms for number sequences. Find the term specified.

    a $n(n + 4)$ 9th term   b $n(n - 6)$ 18th term

    c $n(2n + 9)$ 20th term   d $3n(2n + 7)$ 50th term

    e $n^2(n - 1)$ 10th term   f $n(5n^2 + 3)$ 7th term

(5) You will need **A4.2 Resource sheet 3.1** cut into cards, a dice and two or more players to play this game.

Rules

- Place the cards face down in a pile.
- Each player selects a card from the pile.
- Take turns to throw the dice.
- Substitute the number on the dice for x in the expression on your cards.
- The player with the highest score records that number. If players get the same score, they both record their score.
- Replace the cards at the bottom of the pile.
- The player with the highest total score after five turns wins the game.

Extension problem

(6) Work out the value of the terms.

a x^2y^3	$x = 3, y = 2$	b $3s^4t^2$	$s = 2, t = 7$
c $4p^3q^6$	$p = 5, q = 1$	d $7x^8y$	$x = 2, y = 7$
e $9mn^5$	$m = 9, n = 3$	f $20u^3v^3$	$u = 4, v = 2$
g $10x^0y^5$	$x = 7, y = 3$	h $5ab^4$	$a = 6, b = 0.5$

⊙ Points to remember

- Index notation is used when numbers are multiplied by themselves.

  $3 \times 3 \times 3 \times 3 \times 3 \times 3 = 3^6$

- In algebra, the same notation is used when letters in algebra are multiplied by themselves.

  $a \times a \times a \times a \times a \times a = a^6$

  We say 'a raised to the power of six'.

- The numbers and letters are written in **index form**.

- $5x^2y^3$ means $5 \times x \times x \times y \times y \times y$.

  When $x = 2$ and $y = 3$, $5x^2y^3 = 5 \times 2 \times 2 \times 3 \times 3 \times 3 = 540$.

4 Using algebraic expressions

This lesson will help you to use formulae involving powers.

Exercise 4

1   A teacher asked her class to complete the table for the algebraic expression 'five x plus two squared'. Pupils wrote the expression in four different ways:

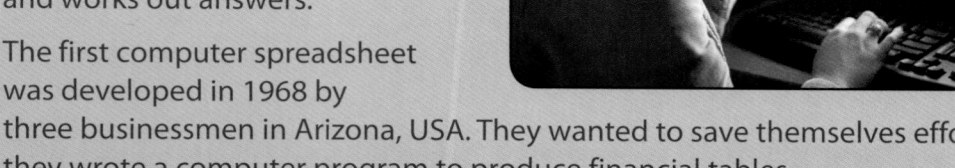

$5x + 2^2$, $(5x + 2)^2$, $5(x + 2)^2$ and $5(x + 2^2)$.

Match the expression to the correct column. Copy and complete the table.

x	Expression A	Expression B	Expression C	Expression D
3	?	35	?	19
2	80	?	144	?
1	?	25	?	9
0	20	?	4	?
−1	?	15	?	−1
−2	0	?	64	?
−3	?	5	?	−11

(2) Let x be the length of a side of a square in cm.

Area of square $= x^2$

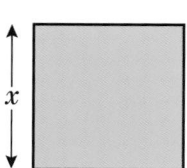

a What is the area of a square when $x = 7$?

b If the area of a square is $169\,cm^2$, what is x?

(3) Let x be the length of a side of a cube in cm.

Volume of cube $= x^3$

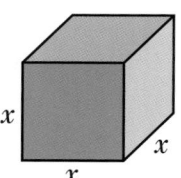

a What is the volume of a cube when $x = 5$?

b If the volume of the cube is $216\,cm^3$, what is x?

c If the volume of the cube is $1\,000\,000\,cm^3$, what is x?

(4) Let r be the radius of a circle in cm.

The area of a circle is approximately $3 \times r^2$.

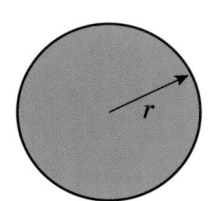

a What is the approximate area of the circle when $r = 8$?

b If the area of a circle is approximately $108\,cm^2$, what is r?

Extension problem

(5) Imagine that you have three discs, one large, one medium and one small, and three rods. You place the discs in order of size on one of the rods, with the smallest on top. You want to transfer the discs to another rod. But:

– you can move only one disc at a time;

– a larger disc must never be placed on a smaller disc.

a What is the minimum number of moves required?

b Investigate the minimum number of moves for different numbers of discs.

⊙ Points to remember

⊙ A **formula** is an algebraic expression in which the letters represent something in real life.

For example, the formula for the area of a square is x^2, where x is the length of each side of the square.

How well are you doing?

(1) *2005 level 5*

a Here is an expression. $\boxed{2a + 3 + 2a}$

Which expression below shows it written as simply as possible?

A $7a$ **B** $7 + a$ **C** $2a + 5$ **D** $4a + 3$ **E** $4(a + 3)$

b Here is a different expression. $\boxed{3b + 4 + 5b - 1}$

Write this expression as simply as possible.

(2) *2007 level 5*

Look at this equation.

$$y = 2x + 10$$

a When $x = 4$, what is the value of y?

b When $x = -4$, what is the value of y?

c Which equation below gives the same value of y for both $x = 4$ and $x = -4$?

A $y = 2x$ **B** $y = 2 + x$ **C** $y = x^2$ **D** $y = \dfrac{x}{2}$

(3) *2007 level 6*

Jenny wants to multiply out the brackets in the expression $3(2a + 1)$.

She writes:

$$3(2a + 1) = 6a + 1$$

Show why Jenny is wrong.

4 *2006 level 6*

Multiply out this expression. Write your answer as simply as possible.

$$5(x + 2) + 3(7 + x)$$

5 *2005 level 6*

About 2000 years ago, a Greek mathematician worked out this formula to find the area of any triangle.

For a triangle with sides a, b and c

$$\text{Area} = \sqrt{s(s - a)(s - b)(s - c)}$$

where $s = \dfrac{a + b + c}{2}$

A triangle has sides, in cm, of 3, 5 and 6.

Use $a = 3$, $b = 5$ and $c = 6$ to work out the area of this triangle.

6 *2004 level 6*

Doctors sometimes use this formula to calculate how much medicine to give a child.

$$c = \frac{ay}{12 + y}$$

c is the correct amount for a child, in ml

a is the amount for an adult, in ml

y is the age of the child, in years

A child who is 4 years old needs some medicine.
The amount for an adult is 20 ml.

Use the formula to work out the correct amount for this child.
You must show your working.

Measures and mensuration

This unit will help you to:

- ◉ convert between metric units;
- ◉ remember the approximate equivalents for metric and imperial measures;
- ◉ know and use formulae for the area of a triangle, parallelogram and trapezium;
- ◉ find the area and perimeter of compound shapes;
- ◉ work out the volume and surface area of cuboids and shapes made from cuboids.

 Did you know that...?

Imperial measurements are still used today. Questions like: 'How tall are you?', 'How much do you weigh?', 'How far is London from Barrow-in-Furness?' are often answered in imperial measurements. The answers might be $5\frac{1}{2}$ **feet**, 8 **stone** or 280 **miles**.

Milk is often sold in **pints**, another imperial measure.

Many sports activities still use imperial measurements.

In football the penalty area is often known as the 18-**yard** box.

The length of a cricket pitch is 22 **yards**, which is one **chain**. Horse racing is measured in **furlongs**. One furlong is 10 chains, or 220 yards, and there are eight furlongs in one **mile**.

The depth of water is measured in **fathoms**, where one fathom is two yards or six **feet**.

Imperial measures of length were originally linked to parts of the body. An **inch** was the width of a man's thumb at the knuckle, a **foot** was the length of a man's foot and a **yard** was the length of the king's outstretched arm. The measures were all slightly different so, in 1844, the Government made a standard yard in bronze, marked in feet and inches, which is still on show in Greenwich.

In a wall in **Trafalgar Square**, London, a plaque from 1876 shows the standards of length for an inch, a foot, two feet and a yard.

1 Converting between units

This lesson will help you to convert between units of measurement.

Length

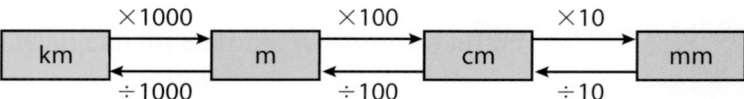

Area

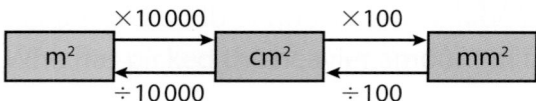

Mass

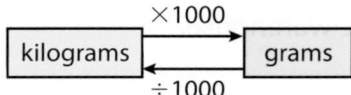

Capacity

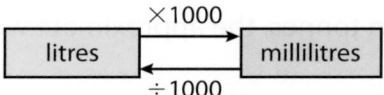

More metric units

Mass 1 tonne = 1000 kg

Area 1 hectare (ha) = 10 000 m²

100 hectares = 1 km²

Example

A car weighs 2150 kg.
Write this in tonnes.

1 tonne = 1000 kg

2150 kg ÷ 1000 = 2.15 tonnes

Exercise 1A

1 Change these measurements into the units given.

  a 36 cm into m   **b** 4.6 m into mm   **c** 4000 g into kg

  d 0.63 litres into ml   **e** 3.4 km into m   **f** 23 000 mm into km

  g 0.34 kg into g   **h** 21 000 000 cm into km

2 Change these measurements into the units given.

  a 7000 m² to cm²   **b** 45 000 cm² to mm²   **c** 2 m² to mm²

  d 900 cm² to m²   **e** 6000 mm² to cm²   **f** 150 000 mm² to m²

3 A gardener leaves a water sprinkler on at a rate of 8 litres per minute.
How many millilitres (ml) of water will be used in 1 hour?

2 Perimeter and area of triangles

This lesson will help you to find the perimeter and area of shapes made from triangles and rectangles.

The **perimeter** of a plane shape is the total length of all its sides.
Area of a triangle $= \frac{1}{2} \times$ base $\times$ height
The height is always perpendicular (at 90°) to the base.

Example

Find the area of each of these triangles.

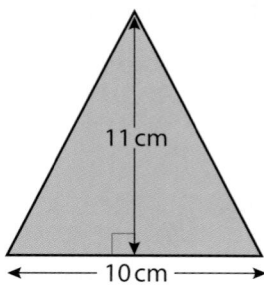

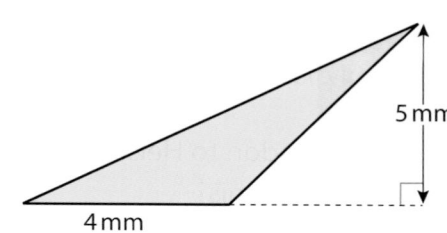

Area $= \frac{1}{2} \times 10 \times 11 = 55$ cm² $\qquad$ Area $= \frac{1}{2} \times 4 \times 5 = 10$ mm²

Exercise 2A

1. Find the perimeter of each of these triangles.

a

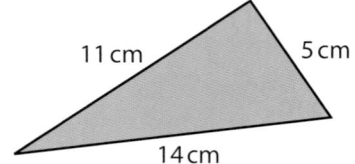

b

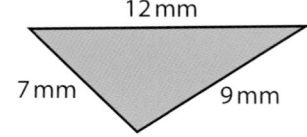

c

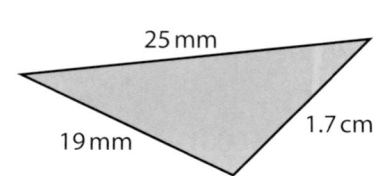

2 **a** What is the perimeter of this triangle?

b Write down a formula, starting $P = \ldots$, for the perimeter P of a triangle.

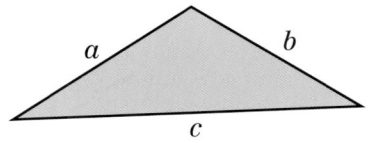

c Write down a formula for the perimeter of an isosceles triangle with sides of length a, b and a.

d Write down a formula for the perimeter of an equilateral triangle with sides of length a.

3 **a** What is the perimeter of this parallelogram?

b Write down the formula for the perimeter of a parallelogram with sides of length l and h.

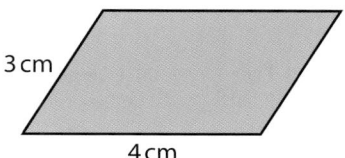

4 **a** What is the perimeter of this trapezium?

b Write down the formula for the perimeter of a trapezium with parallel sides of length w and x, and sloping sides of length y and z.

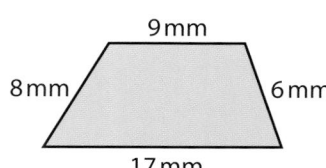

5 Calculate the area of each triangle.

a
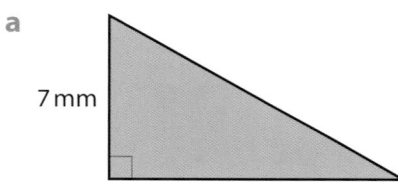

b
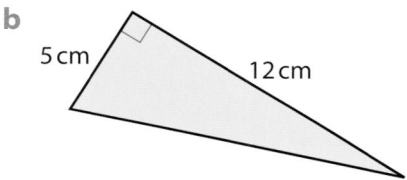

c

d
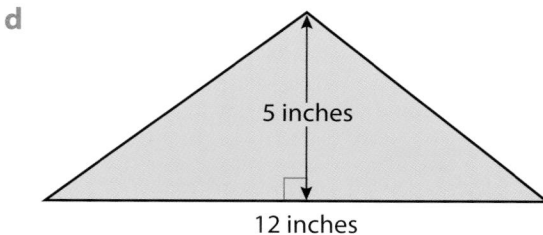

e
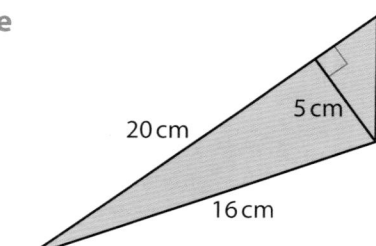

f
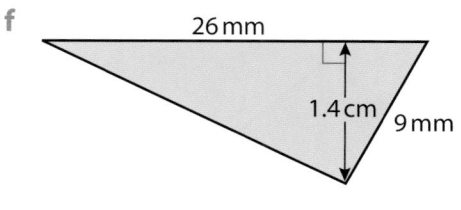

6 Find the perimeter of each shape.

a

7 cm   7 cm
8 cm   8 cm
11 cm

b

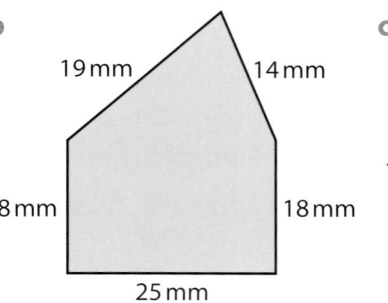

19 mm   14 mm
18 mm   18 mm
25 mm

c

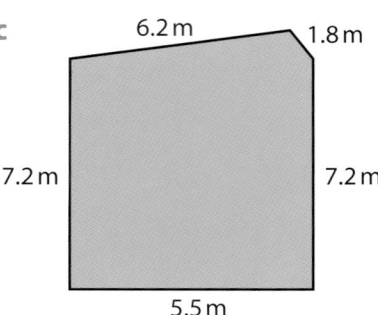

6.2 m   1.8 m
7.2 m   7.2 m
5.5 m

7 Find the area of the shaded triangle inside the rectangle.

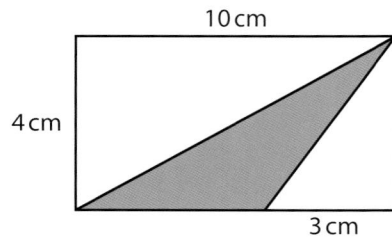

10 cm
4 cm
3 cm

Extension problems

8 The base of a triangle is 6 cm and the area is 12 cm².
Find the perpendicular height of the triangle.

9 The perpendicular height of a triangular sail is 14 feet.
Its area is 49 square feet.
How long is the base of the triangular sail?

10 In this triangle, calculate the length of the
perpendicular height marked x.

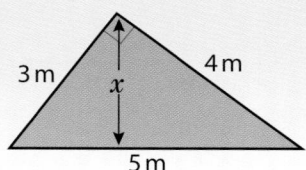

3 m   4 m
x
5 m

Exercise 2B

1 Each of these shapes is made from rectangles and triangles.
Calculate the area of each shape.

a

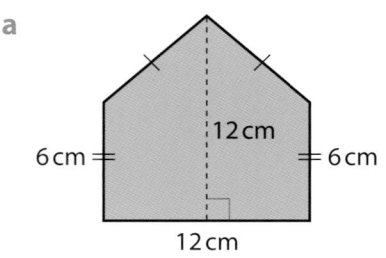

6 cm   12 cm   6 cm
12 cm

b

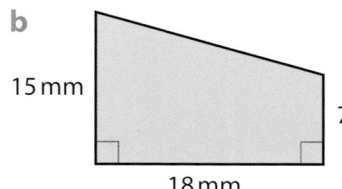

15 mm   7 mm
18 mm

c

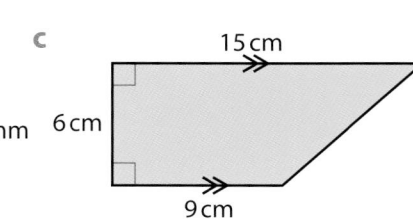

15 cm
6 cm
9 cm

② The diagonals of a rectangle intersect each other at the centre of the rectangle.

Calculate the area of the shaded triangle. Show your method.

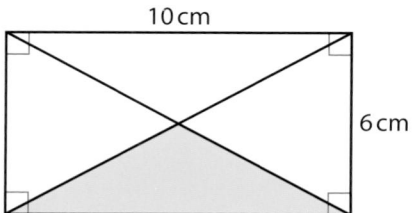

③ a Find the total area of this shape.
b What is the perimeter of the shape?

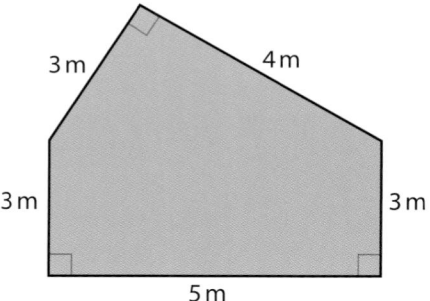

Extension problem

④ The total area of this shape is 230 mm².
Find the length of side x.

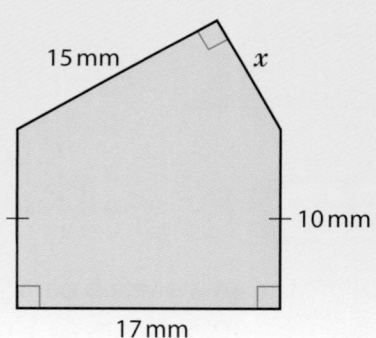

⦿ Points to remember

⊙ Area of a triangle $= \frac{1}{2} \times$ base $\times$ perpendicular height.
⊙ The height is always **perpendicular** to the base.
⊙ The units are always square units.

3 Perimeter and area of quadrilaterals

This lesson will help you to use formulae to find the area of parallelograms and trapeziums.

Area of a parallelogram = base × perpendicular height

Example

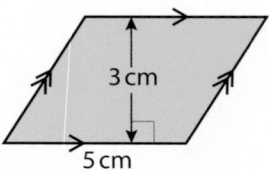

Area = 5 × 3 = 15 cm²

Area of a trapezium = $\frac{1}{2}$ × sum of parallel sides × perpendicular height

Example

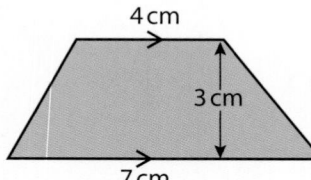

Area = $\frac{1}{2}$ × (4 + 7) × 3 = $\frac{1}{2}$ × 11 × 3 = 16.5 cm²

Exercise 3

1. Calculate the area of each parallelogram.

   a
   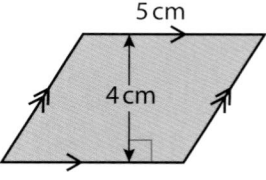

   b
   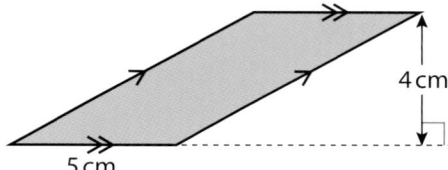

   c
   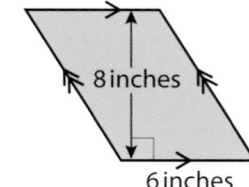

   d
   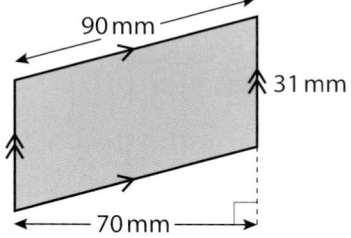

2. A parallelogram has an area of 96 m².
   The base is 8 m long.
   Find the perpendicular height, marked a.

   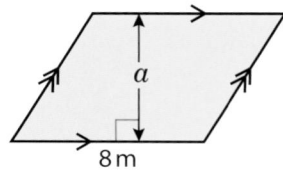

3 The triangle and the parallelogram have the same area and the same perpendicular height. Find the value of x.

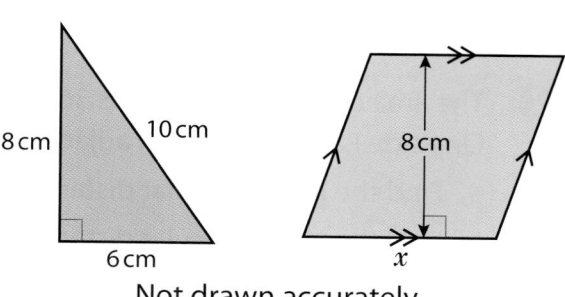

Not drawn accurately

4 Find the area of each trapezium.

a

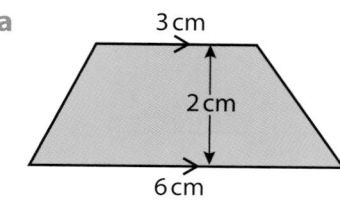

3 cm
2 cm
6 cm

b

3 feet
2 feet
5 feet

c

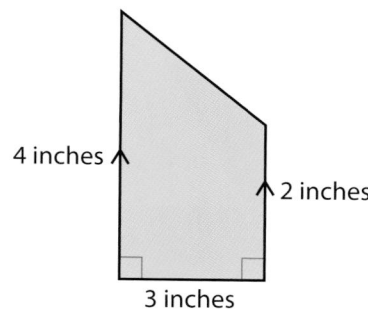

4 inches
2 inches
3 inches

d

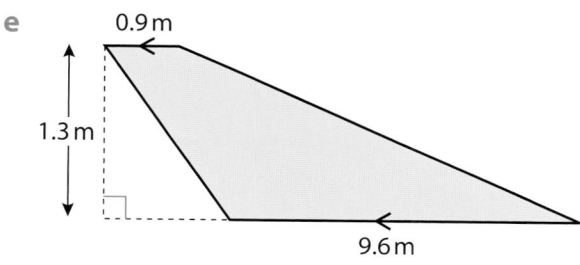

3 m
2 m
5.5 m

e

0.9 m
1.3 m
9.6 m

5 The area of this trapezium is 320 cm². Find the length of side a.

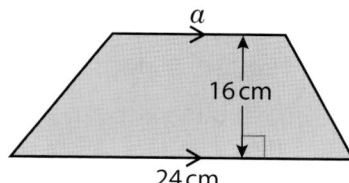

a
16 cm
24 cm

6 The area of this trapezium is 100 mm². Find the perpendicular height, h.

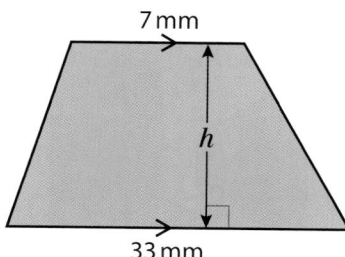

7 mm
h
33 mm

3 Calculate the volume of each cuboid.

a
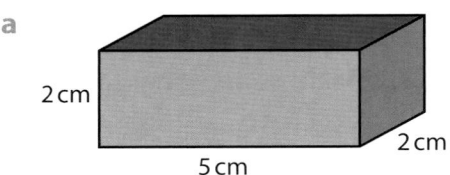
2 cm
5 cm
2 cm

b
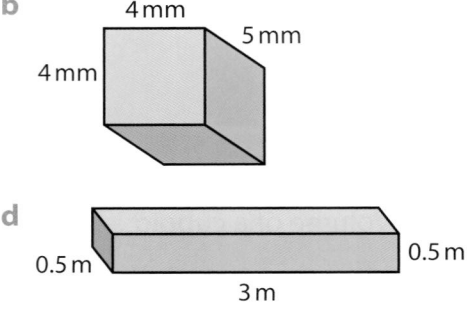
4 mm
5 mm
4 mm

c
8 cm
1 cm
3 cm
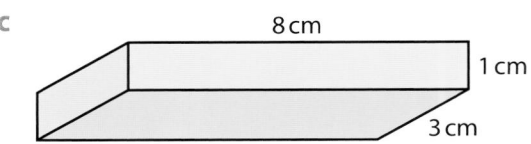

d
0.5 m
3 m
0.5 m

4 The dimensions of a cuboid are 3 cm by 5 cm by 2 cm.
Calculate its volume.

5 The area of the base of a cuboid is 24 mm². Its height is 3 mm.
What is the volume of the cuboid?

6 A cuboid has a volume of 36 m³. The lengths of two of the edges are 3 m and 4 m.
What is the length of the third edge?

7 Each of these shapes is made from cuboids. Calculate the volume of each shape.

a
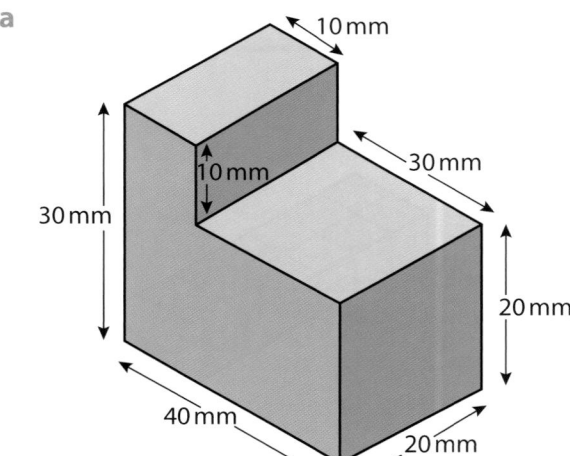
10 mm
10 mm
30 mm
30 mm
30 mm
20 mm
40 mm
20 mm

b
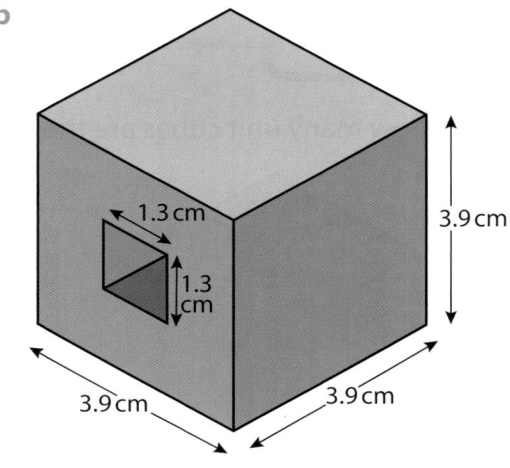
1.3 cm
1.3 cm
3.9 cm
3.9 cm
3.9 cm

8 A cuboid has a volume of 72 cm³. One edge is 3 cm long.
What are the dimensions of the other two edges?
Investigate.

Extension problems

9 Containers come in three lengths: 24 m, 18 m and 12 m.
Each is 4.6 m wide and 4.6 m tall.
How many crates measuring 2.2 m by 2.2 m by 5.8 m will fit in each of the three containers?

10 A box of paperclips has dimensions
2.3 cm by 4.4 cm by 6.2 cm.

A shopkeeper puts boxes of paperclips in an open display tray with dimensions
2.3 cm by 8.8 cm by 31 cm.

What is the largest number of boxes of paperclips that can lie flat in the tray?

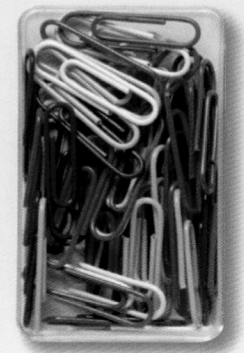

11 How many different cuboids can you make using exactly 100 identical cubes each time?

Investigate.

> ### Points to remember
>
> - The volume of a cuboid is length × width × height, or area of base × height.
> - Volume is measured in cubic units, such as cubic millimetres (mm^3), cubic centimetres (cm^3) or cubic metres (m^3).
> - When you find the volume of a cuboid, the edges must all be in the same units.
> - To find the volume of a shape made from cuboids, divide the shape up into cuboids and add the volumes together.

5 Surface area of cuboids

This lesson will help you to find the surface area of cuboids and solve problems involving surface area and volume.

1 millilitre = 1 cm^3
1 litre = 1000 cm^3
1000 litres = 1 m^3

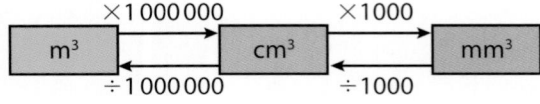

Example

A swimming pool holds 295 m^3 of water. How many litres is this?

1 m^3 = 1000 litres
295 m^3 = 295 × 1000 = 295 000 litres

Exercise 5A

1 Change these to cubic centimetres.

   a 2 litres of cola

   b $\frac{1}{2}$ litre of cooking oil

   c 0.7 litres of wine

   d 5 litres of car oil

2 **a** A car has a maximum boot space of 460 litres.
How many cubic metres (m^3) is this?

   b The same car has a fuel tank that can hold 63 000 cm^3 of unleaded petrol.
How many litres is this?

   c A car's engine capacity is 1896 cm^3. How many litres is this?

3 An Olympic-sized swimming pool holds 2 500 000 litres of water.
How many cubic metres is this?

The **surface area of a cuboid** is the total area of all the faces. You can calculate this by working out the area of each face and then adding them together, or by using:

$$\text{surface area} = 2 \times a \times b + 2 \times a \times c + 2 \times b \times c$$

where a, b and c are the dimensions of the cuboid.

Surface area is measured in **square units**, such as square millimetres (mm^2), square centimetres (cm^2) or square metres (m^2).

When you find the surface area of a cuboid, the edges must all be in the same units, e.g. all in metres, or all in centimetres, or all in millimetres.

Example

Calculate the surface area of this cuboid.

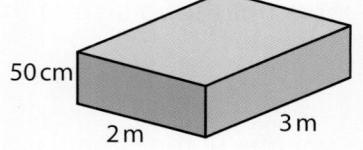

The lengths of the edges are 0.5 m, 2 m and 3 m.
The surface area is:
$$2 \times (0.5 \times 2) + 2 \times (0.5 \times 3) + 2 \times (2 \times 3) = 2 + 3 + 12 = 17 \text{ m}^2$$

1　The small squares on the outside of a 5 cm cube are painted dark blue, light blue and white.

  a　How many small squares are coloured dark blue?

  b　How many small squares are coloured light blue?

  c　How many small squares are coloured white?

2　Find the surface area of each cuboid.

  a

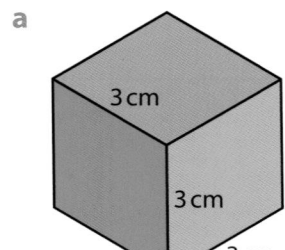

  b

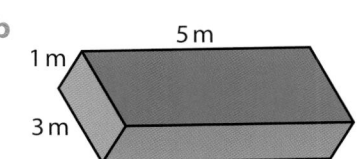

  c

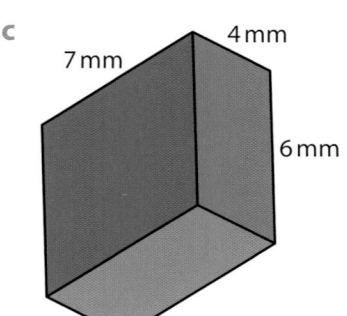

  d

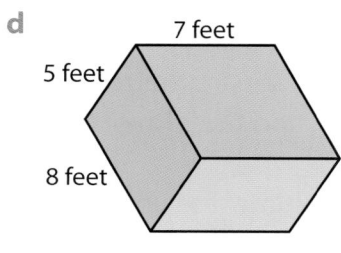

3 A cuboid has length 7 cm, width 5 cm and total surface area of 118 cm².
Find the height of the cuboid.

4 A cube has a surface area of 384 cm².
  a Find the length of an edge of the cube.
  b Find the volume of the cube.

5 The areas of three of the faces of a
cuboid are shown on this diagram.
  a Work out the dimensions of this cuboid.
  b Work out the volume of the cuboid.

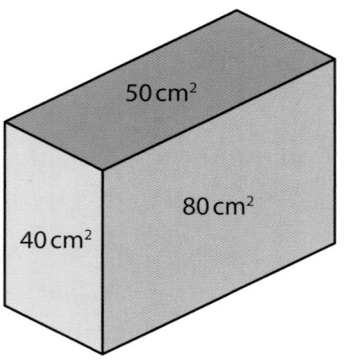

50 cm²

80 cm²

40 cm²

6 The volume of the cuboid is 36 mm³.
The height is 3 mm.
The length and width are each a whole number of millimetres.
What could they be? Investigate.

Work out the surface area for each possible cuboid.
Copy the table and use it to record your findings for each different cuboid.
One example has been completed for you.

Height (mm)	Length (mm)	Width (mm)	Surface area (mm²)
3	1	12	$(2 \times 3 \times 1) + (2 \times 3 \times 12) + (2 \times 1 \times 12) = 102$
3			

● Points to remember

⊙ Surface area is measured in square units, such as square millimetres (mm²), square centimetres (cm²) or square metres (m²).
⊙ To find the surface area of a solid, find the sum of the areas of each face.
⊙ In problems involving area and volume, the units of the sides or edges of shapes must be the same.

How well are you doing?

Conversion between units

1 *2007 level 5*

Here are two containers and the amounts they hold.

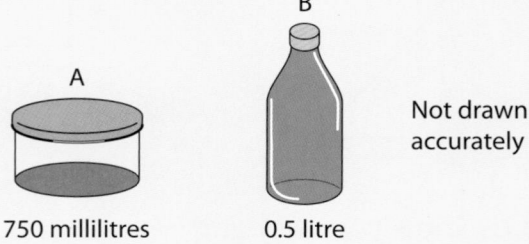

A
750 millilitres

B
Not drawn accurately
0.5 litre

a Which container holds the greater amount, A or B?

b How much more does it hold? Give your answer in millilitres.

2 *2006 level 5*

Copy and complete these sentences.

a 120 mm is the same as ... cm.

b 120 cm is the same as ... m.

c 120 m is the same as ... km.

3 *2004 level 5*

A box contains bags of crisps.
Each bag of crisps weighs 25 grams.

Altogether, the bags of crisps inside the box weigh 1 kilogram.
How many bags of crisps are inside the box?

Area and volume

4 *2007 level 6*

The diagram shows a shaded parallelogram drawn inside a rectangle.

What is the area of the shaded parallelogram?
Give the correct unit with your answer.

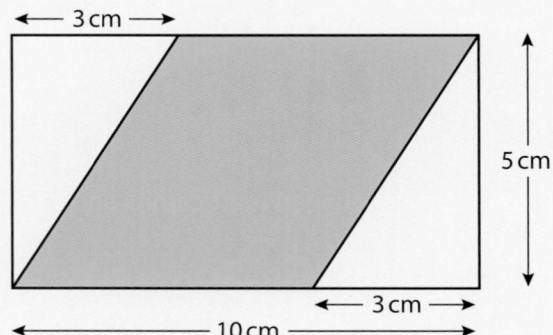

5 *2004 level 6*

The triangle and the rectangle below have the same area.

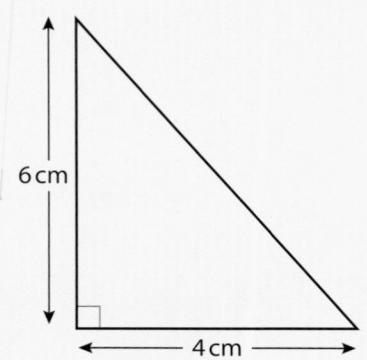
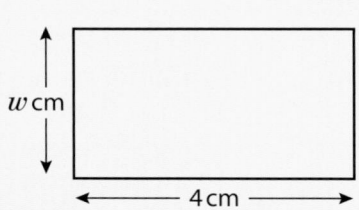

Work out the value of w. Show your working.

6 *2002 level 6*

The drawing shows two cuboids that have the same volume.

Cuboid A

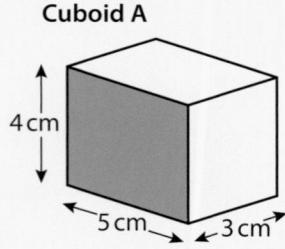

Cuboid B

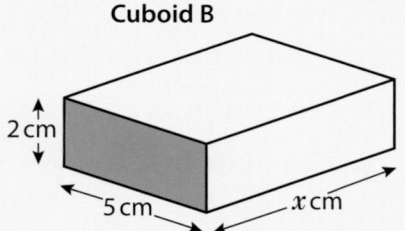

a What is the volume of cuboid A? State your units.

b Work out the value of the length marked x.

c What is the surface area of cuboid A? State your units.

d What is the surface area of cuboid B? State your units.

Fractions, decimals and percentages

This unit will help you to:

- recognise recurring decimals;

- order and calculate with fractions;

- use mental and written methods to multiply and divide by decimals;

- find equivalent fractions, decimals and percentages;

- write one number as a percentage of another;

- work out percentage increases or decreases;

- solve problems involving fractions, decimals and percentages, using a calculator where appropriate.

1 Ordering fractions

This lesson will help you to recognise recurring decimals and put fractions in order.

There are two ways to compare the size of two fractions.

1 Convert each fraction to a decimal by dividing the numerator by the denominator. Then compare the decimals. You can use a calculator to do this.

Example 1

Which is larger, $\frac{3}{8}$ or $\frac{7}{20}$?

$\frac{3}{8}$ as a decimal is 0.375. $\frac{7}{20}$ as a decimal is 0.35.

Since 0.375 is greater than 0.35, $\frac{3}{8}$ is larger than $\frac{7}{20}$.

2 Change each of the fractions to a common denominator.

Example 2

Which is larger, $\frac{3}{8}$ or $\frac{7}{20}$?

The lowest common multiple of 8 and 20 is 40.
Change both fractions to fractions with the denominator 40.

$\frac{3}{8} = \frac{3 \times 5}{8 \times 5} = \frac{15}{40}$ and $\frac{7}{20} = \frac{7 \times 2}{20 \times 2} = \frac{14}{40}$, so $\frac{3}{8}$ is larger than $\frac{7}{20}$.

Exercise 1A

You will need **N4.3 Resource sheet 1.1**.

1 to **3** These questions are on Resource sheet 1.1.

4 Which fraction in each pair is smaller? Show your working.

a $\frac{1}{4}$ or $\frac{1}{5}$ b $\frac{1}{3}$ or $\frac{2}{7}$ c $\frac{5}{9}$ or $\frac{11}{20}$

d $\frac{2}{3}$ or $\frac{7}{11}$ e $\frac{11}{13}$ or $\frac{17}{20}$ f $\frac{8}{17}$ or $\frac{12}{25}$

5 Write each set of fractions in order of size. Start with the smallest fraction.

a $\frac{4}{15}, \frac{1}{3}, \frac{3}{10}$ b $\frac{23}{40}, \frac{7}{10}, \frac{3}{5}, \frac{13}{20}$ c $\frac{3}{5}, \frac{5}{12}, \frac{11}{30}, \frac{7}{15}$

6 John and Sam have identical chocolate bars.

John eats $\frac{3}{4}$ of his chocolate bar.

Sam eats $\frac{7}{8}$ of his chocolate bar.

Who eats more chocolate?
Give a reason for your answer.

7 Rashida says that $\frac{7}{12}$ is bigger than $\frac{5}{6}$ because 7 is bigger than 5.

Is Rashida correct? Explain your answer.

Exercise 1B

A dot over a digit in a decimal place indicates a recurring decimal.

Example

0.8 is $\frac{8}{10}$, but 0.$\dot{8}$, or nought point eight recurring, is 0.8888888…, or $\frac{8}{9}$.

0.16 is $\frac{16}{100}$, but 0.1$\dot{6}$, or nought point one six recurring, is 0.1666666…, or $\frac{1}{6}$.

0.18 is $\frac{18}{100}$, but 0.$\dot{1}\dot{8}$, or nought point one eight all recurring, is 0.18181818…, or $\frac{2}{11}$.

1 Play **Recurring decimals** with a partner.
   You will need a copy of **N4.3 Resource sheet 1.2**, a calculator and some counters in two colours.

0.6	0.8̇	0.7̇3̇	0.5̇	0.4̇
0.75	0.4̇	0.8̇1̇	0.83̇	0.3̇8̇
0.8	0.6̇3̇	0.5	0.5̇4̇	0.9
0.4̇6	0.6̇1̇	0.7̇2̇	0.3̇	0.53̇
0.7	0.6̇	0.583̇	0.7̇	0.9̇0̇

Rules

◉ Take turns.

◉ Choose any two of these numbers.

◉ Divide the smaller number by the larger.
   If the answer is on the grid, cover it with one of your counters.

◉ If the answer is not on the grid, or is already covered with a counter, miss that turn.

◉ The winner is the first player to get four of their counters in a straight line in any direction, horizontal, vertical or diagonal.

2 Try this investigation into sevenths.

Copy and complete the table on the right.
Change each fraction to a decimal. Use your calculator.

$\frac{1}{7}$	
$\frac{2}{7}$	
$\frac{3}{7}$	
$\frac{4}{7}$	
$\frac{5}{7}$	
$\frac{6}{7}$	

a What do you notice about the first six digits after the decimal point?

b Without using your calculator, write $\frac{8}{7}$, $\frac{9}{7}$ and $\frac{16}{7}$ as decimals.

c What would be the first 12 digits after the decimal point for $\frac{1}{7}$?

(3) A fraction with numerator and denominator each less than 20 is turned into a decimal. The calculator display shows:

$$0.7857142$$

What was the fraction?

Points to remember

- Convert a fraction to a decimal by dividing the numerator by the denominator. You can use a calculator to do this.
- Put fractions in order:
  - by converting each fraction to a decimal and comparing the decimals,
  - or by changing all the fractions to a common denominator.

2 Calculating with fractions

This lesson will help you to calculate simple fractions.

Exercise 2A

Play these two games with a partner.

GAME 1

For **Fraction products** you need two dice and a calculator.

Rules

- Take turns to roll the two dice.
  If the two numbers are the same, roll again.

- If the two numbers are different, write down a fraction, with the smaller of the two numbers as the numerator and the larger as the denominator.
  Repeat, and write down a second fraction. It can be the same as or different from the first fraction.

- Multiply the two fractions to find the product. Write down the answer in its simplest form. The other player should check the answer with the calculator.

- The winner is the first player to make five different products.

GAME 2

For **Divide it!** you need a copy of **N4.3 Resource sheet 2.1** and some counters in two colours.

$\frac{1}{15}$	$\frac{2}{27}$	$\frac{1}{33}$
$\frac{2}{35}$	$\frac{1}{40}$	$\frac{1}{45}$
$\frac{4}{75}$	$\frac{3}{140}$	$\frac{1}{88}$
$\frac{1}{50}$	$\frac{2}{45}$	$\frac{1}{14}$
$\frac{1}{32}$	$\frac{1}{60}$	$\frac{1}{18}$

Rules

- Take turns to choose a fraction in the top line below and an integer in the second line below.

$$\boxed{\frac{2}{3}} \quad \boxed{\frac{4}{5}} \quad \boxed{\frac{3}{8}} \quad \boxed{\frac{6}{7}} \quad \boxed{\frac{8}{9}} \quad \boxed{\frac{5}{11}}$$

$$\boxed{12} \quad \boxed{15} \quad \boxed{40}$$

- Divide the fraction by the integer. If the answer is on the grid, you can cover the answer with one of your counters.
  If not, miss that turn.

- The other player checks with the calculator that you are right.

- The winner is the first player to cover three fractions in a line, horizontally, vertically or diagonally.

Exercise 2B

The diagram shows that $\frac{2}{3}$ of $\frac{4}{5}$ is $\frac{8}{15}$, or $\frac{2}{3} \times \frac{4}{5} = \frac{8}{15}$.

We can work this out as: $\frac{2}{3} \times \frac{4}{5} = \frac{2 \times 4}{3 \times 5} = \frac{8}{15}$

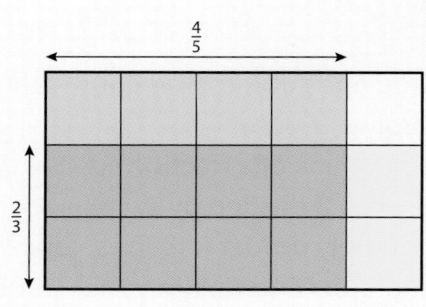

Example 1 $\quad \frac{5}{8} \times \frac{7}{12}$

$\frac{5}{8} \times \frac{7}{12} = \frac{5 \times 7}{8 \times 12}$ Multiply the numerators and multiply the denominators.

$\qquad = \frac{35}{96}$

Example 2 $\quad \frac{21}{40} \times \frac{15}{28}$

$\frac{21}{40} \times \frac{15}{28} = \frac{^{3}21}{^{8}40} \times \frac{15^{3}}{28^{4}}$ Cancel the 21 and 28 by 7, and the 15 and 40 by 5.

$\qquad = \frac{3 \times 3}{8 \times 4}$ Multiply the numerators and multiply the denominators.

$\qquad = \frac{9}{32}$

You can also use a calculator to multiply fractions.

Example 3

To work out $\frac{2}{3} \times \frac{3}{5}$, enter $\boxed{2}$ $\boxed{a^{b}/_c}$ $\boxed{3}$ $\boxed{\times}$ $\boxed{3}$ $\boxed{a^{b}/_c}$ $\boxed{5}$ $\boxed{=}$.

This will produce a display showing something like $\boxed{2 \lrcorner 5}$ or $\boxed{\frac{2}{5}}$.

1. Multiply these fractions **without using a calculator**.
   Show your working.

   a $\frac{3}{5} \times \frac{2}{9}$ b $\frac{6}{7} \times \frac{3}{11}$ c $\frac{4}{5} \times \frac{20}{21}$ d $\frac{3}{8} \times \frac{7}{12}$

   e $\frac{3}{5} \times \frac{20}{27}$ f $\frac{4}{11} \times \frac{33}{44}$ g $\frac{15}{28} \times \frac{42}{65}$ h $\frac{35}{39} \times \frac{52}{84}$

2. **Use a calculator** to find the answers to these calculations.

   a $\frac{13}{20} \times 230$ b $\frac{17}{40} \times 70$ c $\frac{5}{32} \times 80$ d $\frac{6}{25} \times 1440$

   e $\frac{7}{8} \div 210$ f $\frac{15}{22} \div 55$ g $\frac{3}{16} \div 27$ h $\frac{35}{48} \div 140$

Points to remember

⊙ To add and subtract fractions without a calculator, change them to the same denominator.
⊙ We can think of a fraction such as $\frac{8}{3}$ as eight thirds, or as one third of 8, or as 8 divided by 3.
⊙ To multiply proper fractions, cancel first, then multiply the numerators and multiply the denominators.

3 Multiplying and dividing decimals 1

This lesson will help you to use mental and written methods to multiply and divide by decimals.

Multiplying by 0.1 is equivalent to dividing by 10. The digits move one place to the right.

Example 1   Calculate 35×0.1

$35 \times 0.1 = 35 \times \frac{1}{10} = \frac{35}{10} = 3.5$

Multiplication and division are inverse operations, so $3.5 \div 0.1 = 35$.

Dividing by 0.1 is equivalent to multiplying by 10. The digits move one place to the left.

Example 2   Calculate $23 \div 0.1$

$23 \div 0.1 = 23 \times 10 = 230$

Summary

	Equivalent to	Digits move right		Equivalent to	Digits move left
$\times\ 0.1$	$\div\ 10$	1 place	$\div\ 0.1$	$\times\ 10$	1 place
$\times\ 0.01$	$\div\ 100$	2 places	$\div\ 0.01$	$\times\ 100$	2 places
$\times\ 0.001$	$\div\ 1000$	3 places	$\div\ 0.001$	$\times\ 1000$	3 places

Exercise 3A

1 Write the answers to these calculations.

    a 14×100 **b** $3.7 \div 10$ **c** 5×0.1

    d $0.9 \div 0.01$ **e** $3 \div 0.001$ **f** 0.07×0.1

    g $24 \div 100$ **h** 2.4×1000 **i** 28×0.01

    j $5.6 \div 0.1$ **k** 1.6×0.01 **l** 0.06×10

    m 720×0.001 **n** $650 \div 1000$ **o** $0.68 \div 0.001$

Exercise 3B

Multiply simple decimals by using equivalent calculations.

Example 1   Calculate 0.7×0.3

Think of this as $\frac{7}{10} \times \frac{3}{10} = \frac{21}{100}$ or 0.21,

or as $7 \times 3 \div 10 \div 10 = 0.21$

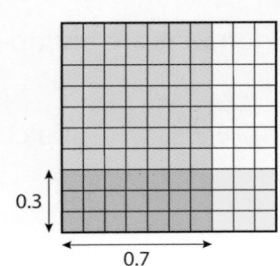
0.3

0.7

Example 2   Calculate 0.7 × 0.04

This is equivalent to $\frac{7}{10} \times \frac{4}{100} = \frac{28}{1000}$, or 0.028.

You can also think of it as 7 × 4 ÷ 10 ÷ 100 = 0.028

Notice that there are the same number of decimal places in the answer as there are in the product.

① Write the answers to these calculations.

a 0.3 × 0.4   b 0.5 × 0.6   c 0.02 × 0.4

d 0.03 × 0.2   e 0.5 × 0.8   f 0.2 × 0.05

g 0.03 × 0.3   h 0.4 × 0.09   i 0.05 × 0.4

② Now write the answers to these calculations.

a 6000 × 0.3   b 200 × 0.04   c 500 × 0.8

d 30 × 0.5   e 9000 × 0.07   f 80 × 0.02

Exercise 3C

Divide by multiples of 10 or 100 by using equivalent calculations.

Example 1   Calculate 1200 ÷ 30

$$1200 \div 30 = \frac{1200}{30} = \frac{1200 \div 10}{30 \div 10} = \frac{120}{3} = 40$$

or

$$1200 \div 30 = \frac{120\cancel{0}}{3\cancel{0}} = 40$$

Divide by simple decimals by using equivalent calculations.

Both numbers are multiplied by the same power of 10 to make the divisor an integer.

Example 2   Calculate 5.6 ÷ 0.8

$$5.6 \div 0.8 = \frac{5.6}{0.8} = \frac{5.6 \times 10}{0.8 \times 10} = \frac{56}{8} = 7$$

Example 3   Calculate $1.2 \div 0.03$

$$1.2 \div 0.03 = \frac{1.2}{0.03} = \frac{1.2 \times 100}{0.03 \times 100} = \frac{120}{3} = 40$$

① Write the answers to these calculations.

  a $6000 \div 30$ b $200 \div 40$

  c $8000 \div 200$ d $500 \div 50$

  e $4900 \div 70$ f $30 \div 50$

② Write the answers to these calculations.

  a $20 \div 0.4$ b $35 \div 0.7$

  c $400 \div 0.8$ d $3.5 \div 0.5$

  e $32 \div 0.08$ f $150 \div 0.3$

  g $56 \div 0.07$ h $0.42 \div 0.6$

  i $0.04 \div 0.8$

◉ Points to remember

- Multiplying by 0.1 is equivalent to dividing by 10; dividing by 0.1 is equivalent to multiplying by 10.
- Multiplying by 0.01 is equivalent to dividing by 100; dividing by 0.01 is equivalent to multiplying by 100.
- 0.7×0.04 is equivalent to:

  $7 \times 4 \div 10 \div 100 = 0.028$

  The answer has the same number of decimal places as the product.
- $3.5 \div 0.7$ is equivalent to:

  $(3.5 \times 10) \div (0.7 \times 10) = 35 \div 7 = 5$

  Both numbers are multiplied by the same power of 10 to make the divisor an integer.

4 Multiplying and dividing decimals 2

This lesson will help you to use mental and written methods to multiply and divide by decimals.

Example

Calculate 6.42×7

The answer lies between $6 \times 7 = 42$ and $7 \times 7 = 49$.

The calculation is equivalent to $642 \times 7 \div 100$.

Work out 642×7.

Divide the answer of 4494 by 100 to get 44.94.

$$\begin{array}{r} 642 \\ \times \quad 7 \\ \hline 4494 \\ \tiny 2\,1 \end{array}$$

Answer: 44.94

Notice that there are the same number of decimal places in the answer as there are in the product.

Use the estimate to check where the decimal point should be in the answer.

You can also do the calculation without using equivalent calculations. Use a grid method or a short-multiplication method. Take care to line up the digits in columns so that the decimal point is in the right place in the answer.

Grid method

×	6	0.4	0.02
7	42	2.8	0.14

Answer:
$42 + 2.8 + 0.14 = 44.94$

Short-multiplication method

$$\begin{array}{r} 6.42 \\ \times \quad 7 \\ \hline 44.94 \\ \tiny 2\,1 \end{array}$$

Answer: $642 \times 7 = 4494$

So $\qquad 6.42 \times 7 = 44.94$

Exercise 4A

Do these calculations **without using a calculator**. Estimate first.

1. Multiply:

   a 52.7×6 b 9.83×7

   c 23.72×3 d 48.1×9

   e 0.46×5 f 3.65×8

Exercise 4B

Example 1   Calculate $47.2 \div 8$

The answer will lie between $40 \div 8 = 5$ and $48 \div 8 = 6$.

The calculation is equivalent to $472 \div 8$ divided by 10.

Work out $472 \div 8$.

$$
\begin{array}{r}
59 \\
8\overline{)472} \\
400 \\
\hline
72 \\
72 \\
\hline
0
\end{array}
$$

Divide the answer of 59 by 10 to get 5.9.

Line up the digits, with units under units, and so on.

Use the estimate to check where the decimal point should be in the answer.

You can also do the calculation without using equivalent calculations using short division.
Take care to line up the digits so that the decimal point is in the right place in the answer.

Short-division method

$$
\begin{array}{r}
5.9 \\
8\overline{)47.^72}
\end{array}
$$

Answer: 5.9

Sometimes you need to continue the division by adding one or more extra zeros.

Example 2   Calculate $38.3 \div 5$

$$
\begin{array}{r}
7.66 \\
5\overline{)38.^33^30}
\end{array}
$$

Answer: 7.66

Sometimes you want the answer correct to one decimal place. Continue the division to two decimal places, rounding the answer correct to one decimal place.

Example 3   Calculate $32.17 \div 9$

$$
\begin{array}{r}
3.57 \\
9\overline{)32.^51^67}
\end{array}
$$

Answer: 3.6 (correct to 1 d.p.)

---

(1) Divide:

   a $87.6 \div 3$ **b** $6.16 \div 4$

   c $2.95 \div 5$ **d** $58.32 \div 8$

(2) Give your answers to these calculations correct to one decimal place.

   a $48.9 \div 7$ **b** $23.7 \div 9$

   c $15.62 \div 6$ **d** $8.29 \div 8$

When you solve word problems involving decimal measurements:

○ make sure that all quantities are in the same unit;

○ check that the answer makes sense in the context of the problem;

○ if appropriate, round answers to a suitable number of decimal places.

Solve these problems **without using a calculator**. Show your working.

1 A dishwasher uses 48.63 litres of water to wash the dishes five times.
How much water is used to wash the dishes once?

2 A rectangular patio measures 3.26 metres by 4 metres.
What is its area?

3 A lawn is in the shape of a regular hexagon.
The length of its perimeter is 20.91 metres.
What is the length of one side of the lawn?

4 Nine DVDs cost £80.55. How much does one DVD cost?

5 A box of golf balls costs £12.85. Amelia buys 7 boxes of golf balls.
How much change does she get from £100?

6 A large box holds 3 kg pasta shells.
Each of six jars is filled with 0.475 kg pasta shells from the box.
How much pasta is left in the box?

7 Eight friends spend a weekend clearing up an overgrown garden.
They are paid a total of £23.80 per hour.
They work for 6 hours and share their total earnings equally among them.
How much does each of the friends get paid for the job?

● Points to remember

For multiplication or division of a decimal by an integer:

⊙ estimate the answer;

⊙ do the equivalent whole-number calculation, then adjust the answer
by dividing by the appropriate power of 10;

⊙ for multiplication, make sure that the number of decimal places in
the answer is the same as in the product;

⊙ for division, add zeros to the number you are dividing if necessary;

⊙ use the estimate to check the size of the answer and to make sure
that the decimal point is in the right place.

5 Calculating percentages

This lesson will help you to:

- find equivalent fractions, decimals and percentages;
- write one number as a percentage of another;
- solve problems involving percentages.

 Did you know that...?

Percentage means 'per hundred', or 'in every hundred'.

The percent sign, %, has probably evolved from a symbol in an anonymous Italian manuscript of 1425. By about 1650, instead of 'per 100' or 'per cento', a percentage was written as 'per $\frac{0}{0}$'.

Later, the 'per' was dropped so that the symbol $\frac{0}{0}$ stood alone. Eventually it became %.

To change a decimal to a percentage, multiply it by 100.

Example 1   0.46 is equivalent to 46%, because 0.46 × 100 = 46.
3.456 is equivalent to 345.6%, because 3.456 × 100 = 345.6.

To change a fraction to a percentage, multiply it by 100.

Example 2 $\frac{3}{10}$ is equivalent to 30% because $\frac{3}{10}$ × 100 = 30.

To change a percentage to a decimal, divide it by 100 to express it in hundredths.

Example 3   47% is equivalent to 0.47, because 47 ÷ 100 = 0.47.
103% is equivalent to 1.03, because 103 ÷ 100 = 1.03.

To change a percentage to a fraction, write it as a fraction with a denominator of 100. Simplify the fraction if you can.

Example 4   25% can be written as $\frac{25}{100}$, which simplifies to $\frac{1}{4}$.

1 Work with a partner. You will need scissors and **N4.3 Resource sheet 5.1**.

Cut out the cards from the bottom of the resource sheet.
Place them in the boxes to make four true statements.

When you are sure that all statements are correct, write the numbers in the boxes.

Do questions 2–6 **without using a calculator**.

2 Write each of these decimals as a percentage.

    a 0.37   b 0.7   c 0.02   d 0.625   e 1.04   f 8.1

3 Write each of these percentages as a decimal.

    a 85%   b 62%   c 9%   d 150%   e 13%   f 17.5%

4 Write each of these percentages as a fraction in its simplest form.

    a 90%   b 84%   c 5%   d 175%   e 41%   f 56%

5 Write each of these fractions as a percentage.

    a $\frac{3}{50}$ b $\frac{9}{25}$ c $\frac{4}{5}$ d $\frac{9}{20}$ e $2\frac{1}{4}$ f $\frac{3}{8}$

6 Write the answers to these calculations.

    a 40% of £250   b $66\frac{2}{3}$% of 600 kg   c 5% of 440 cm

    d 10% of 168 g   e 30% of 200 litres   f 15% of £900

    g 75% of 500 ml   h 70% of 400 m

For questions 7 and 8, you may **use a calculator**.

7 Solve these problems.

    a 50 people were asked what music they preferred.
        14 of them said they liked jazz. What percentage of the people liked jazz?

    b Rob scored 36 marks out of 40 in a test. What was his percentage score?

    c Rachel asked 48 people to name their favourite football club.
        30 of them said Chelsea. What percentage of the people said Chelsea?

    d Seven of the nine snakes in a snake pit are poisonous.
        What percentage of the snakes are poisonous?

    e 150 young children attend a day care centre.
        72 of them are boys.
        What percentage are girls?

    f Edward did a survey of 180 pupils at his school.
        50 of them were left-handed.
        What percentage of the pupils were right-handed?

(8) Write the answers to these calculations.

  a 65% of 920   b 52% of £1200

  c 59% of 64 kg   d 95% of 225 m

  e 70% of 180°   f 55% of 1.6 litres

  g 34% of £28.50   h 45% of 3 hours

⊙ Points to remember

- **Percentage** means 'per hundred', or 'in every hundred'.
- 47% is equivalent to $\frac{47}{100}$ or 0.47.
- A quick way to find 20% of a quantity is to find 10% by dividing by 10, then multiply the result by 2 to find 20%. You can find 30%, 40%, 50%, … similarly.
- If there is no quick method for finding a percentage of a quantity, first find 1%, then multiply by the percentage.
- Always include any units in the answer.

6 Percentage increases and decreases

This lesson will help you to work out percentage increases or decreases, and break problems into manageable parts.

To find the sale price, work out the discount then subtract it from the original price.

Example 1

A £350 refrigerator is reduced by 12% in a sale. What is its sale price?

Calculate 12% of 350: $\frac{12}{100} \times 350 = 42$

Subtract £42 from the original price: £350 − £42 = £308.   **Answer: £308**

Another way to do it is to subtract the percentage discount from 100%, then calculate this percentage of the original price.

Calculate 88% of 350: $\frac{88}{100} \times 350 = 308$.   **Answer: £308**

To work out a percentage increase, find the increase then add it to the original amount.

Example 2

The price of a £350 refrigerator increases by 4%. What is its new price?

Calculate 4% of 350: $\frac{4}{10} \times 350 = 14$

Add £14 to the original price: £350 + £14 = £364. **Answer: £364**

Another way to do it is to add the percentage increase to 100%, then calculate this percentage of the original price.

Calculate 104% of 350 $\frac{104}{100} \times 350 = 364$ **Answer: £364**

Exercise 6

① Use estimation to match each percentage calculation to its answer.

Example

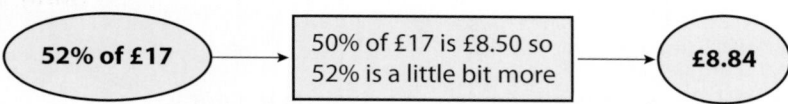

Match these pairs.

② A sports shop is taking 8% off all its prices. What will each of these items cost after the 8% discount?

   a Trainers £35
   b Cricket bat £93
   c Sports bag £22.50
   d Tennis socks £6.75
   e Set of golf clubs £425
   f Tennis racket £85
   g Ice skates £72.50
   h Football £47.25

3 A car showroom is increasing the prices of all its cars by 3%.
How much will each of these cars cost after the 3% increase?

a Sports car £25 300   b Hatchback £12 500

c Convertible £50 000   d Saloon £18 750

e Mini £8000   f People carrier £36 900

g Estate £10 200   h Four-wheel drive £47 250

Extension problems

Amber's mum is organising a holiday for her family.
She hopes to get a discount as she is booking at the last minute.
The travel agent said she could have a 20% discount but she
must also pay 15% for travel insurance.

Should Amber's mum:

claim the discount first and then pay the insurance,

or:

pay the insurance first and then claim the discount?

What do you think? Give reasons for your answer.

5 Rohini is a company director.
Last year, she had a 15% pay rise.
This year, she has been given a 10% pay rise.
The local newspaper has reported her pay rise
as 25% over two years.
Is the newspaper right?
Give reasons for your answer.

◉ Points to remember

- ⊙ There are two ways of finding a selling price after a percentage discount:
  - – calculate the discount, then subtract it from the original price;
  - – subtract the discount percentage from 100%, then calculate this percentage of the original price.
- ⊙ There are two ways to find a new amount after a percentage increase:
  - – calculate the increase, then add it to the original amount;
  - – add the percentage increase to 100%, then calculate this percentage of the original amount.
- ⊙ If you are given the original amount and final amount, and are asked to find the percentage increase or decrease, work out the increase or decrease as a percentage of the original amount.

How well are you doing?

can you:

- order, add and subtract fractions?
- multiply and divide fractions by integers?
- multiply and divide by decimals?
- find equivalent fractions, decimals and percentages?
- write one number as a percentage of another?
- work out percentage increases or decreases?
- solve problems involving fractions, decimals and percentages, using a calculator when appropriate?

Fractions, decimals and percentages (no calculator)

1 *2005 level 5*

   a Copy and complete the sentences.

   …… out of 10 is the same as 70%.

   10 out of 20 is the same as ……%.

   b Copy and complete the sentence.

   …… out of …… is the same as 5%.

   Now copy and complete the same sentence using different numbers.

2 *2007 level 6*

   a Which of the fractions below are smaller than $\frac{1}{9}$?

   A $\frac{1}{10}$ **B** $\frac{4}{9}$ **C** $\frac{1}{2}$ **D** $\frac{1}{100}$ **E** $\frac{1}{8}$

   b To the nearest per cent, what is $\frac{1}{9}$ as a percentage?

   A 0.9%   **B** 9%   **C** 10%   **D** 11%   **E** 19%

   c Copy and complete the sentence below by writing a fraction.

   $\frac{1}{9}$ is half of …….

3 Which two of these four numbers, when multiplied together, have the answer closest to 70?

   7.4   8.1   9.4   10

4 *1999 level 6*

a In a magazine there are three adverts on the same page.

> Advert 1 uses $\frac{1}{4}$ of the page
>
> Advert 2 uses $\frac{1}{8}$ of the page
>
> Advert 3 uses $\frac{1}{16}$ of the page

In total, what fraction of the page do the three adverts use?
Show your working.

b The cost of an advert is £10 for each $\frac{1}{32}$ of a page.

An advert uses $\frac{3}{16}$ of a page. How much does the advert cost?

Fractions, decimals and percentages (calculator allowed)

5 Write these fractions in order of size, starting with the smallest.

$\frac{3}{4}$ $\qquad$ $\frac{3}{5}$ $\qquad$ $\frac{9}{10}$ $\qquad$ $\frac{17}{20}$

6 *2005 level 6*

Here is some information about A levels in 2002.

	English	Mathematics
Number of students	72 000	54 000
Percentage gaining grade A	19%	37%

How many more students gained grade A in Mathematics than in English?

7 *2004 level 6*

In 2001 the average yearly wage was £21 842.
On average, people spent £1644 on their family holiday.
What percentage of the average yearly wage is that? Show your working.

Enquiry 1

This unit will help you to:

- discuss a problem and find questions to explore;
- plan how to collect information, how much to collect and how accurate it needs to be;
- calculate and use the range, mean, median and mode (or modal class);
- draw and interpret a range of charts, graphs, tables and diagrams, and decide which are the most useful for a problem;
- relate your conclusions to the question you are exploring;
- write and illustrate a short report of a statistical investigation.

1 Specifying the problem and planning

This lesson will help you to:

- discuss a problem and find questions to explore;
- plan how to collect information, how much to collect and how accurate it needs to be.

Teenagers often want to know what there is to do in their town after school.

When you solve a problem involving data, it is important to consider who might be interested in the problem, and why.
It is also important to know how to collect data and what to do so that you can find out about the problem properly.

Example

Some teenagers want to know: *What is there to do in our town after school?*

A Who might be interested in the answers to this question? Why?

The teenagers themselves so that they have something to do; their parents so that they know their children are safe; the local council and local residents so that the teenagers don't get into trouble.

B What data do you need to collect? How would you do this?

You could use a questionnaire to find out what teenagers in your area do after school and find out what else they would like to do. You might also like to ask local residents and local business people if they think there is a problem and what ideas they have.

You might then be able to persuade the council to help you set something up for teenagers to do after school.

Exercise 1A

Work in a group of four. Answer questions A and B below for these problems.

A Who might be interested in the answer to this question? Why?

B What data do you need to collect? How would you do this?

1. Is it too hot to go on holiday in August?

2. Where should I go if I want sunshine on holiday in February?

3. How many copies of our new dictionary should we publish?

4. Are there any good magazines sold for my age group?

Exercise 1B

Example

The problem is: *What is there to do in our town after school?*

Write down three related questions you would need to ask in order to collect the data you need.

What do you like to do after school?

Where do you like to go after school?

What else would you like to be able to do after school?

Work with a partner.

For each of the problems in Exercise 1A, write down three related questions that you would need to ask in order to collect the data you need.

Points to remember

When you plan how to solve a problem, consider:

- who might be interested in the answer;
- why they might be interested in it;
- what data you will need to collect;
- how you will do this.

2 Processing data

This lesson will help you to draw and interpret pie charts.

Did you know that...?

William Playfair, a Scottish architect, published the first pie chart in 1801. It was part of a bigger chart to show that the British paid more tax than people in other countries. He thought it was easier to take in information if you could see a picture of it. What do you think?

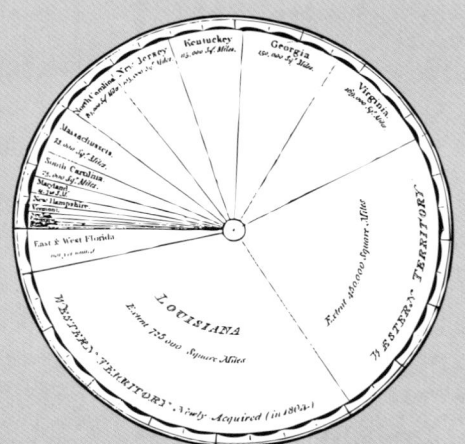

Playfair was very outspoken and a bit of a scoundrel. He tended to put what money he had into dubious schemes. He was convicted of libel in England and swindling in France. His work was less well regarded because of this. Even though he was still publishing fine charts and graphs at a ripe old age, his advice that others should do so too was largely ignored.

In a **pie chart** the angle at the centre of the circle is proportional to the frequency for each category represented.

- ☺ The full circle is 360°. Each person or item in the survey is represented by the same size angle.
- ☺ A table will help you to work out how large the angles need to be for each sector.
- ☺ Remember to mark the centre of the circle, draw a radius and measure each angle round from the last radius you drew so that the sectors don't overlap.
- ☺ A completed pie chart is a full circle. All the angles should add up to 360°.
- ☺ The pie chart needs a key so that it is clear what category goes with each sector.

Example

The frequency table shows the favourite sports of 20 children.

Draw a pie chart to illustrate the data.

Favourite sport	Frequency	Angle
Swimming	3	3 × 18 = 54°
Football	6	6 × 18 = 108°
Tennis	4	4 × 18 = 72°
Cricket	2	2 × 18 = 36°
Netball	1	1 × 18 = 18°
Other	4	4 × 18 = 72°

The angle for each person is 360 ÷ 20 = 18°.
Three people liked swimming so the angle is 3 × 18 = 54°.

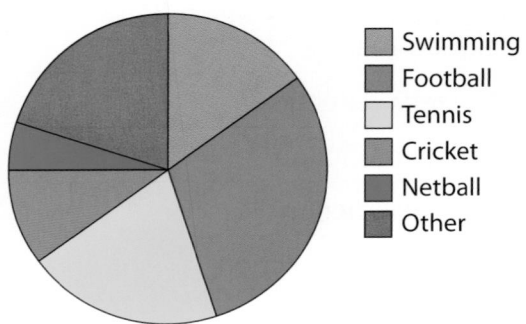

Swimming
Football
Tennis
Cricket
Netball
Other

The data for questions 1, 2 and 4 in this exercise is adapted from www.literacytrust.org.uk.

1 Twenty pupils were asked how much they enjoyed reading.
The results were recorded in a table.

Reading enjoyment	Number of pupils
Very much	4
Quite a lot	6
A bit	8
Not at all	2

a How many degrees will represent one person in a pie chart of this data?

b How many degrees are needed for the sector for 'very much'?

c Work out the angles for the other sectors and draw a pie chart to represent the data.
Your circle should have a radius of approximately 8 cm.

2 Thirty-six pupils were asked how often they read outside school.
The results were recorded in a table.

How often pupils read out of school	Number of pupils
Every day or almost every day	14
Once or twice a week	11
Once or twice a month	5
Never or nearly never	6

a How many degrees will represent one person in a pie chart of this data?

b Work out the angles for the sectors and draw a pie chart to represent the data.

3 A library recorded the type of book borrowed for 60 books and recorded them in a table.

Type of book	Number of books
General fiction	15
Light romance	6
Mystery, detection	8
Adult non-fiction	11
Children's fiction	14
Children's non-fiction	16

a How many degrees will represent one book in a pie chart of this data?

b Work out the angles for the sectors and draw a pie chart to represent the data.

4   In a survey pupils were asked if they thought they read enough.
The results were recorded in a table.

Do you read enough?	Percentage of pupils
Yes	48%
No, but I want to	32%
No, and I don't want to	20%

a   In a pie chart of this data, how many degrees will represent 1%?

b   Work out the angles for the sectors and draw a pie chart to represent the data.

Points to remember

- In a **pie chart** the angle at the centre of the circle is proportional to the frequency for each category.
- The number of degrees per person or item can be calculated by:
  360° ÷ total number of items or people

3 Representing data

This lesson will help you to:

- draw and interpret bar charts and frequency diagrams;
- draw and use stem-and-leaf diagrams;
- design and use two-way tables.

In a **stem-and-leaf diagram** the data is arranged in order in a format a little like a grouped frequency diagram.

- The 'leaves' should be single digits so the other part of the values form the 'stem'.
- All the data should be entered even if a value appears more than once.
- The digits in the leaves should be in order, smallest to largest.
- Try to line up the leaves so that they are underneath one another, perhaps by using squared paper or a table.

Example

This list gives the heights of 20 Year 6 pupils in centimetres:

157, 143, 145, 140, 150, 144, 148, 150, 147, 145, 140, 144, 137, 142, 152, 162, 150, 157, 155, 140.

Draw a stem-and-leaf diagram of this data.

The stem will be the hundreds and tens places in the values: 130, 140, 150 and 160.
The leaves will be the units digits.

13	7
14	0, 0, 0, 2, 3, 4, 4, 5, 5, 7, 8
15	0, 0, 0, 2, 5, 7, 7
16	2

The smallest height is 137 cm and the greatest is 162 cm so the range is 162 – 137 = 25 cm.
The shape of the graph shows us that most of the Year 6 pupils are between 140 and 159 cm tall.

Stem-and-leaf diagrams are very useful because they group the data but you can still see the individual values. This means you can look at the general shape of the data as well as use them to calculate statistics.

Exercise 3A

1 This list gives the birth weights in kilograms for 20 babies:

3.6, 2.7, 3.8, 4.1, 5.0, 3.4, 4.7, 2.9, 4.8, 3.6, 2.8, 3.1, 3.6, 3.9, 4.2, 4.6, 4.5, 2.9, 4.6, 4.4

a Copy and complete this stem-and-leaf diagram.

Stem (kg)	Leaf (0.1 kg)
2	
3	
4	
5	

b What was the weight of the heaviest baby?

c What was the range of the weights?

2 This list shows the number of overdue books recorded in a library for 16 weeks:

44, 44, 28, 35, 33, 40, 25, 32, 45, 29, 41, 44, 29, 32, 25, 44

a Draw a stem-and-leaf diagram for the data.

b Write a sentence to describe what the data shows about the number of overdue library books.

③ This list shows the heights in centimetres of 25 pupils:

165, 157, 143, 155, 155, 179, 154, 162, 165, 157, 145, 154, 145, 161, 167, 170, 134, 190, 130, 160, 140, 150, 153, 171, 145

a Draw a stem-and-leaf diagram to illustrate the data.

b Do you think that the pupils are all from the same year group? Explain your answer.

Exercise 3B

You can read a **two-way table** both across the page and down.
It allows two types of information to be presented and compared in the same form.

Example

This two-way table shows the ages of a group of pupils and whether or not they visit the library.

	Visit the library	Don't visit the library	Totals
Age 11	17	26	43
Age 12	23	19	42
Age 13	19	13	32
Totals	59	58	

How many pupils were surveyed altogether? 117

Do more 12-year-olds visit the library than not visit library? Yes

At what age do more pupils visit the library than not visit the library? 12 and 13

① The table shows the percentages of men and women passing their driving test at the first attempt.

	Pass	Fail	Totals
Female	27%		100%
Male	34%	66%	100%

a Who were more likely to pass their driving test, males or females?

b What percentage of women failed their driving test?

② The table shows the number of children killed or seriously injured in road accidents between 2002 and 2004 (data from www.dft.gov.uk).

Road user type	2002	2003	2004	Totals
Pedestrians	2828	2381	2339	7548
Cyclists	594	595	577	1766
Car	939	885	759	2583
Other road users	235	239	230	704
Total	4596	4100	3905	

a   Is the total number of deaths and serious accidents increasing or decreasing over time?

b   For which type of road users did the number of deaths and serious accidents increase between 2002 and 2003?

c   Which type of road user accounts for the most deaths and serious accidents?

d   How can you check that the totals are correct on a two-way table?

③ The table shows the age of the pedestrians killed or seriously injured between 2002 and 2004 (data from www.dft.gov.uk).

Age	2002	2003	2004	Totals
0–4		271	250	842
5–8	661	567	508	1736
9–11	693		518	1789
12–15	1153	965	1063	3181
Total	2828	2381		

a   How many children aged 0–4 were killed or had serious accidents in 2002?

b   How many fewer children aged 5–8 were killed or had serious accidents in 2004 compared with 2003?

c   What is the total number of children who were killed or had serious accidents in 2004?

d   How many children aged 9–11 were killed or had serious accidents in 2003?

e   Which age group had the highest number of deaths or serious accidents? Can you think of any reasons why?

⊙ Points to remember

⊙ A **stem-and-leaf diagram** is used to group data so that the original data is kept.

⊙ A **two-way table** can be read both across the page and down. It allows two types of information to be presented and compared in the same form.

4 Interpreting data

This lesson will help you to draw and interpret pie charts, scatter graphs, bar charts and frequency diagrams.

 **Did you know that...?**

Florence Nightingale may have been the first person to use diagrams to persuade people of the need for change.

She used diagrams to show that most of the fatalities during the Crimean War of 1853–1856 were from sickness and that improving hygiene dramatically reduced the death rate.

Exercise 4A

Work with a partner.

1. Look at data set 1 or data set 2.
   Think about how you could analyse the data set.
   Write down as many ideas as you can.

   Data set 1: Average rainfall in Paris

Month	Jan	Feb	Mar	Apr	May	Jun	Jul	Aug	Sep	Oct	Nov	Dec
Rainfall (mm)	53	54	38	34	42	67	50	62	57	55	50	49

   Data set 2: Average temperature in Paris

Month	Jan	Feb	Mar	Apr	May	Jun	Jul	Aug	Sep	Oct	Nov	Dec
Temperature (°C)	3	4	8	10	15	17	19	18	16	11	7	5

2. Now join with a pair that looked at the other data set.
   Think about how you could analyse the two data sets together.

A **scatter graph** is used to look for connections between two quantities.
One quantity is put on the horizontal axis and the other on the vertical axis.
Each point on the scatter graph represents a pair of values.

Remember:
- ☺ Your graph needs a title.
- ☺ Use a ruler and pencil.
- ☺ Label the lines on the axes evenly and write what the quantity is next to the axis.

Example

The table shows the rainfall and average temperature (temp.) by month in Paris.

Month	Jan	Feb	Mar	Apr	May	Jun	Jul	Aug	Sep	Oct	Nov	Dec
Rainfall (mm)	53	54	38	34	42	67	50	62	57	55	50	49
Temp. (°C)	3	4	8	10	15	17	19	18	16	11	7	5

Draw a scatter graph for the data.

Each point represents a month.

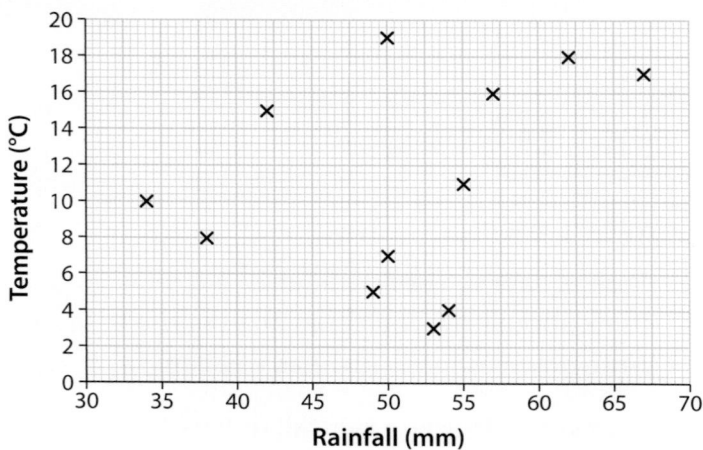

You will need graph paper, a pencil and a ruler.

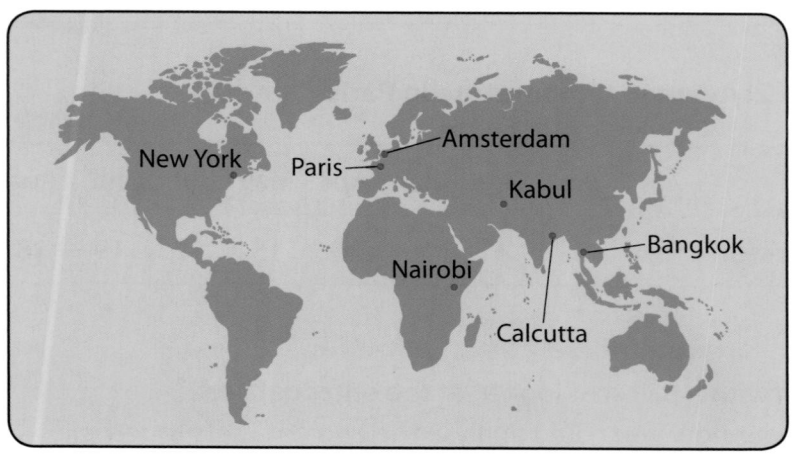

(1) The rainfall and average temperature for each month in Bangkok are shown in the table below.

Month	Jan	Feb	Mar	Apr	May	Jun	Jul	Aug	Sep	Oct	Nov	Dec
Rainfall (mm)	11	28	30	72	189	151	158	187	320	231	57	9
Temp. (°C)	26	27	29	30	30	29	29	28	28	28	27	26

Draw a scatter graph to look for a connection between the rainfall and temperature. Put rainfall on the horizontal axis with a scale of 1 cm to 20 mm from 0 to 320 mm and temperature on the vertical axis with a scale of 2 cm to 1°C from 25 to 31°C.

(2) The rainfall and average temperature for each month in Kabul are shown in the table below.

Month	Jan	Feb	Mar	Apr	May	Jun	Jul	Aug	Sep	Oct	Nov	Dec
Rainfall (mm)	30	35	93	100	20	5	2	2	2	15	20	10
Temp. (°C)	4	1	7	13	20	25	30	32	19	13	9	4

Draw a scatter graph to look for a connection between the rainfall and temperature. Put rainfall on the horizontal axis with a scale of 1 cm to 5 mm from 0 to 100 mm and temperature on the vertical axis with a scale of 1 cm to 2°C from 0 to 32°C.

(3) The rainfall and average temperature for each month in Kiev are shown in the table below.

Month	Jan	Feb	Mar	Apr	May	Jun	Jul	Aug	Sep	Oct	Nov	Dec
Rainfall (mm)	91	76	64	44	31	23	21	24	48	66	62	106
Temp. (°C)	5	6	7	12	16	21	23	29	29	16	12	8

Draw a scatter graph to look for a connection between the rainfall and temperature. Put rainfall on the horizontal axis with a scale of 1 cm to 10 mm from 0 to 110 mm and temperature on the vertical axis with a scale of 1 cm to 2°C from 0 to 30°C.

(4) What could you use these graphs to find out about?

Work in groups of four. Discuss these questions.
Take turns to write down your answers.

1) Which set of bars represents Nairobi and which represents Amsterdam?
Give reasons for your answer.

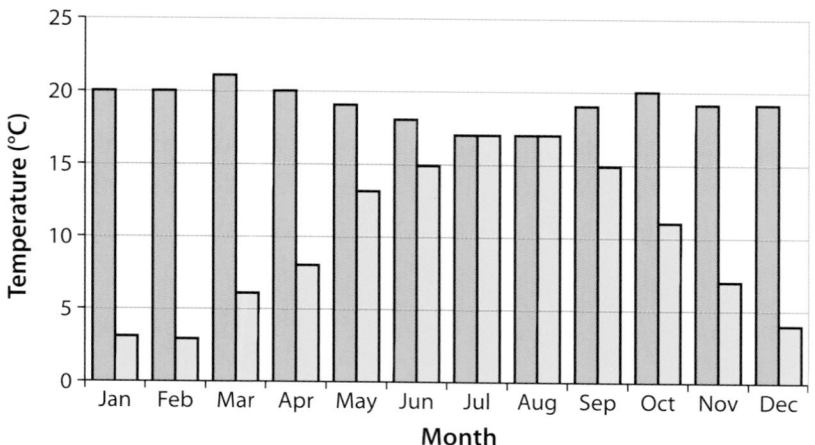

Source: www.worldclimate.com

2) The pie charts show how often children read outside school.
Which pie chart is for boys and which is for girls?
Give reasons for your answer.

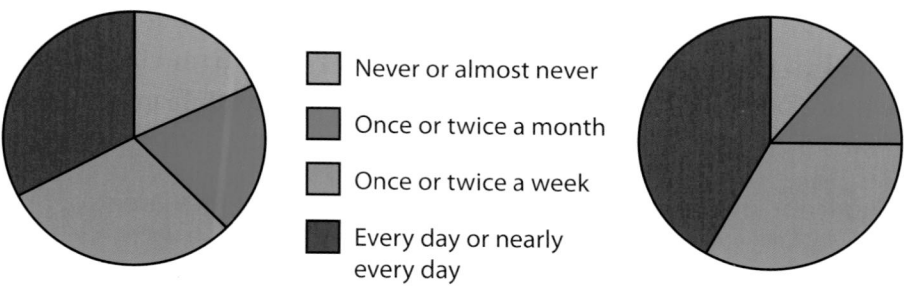

Never or almost never

Once or twice a month

Once or twice a week

Every day or nearly every day

Source: www.literacytrust.org.uk

3) The pie charts show how much children enjoy reading.
Which pie chart is for primary-age pupils and which is for secondary-age pupils?
Give reasons for your answer.

Not at all

A bit

Quite alot

Very much

Source: www.literacytrust.org.uk

(4) Which set of bars represents New York and which represents Calcutta? Give reasons for your answer.

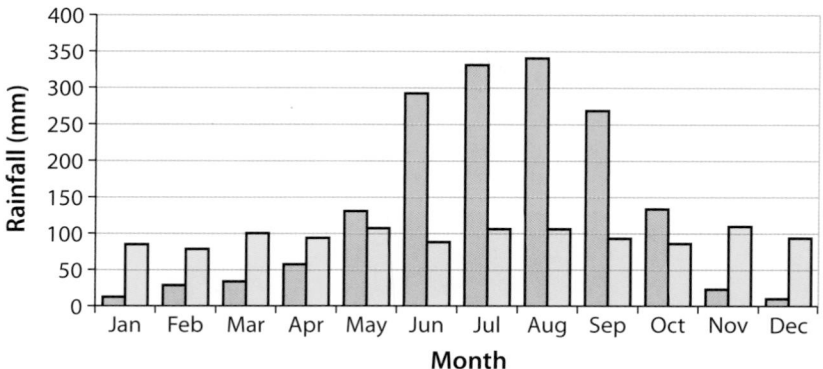

Source: www.worldclimate.com

> ⊙ **Points to remember**
>
> - ⊙ A **scatter graph** allows you to look for a connection between the two quantities. One quantity is put on the horizontal axis and the other on the vertical axis.
> - ⊙ Each point on the scatter graph represents a pair of values.

5 Comparing groups

This lesson will help you to compare groups using a range of charts, graphs and tables.

Exercise 5A

A copy of these photographs is on **S4.2 Resource sheet 5.1** which you could cut up separately if you wish.

There are six photographs. Make sure you know which is which.

- ◉ Group of people of different ages sitting down
- ◉ Group of babies
- ◉ Group of elderly people
- ◉ Tug-of-war team
- ◉ Children swimming
- ◉ Group of runners

1 Age:

  a Which group of people are the youngest?

  b Which group of people are the oldest?

  c Estimate the mean age of the group of children.

  d Estimate the mean age of the group of the runners.

  e Arrange the photographs in order of mean age of the people in them, from youngest to oldest. You will need to agree in your group how to do this.

2 Weight:

  a Which group of people are the lightest?

  b Which group of people are the heaviest?

  c Estimate the mean weight of the mixed-age group.

  d Estimate the mean weight of the runners.

  e Arrange the photographs in order of mean weight of the people in them, from lightest to heaviest. You will need to agree in your group how to do this.

3 Height:

  a Which group do you think has the greatest range of heights? Why?

  b Can you find some groups that might have the same median height?

  c The mean height of the babies is 51 cm. How will the mean height of the group change if you put the group of runners in the same group as the babies?

  d How will the mean height of the group change if you put the group of runners in the same group as the tug-of-war team?

A **grouped frequency diagram** is a type of bar chart used for grouped data.

- All the bars must be the same width.
- The gaps between the bars must be the same.
- The class intervals must not overlap.
- The lines, not the spaces, are labelled evenly on the y-axis.

Example

The table shows the age of the pedestrians killed or seriously injured in 2004 .

Age	Number killed or injured
0–4	250
5–8	508
9–11	518
12–15	1063

(data from www.dft.gov.uk).

Draw a grouped frequency diagram to illustrate the data.

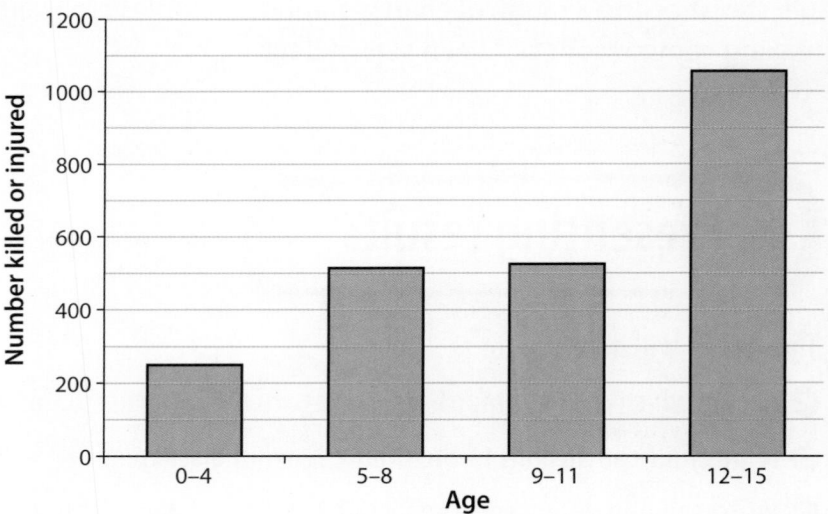

1. The list shows the ages of 40 people:

10, 1, 50, 78, 88, 26, 25, 11, 5, 66, 2, 38, 28, 88, 3, 76, 56, 19, 89, 66, 28, 23, 86, 84, 4, 11, 63, 89, 57, 29, 8, 90, 18, 36, 11, 22, 77, 34, 54, 55

a Draw a table with groups for 1–10, 11–20, …
Tally the ages to find out how many there are in each group.

b Draw a grouped frequency diagram to display the data.

c Which are the modal groups?

d Write a sentence to describe what the graph shows.

② These are the shoes sizes of another 40 people:

2, 7, 4, 6, 6, 8, 9, 7, 4, 9,
4, 12, 5, 7, 11, 6, 3, 7, 4, 8,
8, 9, 4, 8, 5, 3, 1, 6, 9, 6,
4, 7, 3, 4, 12, 6, 7, 8, 8, 3

a Draw a table with groups for 1–2, 3–4, …
Tally the shoe sizes to find out how many
there are in each group.

b Draw a grouped frequency diagram to display
the data.

c Which are the modal groups?

d Write a sentence to describe what the graph shows.

Points to remember

⊙ Simple statistics and a range of charts, graphs and tables are useful
for making comparisons between sets of data.

6 Presenting results

This lesson will help you to:

◉ decide which charts, graphs and tables are the most useful for the problem;

◉ relate your conclusions to the problem being discussed;

◉ write and illustrate a short report of a statistical investigation.

Exercise 6

You will need the data you collected for homework.
Alternatively, you can use the data set on **S4.2 Resource sheet 6.1**.

In your group choose one of these questions to answer, or make up one of your own:

◉ Do women read more books than men?

◉ Do younger people read more books than older people?

◉ Do males and females like different types of book?

◉ How often do most people read?

Your task is to work in pairs to produce a booklet that answers the question you have chosen. Here are some helpful hints and tips:

- You will need to share the data you collected for homework and to add a set of data about each of you.
- You will need to write clearly about what you are doing in your booklet.
- The relevant pieces of data will need putting into tables.
- Decide whether or not you need to group any of the data.
- Choose what type of diagram will illustrate the data best and explain why.
- When you have drawn some diagrams, or done some calculations, you need to write about what they show.
- Make sure you write a clear conclusion saying what you think the answer to your question is. You should also write about any problems you had and how accurate and reliable you think your answer is. You could also write about how you could find out the answer to your question more accurately.

Points to remember

- Choose the best chart type to answer the question that you have been asked.
- A scatter graph is used to look for connections between quantities.

How well are you doing?

Specifying the problem and planning

1 *Now that we have television, computers, the Internet and lots of other electronic media, do we need books and libraries any more?*

   a Who might be interested in the answer to this question?

   b What data would you need to collect to find out the answer to this question? How would you do this?

   c Write down three related questions that you would need to ask in order to collect the data needed to answer the question.

Processing and representing data

2 *2001 level 6*

A teacher asked her class: 'What type of book is your favourite?'
Here are the results (total 20 pupils):

Type of book	Frequency
Crime	3
Non-fiction	13
Fantasy	4

Draw a pie chart to show this information.
Show your working and draw your angles accurately.

3 *2004 level 6*

A teacher asked a class of 24 pupils if they recycled newspapers and glass. Nine pupils answered 'Newspapers only'.

On a pie chart, what would the angle be for the sector 'Newspapers only'? Show your working.

Interpreting and discussing data

4 The stem-and-leaf diagram shows the number of minutes until the first goal is scored in 25 football matches.

```
Stem: tens, leaf: units
0 | 3, 6, 8
1 | 1
2 | 1, 1, 2, 3, 4, 7, 7, 9
3 | 2, 5, 7, 9, 9
4 | 1, 3, 7
5 | 5, 6
6 | 6, 7
7 |
8 | 1
```

a What was the shortest length of time in a match before the first goal was scored?

b In how many matches did the first goal come between 20 and 29 minutes after the start?

c What was the longest wait for a first goal?

d When do you think the first goal in a match is most likely to come? Explain your answer.

5 *2005 level 5*

a Look at these three numbers.

Show that the mean of the three numbers is 10.
Explain why the median of the three numbers is 10.

b Four numbers have a mean of 10 and a median of 10, but none of the numbers is 10.

What could the four numbers be?
Give an example.

Functions and graphs

This unit will help you to:

- plot coordinates;
- know the difference between 'function' and 'equation';
- work out inverse functions;
- draw graphs of linear functions including some representing real situations.

1 Plotting points

This lesson will help you to plot points using coordinates in all four quadrants.

ⓘ Did you know that...?

Cartesian coordinates are named after **René Descartes (1596–1650)**, who was born in France. Because he was clever but often ill as a child, he was allowed to stay in bed until late in the morning.

After he left school, he spent his time travelling around Europe. He settled in Holland when he was 30, where he did his important work.

In 1649 Queen Christina of Sweden persuaded Descartes to go to Stockholm. However, she was a very early riser. After only a few months in the cold northern climate, walking to the palace for 5 o'clock every morning, he died of pneumonia.

A **coordinate pair** is an ordered pair of numbers (x, y).

Example

Write the coordinates of
points A, B, C and D.

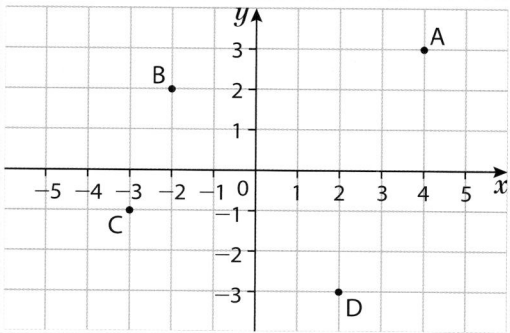

A is (4, 3), B (−2, 2), C (−3, −1) and D (2, −3).

Exercise 1

You will need squared paper, pencil and ruler for this exercise.

1. Write the coordinates of the points A to J shown on the grid below.

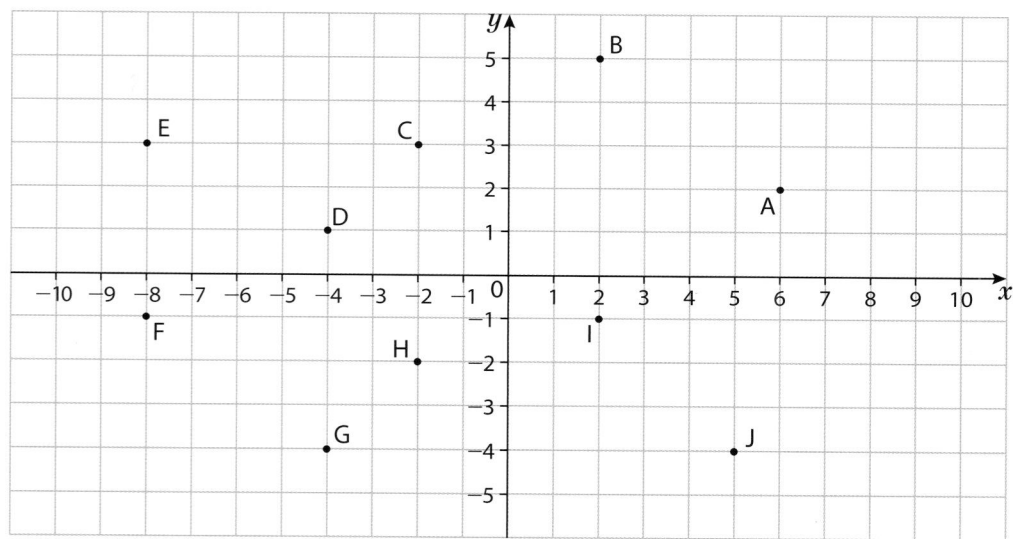

2. Before you start each of these, think about what values of x and y you need and draw a grid.

    a   Points P (−5, −2) and Q (2, −2) are two adjacent vertices of a rectangle
        with an area of 35 square units.
        What are the coordinates of the other two vertices of the rectangle?
        (There are two solutions. Find both of them.)

    b   Points R (−5, 0) and S (−1, 4) are two vertices of a square.
        What are the coordinates of the other two vertices?
        (There are three solutions. Find all of them.)

    c   Points T (−7, 0) and U (−1, 4) are opposite vertices of a square.
        What are the coordinates of the other two vertices?

    d   Points V (−4, −1), W (−1, 1) and X (2, −1) are three vertices of a rhombus.
        What are the coordinates of the fourth vertex?

③ Triangle ABC is drawn on this grid.
Triangle PQR is identical.

What are the coordinates of point R?

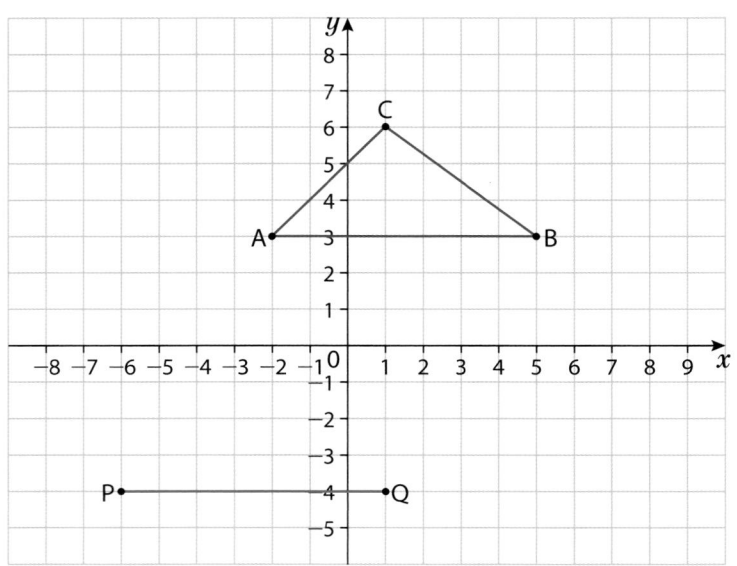

④ Trapeziums A, B and C form a sequence.

What are the coordinates of the vertices of the next trapezium in this sequence?

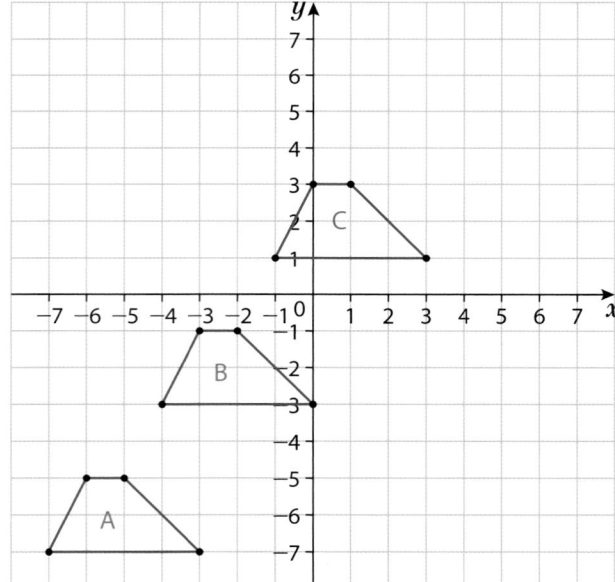

5 Triangle ABC is drawn on this grid.

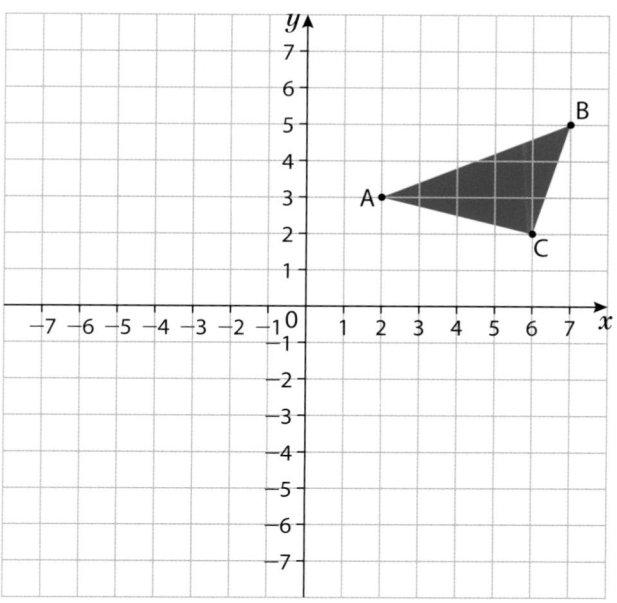

a Triangle ABC is reflected in the y-axis. What are its new coordinates?

b Triangle ABC is reflected in the x-axis. What are its new coordinates?

c Triangle ABC is reflected in the line $y = -x$. What are its new coordinates?

d Triangle ABC is reflected in the line $y = x$. What are its new coordinates?

6 Points L (-8, -4) and M (6, -4) are two vertices of rectangle KLMN.
The area of KLMN is 70 square units.
What are the coordinates of the fourth vertex?
(There are two solutions. Find both of them.)

Extension problem

7 a Points P (-2, -5) and Q (1, 2) are opposite vertices of a square.
What are the coordinates of the other two vertices?

b Find the area of the square.

 Points to remember

⊙ A **coordinate pair** is an ordered pair of numbers (x, y).
⊙ The **x-coordinate** is along the horizontal x-axis.
⊙ The **y-coordinate** is up the vertical y-axis.

2 Functions and inverse functions

This lesson will help you to work with functions and inverse functions.

You can show a relationship between two variables x and y in a **mapping diagram** like this:

$x \to y$
$1 \to 2$
$2 \to 5$
$3 \to 8$
$4 \to 11$
$x \to 3x - 1$

You can also write it as a **function** like this: $\quad x \to$ | multiply by 3 | $\to$ | subtract 1 | $\to y$

The **inverse function** is: $\qquad\qquad\qquad x \gets$ | divide by 3 | $\gets$ | add 1 | $\gets y$

Exercise 2

1 Find the outputs y for the given inputs x for this function:

$x \to$ | add 9 | $\to y$

a $x = 7$	**b** $x = 37$	**c** $x = 15$	**d** $x = 56$
e $x = 25$	**f** $x = 90$	**g** $x = 50$	**h** $x = 44$

2 Find the outputs y for the given inputs x for this function:

$x \to$ | multiply by 7 | $\to y$

a $x = 2$	**b** $x = 4$	**c** $x = 8$	**d** $x = 7$
e $x = 12$	**f** $x = 15$	**g** $x = 50$	**h** $x = 100$

3 Find the outputs y for the given inputs x for this function:

$x \to$ | multiply by 3 | $\to$ | add 7 | $\to y$

a $x = 3$	**b** $x = 11$	**c** $x = 9$	**d** $x = 25$
e $x = 10$	**f** $x = 32$	**g** $x = 35$	**h** $x = 40$

(4) Work out the functions and find the missing numbers in these mappings.

a $x \rightarrow y$
  $1 \rightarrow 7$
  $2 \rightarrow 11$
  $3 \rightarrow 15$
  $4 \rightarrow$
  $5 \rightarrow$
  $6 \rightarrow$
  $x \rightarrow$

b $x \rightarrow y$
  $1 \rightarrow 4$
  $2 \rightarrow 10$
  $3 \rightarrow 16$
  $4 \rightarrow$
  $5 \rightarrow$
  $6 \rightarrow$
  $x \rightarrow$

(5) Write the inverse functions.

a $x \rightarrow$ | add 15 | $\rightarrow y$

b $x \rightarrow$ | subtract 8 | $\rightarrow y$

c $x \rightarrow$ | multiply by 7 | $\rightarrow$ | subtract 3 | $\rightarrow y$

d $x \rightarrow$ | add 19 | $\rightarrow$ | multiply by 12 | $\rightarrow y$

e $x \rightarrow$ | divide by 4 | $\rightarrow$ | subtract 8 | $\rightarrow y$

f $x \rightarrow$ | add 7 | $\rightarrow$ | multiply by 4 | $\rightarrow$ | divide by 3 | $\rightarrow y$

(6) Match the functions (labelled **a** to **h**) to their inverses (labelled P to W).

a $x \rightarrow$ | add 5 | $\rightarrow$ | multiply by 7 | $\rightarrow y$

P $x \leftarrow$ | add 7 | $\leftarrow$ | divide by 5 | $\leftarrow y$

b $x \rightarrow$ | multiply by 5 | $\rightarrow$ | subtract 7 | $\rightarrow y$

Q $x \leftarrow$ | multiply by 7 | $\leftarrow$ | subtract 5 | $\leftarrow y$

c $x \rightarrow$ | subtract 7 | $\rightarrow$ | multiply by 5 | $\rightarrow y$

R $x \leftarrow$ | divide by 7 | $\leftarrow$ | subtract 5 | $\leftarrow y$

d $x \rightarrow$ | divide by 7 | $\rightarrow$ | add 5 | $\rightarrow y$

S $x \leftarrow$ | subtract 7 | $\leftarrow$ | divide by 5 | $\leftarrow y$

e $x \rightarrow$ | multiply by 7 | $\rightarrow$ | subtract 5 | $\rightarrow y$

T $x \leftarrow$ | add 5 | $\leftarrow$ | multiply by 7 | $\leftarrow y$

f $x \rightarrow$ | add 7 | $\rightarrow$ | multiply by 5 | $\rightarrow y$

U $x \leftarrow$ | subtract 5 | $\leftarrow$ | divide by 7 | $\leftarrow y$

g $x \rightarrow$ | multiply by 7 | $\rightarrow$ | add 5 | $\rightarrow y$

V $x \leftarrow$ | divide by 7 | $\leftarrow$ | add 5 | $\leftarrow y$

h $x \rightarrow$ | subtract 5 | $\rightarrow$ | divide by 7 | $\rightarrow y$

W $x \leftarrow$ | divide by 5 | $\leftarrow$ | add 7 | $\leftarrow y$

Extension problem

(7) Find the outputs y for the given inputs x for this function:

$x \rightarrow$ | add 6 | $\rightarrow$ | multiply by 5 | $\rightarrow y$

a $x = 8$ b $x = 9$ c $x = 16$ d $x = 12$

e $x = 22$ f $x = 90$ g $x = 52$ h $x = 27$

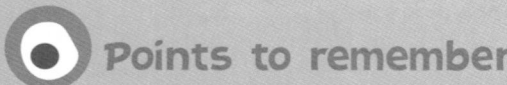

Points to remember

⊙ You can show a relationship between two variables x and y in a **mapping diagram** like this:

$$x \to y$$
$$1 \to 6$$
$$2 \to 10$$
$$3 \to 14$$
$$4 \to 18$$
$$x \to 4x + 2$$

⊙ You can also write it as a **function** like this:

$x \to$ ┌ multiply by 4 ┐ $\to$ ┌ add 2 ┐ $\to y$

⊙ Then the **inverse function** is:

$x \leftarrow$ ┌ divide by 4 ┐ $\leftarrow$ ┌ subtract 2 ┐ $\leftarrow y$

3 Functions, equations and graphs

This lesson will help you to represent information as functions, equations and graphs.

x	0	1	2	3	4	5
y	2	7	12	17	22	27

In the table above the function is $x \to$ ┌ multiply by 5 ┐ $\to$ ┌ add 2 ┐ $\to y$.

This can be written as an equation: $y = 5x + 2$.

A relationship between two variables x and y can be shown as a function like this.

$x \to$ ┌ multiply by 3 ┐ $\to$ ┌ subtract 1 ┐ $\to y$

This relationship can also be written as the **equation** $y = 3x - 1$.

This is a **linear** relationship.
You can draw an accurate graph of the relationship by finding three pairs of values (x, y) and plotting them on rectangular axes.

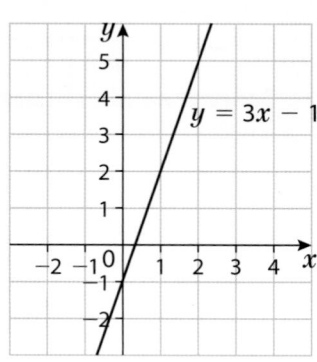

x	0	1	2
$y = 3x - 1$	−1	2	5

Exercise 3

You will need squared paper, a ruler and a pencil for this exercise.

(1) Find the value of each expression when $x = 8$.

   a $9 + 5x$ **b** $5(9 + x)$ **c** $5x - 9$ **d** $5(9 - x)$

   e $\dfrac{x + 9}{5}$ **f** $\dfrac{x}{5} + 9$ **g** $9 - \dfrac{x}{5}$ **h** $\dfrac{9 - x}{5}$

(2) Copy and complete the tables below.

a

x	-3	-2	-1	0	1	2	3	4
$y = 8x + 3$								

b

x	-1.5	-1	-0.5	0	0.5	1	1.5	2
$y = 4x - 1$								

c

x	3.1	3.2	3.3	3.4	3.5	3.6	3.7	3.8
$y = 7x - 4$								

d

x	-6	-5	-4	-3	-2	-1	0	1
$y = 0.5x$								

e

x	-3	-2	-1	0	1	2	3	4
$y = 9x + 7$								

(3) Draw accurate graphs of these linear equations.

   a $y = 3x + 4$ **b** $y = 5x - 2$ **c** $y = x + 7$ **d** $y = 4x - 1$

   e $y = 2x + 9$ **f** $y = 0.5x + 3$ **g** $y = 0.5x + 1$ **h** $y = 2x - 1.5$

Extension problem

(4) Write down the coordinates of three points that lie on this graph.

Use them to work out the equation of the graph.

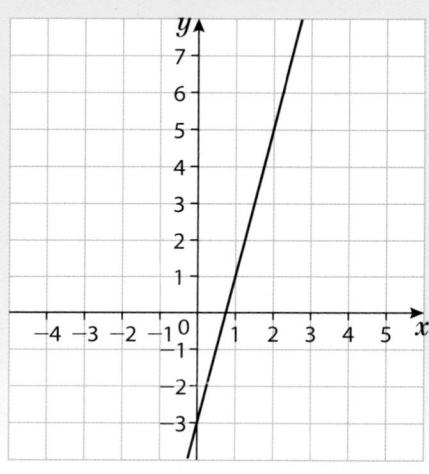

4 Sketching graphs

This lesson will help you to use ICT to generate graphs and to sketch their main features.

Exercise 4

Work with a partner. You will each need squared paper, pencil and ruler.
Each pair will also need a computer with graph-plotting software, or a graphics calculator.

1   Use the computer or graphics calculator to generate graphs of these equations.

a $y = x$	b $y = x + 1$	c $y = x + 2$	d $y = x + 3$
e $y = x - 1$	f $y = x - 2$	g $y = x - 3$	h $y = x - 4$

2   Study the graphs you generated in question 1.
Write down what you notice about them.

3   Use the computer or graphics calculator to generate graphs of these equations.

a $y = x$	b $y = 2x$	c $y = 3x$	d $y = 4x$
e $y = 7x$	f $y = 0.5x$	g $y = 2.5x$	h $y = 7.2x$

4   Study the graphs you generated in question 3.
Write down what you notice about them.

5   Use the computer or graphics calculator to draw graphs of these equations.

a $y = -x$	b $y = -x + 1$	c $y = -x + 2$	d $y = -x + 3$
e $y = -x - 1$	f $y = -x - 2$	g $y = -x - 3$	h $y = -x - 4$

6   Study the graphs you generated in question 5.
Write down what you notice about them.

On squared paper, **sketch** the graphs of these equations on blank sets of axes.
Check your sketches by drawing them on the computer or graphics calculator.

a $y = x$ b $y = 2x - 3$ c $y = 4x + 5$ d $y = 5x - 2$

e $y = x - 5$ f $y = 3x - 7$ g $y = -x - 1$ h $y = -4x + 3$

● Points to remember

⊙ Graphs of the form $y = ax$, where a is a constant, are straight-line
graphs that pass through the origin.
  − The steepness of the line is called its **gradient**.
  − The number in front of x is called the **coefficient** of x. The larger
    the coefficient of x, the greater the gradient.
⊙ A **sketch** of a graph is a neat drawing that shows some of its
features.

5 Interpreting equations of graphs

This lesson will help you to visualise graphs from their equations, and work out the equations of linear graphs.

Look at this linear equation: $y = 2x + 1$.
The equation is in the form $y = ax + b$.
The **coefficient** of x is 2.
The **gradient** of the graph of this equation is 2.

The **intercept** of the graph with the y-axis is (0, 1).

In the right-angled triangle in the diagram, the
vertical height is 2 units and the base is 1 unit.

The **gradient** of the graph is
$$\frac{\text{vertical height}}{\text{base}} = \frac{2}{1} = 2$$

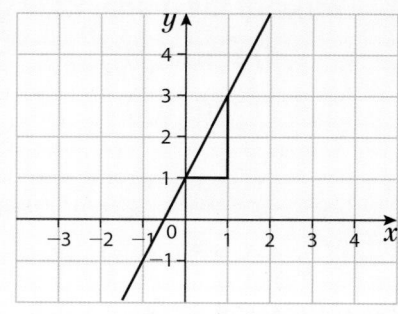

1 Write down the gradient and intercept with the y-axis of the graphs of these linear equations.

   a $y = x$ **b** $y = 2x + 1$ **c** $y = 4x + 8$ **d** $y = 2x - 3$
   e $y = 6x + 2$ **f** $y = 0.5x + 4$ **g** $y = x - 7$ **h** $y = 8x - 10$
   i $y = -x + 1$ **j** $y = -3x - 6$

2 Work out the gradient and intercept of these graphs.

   a 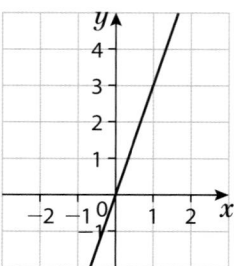   **b**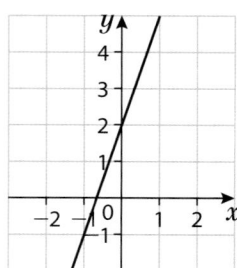

   c 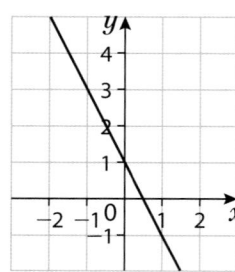   **d**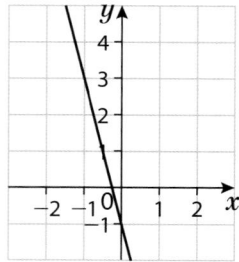

Extension problems

3 Write down the equations of these linear graphs.

   a Gradient 3, intercept $(0, 6)$ **b** Gradient 1, intercept $(0, 9)$
   c Gradient 10, intercept $(0, -2)$ **d** Gradient 0.5, intercept $(0, 5)$
   e Gradient -4, intercept $(0, 7)$ **f** Gradient -1, intercept $(0, 0)$

4 Work out the gradients of the linear graphs that pass through the two given points.

   a $(3, 5)$ and $(1, 1)$ **b** $(3, 6)$ and $(2, 1)$ **c** $(4, 4)$ and $(0, 0)$
   d $(4, 1)$ and $(1, 0)$ **e** $(-3, 5)$ and $(-2, 2)$ **f** $(2, -1)$ and $(1, -4)$

◉ Points to remember

- ⊙ Every linear function can be represented as a straight-line graph with an equation of the form $y = ax + b$.
- ⊙ The **gradient** is a and the **intercept** on the y-axis is $(0, b)$.

6 Interpreting real-life graphs 1

This lesson will help you to draw and interpret graphs of real situations.

Exercise 6

1. Natasha went for a bike ride with her friends.
   She started and ended her journey at home.

This graph records Natasha's bike ride.

a Natasha started her bike ride at 9:30 am.
   At what time did she make her first stop?

b How far had Natasha travelled when she first stopped?

c How long did it take for Natasha to get from her first to her second stop?

d How many miles was it from Natasha's first to her second stop?

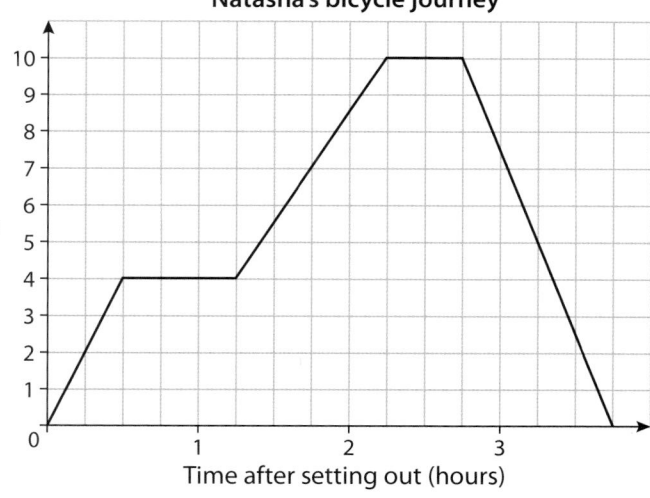

e What average speed was Natasha doing between her first and second stop?

f At what time did Natasha leave her second stop?

g At what time did Natasha get home?

h What was Natasha's average speed on the way home?

(2) This graph shows the conversion between miles and kilometres.

a Estimate from the graph how many kilometres there are to five miles.

b Estimate from the graph how many miles there are to five kilometres.

c Shannon is on holiday in France.
She drives 250 miles on the first day.
How many kilometres is this?

d The speed limit on a French motorway is 110 km per hour.
What is this in miles per hour?

e Boris is driving his German car in England.
He sees that the speed limit in a town is 30 mph. What is this in km per hour?

f Ayesha lives 0.25 miles from her school. What is this in metres?

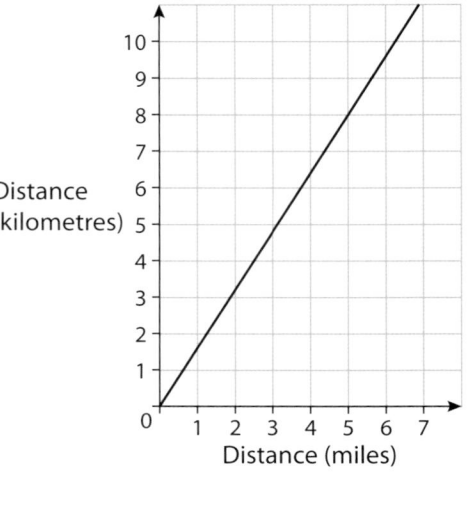

(3) This graph shows how much people get paid for picking daffodils.

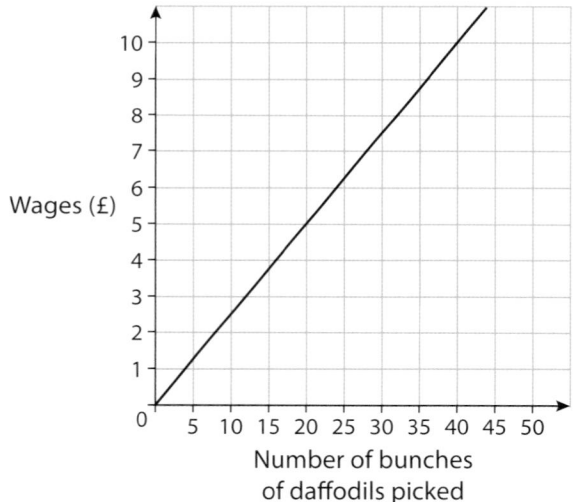

a Estimate from the graph how much a person is paid for picking 10 bunches of daffodils.

b Phoebe earned £50 one day.
How many bunches of daffodils did she pick?

c Zoe earned £560 one week.
How many bunches of daffodils did she pick?

d Owen picked 1255 bunches of daffodils in one week.
How much did he earn?

(4) A speciality tea shop sells loose tea by the gram.
This graph shows the cost of the tea per gram.

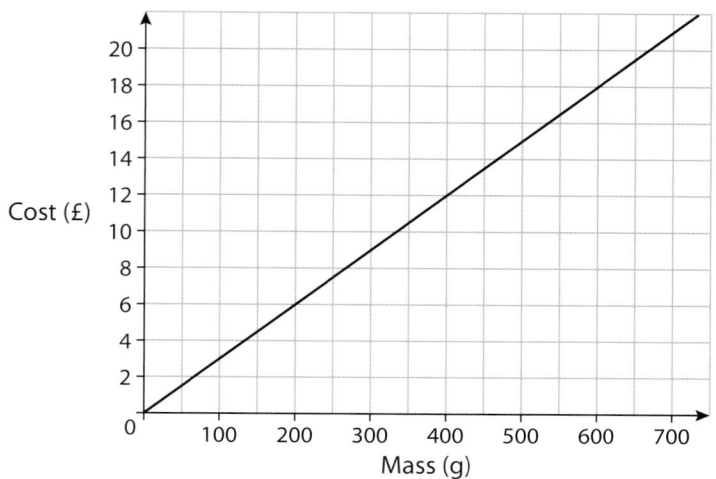

Use the graph to estimate the cost of these masses of tea.

a   200 g   b   100 g

c   10 g   d   1 g

e   500 g   f   1 kg

g   75 g   h   40 g

 Points to remember

⊙ A **distance-time graph** or **travel graph** describes stages in a journey.
⊙ A **conversion graph** shows how to change one unit to another.
⊙ When you draw or interpret graphs of real situations, take care with the scales on the axes.

How well are you doing?

Can you:
- work with functions and inverse functions?
- plot coordinates on rectangular axes?
- visualise, sketch and draw linear graphs from their equations?
- draw graphs of real situations?

You will need squared paper, pencil and ruler for these questions.

1 *2002 level 5*

Some people use yards to measure length.
The diagram shows one way to change yards to metres.

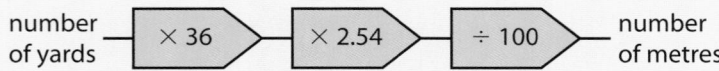

number of yards → × 36 → × 2.54 → ÷ 100 → number of metres

  a Change 100 yards to metres.   **b** Change 100 metres to yards.

2 *2005 level 6*

The graph shows the straight line with equation $y = 3x - 4$.

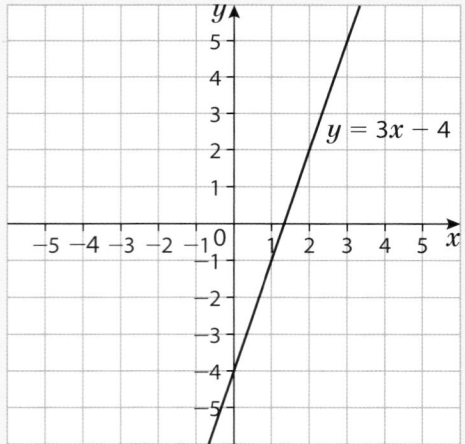

  a A point on the line $y = 3x - 4$ has an x-coordinate of 50.
     What is the y-coordinate of this point?

  b A point on the line $y = 3x - 4$ has a y-coordinate of 50.
     What is the x-coordinate of this point?

  c Is the point $(-10, -34)$ on the line $y = 3x - 4$?
     Write **Yes** or **No**. Show how you know.

3 *2004 level 6*

The graph shows a straight line.

a Write an equation of the straight line.

b On squared paper, draw the straight line that has the equation $x + y = 6$.

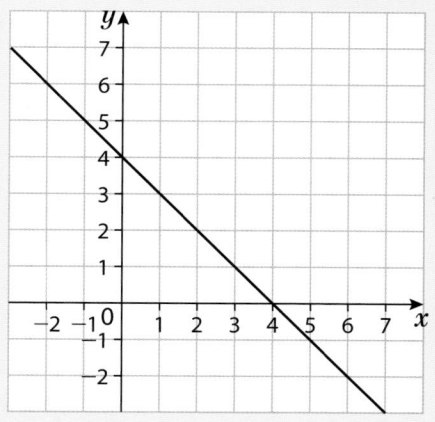

4 Imagine the graph of the linear equation $y = 5x + 7$.

a What is the gradient of the graph?

b What is the intercept on the y-axis?

5 *2004 level 6*

a A function maps the number n to the number $n + 2$.

Copy this table and complete the missing values.

n	$\rightarrow$	$n + 2$
4	$\rightarrow$	...
...	$\rightarrow$	20

b A different function maps the number n to the number $2n$.

Copy this table and complete the missing values.

n	$\rightarrow$	$2n$
4	$\rightarrow$	...
...	$\rightarrow$	20

Many different functions can map the number 25 to the number 5.

Copy and complete the tables by writing two different functions.

n	$\rightarrow$	...
25	$\rightarrow$	5

n	$\rightarrow$	...
25	$\rightarrow$	5

6 1 kilogram is about 2.2 pounds.

On squared paper, draw a conversion graph for kilograms to pounds.

Proportional reasoning

This unit will help you to:

- understand the relationship between ratio, proportion and fractions;
- simplify ratios;
- divide a quantity into two or more parts in a given ratio;
- interpret simple scale drawings;
- solve problems involving ratio or proportion;
- use equivalent fractions, decimals and percentages to find and compare proportions.

1 Dividing a quantity in a given ratio

This lesson will help you to understand the relationship between ratio, proportion and fractions. You will learn to simplify ratios and divide a quantity in a given ratio.

Did you know that...?

A **ratio** compares two quantities measured in the same units.

This map has a ratio of 1 : 50 000.

This means that 1 cm on the map represents 50 000 cm, or 500 m, on the ground.

We usually use whole numbers in a ratio and write them without units.

The colon **:** was first used in England in 1633 in Johnson's *Arithmetick in two Bookes*. It appeared as 3 : 4 to represent the fraction three quarters.

The colon was first used for ratio in 1651 in a book on astronomy by Vincent Wing.

Ratios are used to compare quantities. For example, if there are 6 boys and 9 girls in a class, the ratio of the number of boys to the number of girls is 6 : 9.

Ratios can be simplified like fractions. The ratio 6 : 9 can be simplified.
Dividing both 6 and 9 by 3 gives the ratio 2 : 3.

2 : 3 cannot be simplified because 2 and 3 have no common factors.
This is called the **simplest form** of the ratio.

It means that for every 2 boys in the class there are 3 girls.

Sometimes a ratio involves more than two quantities.

Example 1　　What is the ratio of red to green to blue beads?

The ratio of red to green to blue beads is 2 : 4 : 6 = 1 : 2 : 3.

Example 2　　Simplify the ratio 8 : 12.

4 divides into both 8 and 12, so $8:12 = \frac{8}{4}:\frac{12}{4} = 2:3$.

Example 3　　Simplify the ratio £2 to 50p.

The ratio of £2 to 50p is written as 200 : 50 = 4 : 1.

Exercise 1A

1　**a**　Which of the rows on the right have the same ratio of red squares to blue squares?

A	■■	■■■
B	■	■■
C	■■■■	■■
D	■■■■	■■■■■■
E	■■■	■■■■■

A	■■	■■■
B	■■■	■■
C	■	■■
D	■■■■	■■
E	■■	■■■■

b　Which of the rows on the left have two green squares for every one blue square?

2　Simplify these ratios.

　　a　14 : 35　　　　　　**b**　88 : 55　　　　　　**c**　100 : 20

　　d　30 : 18　　　　　　**e**　12 : 18 : 24　　　　**f**　25 : 10 : 50

3　Simplify these ratios.

　　a　1 day : 8 hours　　**b**　75p : £4.25　　　　**c**　5 kg : 500 g

　　d　3 weeks : 14 days　**e**　2.5 litres : 1750 ml　**f**　750 mm : 50 cm : 1.5 m

(4) Find a partner to play **Matching ratios**.
You will need a set of cards made from
N4.4 Resource sheet 1.1.

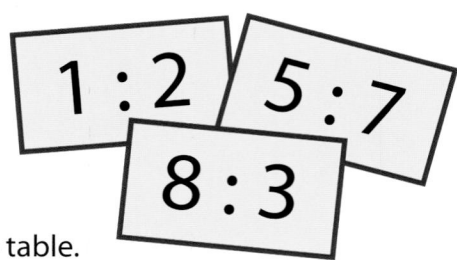

Rules

- Shuffle the cards. Spread them out face down on the table.
- Take turns to turn over two of the cards.
- If the cards are a pair of equivalent ratios, you can keep the cards and have another turn.
- If the ratios on the cards are not equivalent, turn the cards back face down. It is then the other player's turn.
- The winner is the player with most cards when all the pairs have been found.

Exercise 1B

To divide a quantity into two parts in the ratio $a : b$, begin by dividing the quantity into $a + b$ equal shares. Put a shares in one part, and b shares in the other part.

This is the same as finding the fractions $\dfrac{a}{a + b}$ and $\dfrac{b}{a + b}$ of the quantity.

Example 1

Divide 45 cm into two parts in the ratio 2 : 7.

There are $2 + 7 = 9$ equal shares.

Two shares are $\frac{2}{9}$ of 45 cm, or $\frac{2}{{}_1\cancel{9}} \times \dfrac{\overset{5}{\cancel{45}}}{1} = 10\,\text{cm}$.

Seven shares are $\frac{7}{9}$ of 45 cm, or $\frac{7}{{}_1\cancel{9}} \times \dfrac{\overset{5}{\cancel{45}}}{\cancel{1}} = 35\,\text{cm}$.

So the two parts are 10 cm and 35 cm.

Example 2

Joe, Mark and Paul divide £40 in the ratio 1 : 3 : 4.
How much money does each boy get?

There are $1 + 3 + 4 = 8$ equal shares.

Joe gets $\frac{1}{8}$ of £40, or £5.

Mark gets $\frac{3}{8}$ of £40, or £15.

Paul gets $\frac{4}{8}$ of £40, or £20.

Solve these problems **without a calculator**. Show your working clearly.

(1) Anna and Daniel shared £1200.
Anna got twice as much money as Daniel.
How much money did Anna get?

(2) Rectangle ABCD has a perimeter of 48 cm.
Sides AB and DC are three times as long as sides AD and BC.
Find the length of side AD.

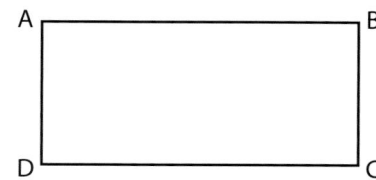

(3) B is a point on the line AC.
The distance AC is 60 cm.
The distance AB is four times the distance BC.
What is the distance from A to B?

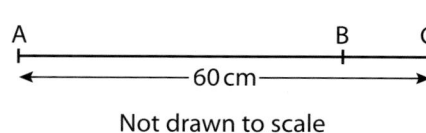

Not drawn to scale

(4) A drink uses tomato juice and carrot juice in the ratio 2 : 3.
I want to make 1 litre of this drink.

   a   How many millilitres of tomato juice should I use?

   b   How many millilitres of carrot juice should I use?

(5) A 5-litre tin of pale green paint contains 1.25 litres of white paint,
3 litres of blue paint and 750 millilitres of yellow paint.
What is the ratio of white to blue to yellow paint?

(6) The instructions for a fruit drink say to mix one part strawberry juice with three parts
raspberry juice and six parts water.
I want to make 1 litre of this fruit drink. How much of each of these should I use?

   a   strawberry juice   b   raspberry juice   c   water

Give your answers in millilitres.

(7) The audience at a cinema consisted of men, women and children in the ratio 3 : 5 : 2.
There were 350 people altogether at the cinema.
How many men, women and children were there?

Extension problems

⊙ '2 in every 3' means that there are 3 units.
The parts are $\frac{2}{3}$ and $\frac{1}{3}$ of the whole.
The ratio of these two parts is 2 : 1.

⊙ '2 for every 3' means that there are 5 units.
The parts are $\frac{2}{5}$ and $\frac{3}{5}$ of the whole.
The ratio of these two parts is 2 : 3.

8 Alex has a good recipe for a tomato sauce.
When he is asked for the recipe, he gives a clue.

I use a whole number of peppers and a whole number of tomatoes. For one litre of tomato sauce, I use a total of 12 peppers and tomatoes in one of these ratios:

A 3:2 **B** 2:3 **C** 2:4 **D** 3:4 **E** 1:6

How many peppers and how many tomatoes does it take to make Marco's sauce?

9 Nicole has a box of chocolates.

For every 2 hard centres in her box, there are 5 soft centres.

There are 8 hard centres in the box. How many soft centres are there?

Liam also has a box of chocolates.
For every 2 hard centres in his box, there are 3 soft centres.

There are 12 soft centres in the box. How many hard centres are there?

Nicole and Liam decide to mix their boxes of chocolates together. What is the ratio of hard centres to soft centres in the combined box?

⦿ Points to remember

- ⦿ A **proportion** is a fraction or percentage.
  If 1 in every 4 beads is red, the proportion of red beads is $\frac{1}{4}$ or 25%.
- ⦿ A **ratio** is a way of comparing quantities.
  We usually use whole numbers in a ratio and write them without units.
- ⦿ Ratios are simplified like fractions.
- ⦿ To divide a quantity into two parts in the ratio $a : b$, begin by dividing the quantity into $a + b$ equal shares.
  Put a shares in one part, and b shares in the other part.

  This is the same as finding the fractions $\dfrac{a}{a + b}$ and $\dfrac{b}{a + b}$ of the quantity.

2 Solving ratio problems

This lesson will help you to solve problems involving ratio or proportion.

A unitary ratio is written in the form $1 : n$. Unitary ratios are useful for comparing proportions.

Example 1

Convert the ratio of $2 : 15$ to the form $1 : n$.

Divide both sides by 2 to get $\frac{2}{2} : \frac{15}{2} = 1 : 7.5$.

Example 2

Lewis does not like to eat too much fat.
A mix for a sponge cake has 6 parts of fat to 9 parts flour.
A mix for fruit cake has 5 parts of fat to 8 parts of flour.
Which mix should Lewis choose?

In the mix for sponge cake, the ratio of fat to flour is $6 : 9$ or $\frac{6}{6} : \frac{9}{6} = 1 : 1.5$.

In the mix for fruit cake, the ratio of fat to flour is $5 : 8$ or $\frac{5}{8} : \frac{8}{5} = 1 : 1.6$.

There is more flour (and less fat) in cake mix B.

Exercise 2A

1 Convert these ratios to the form $1 : n$.

    a 2:8   b 3:18   c 4:11

    d 4:2   e 8:5   f 4:14

    g 25:7   h 1.5:6   i 2.5:5

2 Which ratio of cups of coffee to girls gives each girl the most cups of coffee?

Key:

  cup of coffee

  girl

(3) Fruit drink A is made from 2 parts orange juice and 7 parts pineapple juice.
Fruit drink B is made from 1 part orange juice and 4 parts pineapple juice.
Which has more pineapple juice, 1 litre of fruit drink A or 1 litre of fruit drink B?
Explain how you know.

(4) Cake mix A uses currants and raisins in the ratio 2:3.
Cake mix B uses currants and raisins in the ratio 4:5.
Which cake has the greater proportion of raisins?
Explain how you know.

Exercise 2B

Given a ratio and the size of one part, you can find the other part.

Example

A line segment is divided in the ratio 3:5. The shorter part of the line is 18 cm long.
What is the length of the longer part? How long is the line segment?

Method 1

18 cm represents three shares of the line.
For one share we calculate 18 cm ÷ 3 = 6 cm.
For five shares we calculate 6 cm × 5 = 30 cm.

So the longer part of the line is 30 cm. The whole line is 18 cm + 30 cm = 48 cm.

Method 2

The ratio 3:5 is equivalent to the ratio 18 : ?
To get 18, we have to multiply 3 by the scale factor 6.
So the ratio 3:5 is equivalent to the ratio 3 × 6:5 × 6 or 18:30.
So the longer part of the line is 30 cm. The whole line is 18 cm + 30 cm = 48 cm.

(1) Joseph and Paige share some money in the ratio 3:8.
Joseph's share is £60. How much is Paige's share?

(2) A tennis club's members are men and women in the ratio 4:5.
There are 28 men. How many members of the tennis club are there?

(3) To make green paint you mix 3 parts blue paint to 5 parts yellow paint.
Rajesh mixed 4.5 litres of blue paint with some yellow paint to make green paint.
How many litres of yellow paint did he use?

(4) A photo is 8 cm wide and 5 cm tall.
It is enlarged to give a photograph
20 cm wide.
How tall is the enlarged photo?

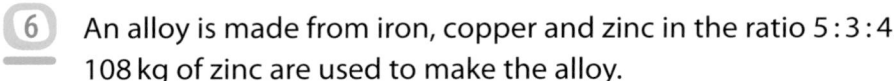

(5) A recipe requires 50 g of sugar for
every 125 g of flour.

   a How much flour is needed for 200 g of sugar?

   b How much sugar is needed for 200 g of flour?

(6) An alloy is made from iron, copper and zinc in the ratio 5 : 3 : 4.
108 kg of zinc are used to make the alloy.

   a How much iron is used?   b How much copper is used?

(7) Imogen, Lily and Alexandra share some money in the ratio 3 : 4 : 7.
Imogen's share is £150.

   a How much money is Lily's share?   b How much money is Alexandra's share?

(8) A type of plaster is made by mixing $1\frac{3}{4}$ parts cement to 3 parts of sand.
How much cement needs to be mixed with 18 kg of sand to make the plaster?

Extension problem

(9) Tin A of purple paint is made by mixing 2 parts of red paint
with 3 parts of blue paint.

   a David has 450 ml of red paint and 450 ml of blue paint.
What is the maximum amount of purple paint that he
can make?

Tin B is a different tin of purple paint. It is the same size as tin A.
It is made by mixing three parts of red paint with seven parts
of blue paint.

   b Tin A and tin B are both poured into a new tin.
What is the ratio of red paint to blue paint in the new tin?

⊙ Points to remember

- ⊙ A **unitary ratio** is written in the form $1 : n$.
To convert a ratio of 2 : 15 to a unitary ratio, divide by 2 to get 1 : 7.5 .
- ⊙ Unitary ratios are useful for comparing ratios.
- ⊙ A **scale factor** tells you how many times bigger one number is than
another.

3 Scale drawings

This lesson will help you to make and interpret scale drawings.

A **scale drawing** is a smaller drawing of an actual object.

The **scale** of a drawing is the relative size of the drawn length to the actual length.

A scale of 1 cm to 1 m means that 1 cm on the drawing represents an actual length of 1 m.

The scale must always be stated next to the drawing.

Example

This is a scale drawing of a room. 1 cm represents 1 m.

On the scale drawing the length of the room is 5 cm so the actual length of the room is 5 m.

On the scale drawing the width of the room is 3.5 cm so the actual width of the room is 3.5 m.

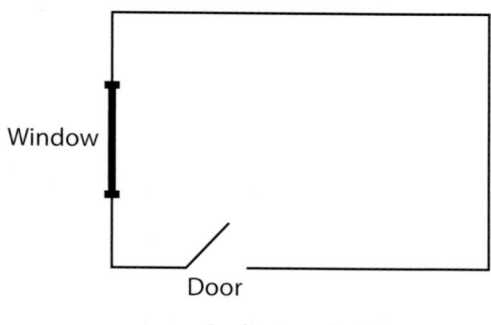

Scale: 1 cm to 1 m

Exercise 3A

1. The lines below are drawn using a scale of 1 cm to 3 m.
   Write the length that each line represents.

   a ────────────

   b ──────────────────────────

   c ─────────────────

   d ──────────────────

   e ──────────────────────────────

2. Sarah has drawn a plan of a shed.
   Clare notices that there is no scale on the drawing but she knows that the shed is 3 metres wide.

   a What scale has Sarah used?

   b What is the actual length of the shed?

   c What is the actual area of the shed?

3 Dave makes a scale drawing of his room.
He uses a scale of 1 cm to 0.5 m.

Measure the length and width of the drawing with your ruler.

a What is the actual length of the room in metres?

b What is the actual width of the room in metres?

c What is the actual length of the diagonal of the room in metres?

Dave decides his drawing is too small. He draws a new rectangle with sides twice as long.

d Write down the length and the width of the new rectangle in centimetres.

e What length in metres does 1 centimetre of the new drawing represent?

Scale: 1 cm to 0.5 m

4 Jacob has drawn a plan of his school field.
He has used a scale of 1 centimetre to represent 6 metres.

a What actual length is represented by 4 cm on Jacob's plan?

b The football pitch is 90 m long.
How long will it be on Jacob's plan?

c How long will the football pitch be on Jacob's plan if he changes the scale so that 1 cm represents 20 metres?

5 Copy and complete the table below for a scale of 5 cm to 1 metre.

	Actual length	Length on scale drawing
a	3 m	
b	1.5 m	
c	50 cm	
d		30 cm
e		12.5 cm
f		1.25 cm

A **map ratio** is the ratio of the distance on the map to the actual distance on the ground. Map ratios are always given in the form $1 : n$ and have no units.

Example

Express the scale 2 cm to 1 km as a map ratio in the form $1 : n$.

Convert 1 km to centimetres: 1 km = 1000 m = 1000 × 100 cm = 100 000 cm
So the scale 2 cm to 1 km can be written as the ratio 2 : 100 000 = 1 : 50 000.

1 What distance does 1 cm represent on maps with these scales?

   a 1 : 5000   b 1 : 300 000   c 1 : 20 000   d 1 : 10 000 000

2 This street map of Winchester City centre has a scale of 1 : 10 000.

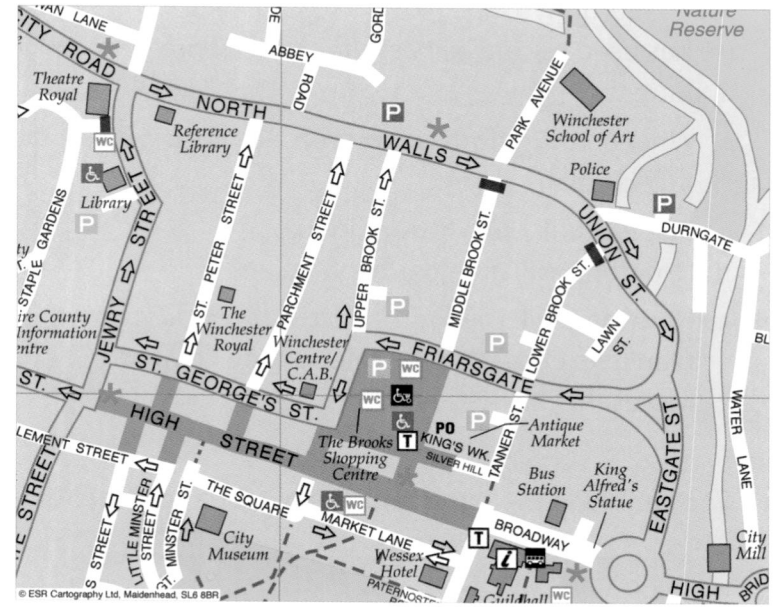

   a What distance does 1 cm on the map represent?

   b Measure first, then estimate the actual length of:
      i   the High Street
      ii St Peter Street

   c Measure first, then estimate the actual distance 'as the crow flies' from the Winchester School of Art to the City Museum.

   d A car drives from the car park on North Walls. It travels around the one-way system along Union Street, Friarsgate and St George's Street to the Library on Jewry Street. Estimate the distance that the car travels. Use a piece of string.

3 Write each of these scales as a map ratio in the form 1 : n.

   a 1 cm to 1 km   b 4 cm to 1 km   c 5 cm to 1 km   d 1 cm to 2 km

4 The following map has a scale of 1 : 25 000.

   a What distance does 1 cm on the map represent?

   b The red dashed line represents a footpath. Estimate the actual distance along the footpath going west from Lower Thurnham to Crook Cottage. Use a piece of string.

   c Use your ruler. Estimate the actual direct distance 'as the crow flies' between:

     i Old Glasson and Norbreck Farm

     ii the Hotel and Hillam

     iii Crook Cottage and Hill House Farm

   d Daisy walks along the road south from Upper Thurnham to Hill House Farm.
She turns west through Hillam.
Just past Bank Houses she turns to follow the road north then east past Gardner's Farm back to Upper Thurnham.

     Estimate the actual distance that Daisy walks. Use your string.

5 Tom has a road map with a scale of 1 : 300 000.

   a Two towns are 9 cm apart on the map. What is their actual distance apart?

   b Two other towns are an actual distance of 60 km apart.
How many centimetres apart are they on Tom's map?

Did you know that...?

Before the metric system started to be taught in British schools in 1974, pupils had to learn by heart tables of weights and measures like this one for length.

3 barleycorns	= 1 inch
12 inches	= 1 foot
3 feet	= 1 yard
22 yards	= 1 chain
10 chains	= 1 furlong
8 furlongs	= 1 mile
5280 feet	= 1 mile
1760 yards	= 1 mile

Extension problem

 Write each of these scales as a map ratio in the form $1 : n$.

a 1 barleycorn to 1 foot

b 1 inch to 1 yard

c 1 inch to 1 mile

d 3 inches to 1 foot

e 4 inches to 1 mile

f 2 yards to 1 furlong

 Points to remember

- A **scale drawing** is a smaller drawing of an actual object.
- The scale gives the relative size of the drawn length to the actual length. For example, a scale of 1 cm to 1 m means that 1 cm on the drawing represents an actual length of 1 m.
- The scale must always be stated next to the drawing.
- A **map ratio** is the ratio of the distance on the map to the actual distance on the ground.
- Map ratios are always given in the form $1 : n$ and have no units. For example, a scale of 1 cm to 50 m is a map ratio of $1 : 5000$, since 50 m is 5000 cm.
- A distance 'as the crow flies' is the shortest distance between two points, measured as a straight line.

4 The unitary method

This lesson will help you to solve problems involving direct proportion.

This table shows some conversions of miles into kilometres.

The ratio of the number of miles to the number of kilometres is always the same.

$25 : 40 = 5 : 8$
$100 : 160 = 5 : 8$
$2.5 : 4 = 5 : 8$

miles	kilometres
5	8
25	40
100	160
2.5	4

We say that the number of miles is **directly proportional** to the number of kilometres since the ratio of number of miles : number of kilometres is always the same.

You can solve straightforward problems involving direct proportion using a **scaling method** in a four-cell diagram.

Example 1

Choc drops costs £1.60 for 75 g.
Jack pays £8 for some choc drops.
How many grams of choc drops does he buy?

Cost (p)	Choc drops (g)	
160	75	
800	?	× 5

Answer: Jack buys 75 g × 5 = 375 g of choc drops.

Harder problems involving direct proportion can be solved using the **unitary method** and a calculator if necessary.

Example 2

The mass of 120 ml of olive oil is 90 g.
What is the mass of 58 ml of olive oil?

Answer: 58 ml of olive oil has a mass of 43.5 g.

	Oil (ml)	Mass (g)
	120	90
÷ 120	1	0.75
× 58	58	43.5

Work out the answers to questions 1–4 **using mental or written methods**.

1 a 4 apples cost 80p. What do 3 apples cost?

   b 5 tomatoes cost 95p. What do 13 tomatoes cost?

   c 9 boxes of asparagus cost £15.30.
      What do 5 boxes of asparagus cost?

   d 10 lettuces cost £5.50.
      What do 7 lettuces cost?

   e 7 oranges cost 56p.
      How many oranges can you buy for £8?

   f 8 marrows cost £9.60.
      How many marrows can you buy for £7.20?

2 a 1 inch is approximately equal to 2.5 cm.
      Roughly how many centimetres are equal to 8 inches?
      How many inches are equal to 30 cm?

   b 4 litres are about the same as 7 pints.
      Roughly how many pints are equal to 10 litres?
      How many litres are equal to 35 pints?

   c 5 kilograms are approximately equal to 11 pounds in weight.
      Roughly how many pounds are equal to 55 kilograms?
      How many kilograms are equal to 55 pounds?

   d 5 miles is about the same as 8 kilometres.
      Roughly how many miles are equal to 20 kilometres?
      How many kilometres are equal to 42.5 miles?

3 A lorry on the motorway travels at a steady speed of 60 miles per hour.

   a How far will it go in 15 minutes?   b How far will it go in 40 minutes?

   c How long will it take to go 45 miles?   d How long will it take to go 90 miles?

4 This recipe makes 12 hot cross buns.

   a Write down the ingredients to make
      16 hot cross buns.

   b What is the ratio of the amounts of
      ingredients to make 12 buns to the
      amounts for 16 buns?

12 hot cross buns
300 g flour
120 g currants
150 g sugar
180 g margarine
1 teaspoon spice
30 ml milk
90 ml beaten egg

   Matthew makes some hot cross buns
   using 450 g flour.

   c How many buns does Matthew make?

   d Write down how much of the other
      ingredients Matthew uses to make his buns.

You may **use a calculator** to help you to answer questions 5–7.
Where appropriate, write your answers correct to two decimal places.

5 A 4-litre container for milk holds about the same as a
7-pint container for milk.

Use this information to copy and complete this
conversion table.

litres	pints
1	
24	
13	
	1
	56
	119

6 James shops at the local deli.
Green olives cost £2.40 for 120 g.

 a What do 100 g of green olives cost?

 b What do 220 g of green olives cost?

 c How many grams of green olives can
 James buy for £12?

Black olives cost £1.80 for 75 g.

 d What do 100 g of black olives cost?

 e What do 220 g of black olives cost?

 f How many grams of black olives can
 James buy for £12?

 g Which are more expensive, green olives or
 black olives? Explain how you know.

 Did you know that...?

The Chinese emperor Shi Huang-ti ordered all
books to be burned in 213 BCE. But people hid
books and some survived. The oldest maths book in
the world is the *Chou-pei*, written about 1100 BCE.

About 200 BCE, after the book burning, **Ch'ang
Ts'ang** edited the *Jiuzhang suanshu or Nine Chapters
on the Mathematical Art*. It has 246 examples of using
maths to solve practical problems in trading, tax
collection, surveying and building.

The problems that are about exchanging grains,
beans and seeds involve proportion and
percentages. Other problems involve ratio and
proportion, mostly to do with travelling or taxes.

We use the same maths today to solve value-for-
money problems.

Shi Huang-ti

7 £1 is about 1.6 euros.
  a How many euros do you get for £7.50?
  b What is 1 euro worth in pence?
  c How many pounds do you get for 56 euros?

Extension problems

8 Which of each of these is the best value for money?

  a 1 pint of milk for 47p
     2 pints of milk for 95p
     8 pints of milk for £3.78

  b 2 kg of potatoes for 75p
     5 kg of potatoes for £1.80
     7 kg of potatoes for £2.59

  c 250 ml of orange juice for 39p
     400 ml of orange juice for 58p
     1 litre of orange juice for £1.50

  d 15 postcards for £7.80
     28 postcards for £14.70
     40 postcards for £21.20

Points to remember

- Two sets of numbers are in **direct proportion** when the ratio of corresponding numbers is the same. For example, (5, 8) and (20, 32) are in direct proportion since $5:20 = 8:32$.
- When you solve direct proportion problems:
  - a four-cell diagram helps you to see the relationships between numbers and decide what calculation to do;
  - the **unitary method** involves reducing the value of one of the variables to 1;
  - corresponding quantities must be in the same units.

5 Fraction, decimal and percentage operators

This lesson will help you to use equivalent fractions, decimals and percentages.

You can write calculations in equivalent ways. For example, these operations are all equivalent.

$\times 5$ then $\div 8$ $\times \frac{5}{8}$ $\times 0.625$ $\times 62.5\%$ $\div 1.6$

When you are solving problems involving fractions, decimals and percentages, decide which is the most efficient way to calculate.

Example   Find 65% of £82.

You can use your calculator to calculate $\frac{65}{100}$ of £82:

⑥ ⑤ ÷ ① ⓪ ⓪ × ⑧ ② =

or you can use fewer keys to calculate 0.65 × 82:

⓪ · ⑥ ⑤ × ⑧ ② =

Exercise 5

Do questions 1–7 **without using your calculator**.

1) Copy and complete this table. It shows the marks in a test out of 40.

Pupil	Mark	Fraction in lowest terms	Decimal	Percentage
Lena	21			
Stacey	37			
Pritam	25			
Michelle	34			
Cole	24			

2) Write each of these calculations in two other ways, one way using a fraction and one way using a decimal. Then write the answer to the calculation.

   a 23% of 700   b 82% of 600   c 68% of 900

3) Write each of these calculations in two other ways, one way using a fraction and one way using a percentage. Then write the answer to the calculation.

   a 0.9 × 420   b 0.35 × 180   c 1.25 × 560

4) Write each of these calculations in two other ways, one way using a percentage and one way using a decimal. Then write the answer to the calculation.

   a $\frac{5}{8}$ of 1400   b $\frac{3}{5}$ of 95   c $\frac{9}{20}$ of 510

5 There are six calculation cards and six answer cards below.

Estimate the answer to each calculation. Match each question to its answer.

Write the calculations and answers in your book.

| 61% of 410 | 35% of 930 | 42% of 520 |

| 94% of 165 | 16% of 420 | 86% of 515 |

| 325.5 | 155.1 | 67.2 |

| 218.4 | 250.1 | 442.9 |

6 What are the mystery functions below? Find each function from the inputs and outputs.
Write as many different ways as you can to describe each function.

a **Mystery function 1**

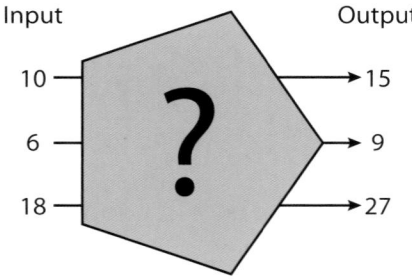

b **Mystery function 2**

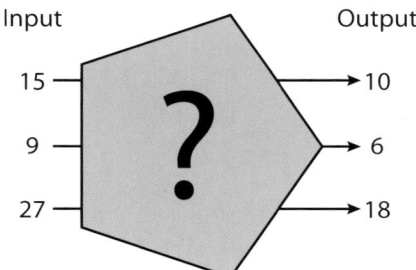

c **Mystery function 3**

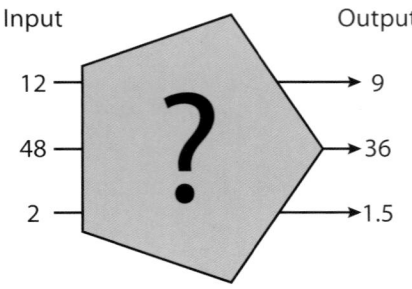

d **Mystery function 4**

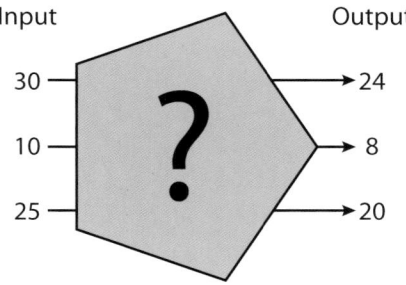

For each mystery function, write another pair of numbers for the input and output.

Use your calculator to work out these calculations.

a 96% of 7400   b 36% of 189   c 55% of 1350

d 12.5% of 94   e 7% of 275   f 17.5% of 376

Explain how you used your calculator to do the calculations.

> ## Points to remember
>
> ⊙ An operation can be described in different ways.
>   For example, for 16 → 10, the relationship could be described as
>   '×5 then ÷8', '×$\frac{5}{8}$', '×0.625', '×62.5%', '÷1.6'.
>
> ⊙ When you solve problems involving fractions, decimals and
>   percentages, decide which is the most efficient way to calculate.

6 Solving problems

This lesson will help you to solve problems involving fractions, decimals and percentages.

Exercise 6

You need a set of cards from **N4.4 Resource sheet 6.2**. Work in groups of four.

Nominate a recorder and a chair-person.

Share out the cards among the members of your group.

Look together at the information on the cards.

Work out how much of each ingredient is used for a batch of cakes.

> ## Points to remember
>
> ⊙ When you solve word problems, read the question to yourself and
>   decide what information to use.
>
> ⊙ Choose a calculation method that is easy to use with the numbers in
>   the problem.
>
> ⊙ Always write down the calculations that you will do.
>
> ⊙ Decide how you will check your work.

How well are you doing?

Proportional reasoning (no calculator)

1. Write the ratio 40 : 48 in its simplest form.

2. *2000 level 4*

    a Peanuts cost 60p for 100 grams.
      What is the cost of 350 grams of peanuts?

    b Raisins cost 80p for 100 grams.
      Jack pays £2 for a bag of raisins.
      How many grams of raisins does he get?

3. *2000 level 5*

    Here is a map of part of France. The map shows that the distance from Calais to Paris is 200 miles.

    5 miles is approximately 8 kilometres.

    Use these facts to calculate the approximate distance in kilometres from Calais to Paris.

    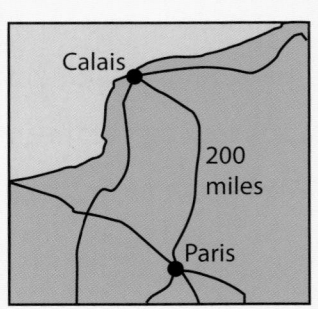

4. *2005 level 5*

    Sapna makes a fruit salad using bananas, oranges and apples.
    For every 1 banana, she uses 2 oranges and 3 apples.

    Sapna uses 24 pieces of fruit.
    How many oranges does she use?

Proportional reasoning (calculator allowed)

5 *Y7 Optional Test level 6*

The arrow on the speedometer of my car turns through 90 degrees when the speed increases from 20 mph to 70 mph.

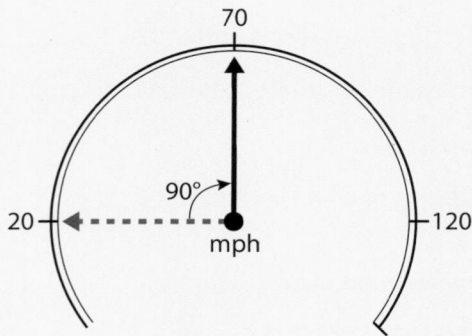

Through how many degrees does the arrow turn when the speed increases from 30 mph to 50 mph?

Show your working.

6 *2003 level 6*

Paul is 14 years old.

His sister is exactly 6 years younger, so this year she is 8 years old.

This year, the ratio of Paul's age to his sister's age is 14 : 8.

14 : 8 written as simply as possible is 7 : 4.

a   When Paul is 21, what will be the ratio of Paul's age to his sister's age?
Write the ratio as simply as possible.

b   When his sister is 36, what will be the ratio of Paul's age to his sister's age?
Write the ratio as simply as possible.

7 *1997 level 6*

Some pupils were asked to choose between a safari park and a zoo for the school trip.

They had a vote.

The result was a ratio of 10 : 3 in favour of going to a safari park.

130 children voted in favour of going to a safari park.

How many children voted in favour of going to the zoo?

G 4.3 Transformations

This unit will help you to:

- describe reflections, rotations and translations;
- use transformations to create tessellations;
- enlarge 2D shapes;
- find the midpoint of a line segment.

1 Repeated transformations

This lesson will help you to describe reflections, rotations and translations

A **transformation** is the movement of a shape from one position to another.

A **reflection** is the mirror image of an **object** in a given **mirror line**.

The diagram shows a white triangle, which is the original object. The coloured triangle is the reflection or **image**.

When an object is reflected:

- the image is the same distance from the mirror line as the object;
- the object and the image are **congruent** (i.e. the same shape and size).

A **rotation** turns a shape about a fixed point, called the **centre of rotation**.

The **angle of rotation** is the amount of turn, usually in degrees, clockwise or anticlockwise.

This diagram shows the image after the object is rotated through 180° clockwise about (0, 0). The centre of rotation is (0, 0).

When an object is rotated, the object and the image are **congruent**.

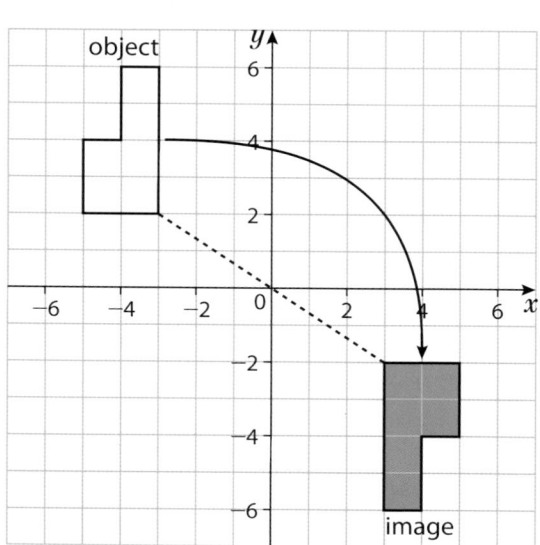

A **translation** is the movement of a shape in the x-direction (horizontally) and the y-direction (vertically).

The diagram shows the image after the object is translated 6 units to the right and 4 units down.

When an object is translated:

- every point in the shape moves in the same direction and through the same distance;
- the object and its image are **congruent**.

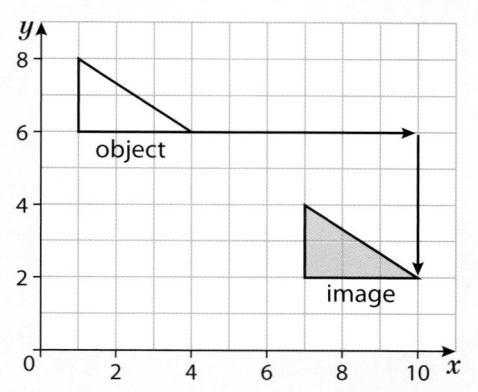

One transformation may be followed by another.

In this diagram, shape A is reflected in the y-axis to create shape B.

Then shape B is reflected in the x-axis to create shape C.

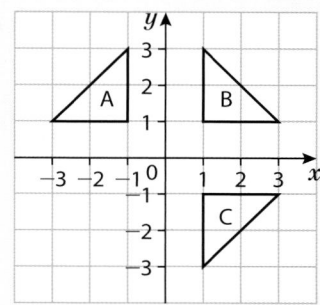

Example

What single transformation is equivalent to a rotation of 120° clockwise followed by a rotation of 50° anticlockwise?

It is equivalent to a rotation of 70° clockwise.

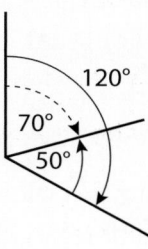

Exercise 1

You will need some squared paper and **G4.3 Resource sheet 1.1**.

1 – 3 These questions are on **Resource sheet 1.1**.

4 Copy this diagram onto squared paper.
Reflect the object in AB, then reflect its image in CD.

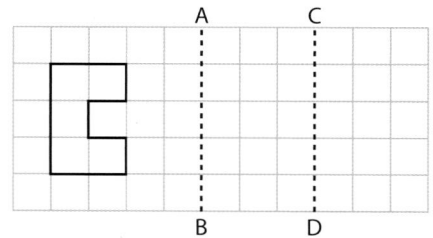

(5) Write down the single transformation equivalent to:

  a a rotation of 90° clockwise followed by a rotation of 63° anticlockwise;

  b a rotation of 300° clockwise followed by a rotation of 40° anticlockwise;

  c a rotation of 58° clockwise followed by a rotation of 32° clockwise;

  d a rotation of 132° clockwise followed by a rotation of 150° anticlockwise.

(6) Copy this diagram onto squared paper.

Rotate flag shape A 90° clockwise about the
centre of rotation to form image B.
Repeat the same rotation on image B to form image C.
Repeat on image C to form image D.

Write down the single transformation that moves
flag A to flag D.

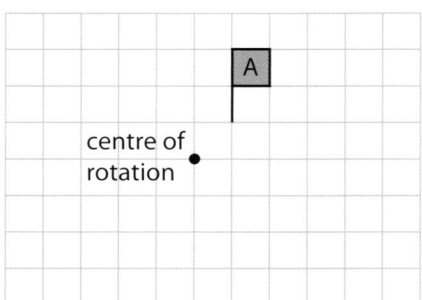

Extension problem

(7) Shape A has been reflected in a vertical mirror line.
The image has then been reflected in a second
mirror line (that is two reflections) to make shape B.

Copy the diagram onto squared paper.
Draw in the two mirror lines.

Investigate if there are any other possible answers.
Use a different colour to draw the pair of mirror lines for any new answer.

⊙ Points to remember

- ⊙ The object and image after reflection, rotation or translation are congruent.
- ⊙ You can replace repeated rotations about the same centre of rotation by a single rotation.
- ⊙ You can replace repeated translations by a single translation.

2 Combining transformations

This lesson will help you to describe and combine transformations

In this diagram, shape A has been reflected in the x-axis to create shape B. Shape B has then been rotated 180° anticlockwise (or clockwise) about (0, 0) to create shape C.

The movement of shape A to shape C can be described by the single transformation of reflection in the y-axis.

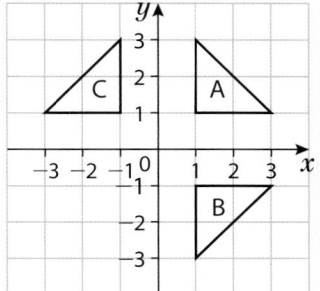

Example

a Find a single transformation that moves A to D.

Rotation through 90° anticlockwise about the origin.

b Find two transformations that move A to B.

Reflection in the x-axis followed by reflection in the line $x = 3$

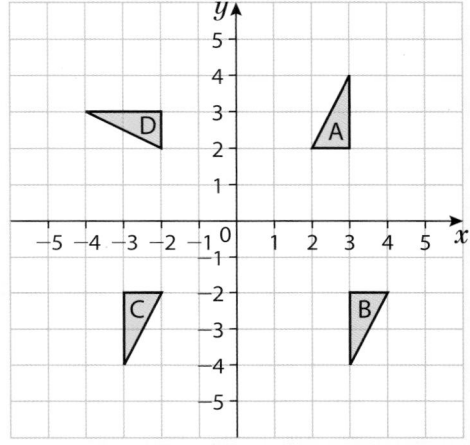

Exercise 2

You will need squared paper.

1 a Copy this grid onto squared paper.
Plot the point A (2, 1).
Reflect A in the y-axis, then translate the image 1 unit up.
Label this image A′.

b The same transformation could be produced by a translation followed by a reflection. Describe the translation and the reflection.

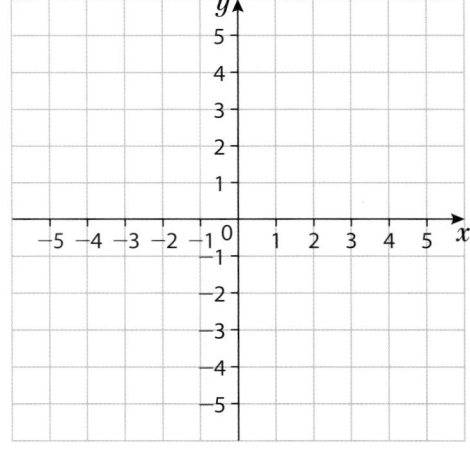

2 a Make another copy of the grid in question 1. Plot the point B (4, 3). Rotate B 90° clockwise about the origin, then translate the image 1 unit right. Label this image B′.

b You can also move B to B′ by a translation followed by a rotation through 90° clockwise about the origin. What is the translation?

3 **a** Make another copy of the grid in question 1. Plot the point C (−3, 2).
Reflect C in the x-axis, then rotate the image through 90° anticlockwise about the origin.
Label this image C′.

 b You can also move C to C′ by a rotation about the origin followed by a reflection in the x-axis. Describe the rotation.

4 Triangles A, B, C and D are drawn on a grid.

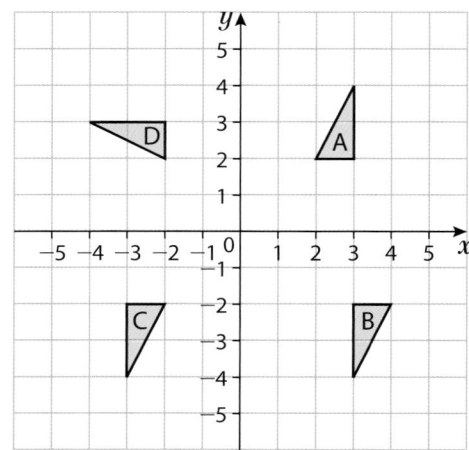

 a Find a single transformation that will map A onto B.

 b Find a single transformation that will map A onto C.

 c Find a single transformation that will map C onto B.

 d Find a single transformation that will map D onto A.

 e Find a combination of two transformations that will map A onto C.

Extension problem

5 Use the diagram from question **4** .

 a Find a combination of two transformations that will map B onto C.

 b Find a combination of two transformations that will map C onto D.

Points to remember

⊙ Reflection, rotation and translation can be combined to transform an object.

⊙ Transformations can be combined in any order.

⊙ Different combinations of transformations may have different effects.

This lesson will help you to use transformations to create tessellations.

 Did you know that...?

The famous Dutch artist **M. C. Escher** (1898–1972) used tessellating shapes to create many pieces of work.

Some of his tessellations, like this one, were of single shapes but others involved more than one shape.

Exercise 3

You will need squared paper.

1   Using squared paper, show how this L-shape will tessellate.

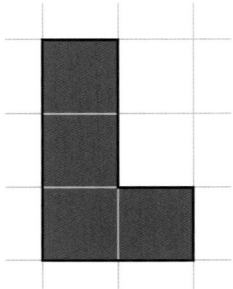

Draw at least eight more L-shapes.

2   Using squared paper, show how this kite will tessellate.

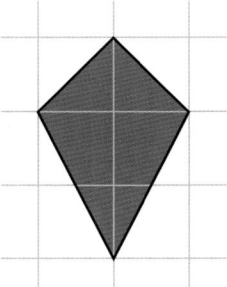

Draw at least eight more kites.

3   **a** Draw a diagram to show how a rectangle could tessellate.

   b Explain why it is possible to create a tessellation of a rectangle.

4   **a** Draw a diagram to show how a rhombus could tessellate.

   b Explain why it is possible to create a tessellation of a rhombus.

(5) Create your own tessellating pattern.

Step 1

Draw a rectangle on card and cut it out. Along one short edge, draw an irregular line from corner to corner.

Step 2

Cut this small section out and use sticky tape to stick it onto the other edge.

 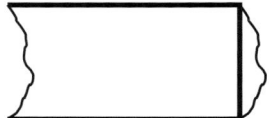

Step 3

Now repeat the process with a long edge, again using sticky tape to stick the part you cut out onto the other edge.

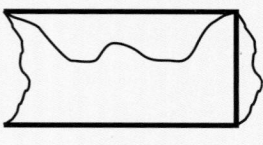 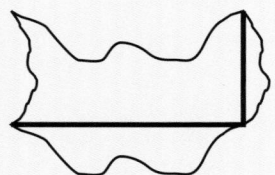

Step 4

Trace the shape onto blank paper and cut out copies. Use these to create a tessellating pattern.

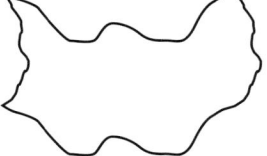

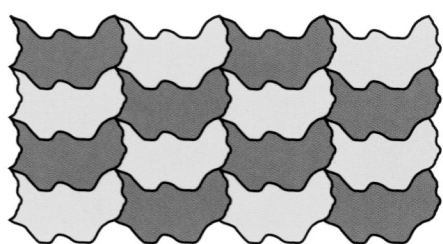

You could use ICT to try this out with more complicated tessellations.

⦿ Points to remember

- ⊙ You can generate tessellations by using reflections, rotations or translations.
- ⊙ Some regular polygons will tessellate, e.g. equilateral triangles, squares, regular hexagons.
- ⊙ Some regular polygons will not tessellate, e.g. regular pentagons.
- ⊙ Some regular polygons will tessellate when combined with other regular polygons, e.g. octagons and squares.

4 Scale factor

This lesson will help you to enlarge 2D shapes using a scale factor.

The scale drawing of this rowing boat has been enlarged.

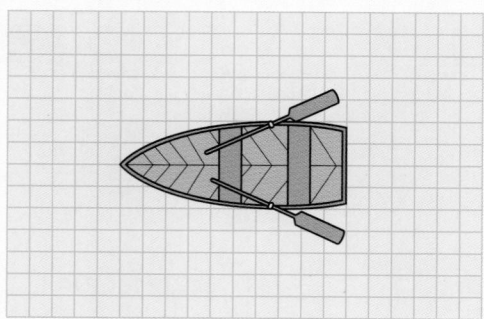 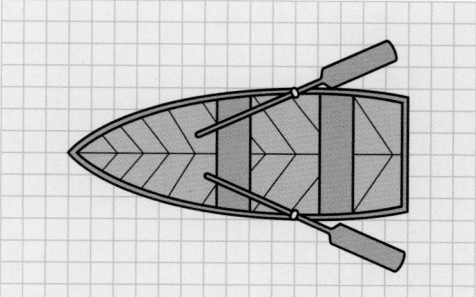

When a shape is enlarged, corresponding sides of the object and image are in the same ratio.

Example 1

The image is an enlargement of the object.
What is the scale factor?

The scale factor is $\frac{12}{6} = \frac{4}{2} = 2$.

Example 2

The image is an enlargement
of the object.
What is the scale factor?

The scale factor is $\frac{10.5}{3.5} = \frac{7.5}{2.5} = \frac{9}{3} = 3$.

The easiest calculation comes from the
sides of lengths 9 cm and 3 cm. Always
check to see if there are easy numbers.

Example 3

Enlarge the object with scale factor 3 so
that point A is transformed to point A′.

The enlarged image is shown on the right.

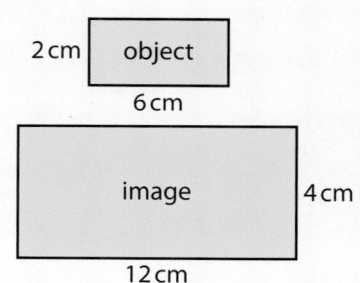

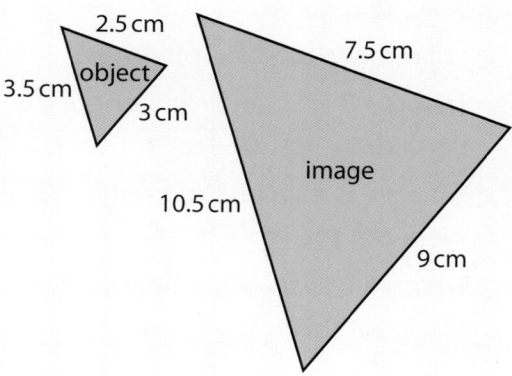

You will need squared paper.

1. Copy each shape onto squared paper. Enlarge the shape by the given scale factor so that point A of the object is transformed to point A′.

a scale factor 2

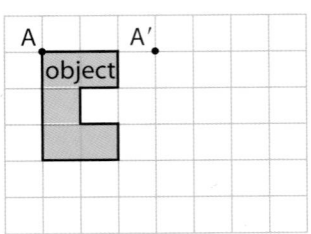

b scale factor 3

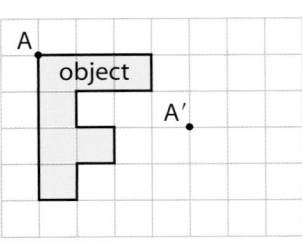

c scale factor 2

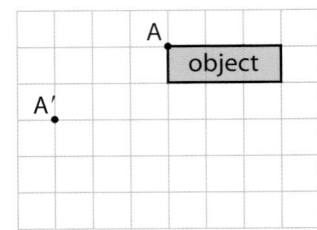

d scale factor 3

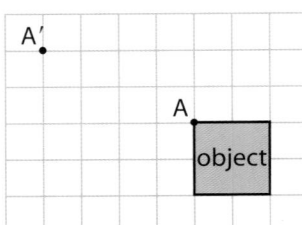

e scale factor 3

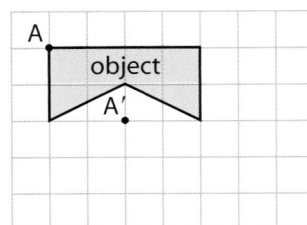

f scale factor 2

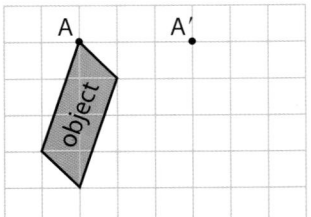

2. The diagram shows four triangles.

a Triangle B is an enlargement of triangle A.
   Work out the scale factor.

b Triangle C is an enlargement of triangle D.
   Work out the scale factor.

c Triangle C is an enlargement of triangle A.
   Work out the scale factor.

d Triangle D is an enlargement of triangle A.
   Work out the scale factor.

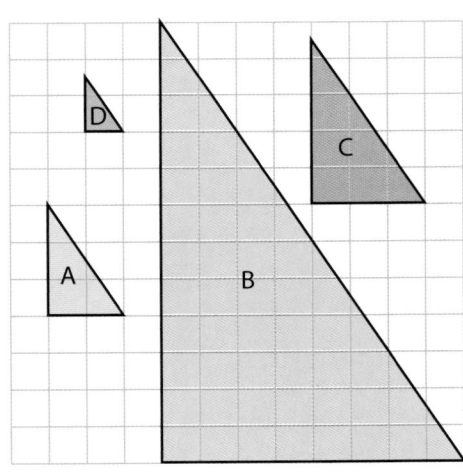

③ The L-shapes below are enlargements of each other.

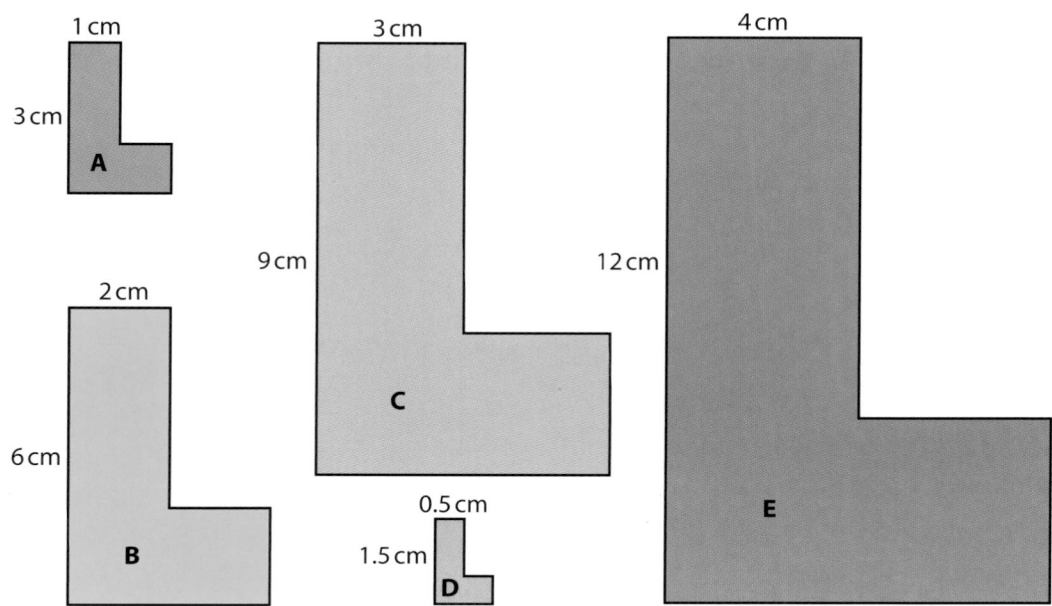

What is the scale factor for each of these enlargements?

a object A to image B

b object A to image C

c object A to image E

d object B to image E

e object D to image A

f object D to image B

g object D to image C

h object D to image E

i object B to image C

j object C to image E

Extension problem

④ What is the scale factor for each of these enlargements?

a object B to image D

b object B to image A

c object E to image B

d object C to image A

Points to remember

⊙ To describe an enlargement, give the centre of enlargement and the scale factor.

⊙ Multiply lengths in the object by the scale factor to find corresponding lengths in the image.

⊙ When corresponding points on the object and the image are linked by lines, the lines meet at the centre of enlargement.

⊙ The object and image are similar shapes. Corresponding angles are the same.

5 Centre of enlargement

This lesson will help you to describe an enlargement, giving the centre of enlargement and the scale factor.

Example

Enlarge this triangle by scale factor 2 with centre of enlargement (0, 0).

For an enlargement of scale factor 2:

- the length of each side of the triangle is multiplied by 2;
- the distance from the centre of enlargement to each point on the object is multiplied by 2.

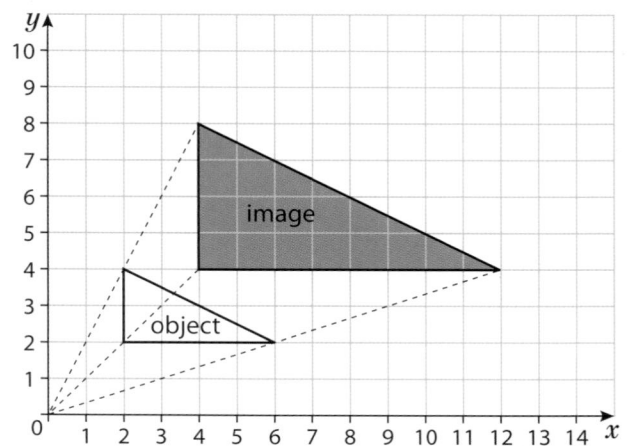

Exercise 5

You will need squared paper.

1. Copy the shape and the centre of enlargement on squared paper. Leave space to draw the enlargement. Enlarge the shape using the given centre of enlargement.

   a scale factor 4

   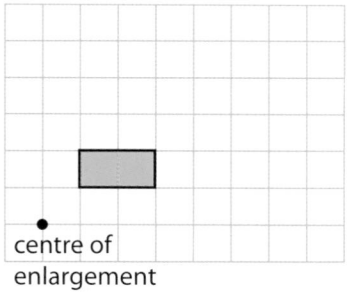

   b scale factor 2

   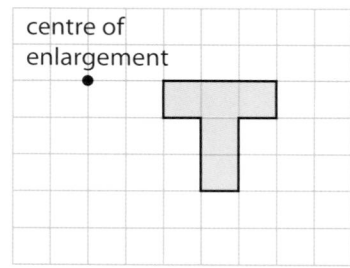

   c scale factor 3

   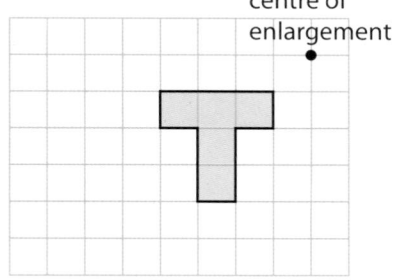

   d scale factor 2

   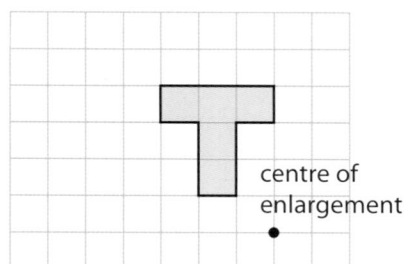

2 Copy this diagram onto squared paper.

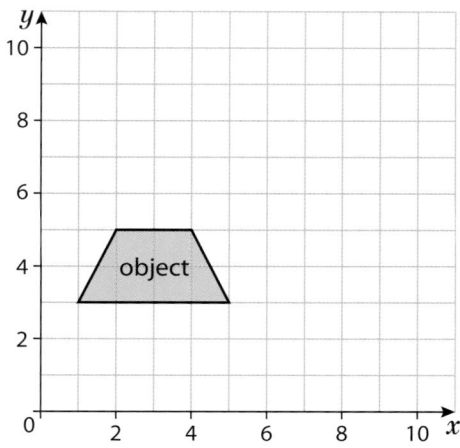

a Enlarge the object by scale factor 2 with centre of enlargement (0, 0).

b On the same diagram, enlarge the object by a scale factor of 2, centre of enlargement (1, 3).

3 For each diagram, describe fully the single transformation that transforms shape A to shape B.

a

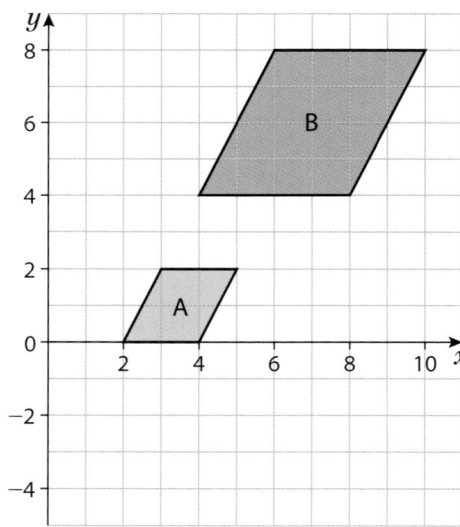

b

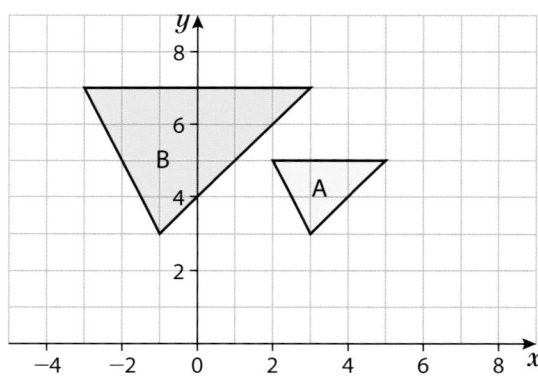

Extension problems

 4 This shape is enlarged by a scale factor of 5.
Copy and complete this table.

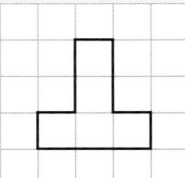

	Perimeter	Area
Original shape		
Enlargement		

For scale factor 5:

a What must you multiply the perimeter of the original shape by to get the perimeter of the enlargement?

b What must you multiply the area of the original shape by to get the area of the enlargement?

5 This shape is enlarged by scale factor 3.
Copy and complete this table.

	Perimeter	Area
Original shape		
Enlargement		

For scale factor 3:

a What must you multiply the perimeter of the original shape by to get the perimeter of the enlargement?

b What must you multiply the area of the original shape by to get the area of the enlargement?

6 What do you notice about your answers to questions 4 and 5?

⊙ Points to remember

- For an enlargement of scale factor 2:
  - the length of each side of the object is multiplied by 2;
  - the distance from the centre of enlargement to each point on the object is multiplied by 2.
- To describe an enlargement, give the centre of enlargement and the scale factor.

6 Enlargement, ratio and proportion

This lesson will help you to understand the effect of enlargement on the lengths of sides, perimeters and areas of shapes

Example 1

The bigger rectangle is an enlargement of the smaller rectangle. Find the value of x.

For the rectangles, the scale factor is $6 \div 4 = 1.5$. So $x = 5 \times 1.5 = 7.5$.

The missing length is 7.5 cm.

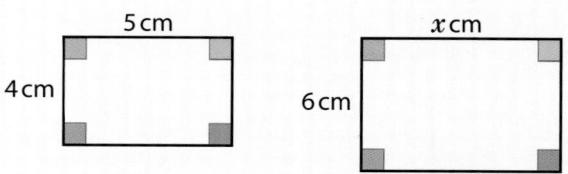

Example 2

The big triangle is an enlargement of the small triangle. Find the values of y and z.

For the triangles, the scale factor is $24 \div 8 = 3$. So $y = 3 \times 3 = 9$.

The missing length in the large triangle is 9 cm. To find z, we know that $z \times 3 = 21$. So $z = 7$.

The missing length in the small triangle is 7 cm.

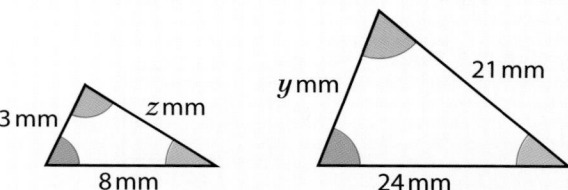

Exercise 6

1 In each pair of shapes the bigger shape is an enlargement of the smaller one. Work out the missing lengths.

a
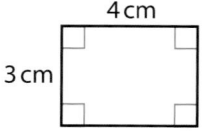
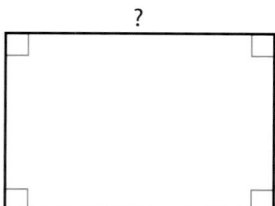

b
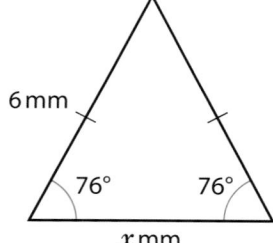
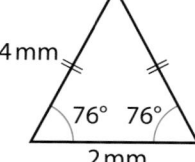

c
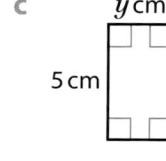
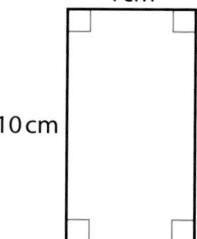

(2) Work out the missing lengths for these enlargements.

a

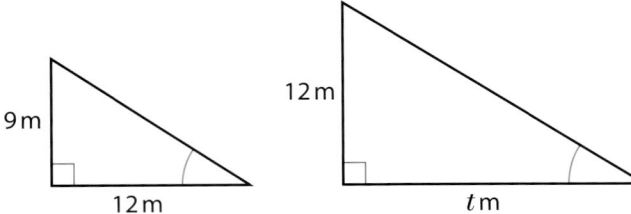

9 m
12 m
12 m
t m

b

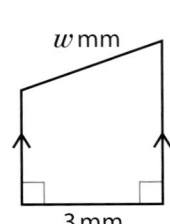

w mm
3 mm

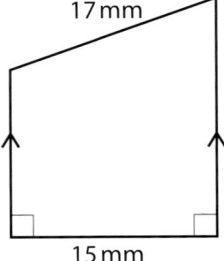

17 mm
15 mm

(3) These three rectangles are all similar. Find the missing lengths.

x cm
12 cm

12 cm
y cm

4 cm
5 cm

Extension problem

(4) These two rectangles are similar. Investigate possible values of *c* and *d*.

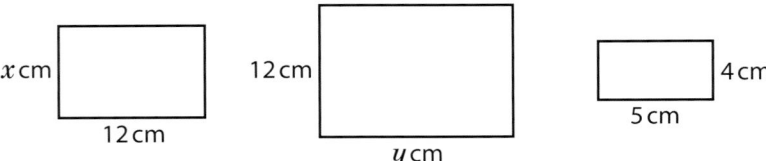

16 cm
c cm

d cm
9 cm

Points to remember

⊙ Similar shapes are enlargements of each other.

⊙ All angles remain unaltered by an enlargement.

⊙ Multiply lengths in the object by the scale factor to find corresponding lengths in the image.

⊙ You can use the unitary method to calculate missing lengths.

7 Finding the midpoint

This lesson will help you to find the midpoint of a line segment.

Example

Find the coordinates of the midpoint of each side of this triangle.

The midpoint of AB is at $\left(\dfrac{11 + 1}{2}, \dfrac{1 + 1}{2}\right) = (6, 1)$.

The midpoint of CA is at $\left(\dfrac{1 + 1}{2}, \dfrac{1 + 7}{2}\right) = (1, 4)$.

The midpoint of BC is at $\left(\dfrac{11 + 1}{2}, \dfrac{1 + 7}{2}\right) = (6, 4)$.

Exercise 7

You will need squared paper.

1. What are the coordinates of the midpoint of each of these line segments?

   a AD

   b BC

   c CD

   d AB

   e BD

   f AC

2. Find the midpoint of each of these line segments.

   a A (3, 0) and B (11, 0)   b A (7, 3) and B (11, 1)   c A (8, −4) and B (−2, 0)

   d A (−3, 4) and B (3, −4)   e A (−9, −1) and B (−3, −4)   f A (6, −2) and B (−7, 1)

3. On squared paper, draw a pair of axes from −5 to 5.
   Plot the points W (1, 3), X (4, −1), Y (1, −5) and Z (−2, −1).
   Join them to make a quadrilateral.

   a What is the special name given to the quadrilateral?

   b What are the coordinates of the midpoint of WY? Show your working.

   c What are the coordinates of the midpoint of XZ? Show your working.

(4) The coordinates of the midpoint of the line LM are (3, 4).
The coordinates of point L are (1, 5). What are the coordinates of M?

(5) The coordinates of the midpoint of the line XY are (7, 2).
The coordinates of X are $(x, 5)$ and the coordinates of Y are $(9, y)$.
Find the values of x and y.

Extension problems

(6) On squared paper, draw a pair of axes from 0 to 8.
Plot the points A (3, 1), B (7, 1), C (7, 5), D (3, 5).
Join the points in order to form quadrilateral ABCD.

a Write down the coordinates of the midpoints of line segments AB, BC, CD, DA.
Label these points E, F, G, H respectively.
Join the points to form a quadrilateral EFGH.

b Write down the coordinates of the midpoints of line segments EF, FG, GH, HE.
Label these points I, J, K, L respectively.
Join the points to form a quadrilateral IJKL.

c What is the area of quadrilateral ABCD?

d What is the area of quadrilateral IJKL?

e What is the scale factor for the enlargement of IJKL to ABCD?

f Write down the coordinates for the centre of enlargement.

(7) Use dynamic geometry software on your
computer to draw a quadrilateral.
Construct the midpoint of each side.
Join these up to form another quadrilateral,
labelled ABCD in this diagram.

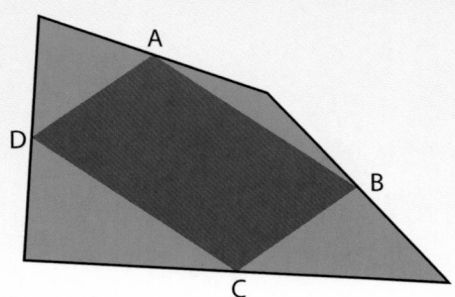

By using the software to change the position of
one or more vertices of the original quadrilateral,
investigate quadrilateral ABCD.

What quadrilateral would you make if you joined the
midpoints of AB, BC, CD and DA, in order?

 Points to remember

Given a line segment AB:

⊙ the x-coordinate of the midpoint is the mean of the x-coordinates of A and B;

⊙ the y-coordinate of the midpoint is the mean of the y-coordinates of A and B.

How well are you doing?

Can you:

- combine reflections, rotations and translations?
- enlarge 2D shapes?
- find the midpoint of a line segment?

Transforming 2D shapes

1. Copy this diagram on squared paper.

   Reflect the object in line 1.
   Label it 'image 1'.
   Reflect image 1 in line 2.
   Label it 'image 2'.

   What single transformation will transform
   the object to image 2?

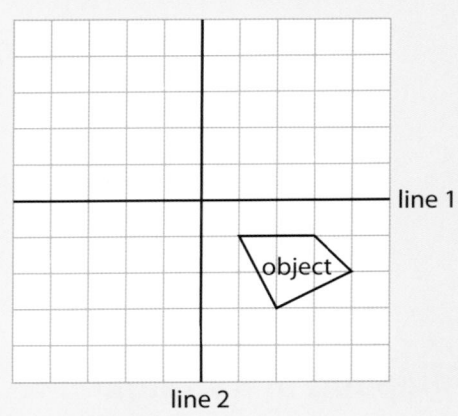

2. Translate the object 3 units to the right and 4 squares up. Label this 'image 1'.
   Translate image 1 3 units to the right and 2 units down. Label this 'image 2'.

   What single transformation transforms the object to image 2?

3   **a**   What is the scale factor of this enlargement?

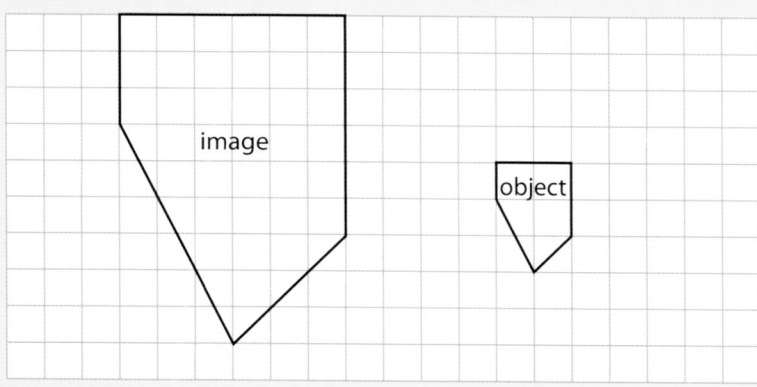

      b   Copy the diagram. Mark on your copy the centre of enlargement.

4   Copy this diagram on squared paper.
Enlarge the object about the centre of
enlargement by a scale factor of 2.

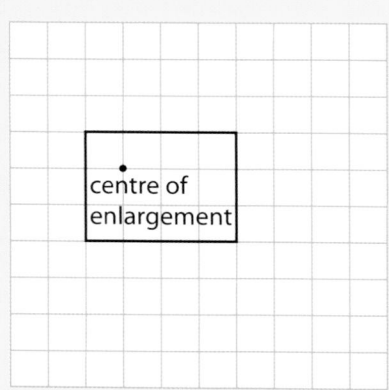

Midpoint of a straight line

5   *2005 level 6*

    a   P is the midpoint of line AB.
What are the coordinates of
point P?

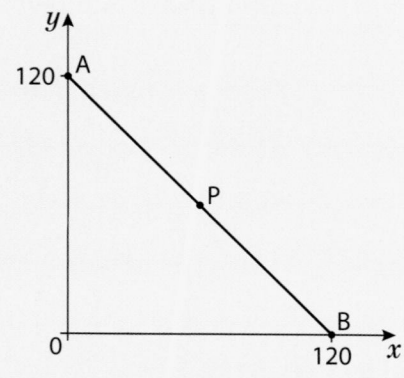

    b   Q is the midpoint of line MN.
The coordinates of Q are (30, 50).
What are the coordinates of M and N?

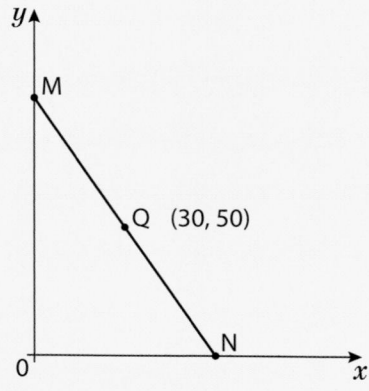

Equations and formulae

This unit will help you to:

- link functions, equations and graphs;
- solve linear equations with brackets or x terms on both sides;
- form algebraic formulae and equations from real situations;
- substitute numbers into formulae;
- link the solution of equations to points on their graphs;
- use algebra to solve problems.

1 Functions, equations and graphs

This lesson will help you to link functions, equations and graphs.

 Did you know that...?

The earliest known use of the word *equation* in the sense that we use it today was in 1202 in Fibonacci's *Liber Abbaci*.

Fibonacci lived in Pisa, in Italy. He was born in 1170 and he died in 1250. This sequence of numbers is named after him: 1, 1, 2, 3, 5, 8, 13, ... Each number is the sum of the two before it. The spirals in seed heads and snail shells are based on the Fibonacci sequence.

A function machine applies one or more **functions** (rules) to an **input** x and gives the **output** y.

When the input values increase by 1 each time, the differences between the output values of a linear relationship can help you to work out the function.

In the example on the right, the differences in the output values are always 3. If the sequence continues in the same way, the function is

$$x \rightarrow \boxed{\text{multiply by 3}} \rightarrow \boxed{\text{add 1}} \rightarrow y$$

Example

Input Output

x	$\rightarrow$	y
1	$\rightarrow$	4
2	$\rightarrow$	7
3	$\rightarrow$	10

You can write the relationship between x and y given by the function $x \rightarrow \boxed{\text{add 6}} \rightarrow y$ as the equation $y = x + 6$.

You can write the relationship between x and y given by the equation $y = 2x - 3$ as the function $x \rightarrow \boxed{\text{multiply by 2}} \rightarrow \boxed{\text{subtract 3}} \rightarrow y$.

You can represent an equation such as $y = 2x - 3$ as a graph.
To draw the graph you need to calculate the values of three ordered pairs (x, y).

Suppose you choose to use the values 0, 2 and 4 for x.
Then the three ordered pairs will be $(0, -3)$, $(2, 1)$ and $(4, 5)$. You need to draw axes, plot these three points and draw the straight line through the points using a pencil and ruler.

Exercise 1

1 Work out the functions and find the missing numbers in these mappings.

a $x \rightarrow y$
1 → 2
2 → 7
3 → 12
4 →
5 →
6 →
7 →
x →

b $x \rightarrow y$
1 → 10
2 → 19
3 → 28
4 →
5 →
6 →
7 →
x →

2 Write these functions as equations in x and y.

a $x \rightarrow \boxed{\text{add 15}} \rightarrow y$

b $x \rightarrow \boxed{\text{subtract 8}} \rightarrow y$

c $x \rightarrow \boxed{\text{multiply by 7}} \rightarrow y$

d $x \rightarrow \boxed{\text{divide by 3}} \rightarrow y$

e $x \rightarrow \boxed{\text{multiply by 4}} \rightarrow \boxed{\text{add 11}} \rightarrow y$

f $x \rightarrow \boxed{\text{multiply by 10}} \rightarrow \boxed{\text{subtract 3}} \rightarrow y$

g $x \rightarrow \boxed{\text{divide by 2}} \rightarrow \boxed{\text{add 4}} \rightarrow y$

h $x \rightarrow \boxed{\text{divide by 5}} \rightarrow \boxed{\text{subtract 1}} \rightarrow y$

3 Write these equations as functions in x.

a $y = x + 13$

b $y = x - 21$

c $y = 9x + 25$

d $y = 7x - 1$

e $y = \frac{x}{3} + 4$

f $y = 19 + 8x$

g $y = 12x - 7$

h $y = 10(x + 2)$

i $y = 9(x - 5)$

j $y = 2 + \frac{x}{10}$

(4) You will need squared paper for this question. Draw accurate graphs of these equations.

  a $y = x + 2$ b $y = x - 1$ c $y = 2x + 5$
  d $y = 3x + 4$ e $y = -x + 1$ f $y = -2x + 3$

(5) For each of the graphs in question 4, write down five ordered pairs (x, y) that lie on the lines.

Extension problem

(6) Write these functions as equations in x and y.

  a $x \rightarrow$ | add 15 | $\rightarrow$ | multiply by 7 | $\rightarrow y$

  b $x \rightarrow$ | subtract 2 | $\rightarrow$ | multiply by 6 | $\rightarrow y$

◉ Points to remember

- ⊙ A function machine applies a rule or **function** to an input x and gives the related output y.

  Example: When the input $x = 4$ is put through the function

  $x \rightarrow$ | multiply by 6 | $\rightarrow$ | add 5 | $\rightarrow y$, the output y is 29.

  This function can be written as the equation $y = 6x + 5$.

- ⊙ You can draw a graph of this linear equation. All the points on the graph are solutions of the equation.

2 Solving linear equations

This lesson will help you to solve simple linear equations.

Every function has an inverse function.

The inverse of addition is subtraction and the inverse of subtraction is addition.

The inverse of multiplication is division and the inverse of division is multiplication.

The inverse function of $x \rightarrow$ | multiply by 3 | $\rightarrow$ | add 9.5 | $\rightarrow y$

is $x \leftarrow$ | divide by 3 | $\leftarrow$ | subtract 9.5 | $\leftarrow y$.

A linear equation is one that can be represented with a straight-line graph.

The equation $y = 3x + 8$ has an infinite number of solutions.
Every point (x, y) on its graph is a solution.

When you read off values of x or y from a graph you can only *estimate* the values because your eyes may not be able to see the exact values.

The equation $3x + 8 = 14$ has a unique solution.

To solve the equation you can use the inverse function.

$$3x + 8 = 14 \qquad x \rightarrow \boxed{\times 3} \rightarrow \boxed{+ 8} \rightarrow 14$$

subtract 8 $3x \quad = 6 \qquad 2 \leftarrow \boxed{\div 3} \leftarrow \boxed{- 8} \leftarrow 14$

divide by 3 $x \quad = 2$

What you do to one side of the equation you must do to the other to keep the equation in balance.

Any letters in the alphabet can be used in an equation in the place of a number.

Normally we use lower-case letters and write them in italic such as $a, m, p, x, \ldots$ Most often we use w, x, y and z to represent variables and a, b, c and d to represent constants, however, any letter can be used. We often use letters such as l for length and w for width in geometrical formulae.

You can use algebra to help you solve problems in real life, in other areas of mathematics or in other subjects. Read through a problem or study a diagram and write an equation. Solve the equation, then go back and use your answer to solve the problem.

Exercise 2

1. Write the inverse functions of these.

   a $x \rightarrow \boxed{\text{add } 52} \rightarrow y$
          b $x \rightarrow \boxed{\text{subtract } 16} \rightarrow y$

   c $x \rightarrow \boxed{\text{multiply by } 31} \rightarrow y$
      d $x \rightarrow \boxed{\text{divide by } 6} \rightarrow y$

   e $x \rightarrow \boxed{\text{multiply by } 8} \rightarrow \boxed{\text{add } 25} \rightarrow y$
      f $x \rightarrow \boxed{\text{multiply by } 102} \rightarrow \boxed{\text{subtract } 15} \rightarrow y$

   g $x \rightarrow \boxed{\text{divide by } 14} \rightarrow \boxed{\text{add } 9} \rightarrow y$
      h $x \rightarrow \boxed{\text{divide by } 3} \rightarrow \boxed{\text{subtract } 0.5} \rightarrow y$

2. a   Draw on graph paper an accurate graph of $y = 2x + 3$.
   b   Use the graph to estimate the value of y when $x = 0$.
   c   Use the graph to estimate the value of x when $y = 0$.
   d   Use the graph to estimate the value of y when $x = 3$.
   e   Use the graph to estimate the value of x when $y = 5$.
   f   Use the graph to estimate the value of y when $x = 2.2$.

3 Use inverse functions to find the value of x for each of these equations.
Check each answer by substituting the value back into the equation.

a $x + 4 = 11$ b $x - 13 = 28$ c $x + 37 = 81$

d $x + 3.5 = 8.3$ e $x - 7.6 = 2.9$ f $x + 7 = -9$

g $15 + x = 34$ h $25 + x = 11$ i $18 = 5 + x$

4 Find pairs of cards where x has the same value.

$x + 7 = 19$ $x + 4 = 11$ $x - 5 = 7$ $x + 19 = 25$

$x + 15 = 17$ $x - 7 = 6$ $x + 27 = 36$ $x + 9 = 16$

$x + 22 = 28$ $x + 16 = 29$ $x - 1 = 1$ $x - 4 = 5$

5 Find the value of x for each equation.
Check your answer by substituting the value back into the equation.

a $9x = 72$ b $6x = 84$ c $13x = 65$

d $27x = 162$ h $\dfrac{x}{9} = 4$ i $\dfrac{x}{8} = 2.5$

6 Find the value of each letter in these equations.

a $p + 16 = 46$ b $m - 24 = 10$ c $7t = 84$

d $a \div 8 = 9$ e $41 + s = 65$ f $w - 34 = 5$

7 a Write an equation in p.

b Solve the equation and work out the value of each of the angles.

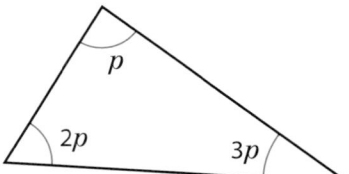

8 a Write an equation in q.

b Solve the equation and work out the value of each of the angles.

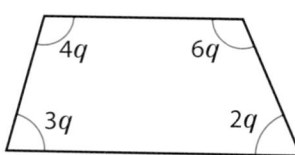

9

Plymouth ←— 19 miles —→←— x miles —→ Truro
←————— 52 miles —————→

A car is travelling from Plymouth to Truro. The driver stops for tea after 19 miles.

a Write an equation in x.

b Work out how much further the car has to go to get to Truro.

Extension problems

10 Write the inverse functions.

    a $x \rightarrow \boxed{\text{add 2.5}} \rightarrow \boxed{\text{multiply by 0.1}} \rightarrow y$

    b $x \rightarrow \boxed{\text{subtract } -1} \rightarrow \boxed{\text{multiply by 2.4}} \rightarrow y$

11 Find pairs of cards where x has the same value.

$4x = 28$	$3x = 48$	$\dfrac{x}{4} = 2$	$5x = 20$
$\dfrac{x}{5} = 3$	$\dfrac{x}{6} = 3$	$8x = 56$	$\dfrac{x}{9} = 2$
$9x = 36$	$5x = 40$	$\dfrac{x}{8} = 2$	$2x = 30$

Points to remember

⊙ The equation $x + 16 = 31$ has a unique solution.

⊙ To solve the equation you can use the inverse function.

$$x + 16 = 31 \qquad x \rightarrow \boxed{+\ 16} \rightarrow 31$$

$$\text{subtract 16} \qquad x = 15 \qquad 15 \rightarrow \boxed{-\ 16} \rightarrow 31$$

⊙ What you do to one side of the equation you must do to the other to keep the equation in balance.

3 More linear equations

This lesson will help you to solve more complicated linear equations.

Exercise 3

1 Find the value of x. Check each answer by substituting the value back into the equation.

    a $3x + 7 = 19$ **b** $5x - 3 = 27$ **c** $9x + 27 = 99$

    d $4x + 56 = 96$ **e** $8x - 1 = 3$ **f** $7x + 33 = 82$

    g $5x - 2.5 = 42.5$ **h** $\dfrac{x}{2} + 16 = 25$ **i** $\dfrac{x}{5} + 6 = 17$

② Find pairs of cards where x has the same value.

$5x - 21 = 24$

$5x + 9 = 24$

$3x - 2 = 28$

$4x + 7 = 47$

$4x + 15 = 43$

$7x - 8 = 27$

$3x - 4 = 23$

$2x + 5 = 21$

$8x - 2 = 62$

$3x + 14 = 23$

$6x - 3 = 39$

$2x + 6 = 16$

③ Find the value of the letter in each equation.

a $7h + 14 = 49$

b $7q + 29 = 92$

c $15 + \dfrac{t}{3} = 19$

d $\dfrac{a}{6} + 8 = 32$

e $2r - 11 = 9$

f $13 + 8b = 33$

g $6m - 3 = -15$

h $75 + 6c = 45$

The diagrams in questions 4, 5 and 6 are not drawn to scale.

④ Rectangle ABCD is made from four identical rectangles with width x cm and height 35 cm. The area of ABCD is 3220 cm².

a Write an equation in x.

b Solve the equation to find the width of each small rectangle.

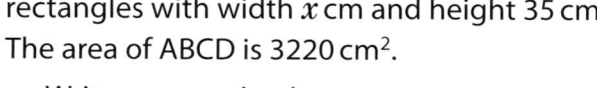
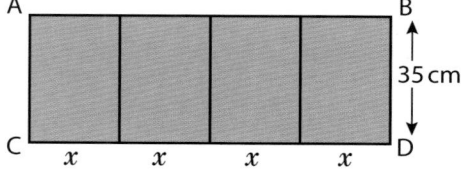

⑤ The perimeter of the triangle is 17 cm.

a Write an equation in x.

b Solve the equation.
Work out the lengths of each side of the triangle.

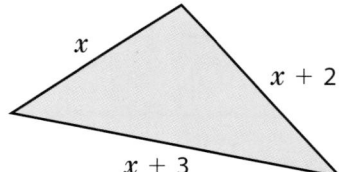

⑥ The perimeter of the pentagon is 125 cm.

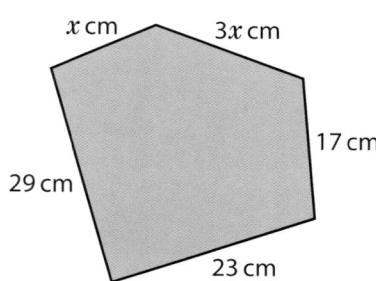

a Write an equation in x.

b Solve the equation. Write down the lengths of the sides marked x and $3x$.

7 The monthly contract for Kate's mobile phone gives 100 free minutes of calls. Every minute after that costs 24 pence. The monthly standing charge is £15. Let the number of minutes of calls a month be x minutes.

    a Write an equation in x to work out the monthly bill.

    b If Kate uses 321 minutes of calls work out her monthly bill.

    c One month Kate's bill is £53.40.
       Work out how many minutes of calls Kate used that month.

Extension problem

8 Kate changes her contract.
She now pays £25 standing charge and gets 250 free minutes per month.
How many minutes of calls does Kate have to make before this contract saves her money?

⦿ Points to remember

⦿ The equation $y = 3x + 5$ has an **infinite** number of solutions.
Any point (x, y) on its graph is a solution.

⦿ The equation $3x + 5 = 17$ has a **unique** solution.
To solve the equation use the inverse function.

$$3x + 5 = 17$$
$$\text{subtract 5} \qquad 3x = 17$$
$$\text{divide by 3} \qquad x = 4$$

$$x \rightarrow \boxed{\times 3} \rightarrow \boxed{+5} \rightarrow 17$$
$$4 \leftarrow \boxed{\div 3} \leftarrow \boxed{-5} \leftarrow 17$$

⦿ What you do to one side of the equation you must do to the other to keep the equation in balance.

4 Forming equations and formulae

This lesson will help you to use algebra to solve problems.

When you use letters in equations and formulae, first define what the letter stands for. You do this using the word 'Let', like this: 'Let the length of a side of a square be l' or 'Let the number be x'.

You can then write expressions and equations using the letters. This can help you solve problems.

Example

Let a number be n. Multiply it by 11, then add 17. The answer is 303. What is n?

$$11n + 17 = 303$$
$$\text{subtract 17} \qquad 11n = 286$$
$$\text{divide by 11} \qquad n = 26$$

Exercise 4

Before trying to solve these problems, use the given letters to write an equation.
Then solve the equation to find the value of the letter.

1 Write equations to match these statements.

   a Let a number be w. Multiply it by 7, then add 25. The answer is 67.

   b Let a number be x. Divide it by 4, then add 7. The answer is 13.

   c Let a number be y. Multiply it by 9, then subtract 13. The answer is 59.

   d Let a number be z. Add 2, then multiply the result by 5. The answer is 45.

2 I am x years old. My brother is 15 and my Dad is 39.
If you add twice my age to my brother's age, then you get my Dad's age.
How old am I?

3 Ravinda is paid £y an hour to stack shelves in a supermarket.

Bradley is paid £2 per hour more than Ravinda for cleaning offices.

Courtney is paid £3 less than Bradley for working in a café.

Natalie is paid twice as much as Bradley for working in an office.

The sum of their hourly pay is £50 per hour.
How much does each person get paid per hour?

4 There are n chocolates in a box of True Chocs.

There are seven more chocolates in a box of High Treats.
There are twice as many chocolates in a box of Sweethearts as in a box of High Treats.

There are 81 chocolates altogether in the three boxes.
How many chocolates are in each box?

5 **Consecutive** means 'following one another in a sequence'.
In the sequence of whole numbers 15 and 16 are consecutive numbers.

   a 75 is the smallest of three consecutive whole numbers. What are the other two?

   b 100 is the largest of three consecutive whole numbers. What are the other two?

   c 34 is the middle of three consecutive whole numbers. What are the other two?

   d n is the smallest of four consecutive whole numbers. What are the other three?

   e n is the largest of four consecutive whole numbers. What are the other three?

   f n is the middle of five consecutive whole numbers. What are the other four?

6 The word **sum** means the result of adding two or more numbers.

    a Find two consecutive whole numbers whose sum is 347.

    b Find three consecutive whole numbers whose sum is 78.

    c Find three consecutive even numbers whose sum is 78.

    d Find two consecutive odd numbers whose sum is 72.

Extension problem

 7 Prove that the sum of three consecutive numbers is always divisible by 3.

 Points to remember

⦿ You can use algebra to solve problems.

⦿ Read through the problem carefully and write an equation.

⦿ Solve the equation, then go back and use this to solve the problem.

5 Equations with brackets

This lesson will help you to solve linear equations with brackets.

 Did you know that...?

The Greek mathematician **Diophantus**, who lived in the third century, is sometimes called 'the father of algebra'.

The title really belongs to the Islamic mathematician al-Khwarizmi, pictured on this Soviet postage stamp.

Mohammed ibn-Musa al-Khwarizmi was born around 800. His name shows that he was 'Mohammed, son of Moses, father of Jafar, from Khwarizm', in central Asia.

The word 'algebra' comes from the title of his book, *Al-jabr wa'l muqabalah*.

Mohammed al-Khwarizmi

If there are no brackets, multiply or divide before adding or subtracting.
Put brackets in only when you want to change the order of operations.
There are two ways of solving equations with single brackets.

Example 1

Solve $5(x + 4) = 55$.

Method 1: Leave the brackets in the equation.

$$5(x + 4) = 55$$

divide by 5 $x + 4 = 11$

subtract 4 $x = 7$

$$x \rightarrow \boxed{+\ 4} \rightarrow \boxed{\times\ 5} \rightarrow 55$$
$$7 \leftarrow \boxed{-\ 4} \leftarrow \boxed{\div\ 5} \leftarrow 55$$

Method 2: Multiply out the brackets first.

$$5(x + 4) = 55$$
$$5x + 20 = 55$$

subtract 20 $5x = 35$

divide by 5 $x = 7$

$$x \rightarrow \boxed{\times\ 5} \rightarrow \boxed{+\ 20} \rightarrow 55$$
$$7 \leftarrow \boxed{\div\ 5} \leftarrow \boxed{-\ 20} \leftarrow 55$$

Sometimes the number outside the bracket is a fraction.

Example 2

Solve $\frac{1}{5}(x - 4) = 4$.

$$\frac{1}{5}(x - 4) = 4$$

multiply by 5 $x - 4 = 20$

add 4 $x = 24$

$$x \rightarrow \boxed{-\ 4} \rightarrow \boxed{\div\ 5} \rightarrow 4$$
$$24 \leftarrow \boxed{+\ 4} \leftarrow \boxed{\times\ 5} \leftarrow 4$$

Sometimes the coefficient of x is greater than 1.

Example 3

Solve $5(3x + 6) = 60$.

$$5(3x + 6) = 60$$

divde by 5 $3x + 6 = 12$

subtract 6 $3x = 6$

divide by 3 $x = 2$

$$x \rightarrow \boxed{\times\ 3} \rightarrow \boxed{+\ 6} \rightarrow \boxed{\times\ 5} \rightarrow 60$$
$$2 \leftarrow \boxed{\div\ 3} \leftarrow \boxed{-\ 6} \leftarrow \boxed{\div\ 5} \leftarrow 60$$

When there is more than one set of brackets in an equation, multiply out the brackets first.
Then simplify the algebraic expression before solving the equation.

Example 4

Solve $7(x + 4) + 6(x + 2) = 79$.

Multiply out: $7x + 28 + 6x + 12 = 79$

Simplify: $13x + 40 = 79$

subtract 40 $13x = 39$

divide by 13 $x = 3$

$$x \rightarrow \boxed{\times\ 13} \rightarrow \boxed{+\ 40} \rightarrow 79$$
$$3 \leftarrow \boxed{\div\ 13} \leftarrow \boxed{-\ 40} \leftarrow 79$$

1 Insert brackets where necessary to make these equations correct.

  a $6 \times 2 + 7 - 3 \times 5 + 4 = 36$
  b $6 \times 2 + 7 - 3 \times 5 + 4 = -8$
  c $6 \times 2 + 7 - 3 \times 5 + 4 = 8$
  d $6 \times 2 + 7 - 3 \times 5 + 4 = 43$

2 Find the value of x.

  a $2(x + 4) = 18$
  b $3(x + 6) = 30$
  c $5(x - 3) = 25$
  d $9(x + 1) = 36$
  e $4(3 + x) = 32$
  f $42 = 7(x + 5)$

3 Find the value of x.

  a $\frac{1}{2}(x + 4) = 5$
  b $\frac{1}{4}(x + 7) = 2$
  c $\frac{1}{5}(x - 3) = 3$
  d $\frac{1}{3}(x + 2) = 5$
  e $\frac{1}{8}(x - 5) = 2$
  f $\frac{1}{5}(6 + x) = 1$

4 Find the value of x.

  a $3(2x + 5) = 33$
  b $4(3x + 2) = 80$
  c $5(6x - 4) = 10$
  d $3(4x + 1) = 51$
  e $8(7x - 5) = 72$
  f $6(2 + 6x) = 30$

5 Find the value of x.

  a $3(x + 1) + 5(x + 5) = 44$
  b $6(x + 4) + 4(x + 5) = 74$
  c $5(x - 2) + 3(x + 2) = 36$
  d $4(x + 3) + 7(x - 1) = 49$
  e $2(x - 5) + 8(x - 7) = 4$
  f $6(x + 6) + 9(x + 2) = 69$

6 Find the cards below that match the expression $6(5x + 4) + 8(2x - 1)$.

$6(7x + 2) + 4(x + 1)$ $3(9x + 4) + 2(5x - 3)$ $6(3x + 2) + 4(7x - 3)$

$5(6x + 2) + 8(10x - 5)$ $4(5x + 2) + 2(13x + 4)$ $2(7x + 8) + 6(8x + 12)$

$9(12x + 6) + 8(3x - 1)$ $4(9x + 5) + 7(4x - 3)$ $4(9x + 5) + 2(5x - 2)$

7 Find the value of the letters in the equations.

  a $5(p + 6) + 7(p + 3) = 111$
  b $3(q + 6) + 7(q + 1) = 45$
  c $8(s - 1) + 3(s + 2) = 31$
  d $2(t + 4) + 5(t - 2) = 47$
  e $10(n - 1) + 3(n - 3) = 46$
  f $9(b + 2) + 4(b + 7) = 124$

Extension problems

8 Find the value of x.

a $8(x + 7) = 96$ b $7(x + 9) = 119$ c $6(x - 10) = 54$

d $11(x + 5) = 121$ e $4(x - 7) = 36$ f $9(4 + x) = 27$.

9 Find the value of x.

a $2(2x + 2) + 4(3x + 1) = 24$ b $5(4x + 1) + 3(2x + 1) = 86$

c $4(3x - 3) + 7(5x + 2) = 96$ d $5(2x + 3) + 6(4x - 2) = 20$

e $3(3x - 4) + 5(6x - 5) = 119$ f $4(4x + 5) + 5(5x + 6) = 91$

 Points to remember

⊙ To solve a linear equation containing brackets, multiply out the brackets and simplify the equation first.

Example
$$2(x + 4) + 5(3x + 7) = 77$$
$$2x + 8 + 15x + 35 = 77$$
$$17x + 43 = 77$$
$$17x = 34$$
$$x = 2$$

6 Equations with x on both sides

This lesson will help you to solve linear equations with x terms on both sides.

To solve an equation that has x terms on both sides, put all the x terms on one side.

Example of removing the x term from the right-hand side by subtraction:

	$5x - 1 = 3x + 3$
subtract $3x$	$2x - 1 = \qquad 3$
add 1	$2x = \qquad 4$
divide by 2	$x = \qquad 2$

$x \rightarrow \boxed{\times 2} \rightarrow \boxed{-1} \rightarrow 3$

$2 \leftarrow \boxed{\div 2} \leftarrow \boxed{+1} \leftarrow 3$

Example of removing the x term from the right-hand side by addition:

	$5x + 7 = 39 - 3x$
add $3x$	$8x + 7 = 39$
subtract 7	$8x = 32$
divide by 8	$x = 4$

$x \rightarrow \boxed{\times 8} \rightarrow \boxed{+7} \rightarrow 39$

$4 \leftarrow \boxed{\div 8} \leftarrow \boxed{-7} \leftarrow 39$

Example of removing the x term from the left-hand-side by subtraction:

$$4x + 3 = 8x - 9$$

subtract $4x$ $\qquad\qquad 3 = 4x - 9$

The equation $3 = 4x - 9$ can be reflected in the equals sign to put the equation in its normal form.

$$4x - 9 = \quad 3 \qquad\qquad x \rightarrow \boxed{\times 4} \rightarrow \boxed{-9} \rightarrow 3$$

add 9 $\qquad\qquad 4x = 12 \qquad\qquad 3 \leftarrow \boxed{\div 4} \leftarrow \boxed{+9} \leftarrow 3$

divide by 4 $\qquad\quad \underline{x = \quad 3}$

Exercise 6

① Copy and complete these statements.

a $16 + \square = 0$ **b** $-16 + \square = 0$ **c** $16 - \square = 0$

d $-16 - \square = 0$ **e** $7x + \square = 0$ **f** $-7x + \square = 0$

② Solve these equations.

a $4x + 5 = 3x + 8$ **b** $2x + 1 = x + 6$ **c** $9x + 4 = 6x + 10$

d $7x - 3 = 5x + 9$ **e** $8x - 11 = 3x + 9$ **f** $8x + 5 = 7x + 6$

③ Solve these equations.

a $x + 5 = 3x + 1$ **b** $7x + 6 = 9x + 4$ **c** $2x + 9 = 7x - 6$

d $4x + 3 = 5x - 2$ **e** $8x + 3 = 12x + 2$ **f** $3x + 4 = 8x + 9$

g $2x + 17 = 9x - 11$ **h** $5x + 3 = 7x - 13$

④ Solve these equations.

a $2x + 5 = 17 - x$ **b** $5x - 4 = 12 - 3x$ **c** $6x + 7 = 34 - 3x$

d $3x + 15 = 5 - 2x$ **e** $3x - 2 = 33 - 4x$ **f** $7x + 1 = 61 - 3x$

g $2x + 14 = 5 - x$ **h** $9x + 4 = 18 - 5x$

⑤ The perimeter of the rectangle 'No footway for 400 yds' is the same as the perimeter of the equilateral triangle.

a Write an equation in x.

b Solve the equation to find the width of the rectangle.

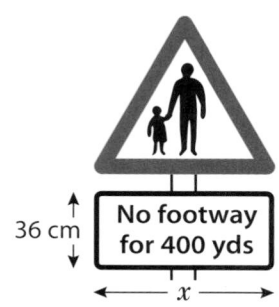

36 cm

No footway for 400 yds

x

6 A piece of land is divided into two rectangles like this.

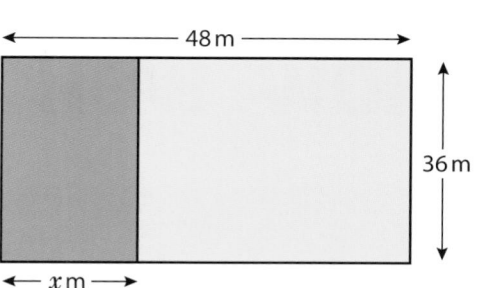

   a The perimeter of the yellow rectangle is double the perimeter of the green rectangle.
What is the value of x?

   b Calculate the value of x when the area of the yellow rectangle is double the area of the green rectangle.

7 An architect is designing two houses shown by the rectangles in this plan.
Calculate the value for x when the area of the pink and blue rectangles are equal.

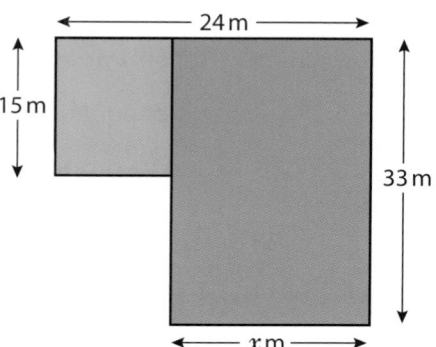

Extension problem

8 Solve these equations.

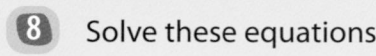

   a $9 - 2x = 5 - x$ **b** $15 - 2x = 20 - 3x$ **c** $8 - x = 14 - 2x$

   d $19 - 3x = 23 - 5x$ **e** $5 - 2x = 15 - 6x$ **f** $7 - 4x = 17 - 12x$

   g $9 - 3x = 7 - 4x$ **h** $21 - 5x = 12 - 2x$

◉ Points to remember

⊙ To solve a linear equation containing brackets, first multiply out the brackets and simplify the equation, then solve.

$$2(x + 4) = 26$$
$$2x + 8 = 26$$

⊙ To solve a linear equation that has x terms on both sides, first collect all x terms together on one side of the equation, then solve.

$$10x + 3 = 6x + 11$$
$$4x + 3 = 11$$

How well are you doing?

Can you:

- link functions, equations and graphs?
- solve linear equations, including equations with brackets and with x terms on both sides?
- substitute numbers into equations and formulae?
- link the solution of equations to points on their graphs?
- use algebra to solve problems?

Equations and formulae

1 Write this function as an equation in x and y.

$x \rightarrow$ [multiply by 14] $\rightarrow$ [subtract 9] $\rightarrow y$

2 Write the inverse function for this function.

$x \rightarrow$ [multiply by 9] $\rightarrow$ [subtract 4] $\rightarrow y$

3 Which of these ordered pairs are solutions to the equation $y = 2x + 3$?
(0, 1), (1, 5), (4, 10), (0.5, 4), (3, 15)

4 *2006 level 5*
Solve these equations.

  a $2k + 3 = 11$ b $2t + 3 = -11$

5 *2001 level 6*
Solve these equations. Show your working.

  a $7 + 5k = 8k + 1$ b $10y + 23 = 4y + 26$

6 *2005 level 6*
I think of a number.
I multiply this number by 8, then subtract 66.
The result is twice the number that I was thinking of.
What is the number I was thinking of?

Enquiry 2

This unit will help you to:

- find questions to explore about a statistical problem;
- decide which information is needed, how accurate it needs to be, and where to find it;
- plan how to collect the information and how big the sample should be;
- collect the data;
- draw a table of results using equal-sized groups;
- draw and interpret a variety of graphs on paper and using ICT;
- calculate statistics and use them to compare two sets of data;
- write and illustrate a short report.

1 Collecting continuous data

This lesson will help you to understand discrete and continuous data, and help you to collect continuous data.

 Did you know that...?

Lengths haven't always been measured in metric or imperial units.

Around 3000 BC the Egyptians used a **cubit** to measure lengths. A cubit was the length of an arm from the elbow to the fingertips, however, since this length varies, the Egyptians developed a standard cubit. This was kept as a black granite rod against which people could check their own measuring rods.

The cubit was subdivided into *digits* for smaller measurements. A digit was the width of a finger. For example, there were 28 digits in a cubit, 4 digits in a *palm* and 5 digits in a *hand*.

The *foot* was also used as a measure of length.

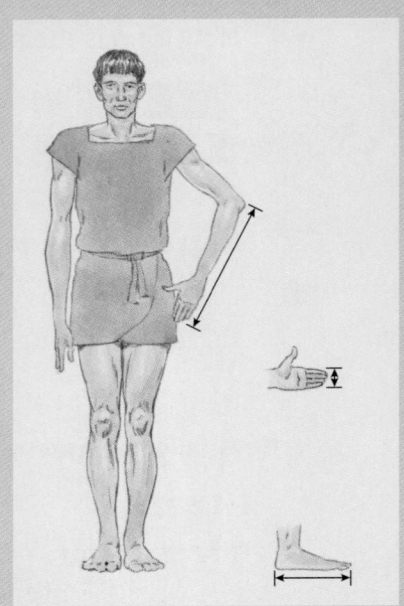

There are two types of data — discrete and continuous.

- ☉ **Discrete data** can be collected by counting.
  The items of data only take integer values. Examples are the number of kittens in a litter, the number of patients in a hospital or the number of spelling errors in an essay.
- ☉ **Continuous data** can be collected by measuring.
  The items of data take any value within an interval and are never exact. Examples are the height of a child, the length of time to walk to school or the weight of a cake.

Exercise 1A

1. a Write down how old you are in years.
   b You aren't that age exactly so write down how old you are in years and months.
   c You aren't this age exactly either so write down your age in years, months and days.
   d Can you write your age more exactly than that?
   e How exact is it possible to write your age?

2. Bethany is measuring the length of a pen in centimetres.
   a She measures the pen with a trundle wheel. How long is the pen?

   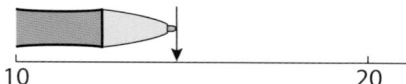

   b Then she measures the pen more accurately using a measuring tape. How long is the pen?

   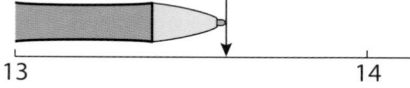

   c Next she measures the pen more accurately using a ruler. How long is the pen?

   d Finally she measures the pen with a micrometer. How long is the pen?

Exercise 1B

Work in a group of six, sharing a copy of **S4.3 Resource sheet 1.1.**

For each person in your group, measure and record on the resource sheet their:

- hand span;
- foot length;
- reaction time;
- standing jump distance;
- height.

You should already have decided as a class how you will make each measurement and how accurate it needs to be.

When you have finished measuring, give your completed resource sheet to your teacher, who will put together all the class data for you to use later in this unit.

Points to remember

- **Discrete data** can be collected by counting and take only integer values. Examples are the number of pupils in a class or the number of weeds on a lawn.
- **Continuous data** can be collected by measuring and take any value within an interval. Examples are quantities such as length, weight, temperature, time and speed.

2 Processing and representing continuous data

This lesson will help you to:

- draw a table of results using equal-sized groups;
- draw and interpret frequency diagrams for continuous data.

You may need to group data before you can represent it using a diagram or a chart.
You need to choose class intervals that don't overlap.

In a frequency diagram for **continuous data**:

⊙ the bars touch, because the data is continuous and so can take any value in the interval;

⊙ the horizontal axis is labelled as a scale, again because the data is continuous and can take any value in the interval;

⊙ frequency always goes on the vertical axis;

⊙ the grid lines, not the spaces, are labelled on the vertical axis.

Example

This list shows the heights of 30 pupils measured in centimetres.

165	157	143	155	155	179	154	162	165	157
145	154	145	161	167	170	134	190	130	160
140	150	153	171	145	165	158	168	154	170

Draw a frequency table for the data. Then plot a frequency diagram.

Height (cm)	Frequency
$130 \leqslant x < 140$	2
$140 \leqslant x < 150$	5
$150 \leqslant x < 160$	10
$160 \leqslant x < 170$	8
$170 \leqslant x < 180$	4
$180 \leqslant x < 190$	0
$190 \leqslant x < 200$	1

Here is a frequency diagram to show the heights of the pupils.

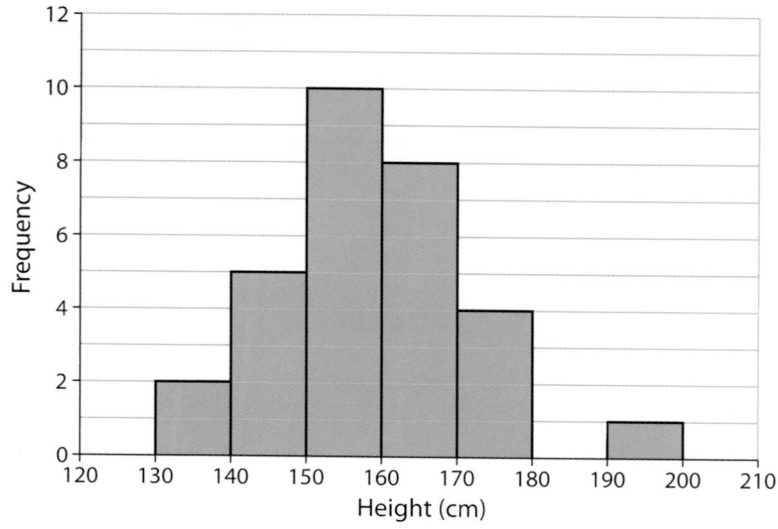

Exercise 2

You will need graph paper. The data for this exercise comes from www.censusatschool.ntu.ac.uk

1 The list shows the heights of 30 pupils measured in centimetres.

172	172	151	161	150	175	156	169	164	148
154	165	145	131	151	157	171	175	171	174
164	187	160	165	147	145	159	152	169	150

a Copy and complete this frequency table.

Height (cm)	Frequency
$130 \leqslant x < 140$	
$140 \leqslant x < 150$	
$150 \leqslant x < 160$	
$160 \leqslant x < 170$	
$170 \leqslant x < 180$	
$180 \leqslant x < 190$	

b Draw a frequency diagram for this set of data.
Draw a horizontal axis for height from 120 cm to 200 cm, using a scale of 1 cm on the graph paper for every 5 cm height.
Draw the vertical axis for the number of people, using a scale of 2 cm on the graph paper for every one person.

2 This list shows the foot lengths for 30 pupils measured in centimetres.

21	23.5	21	27	25	27	24	27	25.5	22
22	21	21	24	30	22	20	29	20	24
20	26	18	25	19	24.5	23	25	23	27

Here is the start of a frequency table.

a Write down three different foot lengths that would be in the first class interval.

b In which class interval would you put a foot length of 23.6 cm?

c In which class interval would you put a foot length of 28 cm?

d Copy and complete the frequency table for the data given.

Foot length (cm)	Frequency
$18 \leqslant x < 20$	
$20 \leqslant x < 22$	
$22 \leqslant x < 24$	
$24 \leqslant x < 26$	
$26 \leqslant x < 28$	
$28 \leqslant x < 30$	
$30 \leqslant x < 32$	

e Draw a frequency diagram for this set of data.
Draw a horizontal axis for foot length from 18 cm to 32 cm, using a scale of 1 cm on the graph paper to every 1 cm foot length.
Use a scale of 2 cm for every one person on the vertical axis.

③ This list shows the wrist circumferences for 30 pupils measured in millimetres.

155	170	160	110	180	200	150	140	155	120
145	150	160	150	190	170	167	160	130	170
178	175	175	170	170	180	180	150	160	120

a Copy and complete this frequency table.

b Draw a frequency diagram for this set of data.
Draw a horizontal axis for wrist circumference from 100 mm to 220 mm, using a scale of 1 cm to 10 mm wrist circumference. Use a scale of 2 cm for every one person on the vertical axis.

Wrist circumference (mm)	Frequency
$110 \leqslant x < 130$	
$150 \leqslant x < 170$	
$190 \leqslant x < 210$	

Points to remember

⊙ In a frequency diagram for continuous data, the bars touch and the horizontal axis is labelled as a scale.

⊙ Groups for continuous data should be of equal width and not overlap.

3 Analysing and interpreting distributions

Did you know that...?

Statistics help people who are planning to analyse trends and make decisions about what to do.

The government provides a website where all kinds of data from surveys is available. This is: **www.statistics.gov.uk**

You can find data about your own neighbourhood or you can see a summary for the UK as a whole.

This lesson will help you to:

● find questions to explore about a statistical problem;

● decide which information is needed and how accurate it needs to be;

● draw and interpret a variety of graphs.

Exercise 3

Work with a partner. Your teacher will give you a copy of the data to use. The data shows:

● hand span
● foot length
● reaction time

● standing jump distance
● height

Your teacher will help you to choose one of these questions to investigate, or will suggest that you make up your own question.

1   Do taller people jump further?

2   Do most people have similar reaction times?

3   Is there a relationship between foot length and hand span?

4   How does hand span vary in the class?

As part of your investigation, you will need to analyse and organise the data, draw a graph, come to some conclusions, and put together a short report. You may use graph plotting software for statistical diagrams to plot your graphs for this work. You will have some time in this and the next lesson to do all this.

Before you begin, think about these points.

Questions 2 and 4 are about the distribution of the data.

● What type of data is it — continuous or discrete?

● Do you need to group the data? If so, what class intervals will you choose?

● What type of chart or diagram will you draw?

Questions 1 and 3 are about looking for a relationship between two quantities.

● What type of chart or diagram will you draw?

You can now start to work on your investigation.

 Points to remember

⊙ Scatter graphs are useful for showing connections between two quantities.

⊙ Frequency diagrams are useful for showing how a set of data is distributed.

4 Communicating findings

This lesson will help you to write and illustrate a short report.

When you report what you have found out in a statistical investigation, explain:

- ☉ the question you were exploring;
- ☉ what you did and what you found out;
- ☉ how you came to your decisions.

Exercise 4

Today you will complete the investigation that you started in Exercise 3. You will analyse and organise data, draw a graph, come to some conclusions, and put together a short report.

You will be presenting your results to the whole class. The points below will help you to plan how to do this. Keep your presentation short and simple. Decide who will present each part. You will need to tell people:

- ⊙ what your question was;

- ⊙ how you answered the question;

- ⊙ what your results were (you might like to make a slide or an overhead transparency of an important graph to show them);

- ⊙ how accurate your results are;

- ⊙ what conclusions you came to;

- ⊙ how your investigation could have been improved.

⊙ Points to remember

- ⊙ The shape of a graph helps you to see important features of a data set.
- ⊙ Choose a chart or diagram that helps you to answer your question.
- ⊙ Explain why you chose it.
- ⊙ Write down what each chart, diagram or calculation shows you about the data.
- ⊙ Make sure that you answer the original question.
- ⊙ In your conclusion say how accurate you think your results are and how you could improve the project another time.

5 Mean, median and range

This lesson will help you to calculate statistics and compare sets of data.

Sometimes it is easier to calculate the mean of a set of numbers by using an estimate of the mean (an **assumed mean**).

Example

Find the mean of 568, 549, 557, 544, 559 and 541.

Assume a mean of 550.
The differences from the assumed mean are: 18, −1, 7, −6, 9 and −9.
The mean of the differences is $(18 − 1 + 7 − 6 + 9 − 9) ÷ 6 = 3$.
So the actual mean is 3 more than the assumed mean. The actual mean is 553.

The mode, median and mean are different ways of finding the average of a set of numbers. The range shows how much the numbers are spread out.

- The **mode** is the number that occurs most often in the set.
- The **mean** is found by adding up all the numbers in the set and dividing by the number of numbers in the set.
- The **median** is the middle number, or the mean of the middle two numbers, when all the numbers in the set are arranged in order.
- The **range** is the highest number in the set minus the lowest number.

Example

The mean height of a group of girls is 149 cm and the range of their heights is 15 cm.
The mean height of a group of boys of the same age is 156 cm.
The range of their heights is 9 cm.
Compare the distribution of heights in the two groups.

On average the boys are 7 cm taller, but the variation in their heights is less than that of the girls.

Exercise 5

Show all your working.

1. Find the mean of 14.8, 13.6, 13.2, 14.9, 14, 13.1, 12.9, 14.8, 15.3 and 14.4 using an assumed mean of 14.0.

2. Eight packets of cheese are priced at £2.29, £2.44, £2.13, £2.09, £2.38, £2.22, £2.25 and £2.35. Use £2.30 as an assumed mean to work out the actual mean.

3 Boxes of paperclips say that they contain '1000 paperclips on average'. The exact number of paperclips in 12 of these boxes are:

1013, 1022, 1019, 997, 988, 1011, 1015, 996, 989, 1022, 1003, 985

Use 1000 as the assumed mean to work out the actual mean number of paperclips in a box.
Do you think the claim on the box is reasonable?

4 The weights of ten adults are 67, 85, 54, 73, 77, 59, 66, 69, 71 and 81 kg.
Choose an assumed mean and use it to work out the actual mean.

5 A box of nails says that the nails are 2 cm long.

Jasmine measures 10 of the nails. The lengths are:

2.1, 1.9, 2.2, 1.8, 1.9, 1.8, 2.2, 2.0, 2.0 and 2.1 cm.

Assume a suitable mean and work out the actual mean.

6 Calculate the mean and range for these two sets of data.

Set 1: 12, 13, 19, 12, 11, 15, 10, 14, 11, 9
Set 2: 12, 9, 9, 13, 16, 16, 10, 14, 13, 14

Describe the differences between the two sets.

7 The shoe sizes for 12 girls and 12 boys were recorded.

Girls: 5, 6, 9, 6, 6, 4, 8, 6, 6, 7, 8, 7
Boys: 6, 8, 7, 10, 9, 8, 7, 8, 8, 9, 6, 11

a Calculate the mode and range for the girls and then for the boys.

b Describe the differences between the shoes sizes of the girls and boys.

c Why is the mode more useful as a measure of the average for shoe size than the mean?

8 A gardener grows two different kinds of courgette. He records the number of courgettes he picks each week for eight weeks from the two different types, A and B.

Week	1	2	3	4	5	6	7	8
Type A	3	2	5	7	6	7	4	2
Type B	2	2	4	4	5	4	5	1

a Calculate the mean, range and mode for both types of courgette.

b Use some of the values to argue that type A is the best type of courgette.

c Use some of the values to argue that type B is the best type of courgette.

(9) The table gives the heights of 15 boys and 15 girls in centimetres.

Girls	138	138	136	135	145	140	135	139	148	135	146	143	137	148	145
Boys	147	146	158	157	142	143	153	158	152	147	143	158	145	148	143

a Calculate the median and the range of both the boys and the girls.

b Use these values to write about the differences in the heights for the two groups.

Extension problem

(10) The data below shows the mean height of men and women in the different countries. Describe the differences.

Country	Gender	Mean (cm)
UK	Men	175
	Women	162
China	Men	169
	Women	155
Japan	Men	169
	Women	156
Netherlands	Men	180
	Women	165
USA	Men	176
	Women	163
France	Men	172
	Women	160
Germany	Men	173
	Women	162
Italy	Men	173
	Women	161

Data source: The Nuffield Foundation www.fsmq.org

Points to remember

⊙ An **assumed mean** can help you to calculate the actual mean of a data set.

⊙ You can use the range and one of the mean, median or mode to compare two sets of data.

6 Comparing probabilities

This lesson will help you to collect data from experiments.

Probability experiments can be used to collect data that can then be analysed.

A **simulation** is a way of collecting data without having to do the actual experiment. The experiment may be too dangerous, too expensive or too difficult.

A simulation is an easy-to-do experiment that behaves in the same way as the real experiment.

In this exercise you will investigate variations of Murphy's law.

Did you know that...?

Murphy's law is named after Captain Edward A. Murphy, an engineer who worked at Edwards Air Force Base in California.

He was working on a project designed to see how much force a person's body can stand in a crash.

One day, Murphy found that an electrical part was wired wrongly. He was annoyed with the technician responsible and said: 'If there is any way to do it wrong, he'll find it.'

MURPHY'S LAW
Anything that can go wrong will go wrong

Exercise 6

Work in a pair. You will need a copy of **S4.3 Resource sheet 6.1**.

Experiment 1

If you drop a piece of buttered toast it will always land butter-side down.

You will need a coin and a piece of Blu Tack for this experiment.

For this experiment you need to imagine that the coin is a piece of toast.

First you will flip the 'toast' with no butter on it. Then you will stick some Blu Tack on one side of the coin to simulate butter on the 'toast' and flip it again.

Flip the coin 50 times. Each time record whether you get a head or tail using the tally chart on **S4.3 Resource sheet 6.1**. Fill in the experimental probabilities on the sheet.

Now try the experiment again but this time stick a piece of Blu Tack on the 'tails' side of the coin.

Fill in the experimental probabilities on the sheet, then answer these questions.

1   **a**   What does the coin represent in the simulation?

     b   What does the Blu Tack represent in the simulation?

     c   When the coin lands on heads is it butter-side-up or butter-side-down?

     d   Did your 'toast' land butter-side-down more often than it did butter-side-up?

     e   What is the theoretical probability of getting a tail with a fair coin?
         What effect do you think the Blu Tack had on the probability of getting a tail?

     f   How realistic do you think this simulation is?

Experiment 2

When you are in a hurry, the traffic lights are more likely to be red.

You will need a dice and some red, green and orange counters in a bag.

An odd score means you are in a hurry.
An even score means that you are not.

For this experiment you will need to imagine that the counters in the bag represent the traffic lights. When you pick a counter out of the bag, the colour of the counter indicates the colour of the traffic lights.

Put two red, two green and one orange counter in the bag.

Roll the dice and pick a counter at random from the bag. Record the results on **S4.3 Resource sheet 6.1**. Repeat the experiment 50 times.

Use a coloured pen to highlight the results where you are in a hurry and the lights are red.

Fill in the experimental probability on the sheet, then answer these questions.

2   **a**   What is your experimental probability of being in a rush?

     b   What is the theoretical probability of being in a rush?

     c   What is your experimental probability of getting a red light?

     d   What is the theoretical probability of getting a red light?

     e   Is the colour of the counter affected by the number rolled on the dice?
         So are the lights more likely to be red if you are in a hurry?

     f   How realistic do you think this simulation is?

Experiment 3

It always rains when I forget to take my umbrella with me.

You will need two dice of different colours.

The score on one of the dice indicates whether or not you remember to take your umbrella with you.

The score on the other die indicates the weather.

Decide for each die what the different numbers will stand for and record this information on **S4.3 Resource sheet 6.1**.

Roll the two dice 50 times. Record the results on **S4.3 Resource sheet 6.1**.

Use a coloured pen to highlight the results where you forget your umbrella and it rains.

Now answer the questions.

(3)   a   What is the experimental probability of forgetting your umbrella and it rains?

     b   Is it possible to work out the theoretical probability of forgetting your umbrella?

     c   Is it possible to work out the theoretical probability of it raining?

     d   Is the score on one die affected by the score on the other? So is forgetting your umbrella affected by the chance of it raining?

     e   How realistic do you think this simulation is?

Points to remember

⊙ A **simulation** is a way of collecting data about a problem without having to carry out the actual experiment.

⊙ A simulation is an easy-to-do experiment that behaves in the same way as the experiment we are unable to do.

⊙ Probability experiments can be simulated.

7 Line graphs for time series

This lesson will help you to collect data using ICT, and draw and interpret line graphs.

A **line graph** is useful for showing continuous data when values are recorded against time.

Time is the independent variable so it goes on the horizontal axis.

The other variable depends on the time. It goes on the vertical axis.

Remember to label the axes as scales.

Example

Sketch a graph to show how the temperature changes over 24 hours from midnight in mid-summer in the UK.

Describe the change in temperature over time.

The temperature increases slowly over the first part of the morning and then more rapidly in the middle of the day. It stays warm for the afternoon and then cools down quickly.

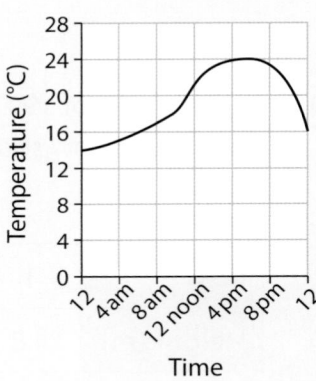

Exercise 7

You will need a copy of **S4.3 Resource sheet 7.1** and some graph paper.

1   Choose one day during the week when you are in school.
    Use the first set of axes to draw a graph to show how your mood changes during the day.
    In the box, write a description of how your mood changes over the day and why.

2   Choose one day during the weekend.
    Use the second set of axes to draw a graph to show how your mood changes during the day.
    In the box, write a description of how your mood changes over the day and why.

(3) This is the tide table for Oahu Island in Hawaii for one day in June 2006.

Time	00:00	01:00	02:00	03:00	04:00	05:00	06:00	07:00	08:00	09:00	10:00	11:00
Height (cm)	6	9	12	18	18	18	15	9	6	6	6	15

Time	12:00	13:00	14:00	15:00	16:00	17:00	18:00	19:00	20:00	21:00	22:00	23:00
Height (cm)	24	37	49	61	67	67	61	52	40	27	18	9

a Plot a line graph to show the height of the tide against time.
   Use a scale of 1 cm to every 2 hours for time on the horizontal axis from 00:00 to 23:00.
   Use a scale of 2 cm to every 10 cm on the vertical axis from 0 cm to 70 cm.

b Describe the shape of the graph and how the height of the tide changes over time.

(4) In the spring of 1997 Red River in Fargo, North Dakota, flooded.
The table below shows how the depth of water increased over the month of April that year.

Day	1	2	3	4	5	6	7	8	9	10
Height (m)	4.8	5.0	5.2	6.1	7.2	8.4	9.2	9.9	10.5	11.0

Day	11	12	13	14	15	16	17	18	19	20
Height (m)	11.2	11.3	11.2	11.3	11.5	11.7	12.0	12.1	12.0	12.0

Day	21	22	23	24	25	26	27	28	29	30
Height (m)	11.9	11.7	11.6	11.4	11.2	11.1	10.9	10.7	10.5	10.3

Data source: www.ndsu.nodak.edu

a Plot a line graph to show the height of the water in the month.
   Use a scale of 1 cm to every 2 days for time on the horizontal axis from 1 to 30.
   Use a scale of 2 cm to every 1 m on the vertical axis from 0 m to 13 m.

b Describe the shape of the graph and how the height of the water changed in the month.

c The level at which flooding occurs is 5.5 m. On which day was this level exceeded?
   Draw a horizontal line on your graph to indicate the flood level.

d On which day was the flooding at its greatest height?

Extension problem

5 The table shows information from the University of East Anglia.
It shows the combined land and sea surface temperature every 10 years from 1900 to 2000.

Year	1900	1910	1920	1930	1940	1950	1960	1970	1980	1990	2000
Temp. (°C)	−0.31	−0.41	−0.31	−0.19	−0.02	−0.09	−0.04	−0.07	0.05	0.21	0.40

Data source: www.cru.uea.ac.uk/cru/data/temperature/. Data taken from Brohan et al (2006), *J. Geophysical Research* **111**, D12106

a Plot a line graph to show the temperature against the year.
Use a scale of 1 cm to every 10 years for time on the horizontal axis.
Use a scale of 2 cm to every 0.1°C on the vertical axis from −0.5°C to 0.5°C.

b Describe the shape of the graph and how the temperature changes over time.

c Do you think that the graph shows any evidence for global warming?
Explain your answer.

Points to remember

⊙ Data can be collected from experiments.

⊙ A line graph is a useful way of displaying continuous data against time.

How well are you doing?

Can you:

- draw a table of results using equal-sized groups?
- draw and interpret a variety of graphs?
- calculate statistics?

Mean, median and range

① Find the mean of this set of numbers.
Show your working.

73, 81, 85, 76, 69, 82, 77, 72, 72, 68

Collecting, representing and interpreting continuous data

② This list shows neck circumferences measured in centimetres for 30 pupils.

46.2	50.7	47.7	32.8	53.6	59.6	44.7	41.7	46.2	35.8
43.2	44.7	47.7	44.7	56.6	50.7	49.8	47.7	38.7	50.7
53.0	52.2	52.2	50.7	50.7	53.6	53.6	44.7	47.7	35.8

a Copy and complete the frequency table.

Neck circumference (cm)	Frequency
$30 \leqslant x < 35$	
$45 \leqslant x < 50$	

b Draw a frequency diagram for the data.
Use a scale of 2 cm to every 5 cm for neck circumference on the horizontal axis from 25 cm to 65 cm.
Use a scale of 2 cm for every one person on the vertical axis.

2007 level 5

The graph shows the average heights of fir trees of different ages.

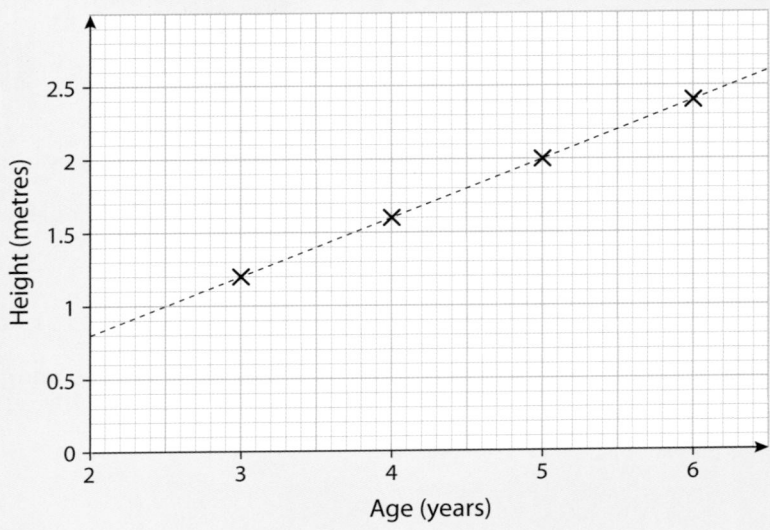

The table shows the cost of fir trees of different heights.

	120 cm to 159 cm	160 cm to 199 cm	200 cm to 239 cm
Cost	£ 20.00	£ 25.00	£ 30.00

a   One of these fir trees is $5\frac{1}{2}$ years old. How much is it likely to cost?

b   One of these fir trees costs £25.00. How old is the tree likely to be?

Constructions

This unit will help you to:

- construct shapes accurately, on paper and with a computer;
- bisect line segments and angles, and draw perpendiculars to lines;
- make scale drawings and use bearings;
- work out the path of a point that moves according to a rule;
- visualise shapes, work logically and explain your reasoning.

1 Drawing arcs and circles

This lesson will help you to use compasses to construct circles and arcs.

Did you know that...?

Leonardo da Vinci was an Italian artist who lived from 1452 to 1519. He is best known for his painting of the Mona Lisa.

He loved geometry and was particularly interested in constructions. He made many drawings, including architectural drawings and scale plans.

Leonardo's drawing of a flying machine was made hundreds of years before the first aeroplane was built.

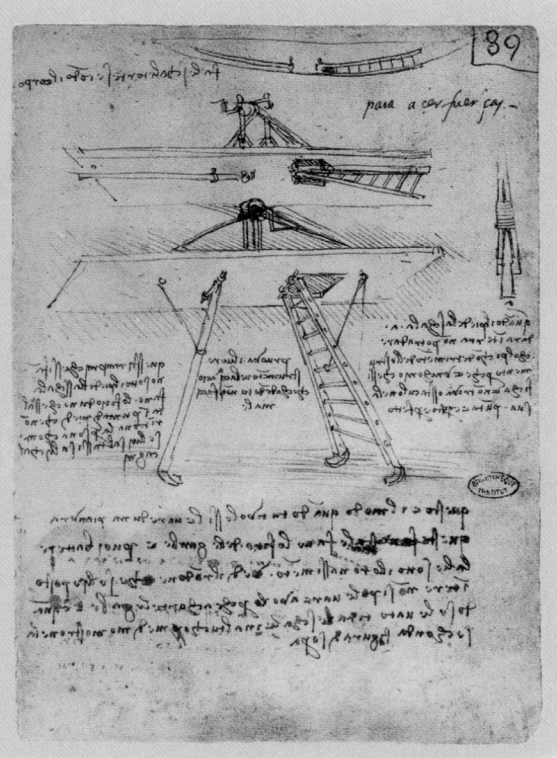

Stars are a common motif in Islamic patterns.

Exercise 1

In this exercise you will draw motifs based on circles.
You will need a ruler, compasses, sharp pencil and plain paper.

1 **Nested stars**

Start by drawing a circle.

Use compasses to draw a hexagon. Remember not to change the radius of the compasses.

Join alternate vertices (corners) to make two overlapping equilateral triangles.

Next join opposite vertices.

Now draw the final pair of triangles using the intersections of these lines and the triangles drawn previously.

You should get the diagram shown here.

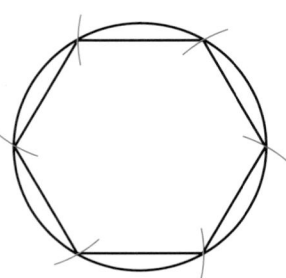

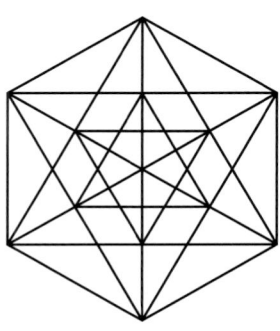

② Eight-pointed stars

Draw a square 14 cm by 14 cm.
Divide each side into quarters.

Join the centres of opposite sides to make four smaller squares.

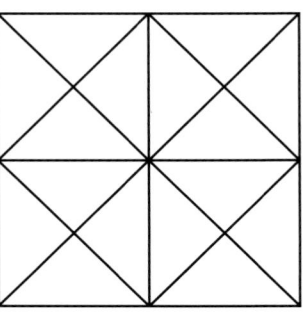

Draw the diagonals for each smaller square.

Use compasses to draw a circle with radius 3.5 cm in the centre of each smaller square.

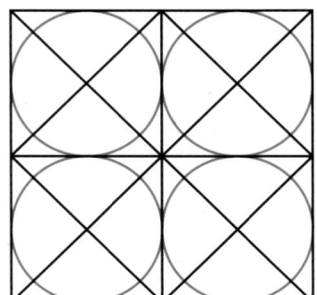

In each smaller square, draw two further squares like this:

- Draw one square by joining the intersection points of the circle and the diagonals of the square.

- Draw the other square by joining the points where the circle touches the large square.

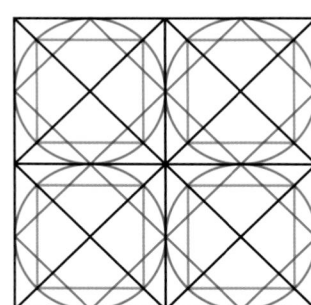

Colour the design to show the eight-pointed stars.

③ Six-pointed stars

Use compasses to draw interlocking circles all with the same radius.

Draw five or six hexagons, as here.

Join alternate vertices in each hexagon to produce two interlocking triangles.

Rub out construction lines to show six-pointed stars.

Colour in your design to show the pattern.

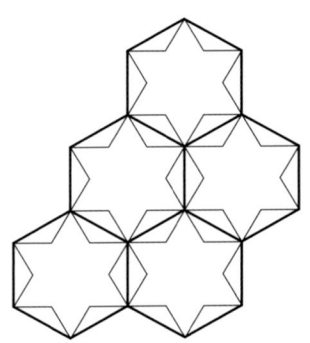

Extension problem

 4 Work out how to arrange the centres of the circles in order to draw the Olympic logo.

 Did you know that...?

The Olympics date back to ancient Greek times, but the Olympic logo was designed by the Frenchmen Pierre de Coubertin in 1913.

The logo has five interlocking circles all the same size, one for each continent.

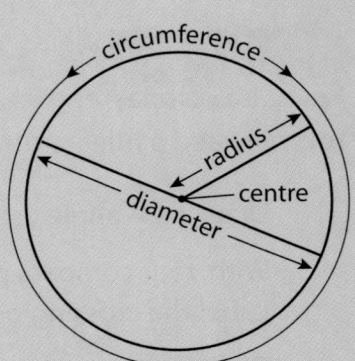 **Points to remember**

- The **circumference** of a circle is the distance all the way round the edge of the circle.
- The **radius** is the distance from the centre to the edge.
- The **diameter** is the distance across the circle through the centre.
- An **arc** is part of the circumference of a circle.

2 Constructing midpoints and bisectors

This lesson will help you to use a straight-edge and compasses to construct bisectors and midpoints.

○ Open the compasses a small distance. Keep them fixed from now on.

○ With the compass point at O, draw an arc crossing both arms of the angle. Label the crossing points A and B.

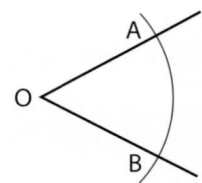

○ With the compass point at A, draw another arc in the middle of the angle.

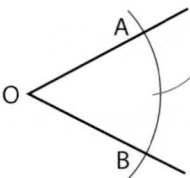

○ With the compass point at B, draw another arc in the middle of the angle. It should cross the second arc. Label this point X.

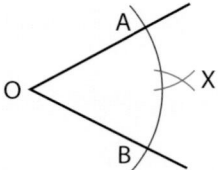

○ Join OX. This line is the **angle bisector**.
Measure the two halves of the angle to check.

○ Leave your construction lines on the diagram.

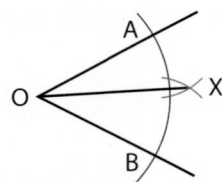

Exercise 2A

You will need a ruler, protractor and compasses.

1. Draw a 45° angle using your protractor. Put your protractor to one side.

   With your compass point at the corner of the angle, draw an arc to cross both arms. Label the crossing points A and B.

   Draw arcs from points A and B to cross each other in the middle of the angle.

   Draw the line that bisects the angle.

(2) Use your protractor to draw a right angle.
Using compasses, bisect this angle.

(3) Use your protractor to draw an angle of 120°.
Using compasses, bisect this angle.

(4) A speedboat sets out from corner X of a boating lake along the bisector of the angle WXY.

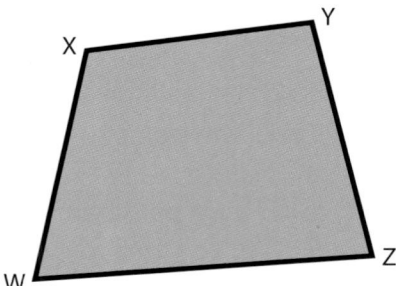

Another speedboat sets out at the same time from corner Y along the bisector of angle XYZ.

Both boats travel at the same speed.

Use your ruler to draw a similar but bigger boating lake. It need not be an exact copy.

Find the point at which the two boats will collide unless they take avoiding action.

Exercise 2B

⊙ Set the compasses to any radius greater than half the length of AB.

⊙ With centre A, draw an arc above and below AB.

⊙ With compasses set at the same radius, and with centre B, draw another arc to cut the first arc at C and D.

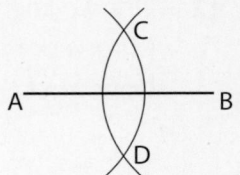

⊙ Join C and D to cut AB at X.

⊙ The line CD is the **perpendicular bisector** of the line AB.
Measure angle AXC to check that it is a right angle.

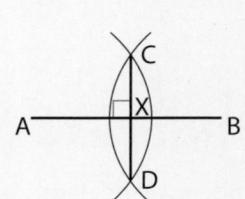

⊙ X is the **midpoint** of the line AB.
Use your ruler to check that AX = XB.

⊙ Leave your construction lines on the diagram.

You will need a ruler, protractor and compasses.

(1) Draw a line segment AB 7.8 cm long. Draw the perpendicular bisector of AB.

(2) Draw an island similar to the island on the map but bigger. It need not be an exact copy.

Put points A, B, C and D on it.

Some treasure is buried on the perpendicular bisector of AB. It is also on the perpendicular bisector of CD.

Find the point at which the treasure is buried. Label the point X.

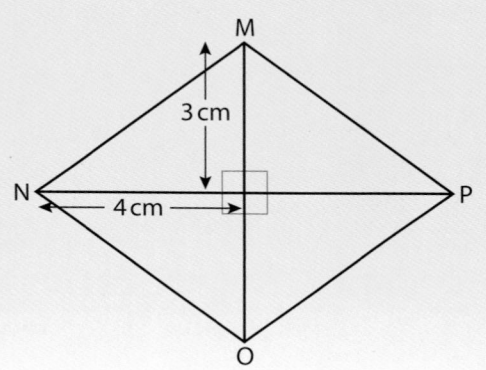

(3) Draw two points 6 cm apart. Label them P and Q.

P •   • Q

Use a straight-edge and compasses to draw all the points that are the same distance from P as from Q.

Extension problems

(4) Draw a line segment NP 8 cm long.
Construct rhombus MNOP such that diagonal NP is 8 cm long and diagonal MO is 6 cm long.

(5) Draw a line AB more than 10 cm long.
Mark a point P a few centimetres above the line.
Construct the perpendicular from P to the line AB.

⊙ Points to remember

⊙ Constructions using a straight-edge and compasses are more accurate than those done by measuring with rulers and protractors.

⊙ Leave construction lines on the diagram.

⊙ Any point on an **angle bisector** is the same perpendicular distance from each of the two arms of the angle.

⊙ Any point on the **perpendicular bisector of a line segment** is the same distance from each end of the line.

3 Constructing triangles on paper

This lesson will help you to use a ruler, compasses and protractor to construct triangles.

⊙ Draw a line segment the length of one of the sides, leaving plenty of room above it.

8 cm

⊙ Set the compasses to the length of one of the other sides. With centre at one end of the line segment, draw an arc.

8 cm

⊙ Set the compasses to the length of the third side. With centre at the other end of the line segment, draw an arc to cross the first arc.

8 cm

⊙ Where the two arcs cross is the third vertex of the triangle. Join the ends of the line segment to the crossing point. Label the triangle.

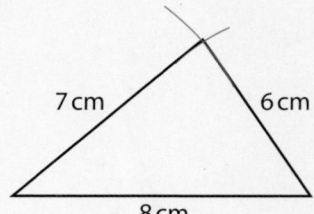

7 cm   6 cm

8 cm

Exercise 3A

You will need a ruler, compasses and sharp pencil.

1. Construct a triangle with sides 5 cm, 8 cm and 9 cm.

2. Construct a triangle with sides 9 cm, 7 cm and 7 cm.

3. Construct a triangle with sides 8 cm, 6 cm and 12 cm.

Constructing a triangle using SAS (side-angle-side)

◉ Draw a line segment the length of one side.
Leave plenty of room above it.

—————————————
8 cm

◉ Use a protractor to mark the size of the angle at one end of the line segment.

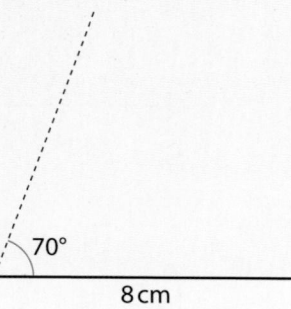

70°
8 cm

◉ Use the ruler to mark off the second side length in the direction of the angle.

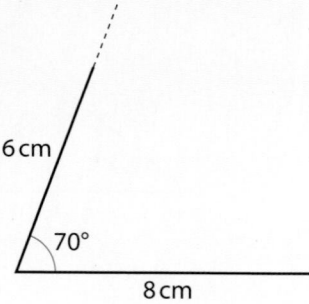

6 cm
70°
8 cm

◉ Join the ends of the two line segments to complete the triangle.

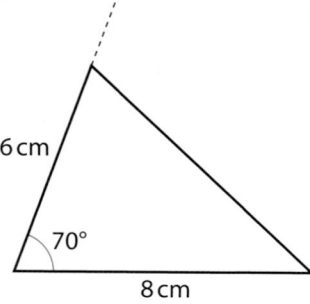

6 cm
70°
8 cm

Constructing a triangle using ASA (angle-side-angle)

◉ Draw a line segment the length of one of the sides, leaving plenty of room above it.

—————————————
8 cm

◉ Use a protractor to mark the size of one of the angles at one end of the line segment.

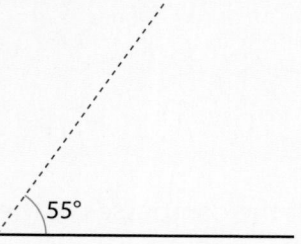

55°

◉ Use a protractor to mark the size of the other angle at the other end of the line segment.

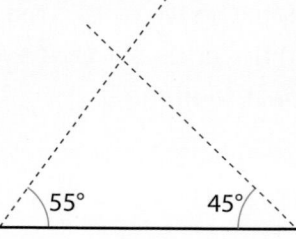

55°   45°

◉ The third vertex of the triangle is where the two dotted lines cross. Join this vertex to the ends of the line segment to complete the triangle.

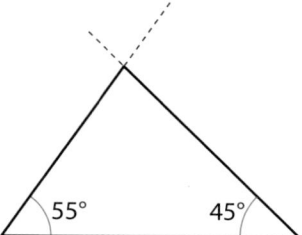

55°   45°

Did you know that...?

Triangles are used in structures to make them rigid, as in these bridges.

You will need a ruler, protractor and sharp pencil.

① This is a sketch of a model bridge.

Use ruler and compasses to make an accurate copy of one of the triangles, using the lengths shown.

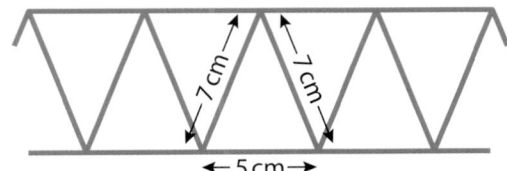

Diagram not to scale

② A football is made up of hexagons and pentagons.

Use a ruler and a protractor to make an accurate copy of the pentagon.

Start by drawing triangle A, then B and finally C.

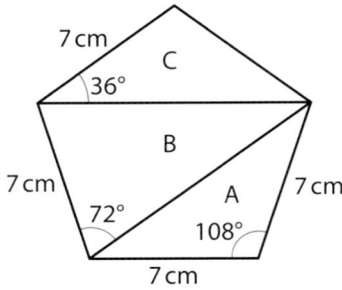

Diagram not to scale

③ Draw each of these triangles using the ASA method.

Triangle A   65°, 6 cm, 70°
Triangle B   60°, 7 cm, 60°
Triangle C   70°, 5.5 cm, 70°

Which triangle has the greatest perpendicular height?

Points to remember

⊙ Triangles that are constructed using these methods are unique:
 – side-side-side (SSS);
 – angle-side-angle (ASA);
 – side-angle-side (SAS).

4 Constructing triangles using ICT

This lesson will help you to use ICT to construct triangles.

Did you know that...?

Many tasks that require accurate drawings are done using computers.

The photograph on the right shows the designer's face reflected in a computer screen displaying a computer-aided design of an engine part.

You can use dynamic geometry software to construct triangles using the three ruler and compasses constructions.
 ⊙ SSS The lengths of all three sides are given.
 ⊙ SAS The lengths of two sides and the included angle are given.
 ⊙ ASA The sizes of two angles and the length of the included side are given.

Work in a pair with a computer and dynamic geometry software.
Either use **G4.4 Resource sheets 4.1 and 4.2** to help you to construct the diagrams
or use The Geometer's Sketchpad file **G4-4_Triangles.**

Write notes and draw sketches to record your work.

1 Take turns to write down three numbers between 2 and 12. They can be decimals if
you like. Use the SSS construction file to try to make triangles with these numbers as
side lengths.

   a Is it possible to make triangles using all your sets of three numbers? If not, why not?

   b Can you find any sets of three numbers that don't make a triangle?

   c Can you make an equilateral triangle? An isosceles triangle? A right-angled triangle?

2 Use the SAS construction file to make some triangles. For each part below, sketch the
triangle in your book. Label the two side lengths and angle size on the sketch.

   a Make an acute-angled triangle.

   b Make an obtuse-angled triangle.

   c Make an isosceles triangle. How do you know the triangle is isosceles?

   d Make an equilateral triangle. How do you know the triangle is equilateral?

   e Make a right-angled triangle.

3 Use the ASA construction file to make some triangles. For each section below sketch your
triangle in your book and add the two angle sizes and side length to the sketch.

   a Make an acute-angled triangle.

   b Make an obtuse-angled triangle.

   c Make an isosceles triangle. How do you know the triangle is isosceles?

   d Make an equilateral triangle. How do you know the triangle is equilateral?

   e Make a right-angled triangle. How do you know the triangle is right-angled?

Points to remember

⊙ Triangles that are constructed using these methods are unique:
   - side-side-side (SSS);
   - angle-side-angle (ASA);
   - side-angle-side (SAS).

5 Making shapes on pinboards

This lesson will help you to solve problems by constructing shapes on pinboards.

You can construct polygons by joining pins on a pinboard.

You can make squares on a 3 by 3 pinboard. Each square has a pin at each corner. Squares that are the same size but in different positions don't count as being 'different'.

The three squares that can be made have areas of 1, 4 and 2 square units.

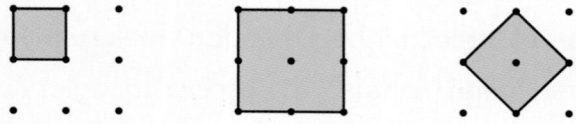

The square with area 2 square units is made up of four triangles, each of which is half of one square unit.

Exercise 5

In this exercise, polygons that are the same shape and size but in different positions don't count as being 'different'.

Only one non-square rectangle can be constructed on a
3 by 3 pinboard.

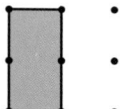

1. **a** How many different sizes of non-square rectangles can you construct on a
   4 by 4 pinboard?

   b What is the area of each of the different rectangles?

2. **a** How many different sizes of non-square rectangles can you construct on a
   5 by 5 pinboard?

   b What is the area of each of the different rectangles?

3. These polygons have been made on a 3 by 3 pinboard.
   Each of them has an area of 2 square units.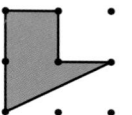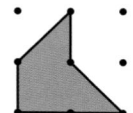

   Using a 3 by 3 pinboard, investigate the different polygons
   you can make, each with an area of 2 square units.
   Each polygon must have a pin at each corner.

A trapezium has one pair of parallel sides.

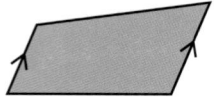
Trapezium

Isosceles trapezium

Using a 3 by 3 pinboard, how many different trapeziums can you make that are not parallelograms, squares or rectangles?

Extension problems

5 Investigate ways of making hexagons on a 3 by 3 pinboard.

Which of your hexagons will tessellate? Here is one example.

6 A heptagon is a seven-sided polygon.
Investigate ways of making heptagons on a 3 by 3 pinboard.

Which of your heptagons will tessellate?

7 Is it possible to make an octagon on a 3 by 3 pinboard?

 Points to remember

⊙ You can use the properties of shapes to help you to make shapes on pinboards.

⊙ You can find the area of a pinboard shape by dividing it into squares, rectangles or triangles, and thinking of triangles as halves of rectangles.

6 Scale drawings

This lesson will help you to make scale drawings.

The **scale** of a drawing gives the relative size of the drawn length to the actual length.
The scale of a map or plan is written as a ratio.

Example 1

Express the scale of 2 cm to 1 km as a ratio in the form $1 : n$.

First convert 1 km to cm.

$$1\,km = 1000\,m$$
$$= 1000 \times 100\,cm$$
$$= 100\,000\,cm$$

The scale is 2 cm to 100 000 cm or $2 : 100\,000 = 1 : 50\,000$

Example 2

Elizabeth is drawing a plan of a swimming pool. She uses a scale of $1 : 250$.

a What actual length does 5 cm on her plan represent?

5 cm represents $\quad 5 \times 250\,cm = 1250\,cm$
$$1250\,cm = 1250 \div 100\,m$$
$$= 12.5\,m$$

b The pool is 30 m long. How long will it be on Jo's plan?

An actual length of 30 m is $30 \times 100\,cm = 3000\,cm$.
$3000\,cm \div 250 = 12\,cm$
The pool will be 12 cm long on Elizabeth's plan.

Exercise 6

You need a ruler, sharp pencil, protractor and compasses for this exercise, and some plain paper.

1. In this question, give the scale in each answer in the form $1 : n$.

   a A plan of the classroom is drawn with 2 cm representing 1 m.
   What is the scale of the plan?

   b The plan of a school's grounds is drawn with 1 cm representing 50 m.
   What is the scale of the plan?

   c A map of the area around the school is drawn with 4 cm representing 1 km.
   What is the scale of the map?

② Nerissa has drawn a plan of her classroom. She has used a scale of 1 : 100.

   a The plan is 7 cm wide. How wide is the classroom?

   b The classroom is 9 m long. How long is the plan?

③ Billy's play house is a scale model of his real house. The scale is 1 : 5.

   a Billy's real house is 10 m tall. How tall is his play house?

   b The play house is 3 m wide. How wide is the real house?

④ Samuel is making a scale model of a radio-controlled aeroplane from a plastic construction kit.
The ratio of lengths on the model plane to lengths on the actual plan is 1 : 10.

Copy and complete the table.

Part	Model plane	Actual plane
length of wing	1 m	
length of plane		20 cm
height of tail	15 cm	
width of door		90 cm
height of door	20 cm	
number of seats		60

⑤ A road map has a scale of 1 : 300 000.

   a Two towns are 8 cm apart on the map. What is their actual distance apart?

   b Two cities are an actual distance of 60 km apart.
How many centimetres are they apart on the road map?

⑥ Malena walks 5 kilometres north and then 8 kilometres east.

Choose a suitable scale. Make an accurate scale drawing of her route.

Use your scale drawing to work out how far Malena is from her starting point.

⑦ Brandon puts a ladder of length 2 metres against a wall.

The foot of the ladder is 1 metre from the wall.

Choose a suitable scale.

Make an accurate scale drawing of the ladder and the wall.

Use your scale drawing to work out how high up the wall the ladder reaches.

(8) A piece of card is 60 cm tall and 40 cm wide.
Two pictures are to be mounted symmetrically on it.
Each picture is 30 cm wide by 20 cm tall.

Using a scale of 1 : 5, make an accurate scale drawing of how the pictures could be arranged.

(9) Using a scale of 2 : 3, make an accurate scale drawing of a triangle with sides 12 cm, 15 cm and 21 cm.
Measure the angle between the two longer sides.

Extension problem

(10) Here is a plan of a ferry crossing.
Choose a suitable scale and make an accurate scale drawing of the ferry crossing.
Use your scale drawing to work out the actual distance between the two piers.

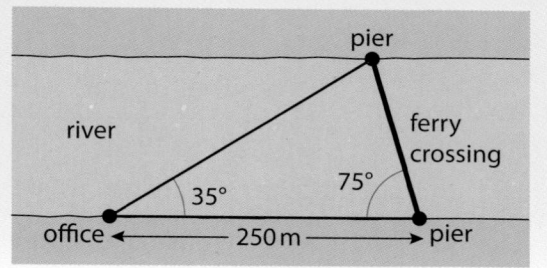

Points to remember

⊙ A **scale drawing** is a smaller drawing of an actual object.

⊙ The **scale** gives the relative size of the drawn length to the actual length.

⊙ State the scale next to the drawing.

⊙ Corresponding measurements in the actual object and the scale drawing are all in the same ratio.

7 Using bearings

This lesson will help you to find the bearing of one point from another and use bearings to solve problems.

A **bearing** is the direction that you travel in to go straight to the object. Bearings are measured clockwise from north in degrees.

When the angle is less than 100°, one or two zeros are written in front of the angle so that the bearing still has three figures.

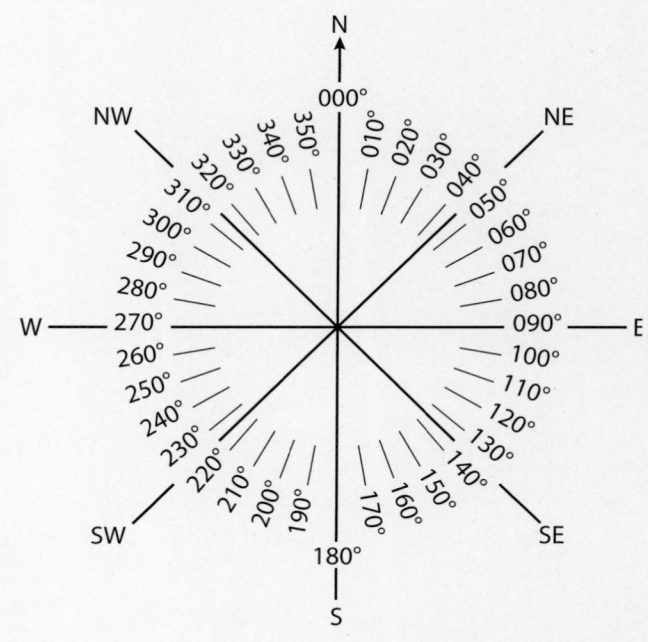

Example 1

Measure the bearing of B from A.

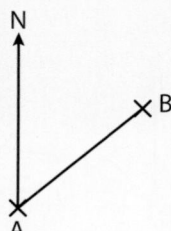

Solution

From north, measure the angle clockwise.

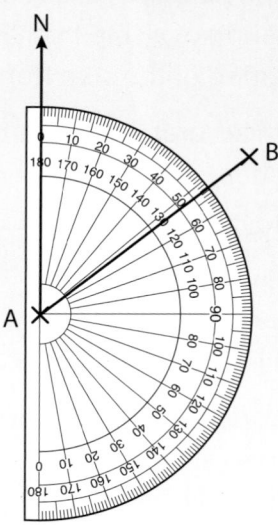

So the bearing of B from A is 052°.

Example 2

Measure the bearing of Q from P.

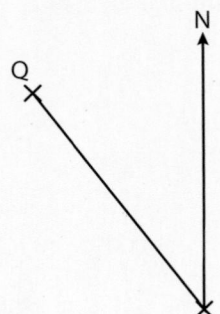

Solution

To find the angle clockwise from north, measure the shaded anticlockwise angle.

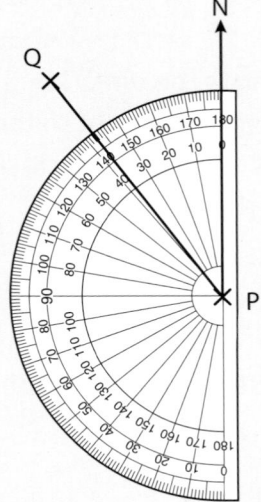

Subtract the anticlockwise angle (38°) from 360°.

$$360° - 38° = 322°$$

The bearing of Q from P is 322°.

Example 3

Folkestone and Dover are shown on the map. The bearing of a ship from Folkestone is 117°. The bearing of the ship from Dover is 209°.

Draw an accurate diagram to show the position of the ship.

Mark the position with a cross X. Label it S.

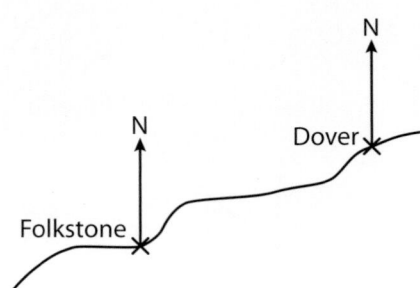

Solution

Draw a line on a bearing of 117° from Folkestone.

Draw a line on a bearing of 209° from Dover by measuring an anticlockwise angle from the north of 360° − 209° = 151°.

Put an X where the lines cross. Label the point S.

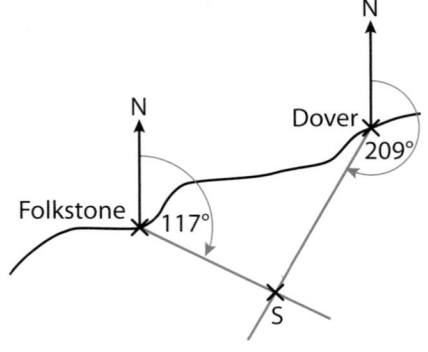

Exercise 7

You will need a ruler, protractor and sharp pencil for this exercise.

① An old schooner is being guided into a harbour. The pilot gives the directions as bearings. The steersman has a compass on board.

What compass direction should he steer for each of these bearings?

a 045°　　　**b** 135°　　　**c** 315°

What bearings should the pilot give so that the steersman steers in these directions?

d W　　　　**e** SW　　　　**f** N

② Write the bearing of B from A in each case.

a 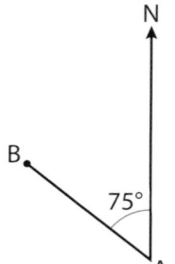　　**b** 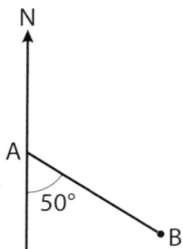　　**c** 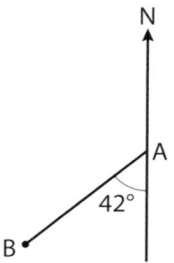　　**d**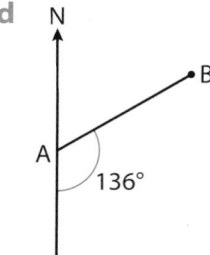

③ Oliver runs from A to B and back again.

a What is the bearing of his outward run from A to B?

b What is the bearing of his return run from B to A? Explain your answer.

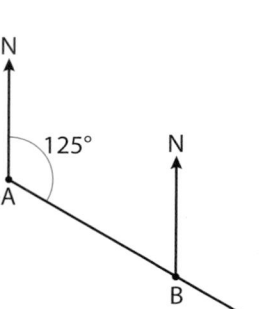

④ Alice runs from A to B and back again.

a What is the bearing of her outward run from A to B?

b What is the bearing of her return run from B to A? Explain your answer.

5 Micheal runs from A to B and back again.

   a What is the bearing of his outward run from A to B?

   b What is the bearing of his return run from B to A? Explain your answer.

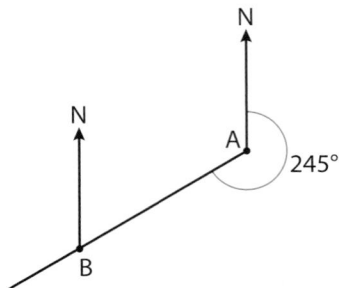

6 The cruise ship *Princess Margaret* was 20 kilometres from the port in Newcastle on a bearing of 030°. At the same time, the ferry *North Star* was 40 kilometres from Newcastle on a bearing of 090°.

Make a scale drawing of the port, the cruise ship and the ferry.

Use the scale drawing to work out the distance and bearing of the *North Star* from the *Princess Margaret*.

Extension problem

7 A plane is flying from Arndale to Bolter. The airfield at Bolter is fogbound. At Corrington, the plane is diverted to land at Dunford. The scale drawing shows the flight path of the plane.

   a What is the scale of the diagram?

   b What is the bearing of the flight path from Arndale to Bolter?

   c How far south of Dunford is Bolter?

   d Find the distance and bearing of the flight path from Corrington to Dunford.

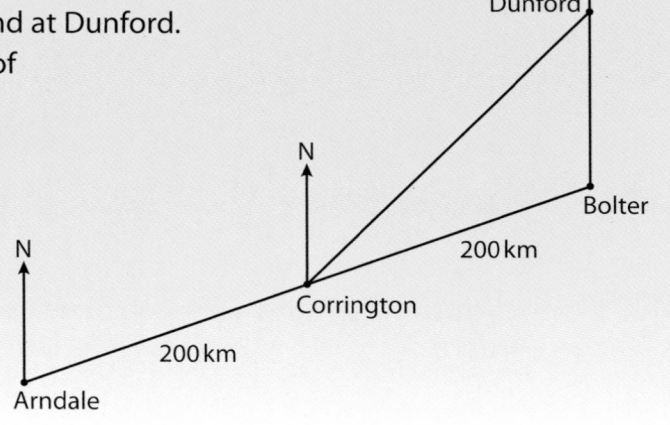

 Points to remember

⊙ A **bearing** is the direction that you travel in to go straight to the object.

⊙ Bearings are measured clockwise from north in degrees.

⊙ Bearings always have three figures.

8 Exploring loci

This lesson will help you to work out the path of an object that moves according to a simple rule.

A **locus** is a path or set of points that follows a rule.

Example 1

The locus of all the points 3 m from a point is a circle of radius 3 m.

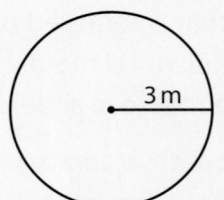

Example 2

The locus of all the points equidistant from points A and B is the perpendicular bisector of the line segment AB.

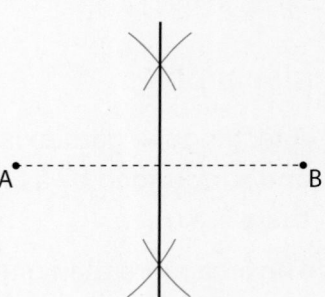

Example 3

The locus of all the points equidistant from the two intersecting lines X and Y is the perpendicular bisector of the angle.

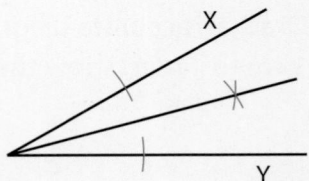

Exercise 8

You will need a ruler, compasses and a sharp pencil.

1. Mark two points A and B on your paper 9 cm apart.
   a Draw the locus of the points that are equidistant from A and B.
   b Draw the locus of the points that are 7 cm from A.
   c Use parts **a** and **b** to help you find the points that are 7 cm from both A and B.

2. A security light is positioned on a long wall.
   Its range is 7 m.

   Draw a scale diagram and shade in the area the light can reach.

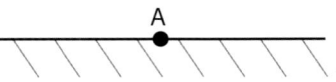

Diagram not drawn to scale

(3) In a building there is a corner where a wall and a window meet at an angle of 120°.

The area nearer the wall than the window is going to be carpeted.

Make an accurate copy of the diagram and shade the area to be carpeted.

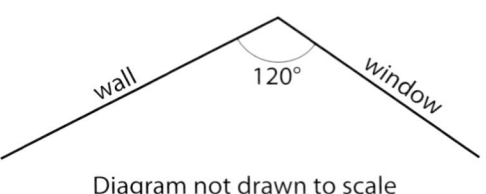

Diagram not drawn to scale

(4) A goat is tethered by a piece of rope 5 m long to a horizontal metal bar 7 m long.
The rope can slide along the metal bar.

Draw an accurate diagram using a scale of 1 cm to 1 m to show the area that the goat can reach. What happens at the ends of the bar?

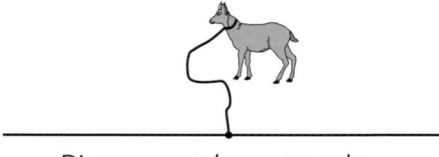

Diagram not drawn to scale

Extension problem

(5) A rectangular garden is 9 m wide and 12 m long and surrounded by a brick wall. In the middle there is a tree.

The area more than one metre from the wall and also more than one metre from the tree is to be a lawn.

Draw an accurate diagram using a scale of 1 cm to 1 m to show the area to be made into a lawn.

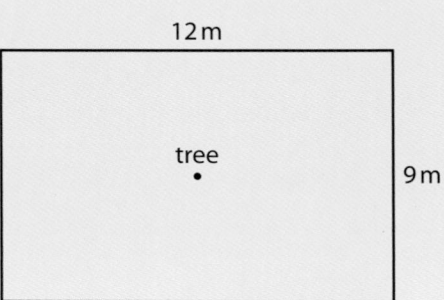

Diagram not drawn to scale

Points to remember

- A **locus** is the set of points, or path, that follows a rule.
- All the points the same distance from a fixed point form a circle.
- All the points equidistant from two fixed points lie on the perpendicular bisector of the line joining the points.
- All the points equidistant from two lines forming an angle lie on the angle bisector.

9 Using ICT to explore loci

This lesson will help you to use ICT to explore loci.

Work with a partner.

You will need a computer with MSW Logo and a copy of **G4.4 Resource sheet 9.1**.

1. What shape do these instructions make?

   FD 100 RT 72
   FD 100 RT 72
   FD 100 RT 72
   FD 100 RT 72
   FD 100

2. Choose another regular polygon and write down the instructions to draw it in Logo.
   Swap your instructions with someone else so that you can check each other's.

3. Type in these instructions. What shape do they make?

   FD 100 RT 90 FD 20 RT 90 FD 40 LT 90
   FD 30 LT 90 FD 40 RT 90 FD 20 RT 90
   FD 100 RT 90 FD 20 RT 90 FD 30 LT 90
   FD 30 LT 90 FD 30 RT 90 FD 20

4. Choose a letter of the alphabet and write the instructions to draw it.
   Swap your instructions with someone else so that you can check each other's.

5. Type in these instructions. What shape do they draw?
   Continue the instructions to continue the pattern.

   FD 10 RT 90
   FD 20 RT 90
   FD 30 RT 90
   FD 40 RT 90
   FD 50 RT 90
   FD 60 RT 90
   ....

Extension problem

 6. Now use logo to make some more spirals.
Make some like these two or some
of your own.

 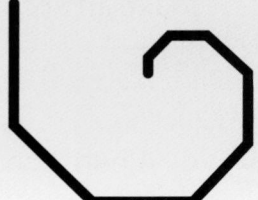

Points to remember

- You can use instructions, or rules, to describe the path of a moving point.
- You can use Logo to explore rules using angles and lengths.

How well are you doing?

You will need a ruler, protractor, compasses and sharp pencil.

Constructions and loci

1 Draw a line AB 7.2 cm long.
Use compasses and straight-edge to construct the perpendicular bisector of AB.

2 Draw an angle of 80°.
Use compasses and straight-edge to draw the bisector of this angle.

3 *2003 level 5*

Use compasses to construct a triangle that has sides 8 cm, 6 cm and 7 cm.
Leave in your construction lines.

4 *1997 level 5*

Here is a rough sketch of a sector of a circle.
Make an accurate full-size drawing of this sector.

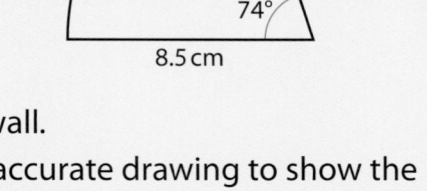

8.5 cm

74°

8.5 cm

5 **a** A path runs so that it is always 5 metres from a wall.
Using a scale of 1 cm to represent 1 m, make an accurate drawing to show the path and the wall.

b A horse is tied to a ring at point X on the wall by a rope 8 metres long.
Choose the point X on the wall and label it X.
Show on your diagram the part of the wall that the horse can reach.
Leave in your construction lines.

6 *1995 level 6*

Shape A is an equilateral triangle.
The instructions to draw shape A are:

FORWARD 5
TURN RIGHT 120°
FORWARD 5
TURN RIGHT 120°
FORWARD 5

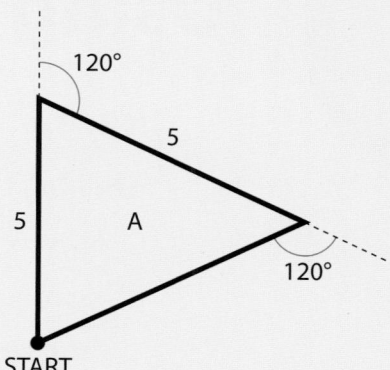

a Write instructions to draw a triangle that has sides double those of shape A.

b Shape B is a parallelogram.
Write the instructions to draw shape B.
The first instruction is:

FORWARD 8

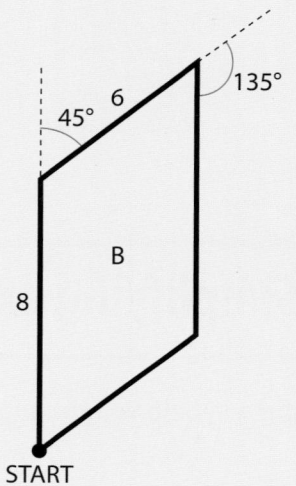

Scale drawings and bearings

7 Mary is drawing a plan of the school field. She uses a scale of 1 : 500.

a What actual length does 4 cm on her plan represent?

b The football pitch is 90 m long. How long will it be on Mary's plan?

8 The scale drawing shows the positions of an airport tower T and a radio mast M.

1 cm on the diagram represents 20 km.

a Measure the distance TM in centimetres.

b Work out the distance in km of the airport tower from the radio mast.

c Measure and write down the bearing of the airport tower from the radio mast.

d Write down the bearing of the radio mast from the airport tower.

North

This unit will help you to:

- revise what you know about 'terms', 'like terms' and 'expressions';
- simplify expressions;
- factorise expressions;
- solve linear equations;
- sketch, draw and interpret linear graphs;
- solve problems using algebra.

1 Simplifying expressions

This lesson will help you to simplify expressions.

A **term** is one or more numbers and/or letters combined by multiplication or division. 3, x, $7a$, $5xy$ are different terms.

Like terms have the same combination of letters. $4y$, $17y$ and y are all like terms.

An **expression** is one or more terms combined by addition or subtraction.

In an **equation** the expression on the left-hand side of the equals sign has exactly the same value as the expression on the right-hand side.

To keep an equation in balance you must always do the same to both sides.

Work out the contents of brackets first.
If there are no brackets, do multiplication and division before addition and subtraction.

You can **simplify an expression** by collecting like terms, like this: $5x + 7 + 3x - 4 = 8x + 3$

You can use a multiplication grid like this to help you to **multiply out brackets**.

$\times$	$7x$	$+$	4
6	$42x$	$+$	24

Exercise 1

1 Work these out.

a $3 + 5 \times (6 - 2 + 4)$ b $(3 + 5) \times 6 - 2 + 4$

c $(3 + 5) \times (6 - 2) + 4$ d $3 + (5 \times 6 - 2) + 4$

2 Simplify these expressions.

a $9x + 1 + 4x + 3$ b $8y + 9 + 3y - 4$

c $2p + 3p + 6 - 4p + 7p$ d $10q - 1 + q - 6q + 11 + 2q - 5$

e $7s + 6r + 3 + 2s - 4r + 8$ f $t + 1 + 7t - 4 + 8t + 1$

g $4 + 3x + 5y + 2 - 2x - 4y$ h $12ab + 5 + 9ab + 3a$

3 Match pairs of cards where the expressions are the same.

$3x + 6 + 5x + 9$ $8x + 9 + x - 8$ $13x + 9 - 7x - 3$ $x - 10 + 2x + 9$

$2x - 1 + 7x + 2$ $7x + 2 + 6x + 8$ $x + 3 + x - 7$ $10x + 7 - 2x + 8$

$x + 12 + 5x - 6$ $4x + 1 - 2x - 5$ $2x + 7 + x - 8$ $15x + 4 - 2x + 6$

4 The expression in each cell is the result of adding the expressions in the two cells beneath it. Copy the diagrams and fill in the missing expressions.

a

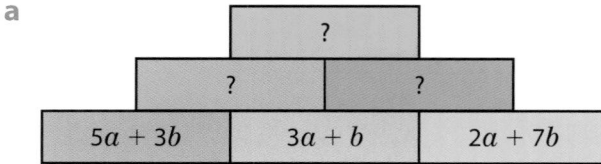

| ? |
| ? | ? |
| $5a + 3b$ | $3a + b$ | $2a + 7b$ |

b

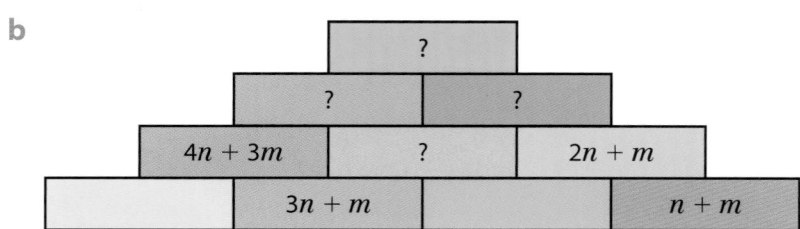

| ? |
?	?
$4n + 3m$	?	$2n + m$
	$3n + m$		$n + m$

5 Multiply out the brackets.

a $5(x + 8)$ b $4(y - 7)$

c $9(3x - 2)$ d $10(5a + 7)$

e $8(7 + 6t)$ f $15(4x - 3)$

g $3(8a + 5b)$ h $12(3p - 2q + r)$

⑥ Multiply out the brackets and simplify these expressions.

   a $5(x + 2) + 4(x + 3)$ b $3(y + 5) + 5(y + 7)$

   c $8(s + 6) + 6(s + 9)$ d $8(p + 10) + 4(p + 8)$

   e $7(4a + 5) + 8(a - 2)$ f $5(7x - 3) + 20(2x + 1)$

   g $12(5t - 4) + 10(9t - 8)$ h $14(3b + 2) + 25(4b - 3)$

⑦ Find the matching pairs.

$5(x + 3) + 7(2x + 1)$ $8(5x + 3) - 6(3x + 4)$ $6(7x + 4) - 2(5x - 8)$

$22x$ $19x + 22$ $48x + 70$ $66x - 65$

$7(6x + 1) + 8(3x - 9)$ $10(2x + 9) + 4(7x - 5)$ $32x + 40$

Extension problems

⑧ The expression in each cell is the result of adding the expressions in the two cells beneath it. Copy the diagram. Fill in the missing expressions.

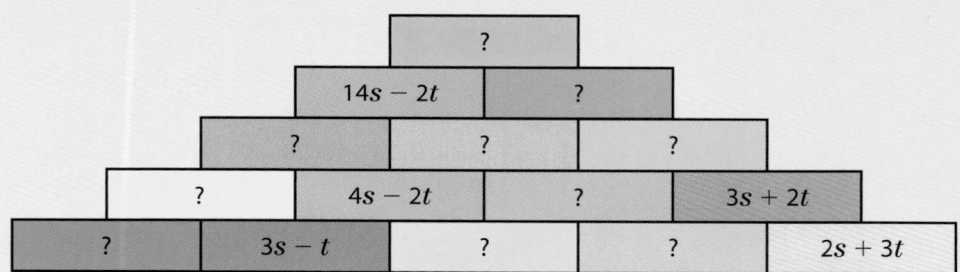

⑨ Multiply out the brackets and simplify these expressions.

   a $7(x + 4) - 2(x + 3)$ b $9(y + 5) - 4(y + 7)$

   c $8(s + 2) + 3(s - 7)$ d $7(p + 4) - (p - 8)$

   e $12(3a - 5) + 7(a - 9)$ f $10(6x - 1) - 3(8x + 11)$

   g $15(2t - 3) - 4(9t - 12)$ h $9(10b - 8) - 5(7b - 1)$

◉ Points to remember

⊙ If there are no brackets, do multiplication and division before addition and subtraction.

⊙ You can simplify an expression by collecting like terms.
   For example, $4x + 3x + 5 + 2x - 3$ can be simplified to $9x + 2$.

⊙ After multiplying out brackets, simplify if you can.

2 Factorising expressions

This lesson will help you to remove common factors from expressions.

The **factors** of a number are all the numbers that divide into it exactly.

Factorising by taking out a common factor is the opposite operation to multiplying out brackets.

The factors of 4 are 1, 2 and 4. The factors of 6 are 1, 2, 3 and 6.

The **common factors** of 4 and 6 are 1 and 2.

The **highest common factor** of 4 and 6 is 2.

Example

Factorise $4c + 6s$.

The highest common factor of 4 and 6 is 2.

$$4c + 6s = \mathbf{2} \times 2c + \mathbf{2} \times 3s$$
$$= \mathbf{2}(2c + 3s)$$

Exercise 2

1   Write down all the factors of these numbers.

    a 12   b 20   c 18

    d 35   e 51   f 99

2   Write down the common factors, excluding 1, of these pairs of numbers.

    a 12 and 18   b 20 and 30   c 60 and15

    d 36 and 42   e 14 and 35   f 16 and 40

3   Write down the highest common factor (HCF) of each of these pairs of numbers.

    a 42 and 60   b 24 and 40   c 45 and 60

    d 45 and 20   e 28 and 63   f 30 and 84

4   Write down all the factors of these terms.

    a $3x$ b $7p$ c $4y$

    d ab e $2xy$ f $13p$

5   Write down the common factors, excluding 1, of these pairs of terms.

    a $2x$ and $7x$ b $4p$ and 10   c $6x$ and $15y$

    d $14t$ and $77t$ e $30s$ and $70s$ f $30m$ and $21m$

6. Write down the highest common factor (HCF) of each of these sets of terms.

   a $10x$ and 70 b $7x$ and $11x$ c $30p$ and $24p$
   d $30q$ and $45q$ e $28m$ and $42m$ f $36t$ and $60t$

7. Factorise these expressions.

   a $5x + 15$ b $6y + 18$ c $7m - 49$
   d $9n + 36$ e $6s + 21$ f $12a - 20$
   g $20t - 30$ h $14v + 22$ i $24x + 40y$

8. Find pairs of matching cards.

   $3x + 6$ $2x + 16$ $3(2x + 5)$ $7(3x + 2)$

   $2(x + 8)$ $7x + 7$ $21x + 14$ $2(4x + 7)$

   $6x + 15$ $3(x + 2)$ $8x + 14$ $7(x + 1)$

9. Play this game of **Substitution** with a partner.
   You will need **A4.5 Resource sheet 2.1** cut into cards and a die.

   Rules

   - Place the cards face down in a pile.
   - Each player selects a card from the pile.
   - Take turns to throw the die.
   - Substitute the number on the die for x in the expression on your card.
   - The player with the highest score records that number.
     If players get the same score, they both record their scores.
   - Players replace their cards at the bottom of the pile.
   - The player with the highest total score after five turns wins the game.

Extension problem

10. Factorise these expressions.

    a $6x + 9y + 3z$ b $28a - 8b + 8$
    c $48 + 12m - 18n$ d $25w - 30x - 20y$
    e $14ax + 35ay$ f $30bp - 40bq$

3 Solving linear equations

This lesson will help you to solve equations.

Example 1   Solve $5x + 7 = 27$.

The equation $5x + 7 = 27$ has a unique solution.
To solve the equation you can use the inverse function.

$$5x + 7 = 27 \qquad x \rightarrow \boxed{\times 5} \rightarrow \boxed{+ 7} \rightarrow 27$$

subtract 7 $\qquad 5x = 20 \qquad 4 \leftarrow \boxed{\div 5} \leftarrow \boxed{- 7} \leftarrow 27$

divide by 5 $\qquad \underline{x = \;\; 4}$

Example 2   Solve $3(8x + 4) = 60$.

Multiply out first.

$$3(8x + 4) = 60 \qquad x \rightarrow \boxed{\times 8} \rightarrow \boxed{+ 4} \rightarrow \boxed{\times 3} \rightarrow 60$$

divide by 3 $\qquad 8x + 4 = 20 \qquad 2 \leftarrow \boxed{\div 8} \leftarrow \boxed{- 4} \leftarrow \boxed{\div 3} \leftarrow 60$

subtract 4 $\qquad\qquad 8x = 16$

divide by 8 $\qquad\qquad \underline{x = \;\; 2}$

1 Find the value of x in each of these equations.

a $x + 6 = 13$ b $x - 11 = 4$ c $x + 29 = 76$

d $x + 4.3 = 9.1$ e $x - 3.9 = 5.4$ f $x + 1 = 0$

g $17 + x = 45$ h $31 - x = 15$ i $11 = x - 4$

2 Find pairs of cards where x has the same value.

$x + 6 = 11$ $x + 3 = 19$ $x + 14 = 22$ $x + 16 = 22$

$x + 12 = 13$ $x - 3 = 9$ $x + 10 = 16$ $x + 44 = 45$

$x + 19 = 27$ $x - 1 = 4$ $x - 5 = 7$ $x - 7 = 9$

3 Find the value of x in each of these equations.

a $8x = 56$ b $7x = 77$ c $15x = 105$

d $31x = 124$ e $2.1x = 10.5$ f $4.3x = 21.5$

g $\frac{x}{6} = 5$ h $\frac{x}{3} = 2.5$ i $\frac{x}{4} = 0.5$

4 Find pairs of cards where x has the same value.

$5x = 40$ $2x = 28$ $\frac{x}{3} = 3$ $6x = 54$

$\frac{x}{7} = 5$ $\frac{x}{2} = 4$ $12x = 36$ $\frac{x}{5} = 7$

$7x = 35$ $9x = 27$ $\frac{x}{7} = 2$ $9x = 45$

5 Find the value of each letter in these equations.
Check your answers by substituting the value of the letter back into the equation.

a $p + 34 = 81$ b $m - 67 = 15$

c $9t = 72$ d $234 + z = 201$

e $97 + s = 105$ f $7w - 53 = 17$

g $6x + 9 = 57$ h $7a - 11 = 38$

i $10b + 56 = 256$ j $6c + 15 = 3$

6 Find pairs of cards where x has the same value.

$9x - 8 = 19$	$7x + 12 = 47$	$4x - 6 = 22$	$3x + 17 = 38$
$8x + 11 = 43$	$12x - 9 = 15$	$5x + 6 = 1$	$3x + 8 = 5$
$4x - 5 = 7$	$5x + 13 = 33$	$10x - 7 = 13$	$8x + 15 = 55$

7 Find the value of x in each of these.

a $2(x + 5) = 16$

b $3(x + 7) = 36$

c $5(x - 2) = 25$

d $9(x + 6) = 90$

e $7(x - 1) = 35$

f $4(8 + x) = 40$

g $8(5 + x) = 104$

h $126 = 7(x + 9)$

Extension problems

When there is more than one bracket in an equation, work out the brackets first.
Then simplify the algebraic expression before solving the equation.

Example 1   Solve $4(x + 5) + 5(x + 6) = 77$.

Multiply out: $4x + 20 + 5x + 30 = 77$

Simplify: $9x + 50 = 77$ $x \rightarrow \boxed{\times 9} \rightarrow \boxed{+ 50} \rightarrow 77$

  subtract 50 $9x \quad = 27$ $3 \leftarrow \boxed{\div 9} \leftarrow \boxed{- 50} \leftarrow 77$

  divide by 9 $\underline{x \quad = \ 3}$

To solve a linear equation that has x terms on both sides, first rearrange the equation to get all x terms on one side of the equation. Then solve the equation as before.

Example 2   Solve $8x - 3 = 4x + 5$.

                              $8x - 3 = 4x + 5$

  subtract $4x$ $4x - 3 = 5$ $x \rightarrow \boxed{\times 4} \rightarrow \boxed{- 3} \rightarrow 5$

  add 3 $4x = 8$ $2 \leftarrow \boxed{\div 4} \leftarrow \boxed{+ 3} \leftarrow 5$

  divide by 4 $\underline{x = 2}$

8 Find the value of x.

a $5x + 1 = 2x + 7$

b $7x + 1 = x + 7$

c $8x + 5 = 6x + 13$

d $6x - 10 = 3x + 8$

e $x + 7 = 2x + 4$

f $5x + 8 = 7x + 3$

9 Find the value of x.

   a $7(2x + 2) = 28$ **b** $3(4x + 7) = 57$

   c $4(5x - 7) = 52$ **d** $6(3x + 8) = 138$

   e $2(2x - 6) = 12$ **f** $9(6 + 6x) = 162$

 Points to remember

You can:

⊙ multiply out brackets and then simplify by collecting like terms;

⊙ factorise an expression by finding the highest common factor;

⊙ solve linear equations using inverse operations.

4 Sketching linear graphs

This lesson will help you to sketch straight-line graphs.

A **sketch** of a graph is a neat drawing using a pencil and ruler.
Look at the equation of the graph. Think about similar graphs.

The points A (2, 6), B (2, 2), C (2, −1) and D (2, −5) all lie on a line parallel to the y-axis.

The x-coordinate is always 2.

The equation of the line is $x = 2$.

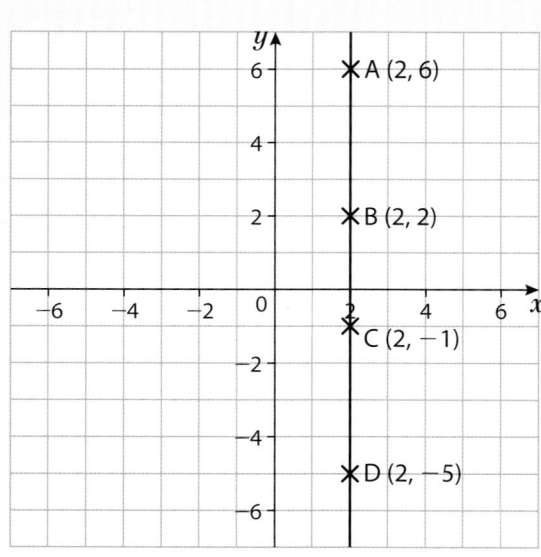

The points P (−5, 3), Q (−2, 3), R (1, 3) and S (4, 3) all lie on a line parallel to the x-axis.

The y-coordinate is always 3.

The equation of the line is $y = 3$.

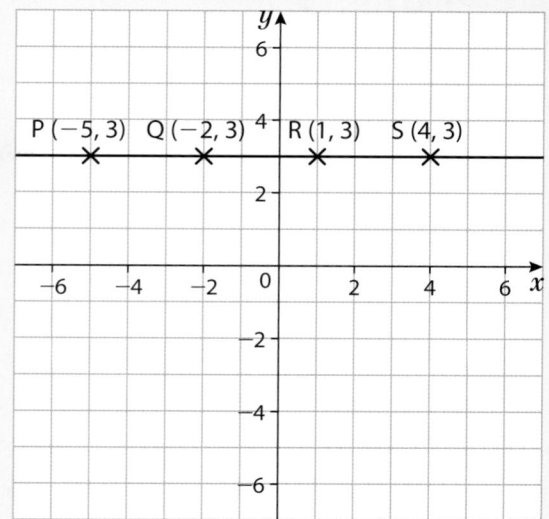

The graph shows a line through the points A (4, 4), B (1, 1), C (−2, −2), D (−5, −5) and the origin O (0, 0).

For each point the y-coordinate is equal to the x-coordinate.

All other points on this line also have the y-coordinate equal to the x-coordinate.

The equation of this line is $y = x$.

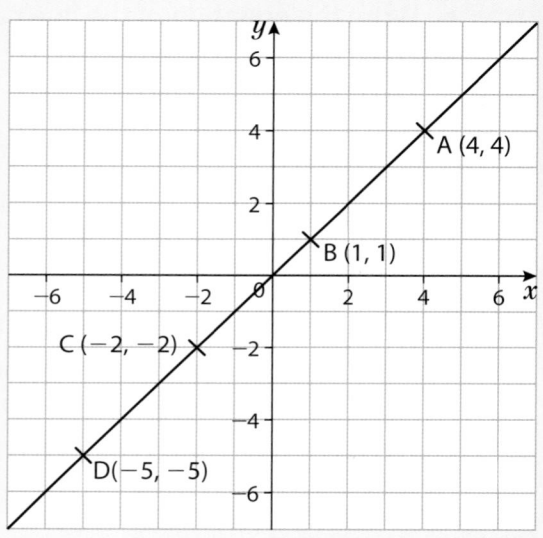

The graph of $y = x + 3$ is a straight line parallel to $y = x$ going through the point (0, 3).

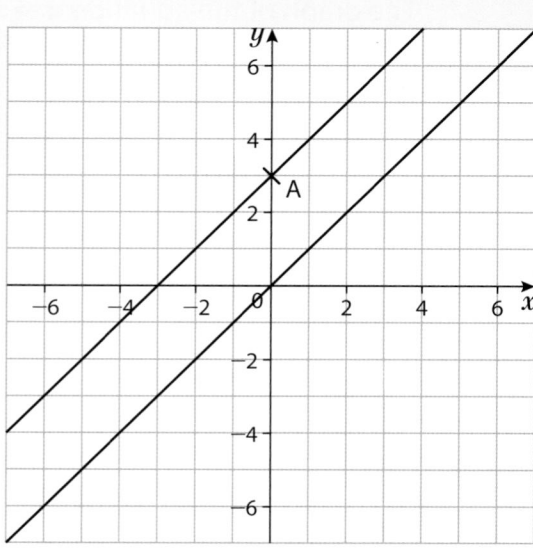

1. ABCD is a square and PQRS is a rectangle.

    a Write down the equation of the line:

        i AB   **ii** BC   **iii** CD

        iv AD   **v** QR   **vi** RS

    b For PQRS, write down the equation of:

        i the horizontal line of symmetry,

        ii the vertical line of symmetry.

    c For square ABCD, write down the equation of:

        i the horizontal line of symmetry,

        ii the vertical line of symmetry.

    d Write the equation of the line parallel to the x-axis passing through $(3, 4)$.

    e Write the equation of the line parallel to the y-axis passing through $(-2, 2)$.

2. This is the graph of $y = x$.

    a At what point does the graph cross the x-axis and y-axis?

    b At what angle is the graph of $y = x$ to the x-axis?

    c What is the gradient of the graph?

    d Which of these points are on the line $y = x$?

        $(-3, -3)$ $(-6, 6)$ $(2, -2)$ $(22, 22)$

    e Which of these equations have graphs parallel to the line $y = x$?

        $y = 2x + 3$ $y = x + 16$ $y = -x + 4$ $y = x - 9$

    f The graph of the equation $y = x + 21$ is parallel to the line $y = x$. Where does it cross the y-axis?

3. This is the graph of $y = x + 4$.

    a Where does the line cross the y-axis?

    b Where does the line cross the x-axis?

    c What is the gradient of the line?

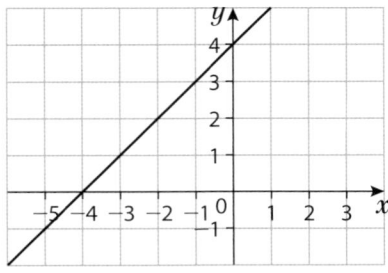

4. Sketch these graphs. Use a new grid for each graph.

    Mark on the graph any points that you use to help you with the sketch.

        a $y = x + 5$ **b** $y = x - 2$ **c** $y = 2x$ **d** $y = 2x + 3$

Extension problem

This graph is a line drawn through the points P $(-5, 5)$, Q $(-3, 3)$, R $(1, -1)$, S $(4, -4)$ and the origin $(0, 0)$.

For each point the y-coordinate is equal to minus the x-coordinate.

All other points on this line also have the y-coordinate equal to minus the x-coordinate. The equation of this line is $y = -x$.

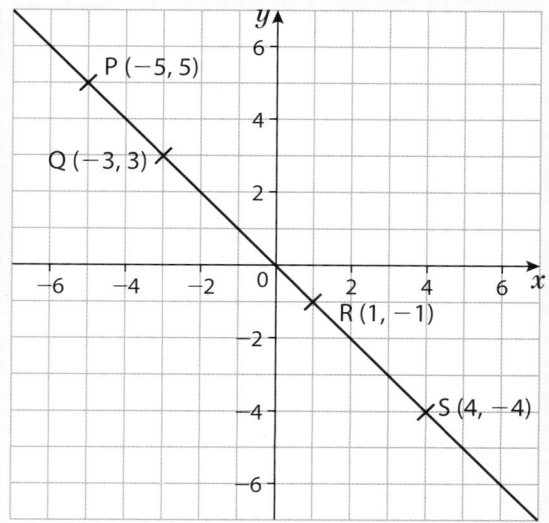

The graph of $y = -x + 3$ is a straight line parallel to $y = -x$ going through the point $(0, 3)$.

Another way to write the equation of this graph is $y + x = 3$.

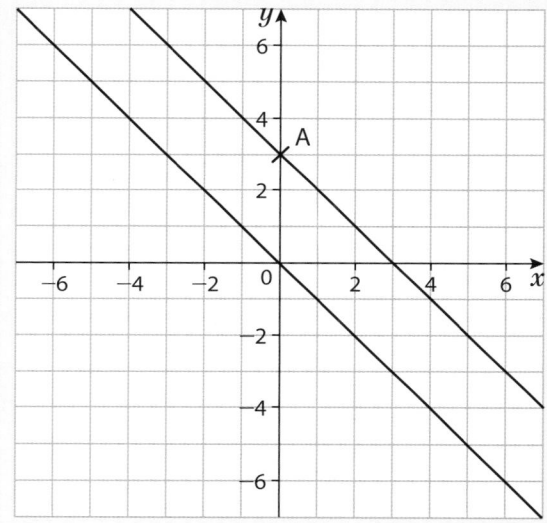

 5 Sketch these graphs. Use a new grid for each graph.

a $x + y = 10$	**b** $y - 2x = 5$	**c** $y - 4x = 2$	**d** $y - 3x - 6 = 0$
e $y - 2x + 4 = 0$	**f** $0 = y - x - 1$	**g** $2y - 6x = 4$	**h** $y = 0.5x + 2$

⊙ Points to remember

- ⊙ A sketch of a graph is a neat drawing using a pencil and ruler.
- ⊙ When you sketch a graph, look at the equation. Base your sketch on what you know about similar graphs.
- ⊙ The graph of $y = ax + b$ is a straight line.
- ⊙ The gradient of the graph is a and the intercept on the y-axis is $(0, b)$.

5 Drawing and interpreting linear graphs

This lesson will help you to draw and interpret straight-line graphs.

To draw a linear graph accurately, first work out the coordinates of three points on the graph.

For example, to draw $y = x + 7$, choose three values of x and work out the values of y.

Plot the points and draw the straight line through them. Continue the line to the edges of the grid.

x	0	1	2
y	7	8	9

Exercise 5

You will need graph paper, pencil and ruler for this exercise.

1. Draw an accurate graph of each equation. Think carefully about the scales on the axes.

   a $y = x$ **b** $y = x + 6$ **c** $y = 3x$ **d** $y = 2x - 1$

   e $y = 4x - 3$ **f** $y = -x$ **g** $y = -x + 5$ **h** $y = -2x - 3$

Extension problems

2. **a** Where does this graph cross the y-axis?

   b Write the coordinates of three points on the graph.

   c What is the gradient of the graph?

   d What is the equation of the graph?

   e What is the y-value of the point on the graph when $x = 4$?

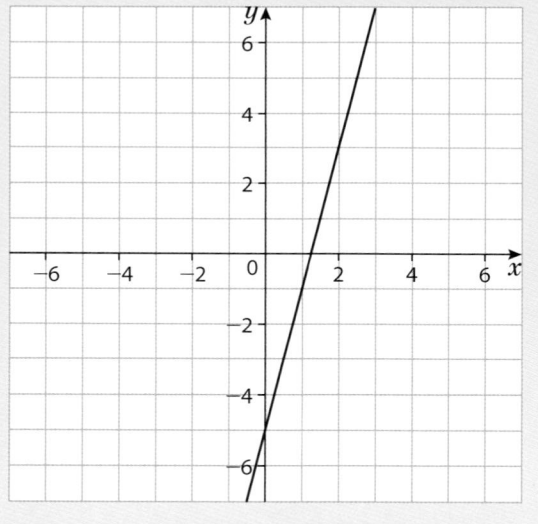

3. Work out the equation of each graph from the given coordinates.

   a

x	0	1	2
y	5	6	7

   b

x	-1	1	3
y	-8	2	12

⊙ Points to remember

- ⊙ To draw a straight-line graph accurately, plot three coordinate pairs.

- ⊙ A sketch of a graph is a neat drawing that shows some of its features.

6 Interpreting real-life graphs 2

This lesson will help you to interpret graphs that represent real situations.

Graphs show relationships between two quantities.
When the two quantities are directly proportional to one another, the graph is a straight line.

You can work out the average speed for a journey by dividing the distance travelled by the time taken.
For example, if a man drives 120 miles in 3 hours, the average speed for the journey is $120 \div 3 = 40$ miles per hour.

Exercise 6

You will need graph paper.

1 The Smiths are going for a week's holiday in Torquay.
   The graph shows part of their journey using average speed.

   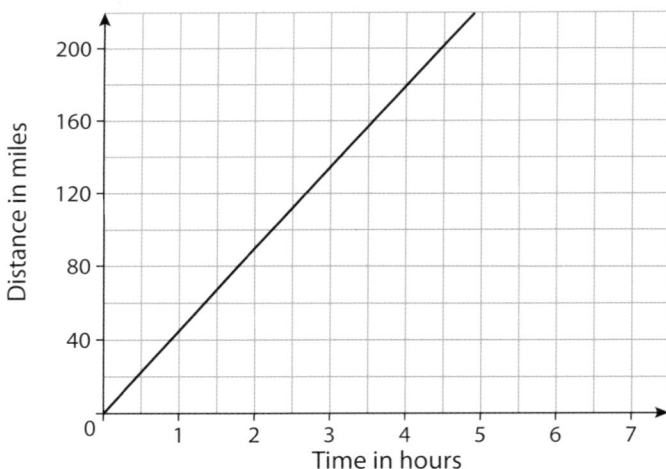

   They set off at 09:30.

   a Use the graph to estimate how far they have
      travelled after one hour.

   b Estimate how long it takes them to travel 180 miles.

   c What is the time when they have travelled 180 miles?

   d Estimate their average speed.

   e Their hotel in Torquay is 270 miles away.
      They continue to travel at the same average speed.
      At about what time will they arrive?

2 In the UK, petrol used to be sold in gallons. This graph converts litres to gallons.

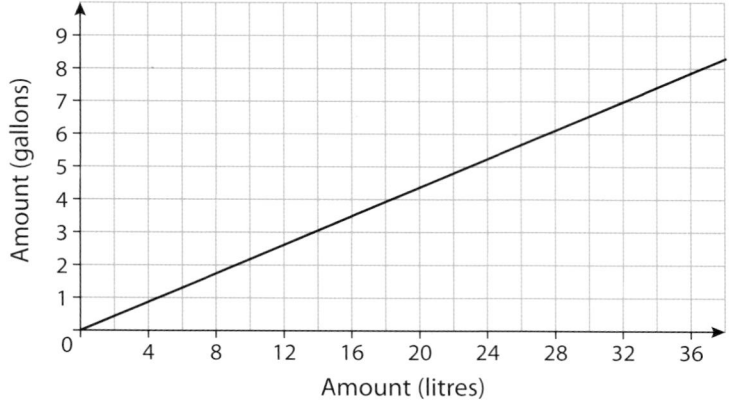

Amount (litres)

a Use the graph to estimate the number of gallons to 20 litres.

b Use the graph to estimate the number of litres to 1 gallon.

c Josh fills his car with petrol. The petrol tank takes 50 litres of fuel. About how many gallons is this?

d Josh has been told that his car should do 48 miles to a gallon of petrol. How many miles can he do on a full tank of petrol?

e There are 8 pints to a gallon. Estimate the number of pints in 14 litres.

f Nicola is buying a watering can. She can choose between one that holds 2 gallons and one that holds 10 litres. Which holds the most water?

3 This graph shows the cost of a length of stair carpet measured in metres.

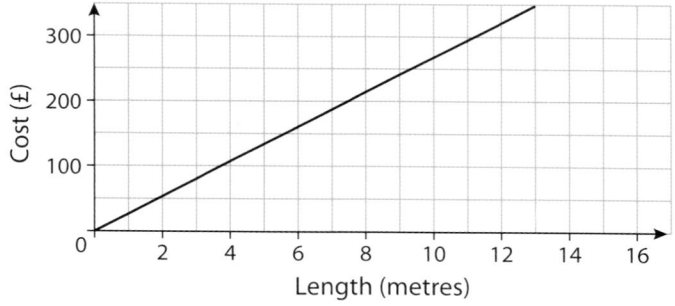

Length (metres)

a Use the graph to estimate the cost of 10 metres of stair carpet.

b Use the graph to estimate the cost of 16 metres of stair carpet.

c John paid £200 for his stair carpet. Estimate the length of carpet he bought.

4 a Use this table to draw an accurate graph on graph paper to show how to calculate Value Added Tax (VAT). Draw axes to show the VAT on goods up to £100.

Cost of goods	0	10	20
VAT at 17.5%	0	£1.75	£3.50

b Use your graph to estimate the VAT on goods worth £50.

c A buyer paid £14.70 VAT. Use your graph to estimate the value of the goods that she bought.

d Dan bought a watch at a duty-free shop at an airport for £96. Estimate how much VAT he saved.

5 A mobile phone company charges
25 pence per minute for calls.

Number of minutes	0	20	40
Cost of calls in pence	0	500	1000

   a Use the table to draw an
accurate graph on graph paper to show how to calculate the cost of using the phone.
Draw axes to show the costs of calls up to 250 minutes.

   b Use your graph to estimate the cost of 55 minutes of calls.

   c Becky made some calls that cost her £62.50. Estimate the number of minutes she used.

Points to remember

⊙ To draw a straight-line graph accurately, plot three coordinate points.
⊙ When you draw or interpret graphs of real situations, take care with the
scales on the axes.

7 Word problems

This lesson will help you to use algebra to solve word problems.

You can use algebra to help you solve problems.

First read the question and identify the unknown quantity.
Represent the unknown quantity by a letter. Form an equation and solve it.

When you have solved the problem, check that you have answered the original question.

Exercise 7

1 In these questions let the unknown number be n.

   a I am thinking of a number. I double it and add 7. I get 12. What is my number?

   b I am thinking of a number. I multiply it by 3 and subtract 8. I get 13. What is my number?

   c I am thinking of a number. I divide it by 7 and add 6. I get 10. What is my number?

   d I am thinking of a number. I divide it by 6 and subtract 9. I get 1. What is my number?

   e I am thinking of a number. I multiply it by 3, add 8 and multiply by 5. I get 55.
What is my number?

   f I am thinking of a number. I multiply it by 4, subtract 7 and multiply by 6. I get 30.
What is my number?

2 a The sum of three consecutive whole numbers is 636.
      What are the three numbers?

   b The sum of five consecutive whole numbers is 85.
      What are the five numbers?

   c The mean of seven consecutive whole numbers is 203.
      What are the seven numbers?

3 Emma and Alex are saving to go on holiday.
   Emma has saved three times as much as Alex.
   Together Emma and Alex have saved £108.
   How much has Alex saved?

4 Ramesh gets £15 a week pocket money.
   He saves three times as much as he spends.
   He also pays £3 a week to belong to the football club.
   How much does Ramesh spend each week?

5 Ben is delivering boxes to the top floor of a building.
   The lift can take a maximum load of 450 kg.
   Each box weighs 9 kg and Ben weighs 72 kg.
   What is the maximum number of boxes that Ben can take in the lift?

6 Nicki's sister is 9 years old.
   Their mother is 48 years old.
   If you add three times Nicki's age to her
   sister's age then you get their mother's age.
   How old is Nicki?

7 Jade's jeans cost £8 more than Amber's jeans.
   Eva's jeans cost twice as much as Jade's jeans.
   Altogether the girls spent £124 on their jeans.
   How much did each girl spend?

8 David travels 2 miles further than Zak to get to school.
   Paul travels three times as far as David.
   Altogether they travel 10.5 miles.
   How far does each boy travel to school?

Extension problem

9 a The sum of two consecutive even numbers is 266.
      What are the two numbers?

b The sum of three consecutive multiples of 3 is 162.
What are the three numbers?

c The result of multiplying a number by 5 and subtracting 8 is the same as multiplying the number by 3 and adding 6.
What is the number?

Points to remember

- Read word problems carefully.
- Define any letters you will use by saying, for example, 'Let x be …'.
- Form an equation and solve it, showing your working.
- Check that your answer fits the problem.

8 Geometrical problems

This lesson will help you to use algebra to solve measurement problems.

If a problem involves a shape, think about the shape's properties.

The properties might include equal or parallel sides, the sum of the angles, and so on.

Or you may need to use a formula for the perimeter or area of the shape.

Exercise 8

The diagrams in this exercise are not drawn to scale.
Use your calculator to solve problems 1–4.

1. The area of a rectangle is 99.2 cm². One side measures 6.4 cm.
What is the length of the other side?

2. The area of a triangle is 27 cm². The base measures 12 cm.
What is its perpendicular height?

3. The perimeter of a regular heptagon is 57.4 cm.
What is the length of one of its sides?

④ The sum of the lengths of the edges of a cube is 114 cm.
How long is each edge?

Use algebra to solve these problems. Show your working.

⑤ Work out the sizes of the three angles in each of these triangles.

a
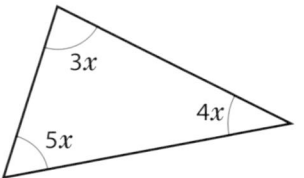

b
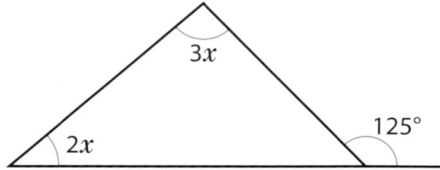

c
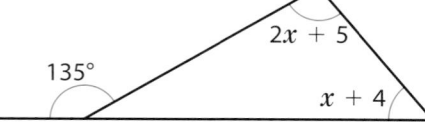

d
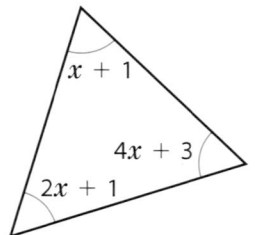

⑥ The perimeter of this hexagon is 89 cm.
Work out the length of each side.

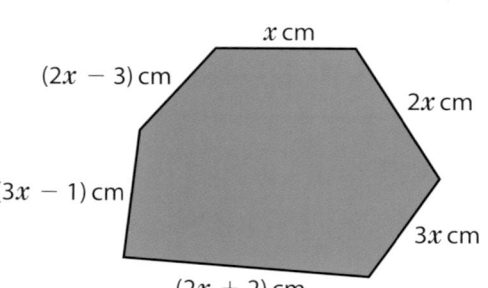

⑦ The lengths on the diagram are in centimetres.
The area of the parallelogram is 105 cm².
Work out the height of the parallelogram.

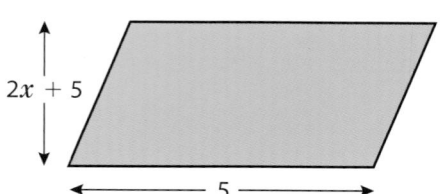

⑧ Work out the sizes of the four angles in each of these quadrilaterals.

a
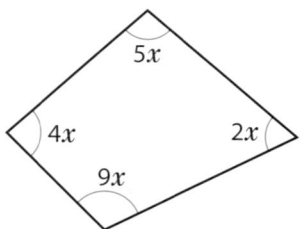

b
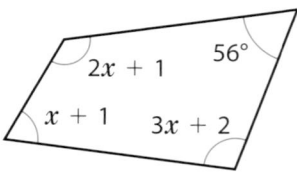

⑨ In a rectangle the ratio length : width is 3 : 1.
The perimeter of the rectangle is 48 cm.
How long are its sides?

10 The base of an isosceles triangle is a third of the length of each of the other two sides.
The perimeter of the triangle is 84 cm.
What are the lengths of the sides?

Extension problems

11 Work out the size of each exterior angle of this pentagon.

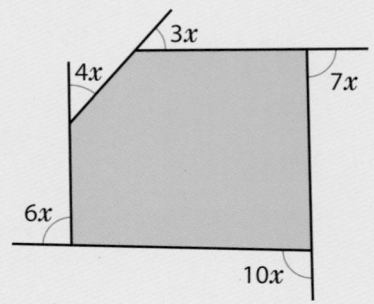

12 Work out the size of each interior angle of this octagon.

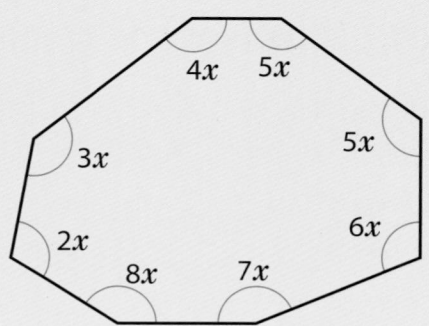

13 The lengths on the diagram are in centimetres.
The area of the rectangle is equal to the area of the triangle.
Work out the height of the triangle.

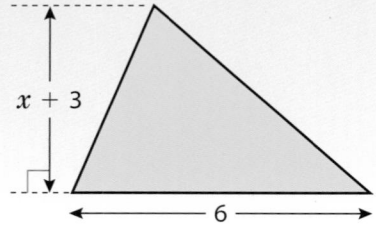 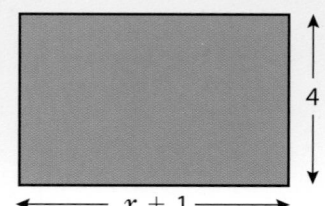

⊙ Points to remember

- ⊙ Take time to read questions carefully.
- ⊙ Define any letters you use by saying, for example, 'Let x be …'.
- ⊙ Form an algebraic expression, equation or formula.
- ⊙ Set out each step of working.
- ⊙ Go back and make sure that you have answered the original question.
- ⊙ Check that your answers are sensible.

How well are you doing?

can you:

- simplify expressions?
- factorise expressions?
- solve linear equations?
- sketch, draw and interpret linear graphs?
- solve problems using algebra?

Expressions, equations and graphs

1 Factorise this expression: $9x - 24$

2 *2006 level 6*

Multiply out this expression. Write your answer as simply as possible.

$$5(x + 2) + 3(7 + x)$$

3 *2007 level 6*

Solve this equation: $2(2n + 5) = 12$

4 *2006 level 6*

Solve this equation: $3y + 14 = 5y + 1$

5 *2005 level 6*

I think of a number. I multiply this number by 8, then subtract 66.
The result is twice the number that I was thinking of.
What is the number I was thinking of?

6 *1999 level 6*

The shape has 3 identical white tiles and
3 identical green tiles.

One of the angles is 70°.

Calculate the size of angle m.

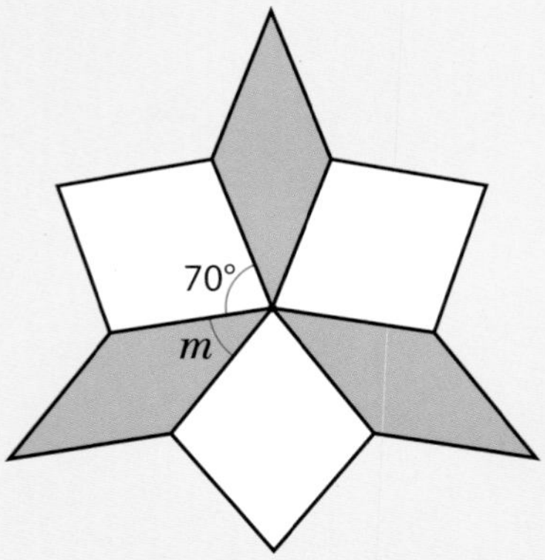

7 *1998 level 6*

Look at this diagram.

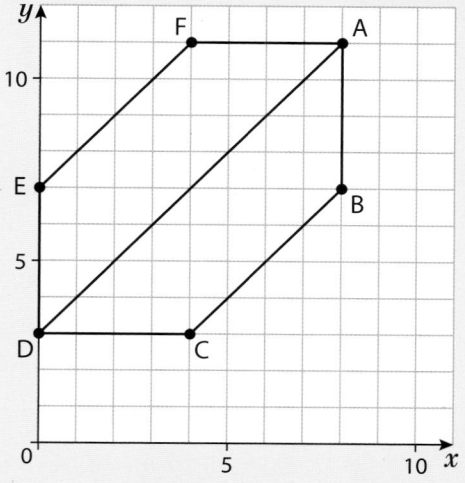

a The line through points A and F has the equation $y = 11$.

What is the equation of the line through points A and B?

b The line through points A and D has the equation $y = x + 3$.

What is the equation of the line through points F and E?

c What is the equation of the line through points B and C?

8 *Y8 Optional Test level 6*

Companies charge different amounts to connect people to the Internet. The graph shows how much three companies charge each month.

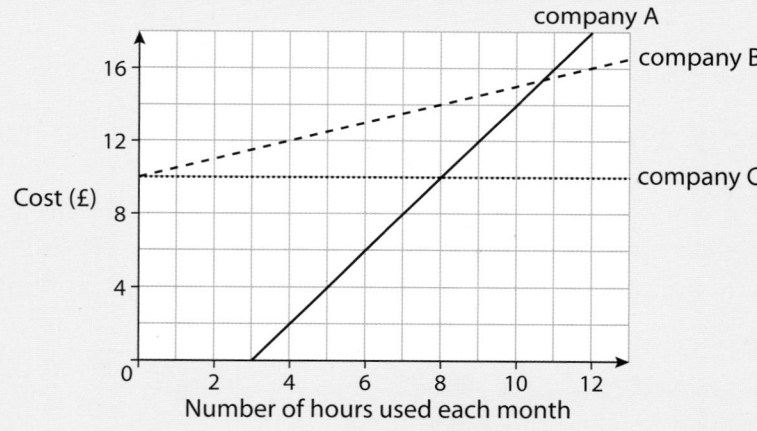

a Copy and complete these sentences.

Company A: The first … hours used every month are free, then they charge £2 for every hour.

Company B: They charge £10 each month, with an extra charge of …p for each hour used.

b Write a sentence to describe the cost each month for company C.

Solving problems

This unit will help you to:

- investigate number problems;
- work logically to find solutions;
- appreciate how different cultures have influenced the development and history of mathematics;
- appreciate that mathematics can be a recreational activity;
- learn about some important problems from the past.

1 Place value puzzles

This lesson will help you to investigate number problems and work logically to find solutions.

Did you know that...?

The Chinese have been writing numbers for thousands of years. Tortoise shells dating from 1500 BCE have been found in China. Numerals scratched on the shells show, for example, the number of prisoners taken in battle or the animals killed on hunts.

Much later, about 400 BCE, the Chinese invented the **counting board**. Numbers were represented by little rods made from bamboo or ivory. The old numerals were changed so that they looked like the little rods.

—	=	≡	≣	≣	⊥	⊥	⊥	⊥
1	2	3	4	5	6	7	8	9

Chinese numerals from 400 BC

The new Chinese numerals formed a place value system like the one we use today but without a symbol for zero. It was the most advanced number system in the world at the time.

The Chinese **abacus** or *suan pan* was not invented until around the 14th century.

The *suan pan*

1 You may find it helpful to use a set of 1–9 digit cards for these calculations. Try to solve the problems without using a calculator.

Arrange the nine cards to complete these calculations. In each problem, use each of the cards once and only once. Write the completed calculations in your book.

a

b

c

d

2 Find a partner and play **Make the most**. You need two sets of 1–9 digit cards.

Rules

- Put the two sets of digit cards face down on the table and shuffle them around.
- Take six cards each.
- Each player uses their six cards to make two products:

  ☐☐ × ☐   ☐☐ × ☐

  Work out the products. Add them together.
- The player who has the largest total scores one point.
- The winner is the first player to get 5 points.

Example

If you have these cards:

2 3 3 5 7 9

you could make:
  72 × 5 and 93 × 3
Work out each product.
  72 × 5 = 360
  93 × 3 = 279
Add them together.
  360 + 279 = 639

③ Take a set of 1–9 digit cards.

| 1 | 2 | 3 | 4 | 5 | 6 | 7 | 8 | 9 |

Use all the cards to make three 3-digit numbers.
Do it so that each of the 3-digit numbers is a multiple of 11.

Points to remember

When you solve problems, remember to:

⊙ be systematic;

⊙ keep a careful record of your findings as you work;

⊙ look for patterns in your findings and draw on these to come to some conclusions that you can explain and justify.

2 Early history of numbers and counting

This lesson will help you to appreciate how different cultures have influenced the development and history of mathematics and to learn about some important problems from the past.

Did you know that...?

The ancient Egyptians used an interesting method for multiplication. It is shown in the **Rhind papyrus**.

The papyrus was written around 1650 BCE by a scribe called Ahmes, who copied a document that was 200 years older.

The papyrus is named after the Scot Henry Rhind, who bought it in Egypt in 1858. It was said to have been found during illegal excavations.

The Rhind papyrus

The Rhind papyrus is very large. It is 33 centimetres tall and over 5 metres long. It is kept at the British Museum in London.

A smaller but older papyrus of a similar kind is kept in the Museum of Fine Arts in Moscow.

The Egyptian method of multiplication is based on doubling.

Assume that we want to multiply 59 by 41.
We take the larger number, 59, and double it repeatedly.

There is no need to double beyond 32 lots of 59, since the next double would be 64 lots of 59, which is more than 41 lots of 59.

$$59 \times 41$$
$$59 \times 1 = 59$$
$$59 \times 2 = 118$$
$$59 \times 4 = 236$$
$$59 \times 8 = 472$$
$$59 \times 16 = 944$$
$$59 \times 32 = 1888$$

Now express 41 as a sum of powers of 2:
$41 = 32 + 8 + 1.$

$$41 - 32 = 9$$
$$9 - 8 = 1$$

Take the products above that correspond to 32, 8 and 1, and add them.

We see that the answer is $59 \times 41 = 2419.$

$$59 \times 1 = 59$$
$$59 \times 8 = 472$$
$$59 \times 32 = 1888$$
$$59 \times 41 = 2419$$

Exercise 2

1 **a** Work out these calculations using the Egyptian method.
   i 56×42 **ii** 25×81 **iii** 72^2

   b Without using a calculator, use your own method to work out 46×37.

   c Which method do you prefer, your own method or the Egyptian method? Explain why.

2 **a** Without using a calculator, use your own method to work out $425 + 348$.

   b Here is a method that some people use for addition.
   Discuss with a partner how it works.
   Try the method by adding 436 and 287.

   c Which method do you prefer, your own method or the other method? Explain why.

```
  384
+249
 500
 120
  13
 633
```

3 **a** Without using a calculator, use your own method to work out $634 - 457$.

   b Here is a method that some people use for subtraction.
   It uses negative numbers.
   Discuss with a partner how the negative numbers are shown and how the method works.
   Try the method by working out $724 - 439$.

   c Which method do you prefer, your method or the other method? Explain why.

```
  453
-287
 234
 166
```

Did you know that...?

The numerals that we use today are called **Hindu-Arabic numerals**. They evolved from the numerals used in India a long time ago. Traders brought the Indian numerals to the Arab world, and from there they came to Europe.

On the right you can see Babylonian numerals, Roman numerals, Hindu numerals, Arabic numerals and the Hindu-Arabic numerals that are used today in almost all countries of the world.

 4 The Hindu-Arabic system of numerals is very efficient.

It uses only ten symbols, the digits 0, 1, 2, 3, 4, 5, 6, 7, 8 and 9, which are used to write any number.

For example, the numerals 3 and 8 are all that are needed to write these numbers:

3, 8, 33, 38, 88

How many different three-digit numbers can you write using only the numerals 3 and 8?

 ## Points to remember

⊙ You can often work out complex calculations by breaking them into simpler calculations.
⊙ When you calculate, try to choose the most efficient method.

3 Missing digits and operations

This lesson will help you to enjoy mathematics as a recreational activity and work logically to find solutions.

Exercise 3

Questions 1−3 are examples of puzzles in which you are given the answer to one calculation and must use it to work out the answer to another calculation.

Do the working in your head and write only the answers.

290 | N4.5 *Solving problems*

Did you know that...?

There are lots of mathematical puzzles in which some of the digits of a calculation are missing and you have to find out what they are.

Sam Loyd (1841–1911), America's greatest puzzlist, invented the division problem on the right. He was also brilliant at chess, conjuring and ventriloquy! The answer to the puzzle is $638\,897 \div 749 = 853$.

```
          *53
   **9)6*8***
      ***2
      *9**
      **4*
      **4*
      ****
```

1. Rebecca knows that $18 \times 19 = 342$.
   Write the answers to these calculations.

   a 180×19 **b** 1800×19 **c** 180×190
   d 18×1.9 **e** 1.8×1.9 **f** 17×19

2. David knows that $28 \times 36 = 1008$.
   Write the answers to these calculations.

   a 56×36 **b** 56×72 **c** 28×18
   d 14×18 **e** 28×37 **f** 29×36

3. Laura knows that $7 \times 11 \times 13 = 1001$.
   Write the answers to these calculations.

   a What is $1001 \div 7$?

   b What is $1001 \div 11$?

   c What is $1001 \div 13$?

   d Which is bigger: $0.7 \times 1.1 \times 1.3$ or 1? Explain why.

   e What is $456 \times 7 \times 11 \times 13$? Explain how you worked it out.

Questions 4–6 are examples of missing-digit or missing-operation puzzles.
Use your calculator to help you to solve them.

4. In these problems, each ■ represents a missing digit.
   Work out what the missing digits are. Write the calculations in your book.

   a ■2■ + ■3 = 316 **b** ■7■ − ■4 = 719 **c** ■9 × 1■ = 228
   d (3■)² = 11■6 **e** 93 × 8■ = 7■■8 **f** 1■2 × 4■ = 5940

5. In these problems, each ● represents a missing operation.
   Work out what the missing operations are. Write the calculations in your book.

   a (78 ● 45) ● 37 = 4551 **b** (1430 ● 65) ● 78 = 100
   c 480 ● (86 ● 71) = 32 **d** 54 ● (12 ● 17) = 258
   e 18 ● (95 ● 56) = 702 **f** 208 ● (156 ● 12) = 195

6 Choose from these numbers: 18, 45, 67, 72, 93.
Work out which number goes in each box. Write the calculations in your book.

a ($\square \times \square$) − $\square$ = 717

b ($\square \div \square$) × $\square$ = 372

c $\square$ − ($\square + \square$) = 30

d $\square$ + ($\square - \square$) = 121

Did you know that...?

In some calculation puzzles the digits 0 to 9 are represented by letters and you have to work out the value of each letter.
A famous example was published in the *Strand Magazine* in July 1924 by **Henry Dudeney**, a British inventor of mathematical puzzles.

```
  S E N D
+ M O R E
─────────
M O N E Y
```

The solution to this puzzle is:

O = 0, M = 1, Y = 2, E = 5, N = 6, D = 7, R = 8, S = 9.

We can see straight away that M must be 1, since it is the only carry-over possible in the sum of S and M. So S must be 8 or 9, because those are the only values that can produce a carry when added to M = 1 (and possibly a carry). And so on..

Extension problems

7 In these puzzles, each letter represents one of the digits from 0 to 9.
Work out what the letters stand for. It is usually best to start from the left-hand end.

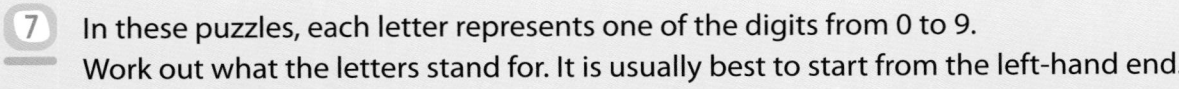

a
```
    N O
    N O
+ T O O
───────
L A T E
```

b
```
    E A T
+ T H A T
─────────
A P P L E
```

c
```
    U N
    U N
+ N E U F
─────────
O N Z E
```

Points to remember

- Decide which information, given or needed, may be useful in solving the problem.
- Look for patterns and relationships in the information that you are given.
- Use your knowledge of number facts and place value to help to solve missing-digit and missing-operation problems.

How well are you doing?

Can you:
- investigate number problems?
- work logically to find solutions?

Solving problems (no calculator)

1 Nadia has four number cards. She says:
'Each card shows a different positive whole number.
I am going to take a card at random.
It is certain that the card will show a number less than 10.
It is impossible that the card will show an odd number.'
What numbers are on the cards?

2 On the board, a teacher has written $12 \times 16 = 192$.
Write the answers to these calculations.

  a 120×16 **b** 1200×16 **c** 120×160

  d 12×1.6 **e** 1.2×1.6 **f** 12×16

3 I think of a number, square it, and subtract 5. The answer is 31.
What is my number?

4 *2003 level 6*
Here are six number cards.

1   **2**   **3**   **4**   **5**   **6**

  a Arrange these six cards to make the calculations below.

$$1164 = \square\square\square + \square\square\square$$

$$750 = \square\square\square + \square\square\square$$

  b Now arrange the six cards to make a difference of 115.

$$115 = \square\square\square - \square\square\square$$

5 *2006 Mental Test level 5*

The answer to 7×58 is 406.

Use this information to help you work out 3.5×58.

6 *2006 level 5*

    a Show that 9×28 is 252.

    b What is 27×28? You can use part **a** to help you.

Solving problems (calculator allowed)

7 Here are some digit cards from 1 to 6.

$$\boxed{1}\ \boxed{2}\ \boxed{3}\ \boxed{4}\ \boxed{5}\ \boxed{6}$$

Use all the cards to make this product.

$$\boxed{}\,\boxed{}\ \times\ \boxed{}\ =\ \boxed{}\,\boxed{}\,\boxed{}$$

Revision unit 1

> **This unit will help you to:**
>
> ⊙ revise the work you have done so far during the year;
>
> ⊙ answer test questions.
>
> Many of the exercise questions are from National Curriculum test papers (SATs).
> In Paper 1, calculators are not allowed. In Paper 2, you may use a calculator.

1 Place value

This lesson will help you to understand decimal place value, to multiply and divide by 0.1 and 0.01 and to find products such as 6×0.7 and 8×0.03.

Multiplying or dividing by 10, 100 or 1000

To multiply by 10, 100 or 1000, move the digits one, two or three places to the left.

To divide by 10, 100 or 1000, move the digits one, two or three places to the right.

For example: $7.36 \times 1000 = 7360$ $\qquad$ $32.8 \div 100 = 0.328$

Multiplying by 0.1 or 0.01

Multiplying by 0.1 is equivalent to multiplying by $\frac{1}{10}$ or dividing by 10.

Multiplying by 0.01 is equivalent to multiplying by $\frac{1}{100}$ or dividing by 100.

For example: $5.9 \times 0.1 = 0.59$ $\qquad$ $5300 \times 0.01 = 53$

Dividing by 0.1 or 0.01

Dividing by 0.1 is equivalent to dividing by $\frac{1}{10}$ or multiplying by 10.

Dividing by 0.01 is equivalent to dividing by $\frac{1}{100}$ or multiplying by 100.

For example: $5.9 \div 0.1 = 59$ $\qquad$ $5300 \div 0.01 = 530\,000$

Exercise 1

Do these **without using a calculator**.

(1) Copy and complete these calculations.

    a 9070 ÷ 100 = …   b 0.7 × … = 700

    c 10.1 × … = 101   d 8006 × 0.001 = …

    e 3 ÷ 0.1 = …   f 4600 × 1000 = …

    g 62 030 ÷ 1000 = …   h 230 ÷ … = 2.3

    i 4 ÷ … = 0.004   j 5.8 × 0.01 = …

(2) Write down the numbers that the arrows are pointing to on the scale.

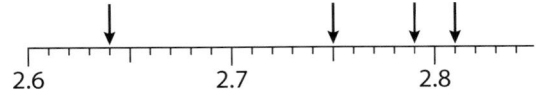

(3) Write these in order, smallest first.

    a 7.53, 7.5, 7.6, 7.65, 7.56   b 8.9, 8.02, 8.09, 8.2, 8.29, 8.92

    c 0.412, 0.421, 1.124, 1.214, 0.241   d 6.067, 6.006, 6.07, 6.077, 6.076

(4) Which pairs of these multiply together to make 1 million?

    10 100 1000 10 000 100 000

(5) Write the number that is ten less than one hundred thousand.

⦿ Points to remember

⊙ Multiplying or dividing by a power of 10 involves moving digits left or right.

2 Solving calculation problems

This lesson will help you to solve number problems.

The questions in this exercise are from the national tests. When you solve them:

⊙ read the question carefully, then write down the calculation that you need to do;

⊙ check that the answer is reasonable in the context of the question;

⊙ indicate your answer clearly, including units where appropriate.

Exercise 2

Answer questions 1−3 **without using your calculator.**

1 *2002 level 4*

A car park charges 15p for 8 minutes.
How much does it cost to park for 40 minutes?

2 *2000 level 5*

a The entrance fee for a museum is £1.20 per person.
240 people paid the entrance fee on Monday.
How much money is that altogether?

b The museum took £600 in entrance fees on Friday.
How many people paid to visit the museum on Friday?

3 *1997 level 5*

a A shop sells plants at 95p each. Find the cost of 35 plants.

b Trees are £17 each.
Mr Bailey has £250. He wants to buy as many trees as possible.
How many trees can Mr Bailey buy?

You may **use a calculator** for questions 3−10. Remember to show your working.

4 *2006 level 4*

A bottle contains 250 ml of cough mixture.

One adult and one child need to take cough
mixture 4 times a day every day for 5 days.

Will there be enough cough mixture in the bottle?
Explain your answer.

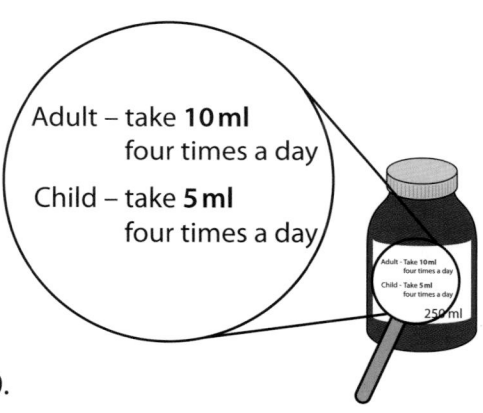

Adult – take **10 ml**
four times a day

Child – take **5 ml**
four times a day

5 *2004 Progress Test level 4*

a Gold ribbon costs 60p for one metre. Tom has £2.40.
How many metres of gold ribbon can he buy?

b Blue ribbon costs 40p for one metre. Nicola buys $3\frac{1}{2}$ metres.
How much does this cost?

6 *Level 4*

A meal in a restaurant costs the same for each person.
For 15 people the total cost is £360.75. What is the total cost for 18 people?

7 *2003 level 5*

A glass holds 225 ml.
An adult needs about 1.8 litres of water each day to stay healthy.
How many glasses is that? Show your working.

(8) *2006 level 5*

A shop sells toilet rolls.
You can buy them in packs of 9 or packs of 6.

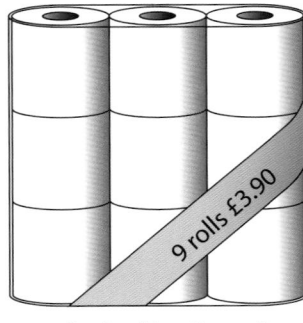
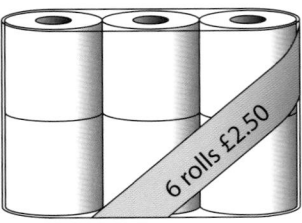

Pack of 9 toilet rolls
£3.90

Pack of 6 toilet rolls
£2.50

Which pack gives you better value for money?
You must show your working.

Extension problem

 2005 level 6

Each year, there is a tennis competition in Australia and another one in France.
The table shows how much money was paid to the winner of the men's competition in each country in 2002.

Country	Money
Australia	1 000 000 Australian dollars (£1 = 2.70 Australian dollars)
France	780 000 euros (£1 = 1.54 euros)

Which country paid more money? Show your working.

 Points to remember

When you solve problems:

⊙ read the question carefully;

⊙ write down the calculation that you need to do and show your working;

⊙ check that the answer is reasonable by fitting it to the question.

3 Expressions and sequences

This lesson will help you to generate sequences, simplify expressions and substitute numbers into expressions.

$3n + 5$ is called an **algebraic expression**.

An algebraic expression must contain at least one letter.

Each part of an expression is called a **term** of the expression.
For the expression $3n + 5$ the terms are $3n$ and $+5$.

The value of an expression can be worked out if the value of each letter is known.

Example 1

Work out the value of the expression $3n + 5$ when $n = 10$.

$3n + 5 = 3 \times n + 5$

When $n = 10$, $3n + 5 = 3 \times 10 + 5$
$$= 30 + 5$$
$$= 35$$

In the expression $3x + 2x + 6$, the terms $3x$ and $+2x$ are called **like terms** because they use the same letter.

$3x$ is $x + x + x$ and $2x$ is $x + x$.
The like terms $3x$ and $+2x$ can be combined.
They become $x + x + x + x + x$, which is written as $5x$.

So the expression $3x + 2x + 6$ can be simplified to $5x + 6$.

$5x$ and $+6$ are not like terms so $5x$ and $+6$ cannot be combined.

Example 2

Simplify $3x + 2y - 3y + 5x$

Collect like terms together to write

$3x + 2y - 3y + 5x = 3x + 5x + 2y - 3y$
$$= 8x - y$$

A **sequence** is a pattern of shapes or numbers that follow a rule.

Here is a sequence of numbers: 3, 5, 7, 9, …

The numbers in the sequence are called **terms** of the sequence.

Example 3

Here is a sequence of numbers: 2, 5, 8, 11, …

The rule for finding the nth term of this sequence is:

$$n\text{th term} = 3n - 1$$

Find the 20th term of the sequence.

To find the 20th term, substitute the value $n = 20$.
The 20th term is $3 \times 20 - 1 = 60 - 1 = 59$

Exercise 3

1 *1995 level 5*

Jo is planting a small orchard.
She plants cherry trees, plum trees, apple trees and pear trees.
n stands for the number of cherry trees Jo plants.

  a Jo plants the same number of plum trees as cherry trees.
    How many plum trees does she plant?

  b Jo plants twice as many apple trees as cherry trees.
    How many apple trees does she plant?

  c Jo plants 7 more pear trees than cherry trees.
    How many pear trees does she plant?

  d How many trees does Jo plant altogether?
    Write your answer as simply as possible.

2 *Year 8 Optional Test level 5*

Simplify these expressions.

  a $n + 1 + 2$ **b** $n + 3n$ **c** $3n + 5 + 4n - 2$

3 *Year 8 Optional Test level 5*

Copy the table and complete the missing values.

x	$x + 1$	$2x$	$2x - 1$	$2(x - 1)$
3		6		
	9			
			29	

4 *2001 level 5*

Copy the cards. Join pairs of algebraic expressions that have the same value when $a = 3$, $b = 2$ and $c = 6$.

One pair is joined for you.

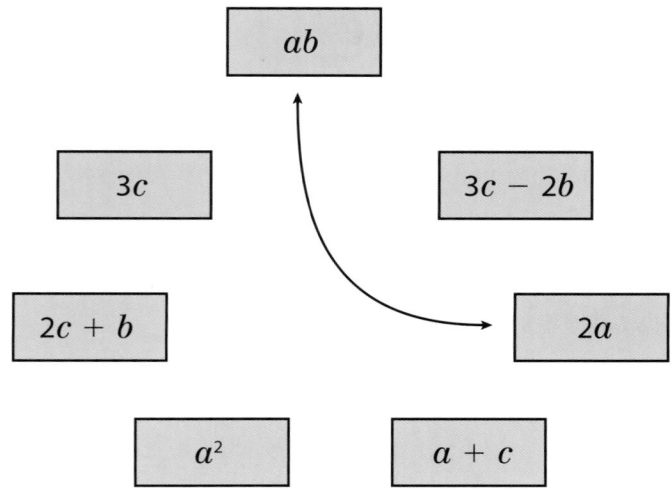

5 *2005 level 4*

Here is a sequence of shapes made with blue and white tiles.

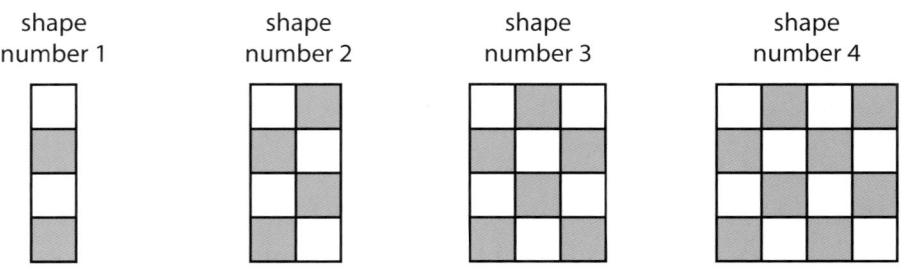

> The number of blue tiles   = 2 × the shape number
>
> The number of white tiles = 2 × the shape number

a   Altogether, how many tiles will be in shape number 5?

b   Altogether, how many tiles will be in shape number 15?

c   Copy and complete the statement below.

> The total number of tiles = … × the shape number

6 *1999 level 5*

Jeff makes a sequence of patterns with red and yellow triangular tiles.

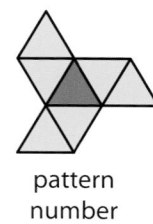
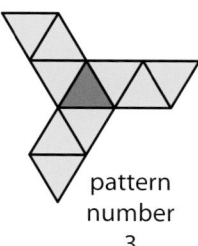

pattern
number
1

pattern
number
2

pattern
number
3

The rule for finding the number of tiles in pattern number N in Jeff's sequence is:

number of tiles $= 1 + 3N$

a The 1 in this rule represents the red tile.
What does the $3N$ represent?

b Jeff makes pattern number 12 in his sequence.
How many red tiles and how many yellow tiles does he use?

c Jeff uses 61 tiles altogether to make a pattern in his sequence.
What is the number of the pattern he makes?

d Barbara makes a sequence of patterns with hexagonal tiles.

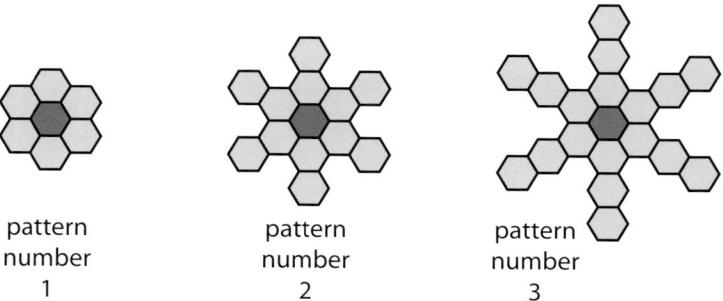

pattern
number
1

pattern
number
2

pattern
number
3

Each pattern in Barbara's sequence has 1 dark blue tile in the middle.
Each new pattern has 6 more light blue tiles than the pattern before.

Write the rule for finding the number of tiles in pattern number N in Barbara's sequence.

◉ Points to remember

- ◉ A **term** is one or more numbers or letters combined by multiplication or division.
- ◉ **Like terms** have the same combination of letters. For example, $2a$ and $5a$ and a are all like terms.
- ◉ An **expression** is one or more terms combined by addition or subtraction. You can simplify an expression by collecting like terms.
- ◉ A **sequence** of numbers follows a pattern. You can find a rule to work out each term in a sequence.

4 Perimeter, area and volume

This lesson will help you to calculate the perimeter and area of 2D shapes and find the volume and surface area of cuboids.

The **perimeter** of a two-dimensional shape is the total distance around the edge or boundary of the shape.

Example 1

Here is a diagram of a garden.
All the corners are right angles.
What is the perimeter of the garden?

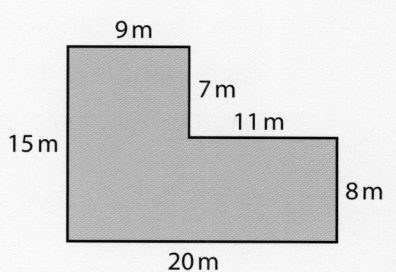

The perimeter is the sum of the lengths of all the sides:

15 m + 9 m + 7 m + 11 m + 8 m + 20 m = 70 m

Area uses square units, such as cm², mm².

- ☉ **Area of a rectangle** = base × height
- ☉ **Area of a triangle** = $\frac{1}{2}$ × base × perpendicular height
- ☉ **Area of a parallelogram** = base × perpendicular height

To find the area of a **compound shape**, split the shape up with straight lines into rectangles and triangles.

Example 2

Work out the area of the trapezium.

The trapezium can be split into a triangle and a rectangle.

The rectangle is 7 cm by 10 cm.

The triangle has a base of (12 − 7) cm or 5 cm and a height of 10 cm.

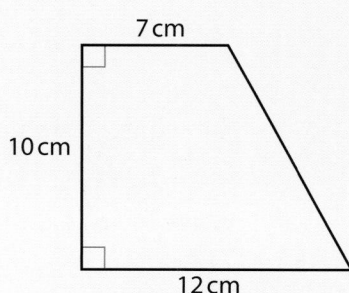

Area of rectangle = base × height
= 7 × 10
= 70 cm²

Area of triangle = $\frac{1}{2}$ × base × height
= $\frac{1}{2}$ × 5 × 10
= 25 cm²

Area of trapezium = 70 + 25
= 95 cm²

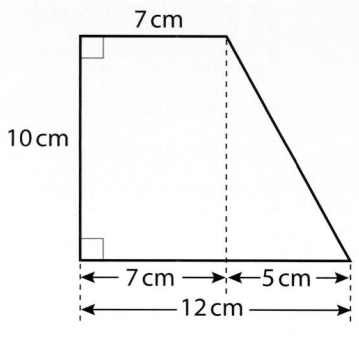

Exercise 4A

1 *2002 level 4*

   a What is the area of this rectangle?

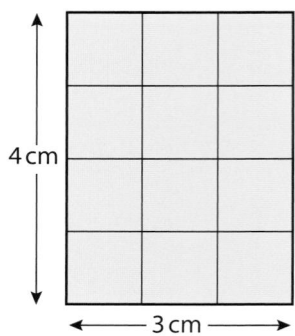

   b I use the rectangle to make four triangles.
       Each triangle is the same size.
       What is the area of one of the triangles?

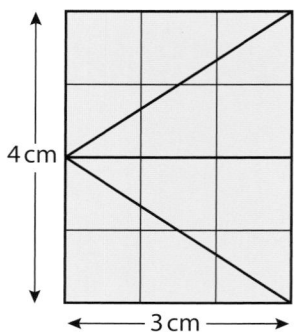

   c I use the four triangles to make a trapezium.
       What is the area of the trapezium?

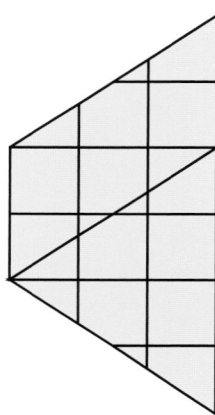

2 *2001 level 5*

I have a square piece of card.

I cut along the dashed line to make two pieces of card.

Do the two pieces of card have the same area?
Write **Yes** or **No**.
Explain your answer.

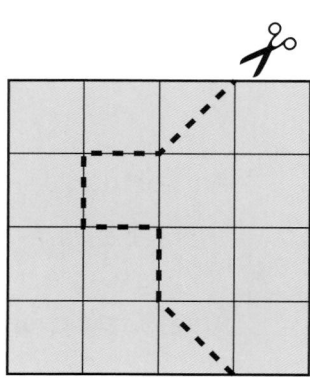

3 *2007 level 5*

Here is a rectangle.

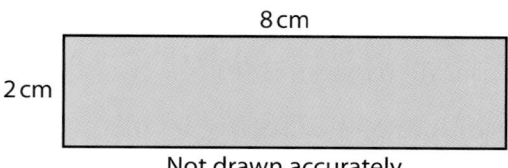

8 cm

2 cm

Not drawn accurately

   a A square has the same area as this rectangle. What is the side length of this square?

   b A different square has the same perimeter as this rectangle. What is the side length of this square?

4 *2004 level 5*

The square and the rectangle below have the same area.

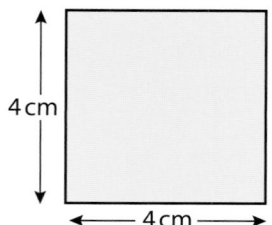

4 cm

4 cm

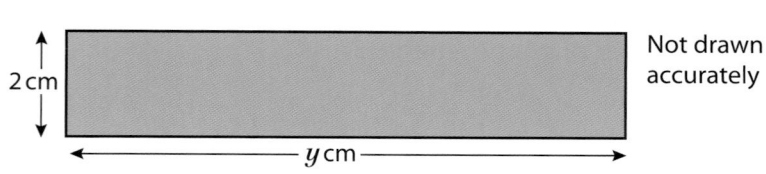

2 cm

Not drawn accurately

y cm

Work out the value of y.

5 *Year 8 Optional Test level 6*

The area of this triangle is 40 cm².

What is the height, h, of the triangle?

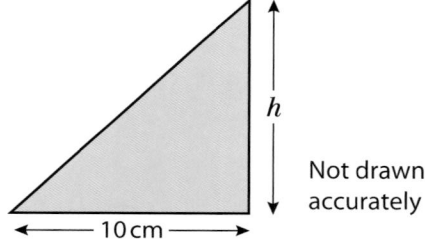

h

Not drawn accurately

10 cm

6 *1998 level 6*

Each shape in this question has an area of 10 cm².

   a Calculate the height of the parallelogram.

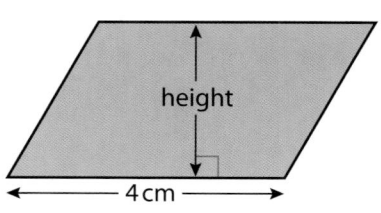

height

4 cm

   b Calculate the length of the base of the triangle.

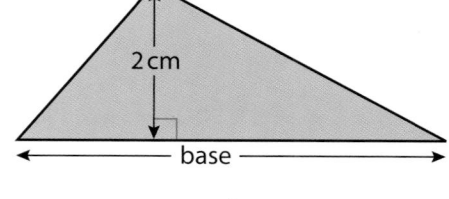

2 cm

base

   c What might be the values of h, a and b in this trapezium?

     (a is greater than b.)

     What else might the values of h, a and b be?

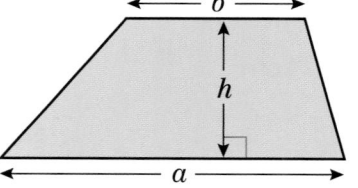

b

h

a

Volume is the amount of space a shape occupies.

Volume uses cubic units, e.g. cm³, mm³.

Volume of a cuboid = length × width × height = area of base × height

Example 1

The diagram shows a cuboid made from centimetre cubes.
Find the volume of the cuboid.

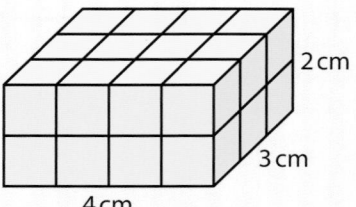

There are 12 centimetre cubes in each layer and there
are two layers.

So the number of centimetre cubes is:
12 × 2 = 24.

The volume of the cuboid is 24 cm³.

Example 2

Work out the volume of the cuboid in the diagram.

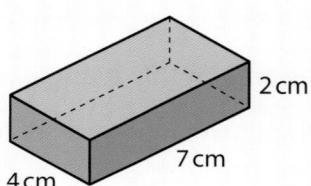

Volume = length × width × height
= 7 × 4 × 2 = 56 cm³

Surface area is the total area of all the faces of a 3D shape.

Surface area uses square units, e.g. cm², mm².

Example 3

The diagram shows a cube of side 2 cm.
Each of its six faces is a square.

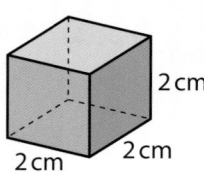

The area of each square face is:
2 × 2 × 4 cm².

So the surface area of the cube is:
4 × 6 = 24 cm².

1 *Year 7 Optional Test level 5*

This shape is made from four cubes joined together.

The table shows information about the shape.

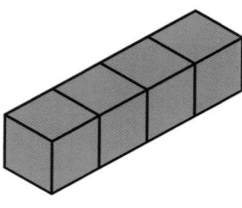

Volume	4 cm³
Surface area	18 cm²

The same four cubes are then used to make this new shape.

Copy and complete the table for the new shape.

Volume	… cm³
Surface area	… cm²

2 *2007 level 6*

Look at the cube.

The area of a face of the cube is $9x^2$.

Write an expression for the total surface area of the cube.

Write your answer as simply as possible.

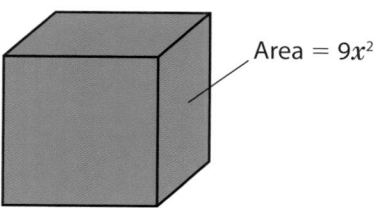

Area = $9x^2$

3 *2002 level 6*

The drawing shows two cuboids that have the same volume.

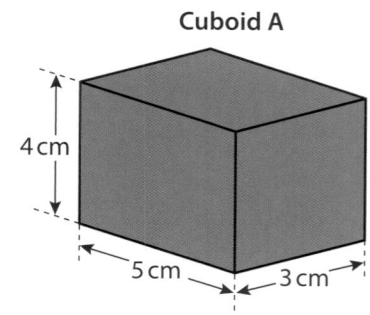

Cuboid A

4 cm

5 cm 3 cm

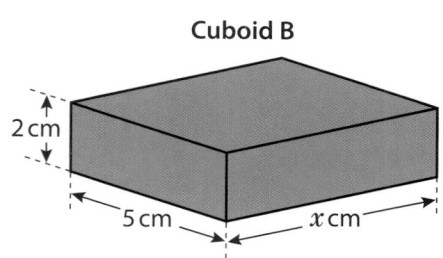

Cuboid B

2 cm

5 cm x cm

a What is the volume of cuboid A? Remember to state your units.

b Work out the value of the length marked x.

4 *2004 level 6*

You can make only four different cuboids with 16 cubes.

	Cuboid A	Cuboid B	Cuboid C	Cuboid D
Dimensions	$1 \times 1 \times 16$	$1 \times 2 \times 8$	$1 \times 4 \times 4$	$2 \times 2 \times 4$

a Which of the cuboids A and D has the larger surface area? Explain how you know.

b How many of cuboid D make a cube of dimensions $4 \times 4 \times 4$?

● Points to remember

⊙ Learn the formulae for the area of a rectangle, the area of a triangle, the area of a parallelogram and the volume of a cuboid.

⊙ To find the area of a compound shape, divide it up with straight lines into rectangles and triangles.

⊙ Triangles on the same base and with the same perpendicular height are equal in area.

⊙ Parallelograms on the same base and with the same perpendicular height are equal in area.

5 Probability

This lesson will help you to find all the possible outcomes for single events and two successive events, and to estimate probabilities from experimental data.

When outcomes are equally likely, the **theoretical probability** of an event is:

$$\frac{\text{number of successful outcomes}}{\text{total number of possible outcomes}}$$

The probability of an event *not* occurring is 1 minus the probability of the event occurring.

The **experimental probability** of an event is:

$$\frac{\text{number of successful trials}}{\text{total number of trials}}$$

Probabilities are written as fractions, decimals or percentages.

Example

A box contains five counters, two of which are white. A counter is picked at random.

There are five possible **equally likely outcomes**.
Two of the outcomes are favourable to the event of picking a white counter.

The **theoretical probability** of picking a white counter is $\frac{2}{5}$.
This can be written as a decimal, 0.4, or a percentage, 40%.

The theoretical probability of *not* picking a white counter is $1 - \frac{2}{5} = \frac{3}{5}$.
This can be written as a decimal, 0.6, or a percentage, 60%.

The counter is returned to the box and another counter is picked at random.
This trial is repeated 100 times.
A white counter is picked 38 times out of 100.

The **experimental probability** of picking a white counter is $\frac{38}{100}$ or 0.38.
This can be written as a percentage, 38%, or a fraction, $\frac{19}{50}$.

The experimental probability of *not* picking a white counter is $1 - 0.38 = 0.62$.
This can be written as a percentage, 62%, or a fraction, $\frac{31}{50}$.

Exercise 5A

(1) *Year 8 Optional Test level 5*

Look at these five cards.

I am going to choose one of these cards at random.

a   What is the probability that the card will show a triangle?

b   What is the probability that the card will show at least one circle?

c   I remove the card with two squares on it. Four cards are left.
I am going to choose one of these four cards at random.
Now what is the probability that the card will show at least one circle?

2 *2000 level 5*

In each box of cereal there is a free gift of a card.
You cannot tell which card will be in a box. Each card is equally likely.
There are four different cards: A, B, C or D.

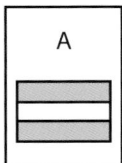 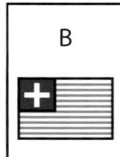 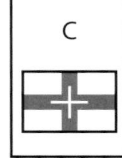 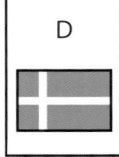

Zoe needs card A. Her brother Paul needs cards C and D.
They buy one box of cereal.

a What is the probability that the card is one that Zoe needs?

b What is the probability that the card is one that Paul needs?

Their mother opens the box. She tells them the card is *not* card A.

c What now is the probability that the card is one that Zoe needs?

d What is the probability that the card is one that Paul needs?

3 *2002 level 5*

A spinner has eight equal sections.

a What is the probability of scoring 4 on the spinner?

b What is the probability of scoring an even number on the spinner?

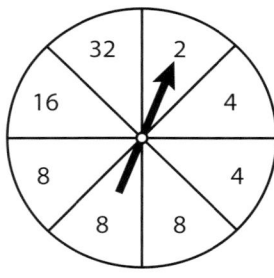

c The arrow is spun 100 times.
A 4 is scored 12 times.
What is the experimental probability of scoring 4?

d A different spinner has six equal sections and six numbers.

On this spinner, the probability of scoring an even number is $\frac{2}{3}$.
The probability of scoring 4 is $\frac{1}{3}$.
Copy this spinner and write what the numbers could be.

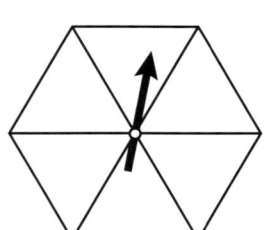

2004 level 5

I buy a box of different size plasters.
Assume each plaster is equally likely to be the top plaster inside the box.

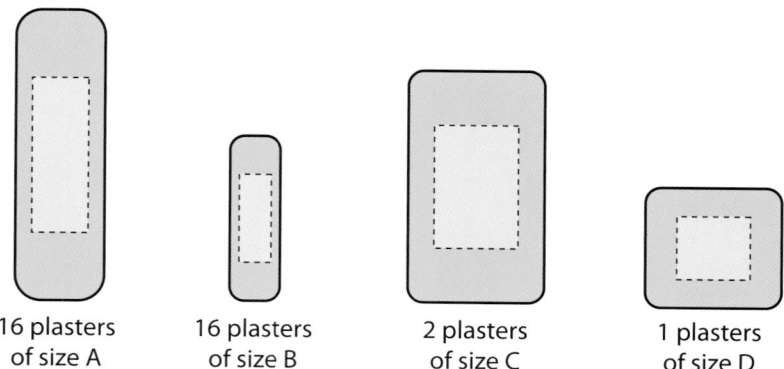

16 plasters   16 plasters   2 plasters   1 plasters
of size A   of size B   of size C   of size D

Altogether there are 35 plasters.
I take the top plaster from inside the box.

a   What is the probability that the plaster is of size D?

b   What is the probability that the plaster is of size A?

c   What is the probability that the plaster is *not* of size A?

Exercise 5B

When two events occur at the same time or one after the other, all the possible equally likely outcomes can be shown in a list or a table.

Example

Tom has two cards, one red and one blue.
He chooses one of the cards at random and writes down its colour.
He puts the card back and shuffles them.
He again picks another card at random and writes down its colour.

The table shows all of the equally likely outcomes.

There are four equally likely outcomes: **RR**, **BR**, **RB** and **BB**.
One of the four outcomes is the event of picking two red cards.

The theoretical probability of picking two red cards is $\frac{1}{4}$.

1 *1997 level 5*

Karen and Huw each have three cards, numbered
2, 3 and 4.

They each take any one of their own cards.
They then add together the numbers on the two cards.

The table shows all the possible answers.

Karen

a   What is the probability that their answer is
    an even number?

b   What is the probability that their answer is a
    number greater than 6?

+	2	3	4
2	4	5	6
3	5	6	7
4	6	7	8

Huw

c   Both Karen and Huw still have their three cards,
    numbered 2, 3 and 4.
    They each take any one of their own cards.
    They then multiply together the numbers on
    the two cards.
    Draw a table to show all possible answers.

d   Use your table to copy and complete these sentences:

    The probability that their answer is a number that is less than … is $\frac{8}{9}$.
    The probability that their answer is a number that is less than … is zero.

2 *1999 level 5*

A coin has two sides, heads and tails.

heads   tails

a   Chris is going to toss a coin.
    What is the probability that Chris will get heads?
    Write your answer as a fraction.

b   Sion is going to toss two coins.
    Copy and complete the table to show the different results he could get.

First coin	Second coin
heads	heads

c   Sion is going to toss two coins.
    What is the probability that he will get tails with both his coins?
    Write your answer as a fraction.

d Dianne tossed one coin. She got tails.
Dianne is going to toss another coin.
What is the probability that she will get tails again with her next coin?
Write your answer as a fraction.

⊙ **Points to remember**

- ⊙ The **theoretical probability** of an event is:

$$\frac{\text{number of successful outcomes}}{\text{total number of possible outcomes}}$$

- ⊙ The **experimental probability** of an event is:

$$\frac{\text{number of successful trials}}{\text{total number of trials}}$$

- ⊙ A probability is written as a fraction, decimal or percentage.

- ⊙ If p is the probability of an event happening, then the probability of the event not happening is $1 - p$.

- ⊙ Use a two-way table to show all the possible outcomes when two events occur at the same time or one after the other.

Revision unit 2

1 Percentages

This lesson will help you to find fractions and percentages of numbers, money and measures, including percentage increases or decreases.

It is easy to find an amount after a **percentage discount**.
First subtract the percentage discount from 100%.
Then calculate this percentage of the original amount.

Example 1

A £350 tumbler drier is reduced by 12% in a sale. What is its sale price?

Take 12% from 100%, which leaves 88%.
Write 88% as 0.88.

Calculate $0.88 \times 350 = 308$.   **Answer: £308**

It is also easy to find an amount after a **percentage increase**.
First add the percentage increase to 100%.
Then calculate this percentage of the original amount.

Example 2

The price of a £425 TV increases by 4%. What is its new price?

Add 4% to 100%, which gives 104%.
Write 104% as 1.04.

Calculate $1.04 \times 425 = 442$ **Answer: £442**

Exercise 1

Answer questions 1–7 **without a calculator**.

1 *1999 level 4*

The cost in June for an adult for one week in a holiday camp is £85.
The cost for a child is 25% less.
What is the cost in June for a child for one week in the holiday camp?

2 *2003 level 5*

a Explain how you know that 12.5% of this diagram is shaded.

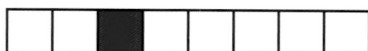

b Copy this diagram. Shade 37.5%.

3 *2005 level 5*

Copy and complete these sentences.

a … out of 10 is the same as 70%.

b 10 out of 20 is the same as … %.

c … out of … is the same as 5%.

Now copy and complete the last sentence again but using different numbers.

4 *Year 8 Optional Test level 5*

a What is 30% of 250?

b I'm thinking of a number. 10% of my number is 84.
Show calculations and explain how you can work out that 15% of my number is 126.

c What is 12.5% of my number?

5 *2005 Mental Test level 6*

Last month my telephone bill was £30.
This month it is 20% more.
How much is this month's bill?

6 *2002 Key Stage 2 level 6*

In Class 8, 80% of the pupils like crisps.
75% of the pupils who like crisps also like chocolate.
In Class 8, what percentage of the pupils like both crisps and chocolate?

7 *1997 level 6*

This pie chart shows the different ways that wood is used in the world.

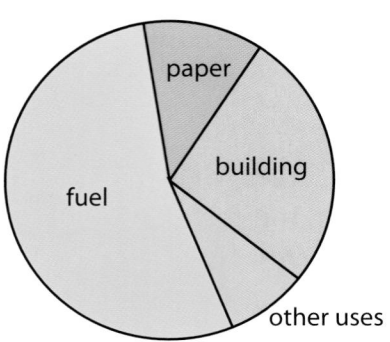

a Use the pie chart to estimate the percentage of wood that is used for paper.

b 55% of the wood is used for fuel.
Calculate the angle for the fuel sector on the pie chart.
Show how you worked out your answer.

You may **use your calculator** to answer questions 8 – 11. Show your working.

8 *2003 level 5*

An adult weighs 80 kg.
60% of his total mass is water.
What is the mass of this water?

9 *2002 level 5*

a In 1976 the average yearly wage was £3275.
On average, people spent 17% of £3275 on their family holiday.
How much is 17% of £3275?

b In 2001 the average yearly wage was £21 842.
On average, people spent £1644 on their family holiday.
What percentage of the average yearly wage is that?

10 *Year 7 Optional Test level 5*

Altogether, the area of the Earth's surface is 510 million km².
Only 29% of this is land.
Calculate how many million km² of land there are on the Earth's surface.

Extension problem

11 *2005 level 6*

Here is some information about A levels in 2002.

	English	Mathematics
Number of students	72 000	54 000
Percentage gaining grade A	19%	37%

How many more students gained grade A in mathematics than in English?

Points to remember

- Percentages such as 10%, 15%, 75%, and so on, can be calculated mentally or by using jottings.
- Other percentages can be found by using a written method or a calculator.

2 Ratio and proportion

This lesson will help you to simplify ratios, divide a quantity in a given ratio and use the unitary method to solve problems involving proportion.

Ratios are used to compare quantities.

For example, the number of yellow stars to the number of blue stars is in the ratio 9 : 3.

The order of the numbers is important.

The ratio 3 : 9 is the ratio of the number of blue stars to the number of yellow stars.

In one kind of ratio problem, you are asked to divide a quantity into two parts in the ratio $a:b$.

Example 1

Divide £28 in the ratio 3 : 4.

There are 3 + 4 = 7 shares.
1 share is £28 ÷ 7 = £4
The first part is 3 shares, or £4 × 3 = £12
The other part is 4 shares, or £4 × 4 = £16

Check: £16 + £12 = £28

In another kind of ratio problem, you are given the ratio and the size of one part, and are asked to find the other part.

Example 2

A sum of money is divided in the ratio 3 : 4.
The smaller part is £15. How much is the other part?

Altogether, there are 3 + 4 = 7 shares.
One part is £15, which is 3 shares.
1 share is £15 ÷ 3 = £5
The other part is 4 shares, or £5 × 4 = £20

Check: £15 : £20 = 3 : 4

Sometimes you are given the difference between the two parts instead.

Example 3

In a class the ratio of boys to girls is 7 : 4.
There are 9 more boys than girls. How many pupils are in the class?

Altogether, there are 7 + 4 = 11 shares.
The difference between the two parts is 7 − 4 = 3 shares.
So 3 shares are 9 pupils.
1 share is 9 ÷ 3 = 3 pupils
11 shares are 3 × 11 = 33 pupils

Check: 7 shares is 21 boys and 4 shares is 12 girls, or 9 more boys than girls.

Exercise 2

1   *Year 8 Optional Test level 5*

   At a theatre there are 900 seats.
   There are twice as many seats downstairs as upstairs.
   How many seats are downstairs?

2   *1999 level 5*

   a   Nigel pours 1 carton of apple juice and 3 cartons of orange juice into a big jug.
       What is the ratio of apple juice to orange juice in Nigel's jug?

   b   Lesley pours 1 carton of apple juice and $1\frac{1}{2}$ cartons of orange juice into another big jug.
       What is the ratio of apple juice to orange juice in Lesley's jug?

   c   Tandi pours 1 carton of apple juice and 1 carton of orange juice into another big jug.
       She wants only half as much apple juice as orange juice in her jug.
       What should Tandi pour into her jug now?

③ *1998 level 5*

You can make different colours of paint by mixing red, blue and yellow in different proportions. For example, you can make green by mixing 1 part blue to 1 part yellow.

a To make purple, you mix 3 parts red to 7 parts blue.
   How much of each colour do you need to make 20 litres of purple paint?
   Give your answer in litres.

b To make orange, you mix 13 parts yellow to 7 parts red.
   How much of each colour do you need to make 10 litres of orange paint?
   Give your answer in litres.

④ *2005 Key Stage 2 level 5*

Sapna makes a fruit salad using bananas, oranges and apples.
For every one banana, she uses 2 oranges and 3 apples.
Sapna uses 24 pieces of fruit. How many oranges does she use?

⑤ *2003 Mental Test level 6*

Jenny and Mark share some money in the ratio 2:3.
Jenny's share is £110.
How much is Mark's share?

⑥ *2004 Mental Test level 6*

The instructions for a fruit drink say to mix 1 part blackcurrant juice with 4 parts water.
I want to make 1 litre of this fruit drink.
How much blackcurrant juice should I use?
Give your answer in millilitres.

⑦ Two numbers are in the ratio 3:2. One of the numbers is 12.
There are two possible answers for the other number.
What are the two possible answers?

Extension problems

⑧ *2001 Key Stage 2 level 6*

Children were asked to choose between a safari park and a zoo for a school trip.
They had a vote. The result was a ratio of 10:3 in favour of going to a safari park.

130 children voted in favour of going to a safari park.
How many children voted in favour of going to the zoo?

⑨ *2000 Key Stage 2 level 6*

Shortcrust pastry is made using flour, margarine and lard.
The flour, margarine and lard are mixed in the ratio 8:3:2 by weight.
How many grams of margarine and lard are needed to mix with 200 grams of flour?

10 *2003 level 6*

Paul is 14 years old.
His sister is exactly 6 years younger, so this year she is 8 years old.

This year, the ratio of Paul's age to his sister's age is 14 : 8.
14 : 8 written as simply as possible is 7 : 4.

a   When Paul is 21, what will be the ratio of Paul's age to his sister's age?
Write the ratio as simply as possible.

b   When his sister is 36, what will be the ratio of Paul's age to his sister's age?
Write the ratio as simply as possible.

c   Could the ratio of their ages ever be 7 : 7?
Write **Yes** or **No**.
Explain how you know.

 11 *2001 Key Stage 2 level 6*

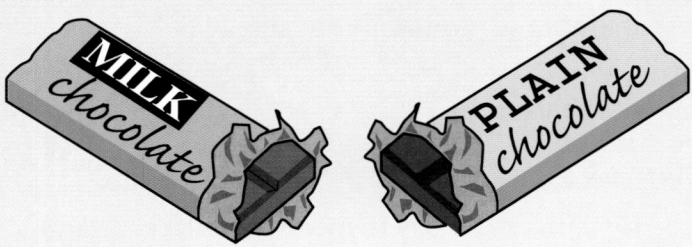

In a survey, the ratio of the number of people who preferred milk chocolate
to those who preferred plain chocolate was 5 : 3.
40 more people preferred milk chocolate to plain chocolate.
How many people were in the survey?

 Points to remember

- If you are asked to divide a given quantity into two parts in the ratio 3 : 7,
  the two parts are $\frac{3}{10}$ and $\frac{7}{10}$ of the whole quantity.

- If you are given a ratio 2 : 7 and the size of the smaller part,
  find one share by dividing the smaller part by 2, then multiply by 7 to
  find the larger part.

3 Equations and graphs

This lesson will help you to solve linear equations and to plot the graphs of linear functions.

The **solution** of an equation is the value of the letter symbol that makes the equation true.

The left-hand side of the equation must always balance the right-hand side.

To keep the balance, do the same to the left-hand side and the right-hand side of the equation.

Example 1

Solve the equation $a - 7 = 19$.

$$a - 7 = 19$$
$$a - 7 + 7 = 19 + 7 \qquad \text{Add 7 to both sides.}$$
$$a = 26$$

Check: When $a = 26$, $26 - 7 = 19$

Example 2

Solve the equation $6x = 72$.

$$6x = 72$$
$$6x \div 6 = 72 \div 6 \qquad \text{Divide both sides by 6.}$$
$$x = 12$$

Check: When $x = 12$, $6 \times 12 = 72$

Example 3

Solve the equation $4n + 3 = 31$.

$$4n + 3 = 31$$
$$4n + 3 - 3 = 31 - 3 \qquad \text{Subtract 3 from both sides.}$$
$$4n = 28.$$
$$4n \div 4 = 28 \div 4 \qquad \text{Divide both sides by 4.}$$
$$n = 7$$

Check: When $n = 7$, $4 \times 7 + 3 = 31$

Exercise 3A

1 *2004 level 4*

Work out the values of x, y and z in the number sentences below.

a $3 \times 10 + 4 = x$ 　　 b $3 \times 10 + y = 38$ 　　 c $z \times 10 + 12 = 52$

2 *2004 level 4*

Solve these equations.

a $s + 12 = 24$ 　　 b $k - 12 = 24$

3 *2006 level 5*

Solve these equations.

a $2k + 3 = 11$ 　　 b $2t + 3 = -11$

4 *2007 level 5*

Solve these equations.

a $32x + 53 = 501$ 　　 b $375 = 37 + 26y$

5 *2002 level 5*

Some people use yards to measure length.
The diagram shows one way to change yards to metres.

a Change 100 yards to metres. 　　 b Change 100 metres to yards.

Extension problem

6 *2003 level 6*

Solve these equations. Show your working.

a $8k - 1 = 15$ 　　 b $2m + 5 = 10$ 　　 c $3t + 4 = t + 13$

Exercise 3B

Graphs can show the relationship between two quantities in real life.

Rhys buys a DVD player. He pays a deposit of £50 and 12 equal monthly amounts. The graph shows the total amount he has paid at the end of each month.

Straight-line graphs are called **linear graphs**.

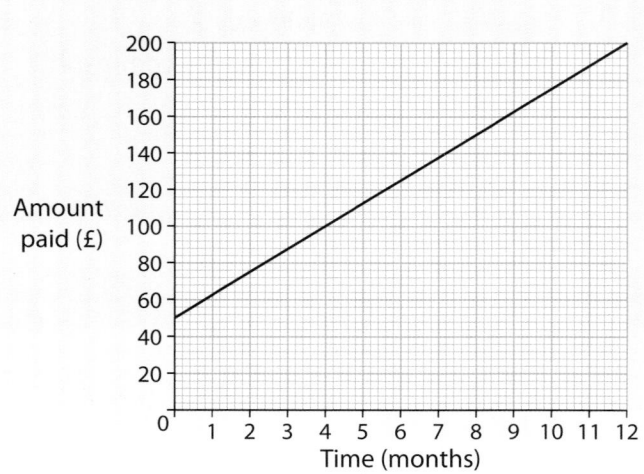

1 *1999 level 5*

The graph shows the average heights of young children.

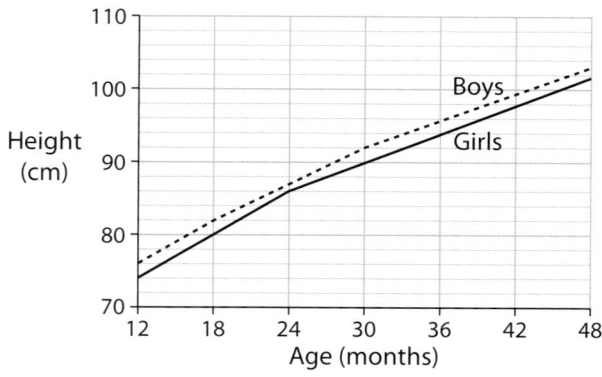

a   What is the average height of girls aged 30 months?

b   What is the average height of boys aged 36 months?

c   Jane is average height for her age. Her height is 80 cm.
Use the graph to find Jane's age.

d   The table shows approximately how much an average girl grows each year
between the ages of 12 and 48 months.

Copy this table. Use the graph to complete it.

Age (months)	Approximate height at start (cm)	Approximate height at end (cm)	Approximate growth (cm)
12 to 24	74	86	12
24 to 36	86		
36 to 48			

e   This formula tells you how tall a boy is likely to be when he grows up.

> Add the mother's and father's heights.
> Divide by 2.
> Add 7 cm to the result.
>
> The boy is likely to be this height, plus or minus 10 cm.

Marc's mother is 168 cm tall. His father is 194 cm tall.

What is the greatest height Marc is likely to be when he grows up?
Show your working.

2   Complete the question on **R4.2 Resource sheet 3.1**.

When you draw a graph of an equation, the coordinates of the points to be plotted are often shown in a **table of values**.

The straight line with equation $y = 2x + 3$ passes through the points $(3, 9)$, since $9 = 2 \times 3 + 3$. It also passes through the points $(2, 7)$, $(1, 5)$, $(0, 3)$, $(-1, 1)$, $(-2, -1)$ and $(-3, -3)$.

The table of values for these points is:

x	-3	-2	-1	0	1	2	3
y	-3	-1	1	3	5	7	9

The graph of $y = 2x + 3$ is shown on the grid.

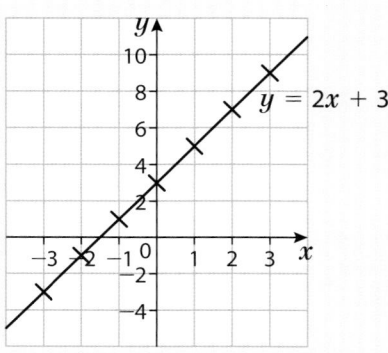

3　*2005 level 6*

The graph shows the straight line with equation $y = 3x - 4$.

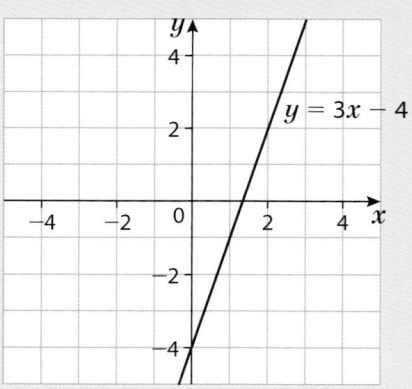

  a A point on the line $y = 3x - 4$ has an x-coordinate of 50.
What is the y-coordinate of this point?

  b A point on the line $y = 3x - 4$ has a y-coordinate of 50.
What is the x-coordinate of this point?

  c Is the point $(-10, -34)$ on the line $y = 3x - 4$?
Write **Yes** or **No**. Explain how you know.

4　*2003 Mental Test level 6*

You need some squared paper, a pencil and a ruler.
Draw this grid on the squared paper.

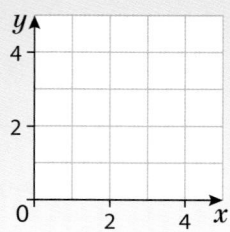

  a On the grid, sketch the straight line with equation $y = 3$.
Label the line.

  b On the grid, sketch the straight line with equation $y = x$.
Label the line.

5 *2003 level 6*

The diagram shows a square drawn on a square grid.

Points A, B, C and D are at the vertices of the square. The equation $y = 0$ is the line through A and C.

Which line is each of these equations?

a $x = 0$

b $x + y = 2$

c $x + y = -2$

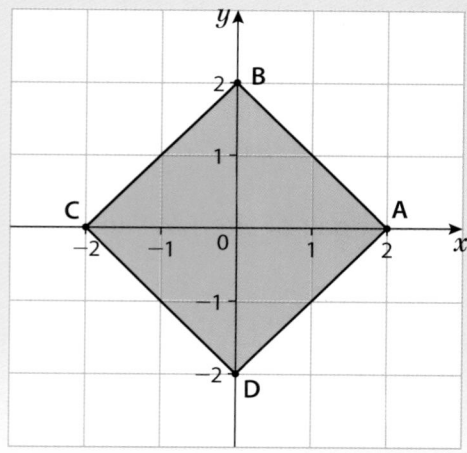

 Points to remember

⊙ The equation $3x + 7 = 10$ has a unique solution, when $x = 1$.

⊙ The equation $3x + 2y = 10$ has an infinite number of solutions. The value of y depends on the value of x.

⊙ When you interpret graphs, first inspect the axes and work out the scales.

⊙ When a graph represents a real situation, make sure that you understand what it is about before you answer questions.

4 Angles and transformations

This lesson will help you to identify alternate angles and corresponding angles, and to transform 2D shapes using reflection, rotation, translation or enlargement.

In the diagrams below a straight line crosses two parallel lines.

Pairs of **corresponding angles** that are equal to each other are shaded.

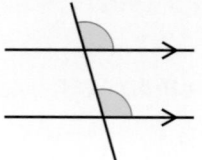 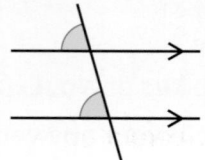 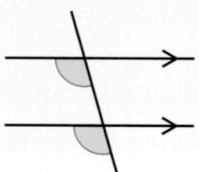 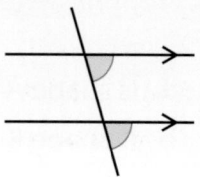

In the diagram on the right, a straight line crosses two parallel lines.

The shaded angles are called **alternate angles** and are equal to each other.

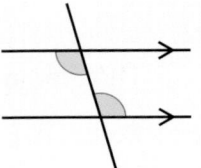

Another pair of alternate angles has been shaded in this diagram.

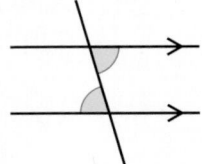

Exercise 4A

You will need some squared paper.

1. *Level 5*

   A, B and C are the coordinate points of three vertices of a quadrilateral.

   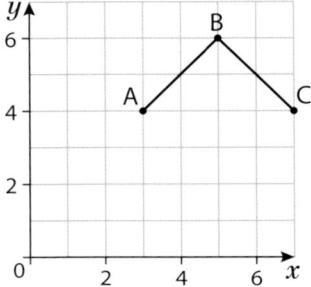

   a What are the coordinates of point D so that shape ABCD is a square?

   b What are the coordinates of point E so that shape ABCE is a trapezium?

2. *2004 level 5*

   Draw these shapes on squared paper.

   a A quadrilateral that has exactly two right angles.

   b A quadrilateral that has exactly one right angle.

3. *2004 level 5*

   The shapes below are drawn on square grids.

   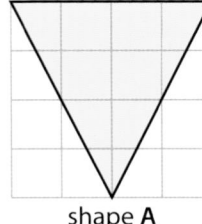
   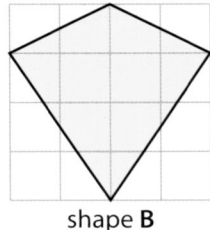
   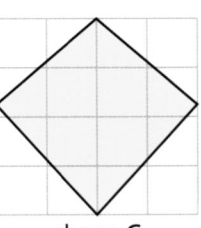

   shape **A**　　　　shape **B**　　　　shape **C**

   a Is shape A an equilateral triangle? Write **Yes** or **No**. Explain your answer.

   b Is shape B a kite? Write **Yes** or **No**. Explain your answer.

   c Is shape C a square? Write **Yes** or **No**. Explain your answer.

4 *2005 level 5*

The diagram shows triangle PQR.

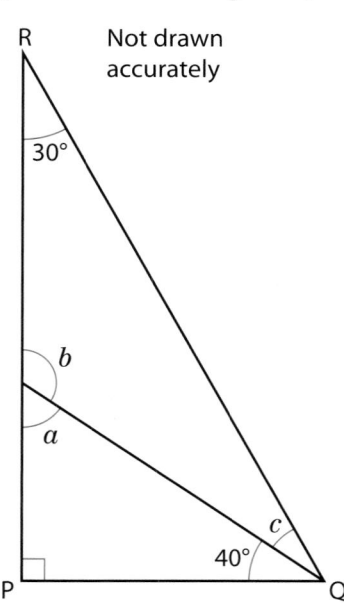

Not drawn accurately

Work out the sizes of angles a, b and c.

5 *Level 6*

Copy this diagram.

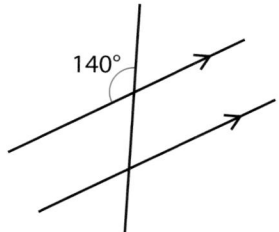

Mark on it two different angles each equal to 40°.

Extension problem

6 *2002 level 6*

The diagram shows a rectangle.

Work out the size of angle a.

Show your working.

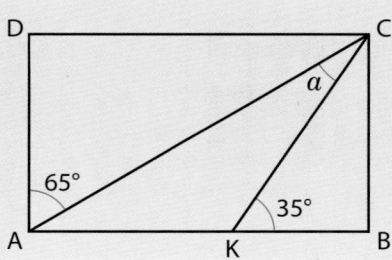

Exercise 4B

Rotations

To describe a **rotation** give:
- the angle of turn;
- the direction of turn (**clockwise** or **anticlockwise**);
- the point the shape turns about (**the centre of rotation**).

Example

Describe the transformation that maps L-shape A onto L-shape B.

The pink L-shape has been rotated 90° clockwise about the centre of rotation O.

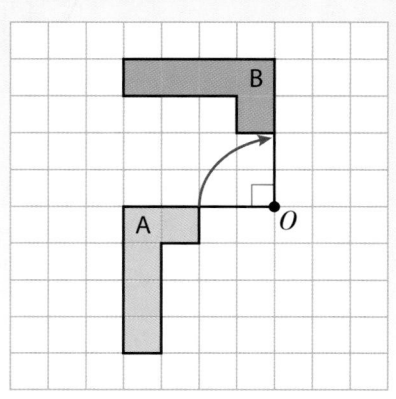

You will need squared paper and triangular dotty paper.

1 *1999 level 5*

You can rotate the blue triangle onto the cream triangle.
The rotation is anticlockwise.

   a Which point is the centre of rotation?

   b What is the angle of rotation?

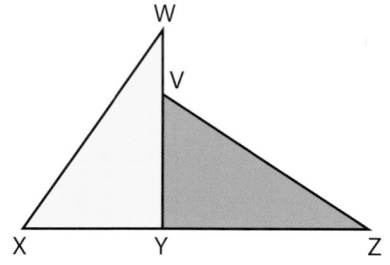

2 *2004 Progress Test level 4*

All the shapes in this question are made from nine squares.

This shape will look the same when it is turned through
two right angles.

Which of the shapes below will look the same when they are turned through two right
angles? Write the letters.

  a 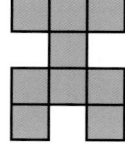   **b** 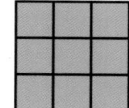   **c** 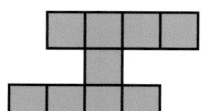   **d**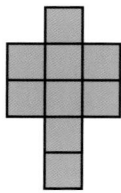

3 *2000 level 4*

   a What are the coordinates of point B?

   b The blue shape is reflected onto the cream
shape in a mirror line.

      Point A stays in the same place.

      Where is point B reflected to?
Write the coordinates.

   c Now the blue shape is rotated onto the
cream shape.

      Point A stays in the same place.

      Where is point B rotated to?
Write the coordinates.

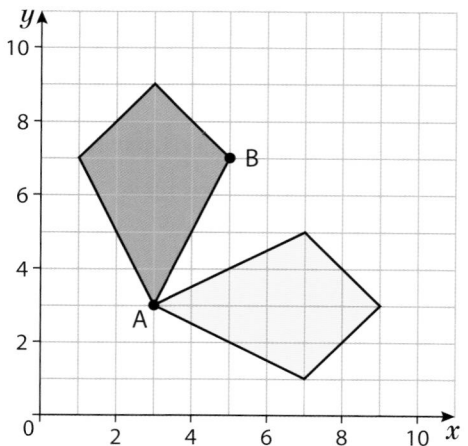

4   *2005 level 5*

The shapes below are drawn on square grids.
The diagrams show a rectangle that is rotated, then rotated again.
The centre of rotation is marked with a dot.

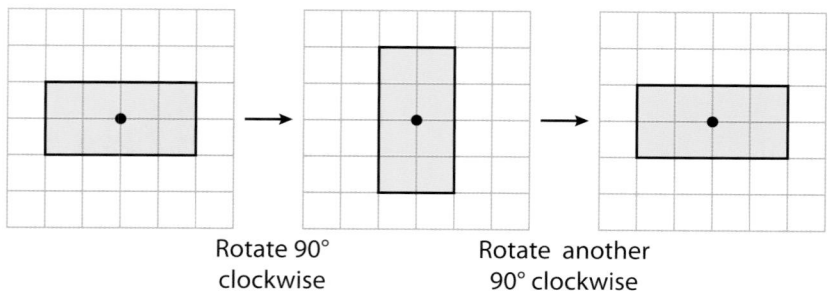

Rotate 90°   Rotate another
clockwise   90° clockwise

Copy the diagrams below on squared paper. Show the triangle when it is rotated, then rotated again. The centre of rotation is marked with a dot.

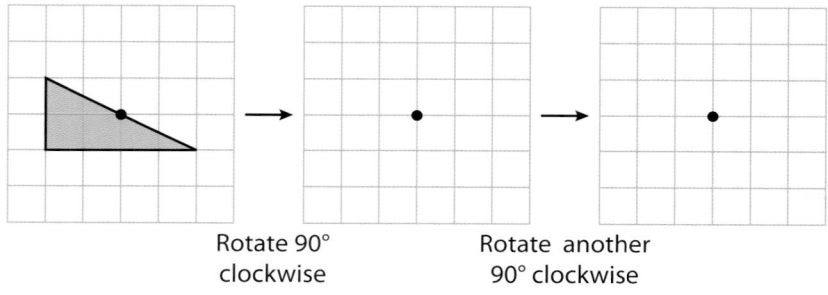

Rotate 90°   Rotate another
clockwise   90° clockwise

5   *1999 level 5*

a   This cuboid is made from 4 small cubes.

On triangular dotty paper draw a cuboid which is twice as high, twice as long and twice as wide.

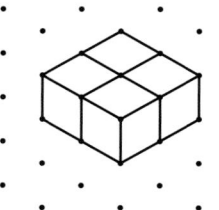

b   Graham made this cuboid from 3 small cubes.

Mohinder wants to make a cuboid which is twice as high, twice as long and twice as wide as Graham's cuboid.

How many small cubes will Mohinder need altogether?

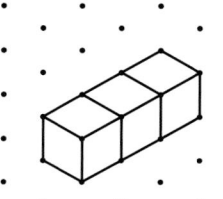

Extension problem

Enlargements

Here is a photograph of a farm gate in Scotland.

Here is an **enlargement** of the photograph.

The gates in the two photographs are the same shape but lengths in the enlargement are 3 times the lengths in the original photograph.

For example, the length of a bar of the gate in the enlargement is 3 times the length of the same bar in the original photograph.

So the larger photograph is an enlargement with **scale factor 3** of the smaller photograph.

In an enlargement:

- the lengths of the sides of a shape change;
- the angles of the shape do not change;
- the sides of the shape and the enlargement are parallel.

In the diagram, triangle P has been enlarged by a scale factor of 2 to give triangle Q.

The corner A of triangle P is mapped onto the corner A' of triangle Q. A line has been drawn through A and A'. Lines have also been drawn joining the other pairs of corners of triangles P and Q.

The lines meet at a point C, called the **centre of enlargement**.

C to A is 2 squares across and 3 squares up.   C to A' is 4 squares across and 6 squares up.

You can find the point A' by joining and extending CA to make CA' the length of CA multiplied by the scale factor 2.

6   *2002 level 6*

The grid shows an arrow and a point marked C.
Copy the arrow and point C on squared paper.

Draw an enlargement of scale factor 2 of the arrow.
Use point C as the centre of enlargement.

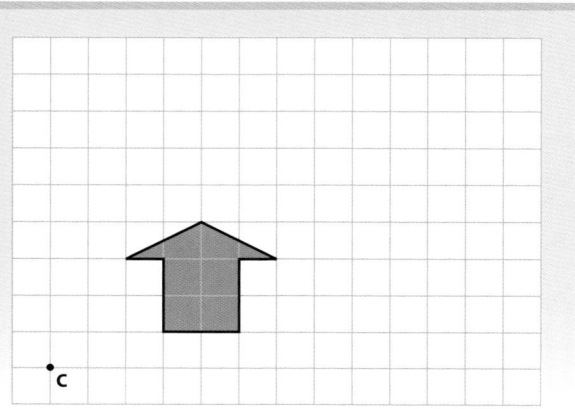

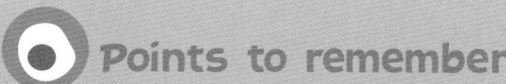

Points to remember

- When you identify equal angles, always give your reasons.
- Look out for vertically opposite angles, corresponding angles and alternate angles.
- Also look out for angles on a straight line, in a triangle and around a point.
- Reflection, rotation and translation leave the size and shape of the object unchanged.
- Enlargement changes the size of the object but not its shape.

5 Representing and interpreting data

This lesson will help you to represent and interpret data in tables, bar charts, line graphs and pie charts.

Interpreting two-way tables

A two-way table can be read both across the page and down.
It allows two types of information to be presented and compared in the same form.

Interpreting line graphs

Make sure you know which quantity is on each axis.

Look at the numbers on the scales to work out how much each small division on the scales is worth. Use a ruler to help you to follow up from the horizontal axis and across from the vertical axis.

Interpreting pie charts

The whole circle is 100% and represents the total.

A sector that is one tenth of the whole circle represents 10% of the total.
For this sector, the angle at the centre of the circle is
$360° ÷ 10 = 36°$.

To help you to estimate the percentages represented by the sectors, imagine splitting the circle into quarters, or smaller parts.

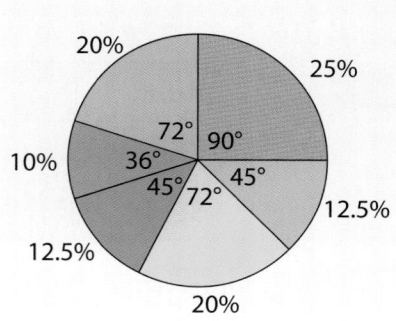

Exercise 5

1 *2003 level 4*

Mark did a survey. He asked pupils in his school:
'Do you like the colour of the school uniform?'

The table shows his results.

	Yes	No	Don't know
Year 7	35	17	2
Year 8	20	24	5
Year 9	19	17	6

a How many pupils from Year 7 took part in the survey?

b Altogether, more pupils said 'Yes' than said 'No'. How many more?

c Mark asked the same question to 40 pupils in Year 11.
25% said 'Yes'. 50% said 'No'. The rest said 'Don't know'.
Copy and complete the table to show how many pupils from Year 11 gave each answer.

	Yes	No	Don't know
Year 11	…	…	…

d Anna does a different survey with pupils in Year 9.
She wants to know if more boys than girls have pets.
She asks: 'Do you have a pet?'

What labels should Anna use on her results table?
Copy the table and fill in the missing labels.

	…………	…………
…………		
…………		

2 *2003 level 4*

The table shows how much it costs to go to a cinema.

	Before 6:00 pm	After 6:00 pm
Adult	£3.20	£4.90
Child (14 or under)	£2.50	£3.50
Senior citizen (60 or over)	£2.95	£4.90

Mrs Jones (aged 35), her daughter (aged 12), her son (aged 10) and a friend (aged 65) want to go to the cinema. They are not sure whether to go before 6:00 pm or after 6:00 pm.

How much will they save if they go before 6:00 pm? Show your working.

3 *1997 level 4*

This table shows the distances between some towns.

Distance in miles

	Hull	Exeter	Bangor	Dover
Hull				
Exeter	305			
Bangor	199	289		
Dover	261	248	331	

a Which two towns are the shortest distance from each other?

b Mrs Davis drove from Bangor to Exeter.
What is the distance between Bangor and Exeter?

c Then Mrs Davis drove from Exeter to Dover.
What is the distance between Exeter and Dover?

d How far did Mrs Davis drive altogether?

4 *2005 level 4*

A survey showed these results about the number of mobile phones used in the UK.

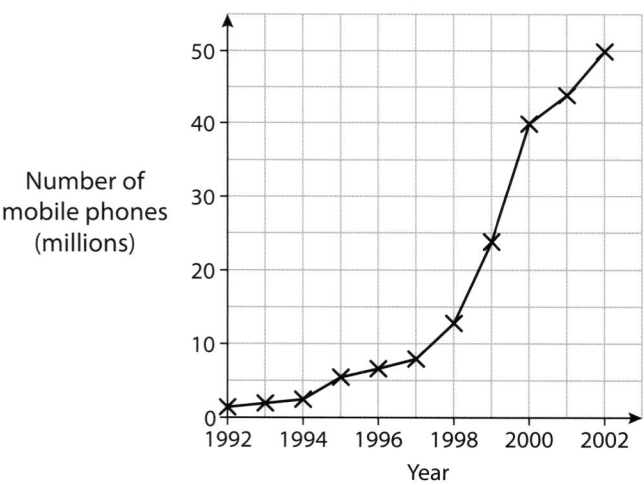

As reported in the Metro newspaper, April 2003

Use the graph to answer these questions.

a How many million mobile phones were there in 1992?

b Ten years later, how many million mobile phones were there?

c From 1998 to 1999, the number of mobile phones increased by about how many million?

(5) *2000 level 5*

Maria and Kay ran a 1500 metres race.
The distance-time graph shows the race.

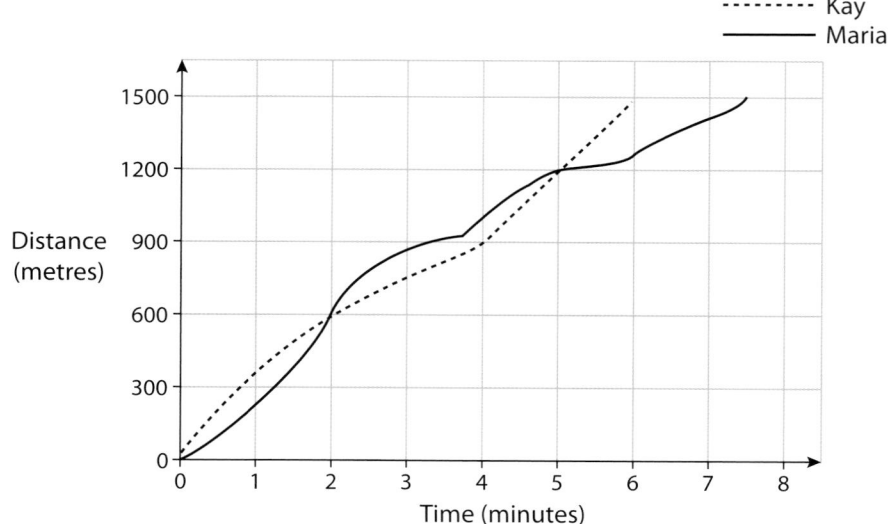

Just after the start of the race, Maria was in the lead.

At 600 metres, Maria and Kay were level.

Use the graph to help you copy and complete these sentences.

a   After 600 metres, Kay was in the lead for .... minutes.

b   At .... metres, Maria and Kay were level again.

c   .... won the race. Her total time was .... minutes.

d   .... finished .... minutes later.

(6) *2004 level 5*

The graph shows at what time the sun rises and sets in the American town of Anchorage.

The day with the most hours of daylight is called the longest day.

Use the information from the graph to answer the questions.

a   The longest day is in which month?

b   How many hours of daylight were there on this day?

c   The shortest day is in which month?

d   How many hours of daylight were there on this day?

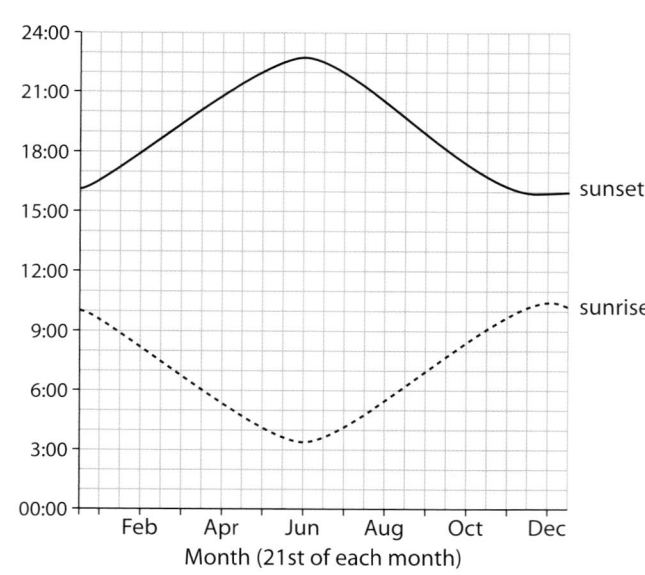

7 *2004 level 4*

The pie charts show what percentage of household rubbish is recycled in different countries.

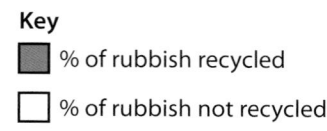

Key
■ % of rubbish recycled
□ % of rubbish not recycled

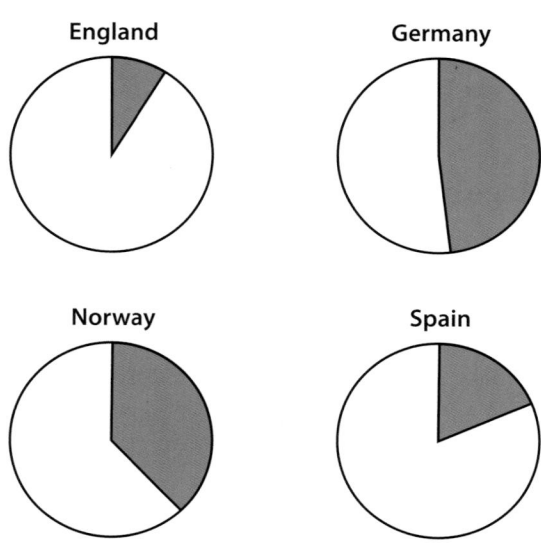

a In England, about what percentage of rubbish is recycled?

b England wants to recycle 30% of rubbish by the year 2010.

Which countries already recycle more than 30% of their rubbish?

8 *2005 level 5*

a Look at this information.

> In 1976, a man earned £16 each week.

The pie chart shows how he spent his money.
How much did the man spend on food each week?

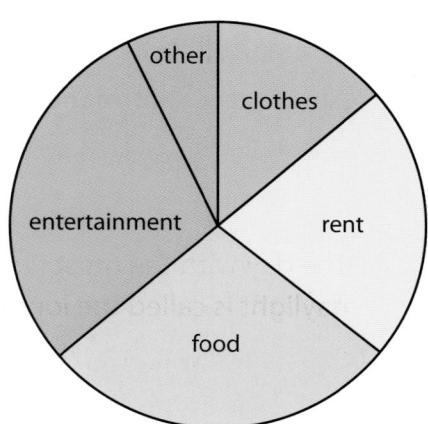

b Now look at this information.

> In 2002, a man earned £400 each week.

The table shows how he spent his money.
Draw a pie chart to show how the man spent his money.
Remember to label each sector.

Rent	£200
Food	£100
Entertainment	£50
Other	£50

9 *1995 level 5*

These pie charts show the area of the Earth's surface covered by water and land north and south of the equator.

North of the equator

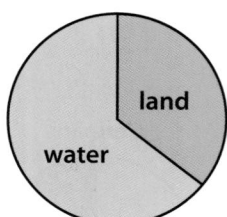

South of the equator

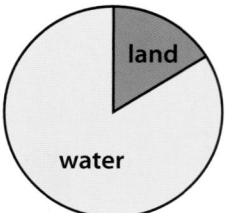

a About what percentage of the Earth's surface north of the equator is covered by land?

b About what percentage of the Earth's surface south of the equator is covered by land?

c Sketch a pie chart to show the area of the whole Earth's surface covered by water and by land. Label the parts of your pie chart 'water' and 'land'.

⊙ **Points to remember**

- ⊙ In a pie chart the angle at the centre of the circle is proportional to the frequency for each category.
- ⊙ A pie chart shows proportions or percentages of the whole.
- ⊙ A two-way table is read across the page and down. It shows two or more sets of information in the same form so that comparisons can be made.
- ⊙ A line graph is a useful way of displaying continuous data against time.
- ⊙ Use the scales to read information from a graph as accurately as you can.

Answers to
How well are you doing?

N4.1 Properties of numbers

1. a $3 + (-2) = 1$, or $6 + (-5) = 1$
   b $(-8) - (-2) = -6$, or $(-5) - 1 = -6$
   c $(-5) \times (-1) = 5$
   d $6 \div (-2) = -3$
2. 36 and 64
3. $24^3 = 24 \times 24 \times 24$
   The last digit of 24^3 is the last digit of $4 \times 4 \times 4$, which is 4.
4. $5 \times 7 \times 13 = 455$
5. 450 or 405

G4.1 Angles and shapes

1. $a = 50°$ (angles on a straight line)
   $b = 60°$ (opposite angles)
   $c = 72°$ (angle sum of triangle)
2. Angle BCK $= 180° - 90° - 45° = 45°$
   (angle sum of triangle BCK)
   Angle ACD $= 180° - 90° - 55° = 35°$
   (angle sum of triangle ACD)
   $a = 90° -$ angle BCK $-$ angle ACD $= 10°$
3. A, F and G are congruent.
4. JK = 5 mm, KL = 6 mm, LM = 7 mm, MJ = 10 mm
5.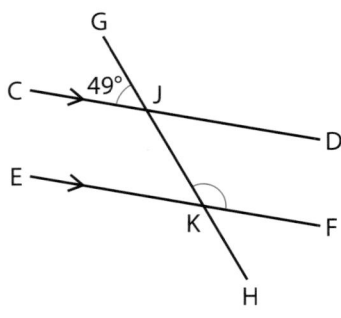
   Angle CJK = 131° (angles on a straight line)
   Angle JKF = 131° (alternate angles)
6.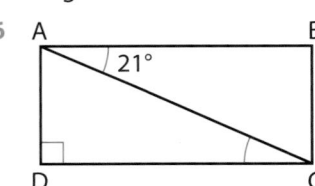
   Angle ACD = 21° (alternate angles)

A4.1 Linear sequences

1. 30, 37, 44, 51, 58
2. Subtract 11
3. 103, 98, **93, 88**, 83, 78, **73**
4. 2, 5, 8, 11, 14
5. a $4n + 2$
   b $\frac{1}{2}(6n + 6)$
   c $2(5n - 3)$
6.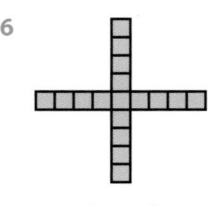

   $4n + 1$

N4.2 Whole numbers, decimals and fractions

1. a 0.6   b $\frac{10}{15}$ and $\frac{6}{9}$
2. a 0.035   b 0.65 and 0.35
3. a $\frac{1}{4} + \frac{6}{8} = 1$ b $\frac{1}{3} + \frac{8}{12} = 1$
4. a 12 558   b 24.669   c 26
5. a 18   b 9.85   c 19.5
6. 0.15 g
7. a 135 metres   b 222 paper clips

S4.1 Probability

1. 0.61
2. 0.15
3. a $\frac{12}{40}$ or $\frac{3}{10}$ b $\frac{13}{40}$ c $\frac{30}{40}$ or $\frac{3}{4}$
4. a

First coin	Second coin
heads	heads
heads	tails
tails	heads
tails	tails

   b $\frac{1}{4}$
   c $\frac{1}{2}$

5 a $\frac{5}{9}$ b $\frac{3}{9}$ or $\frac{1}{3}$

c

×	2	3	4
2	4	6	8
3	6	9	12
4	8	12	16

d 16

A4.2 Expressions and formulae

1 a Expression D $4a + 3$ b $8b + 3$

2 a 18   b 2

c Equation C $y = x^2$

3 $3(2a + 1) = 3 \times 2a + 3 \times 1 = 6a + 3$

4 $8x + 31$

5 Area = $\sqrt{56}$ cm^2 = 7.48 cm^2 (to 2 d.p.)

6 $c = \frac{4 \times 20}{12 + 4} = \frac{80}{16} = 5$

The correct amount for this child is 5 ml.

G4.2 Measures and mensuration

1 a Container A holds more.

b 250 ml

2 a 120 mm is the same as **12** cm.

b 120 cm is the same as **1.2** m.

c 120 m is the same as **0.12** km.

3 40 bags

4 35 cm^2

5 Area of triangle = $\frac{1}{2} \times 6 \times 4 = 12$ cm^2

Area of rectangle = area of triangle, so

$4w = 12$

$w = 3$

6 a 60 cm^3 b $x = 6$

c 94 cm^2 d 104 cm^2

N4.3 Fractions, decimals and percentages

1 a **7** out of 10 is the same as 70%.

10 out of 20 is the same as **50**%.

b e.g. **1** out of **20** is the same as 5%.

5 out of **100** is the same as 5%.

2 a A, D

b D

c e.g. $\frac{1}{9}$ is half of $\frac{2}{9}$.

3 7.4×9.4

4 a $\frac{7}{16}$ b £60

5 $\frac{3}{5}$ $\frac{3}{4}$ $\frac{17}{20}$ $\frac{9}{10}$

6 6300 students

7 7.5% (to 1 d.p.)

S4.2 Enquiry 1

1 a e.g. libraries, publishers, schools, colleges

b One possibility is to ask people about the different sources of information they use. Alternatively you could look for data about how book sales or library use has changed over time.

c For example:

What do you use the Internet for?

What do you use books for?

Do you think books are still useful? Why?

2

Type of book	Angle
Crime	54°
Non-fiction	234°
Fantasy	72°

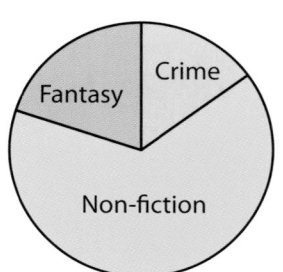

3 135°

4 a 3 minutes

b 8 matches

c 81 minutes

d Between 20 and 29 minutes after the start; this is the modal group.

5 a Mean = (9 + 11 + 10) ÷ 3 = 30 ÷ 3 = 10

The median, 10, is the middle value when the data is arranged in order: 9, 10, 11.

b e.g. 8, 9, 11, 12

A4.3 Functions and graphs

1 a 91.44 metres

b 109.36 yards (to 2 d.p.)

2 a 146

b 18

c Yes, because substituting $x = 10$ in $3x - 4$ gives -34, the y-coordinate.

3 a $x + y = 4$

b

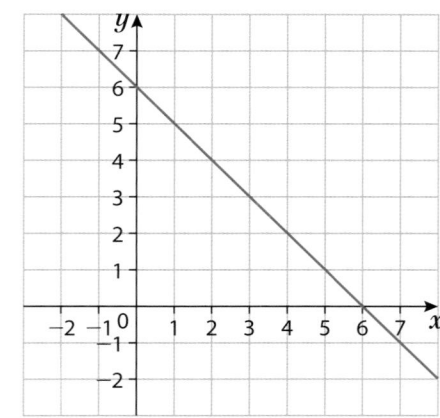

4 a Gradient 5   **b** y-intercept $(0, 7)$

5 a

n	$\rightarrow$	$n + 2$
4	$\rightarrow$	**6**
18	$\rightarrow$	20

b

n	$\rightarrow$	$2n$
4	$\rightarrow$	**8**
10	$\rightarrow$	20

c e.g. $n \rightarrow n - 20, n \rightarrow n \div 5$

6

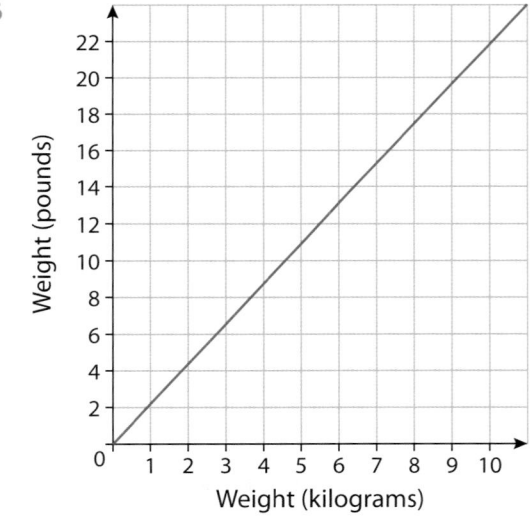

N4.4 Proportional reasoning

1 5:6

2 a £2.10   **b** 250 g

3 320 km

4 8 oranges

5 36°

6 a 7:5   **b** 7:6

7 39 voted in favour of the zoo.

G4.3 Transformations

1

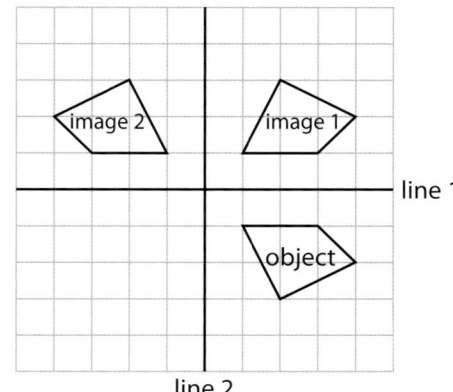

A rotation through 180° about the point where the two lines intersect

2

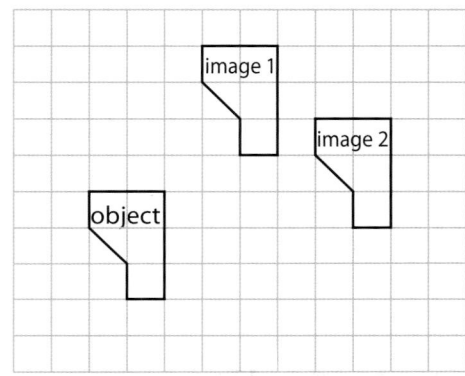

A translation of 6 units to the right and 2 units up

3 a Scale factor 3

b

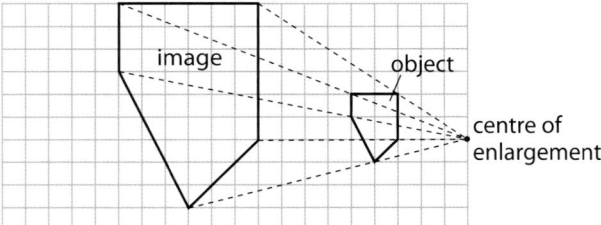

4

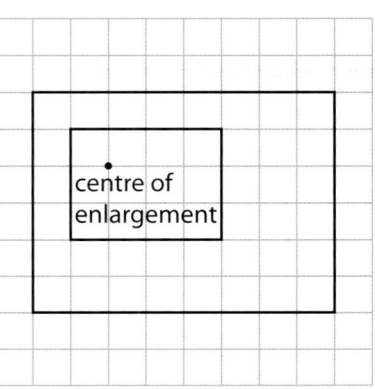

5 a P (60, 60)   **b** M (0, 100), N (60, 0)

A4.4 Equations and formulae

1   $y = 14x - 9$

2   $x \leftarrow$ | divide by 9 | $\leftarrow$ | add 2 | $\leftarrow y$

3   (1, 5) and (0.5, 4)

4   a $k = 4$ b $t = -7$

5   a $k = 2$ b $y = \frac{1}{2}$

6   11

S4.3 Enquiry

1   75.5

2   a

Neck circumference (cm)	Frequency
$30 \leqslant x < 35$	1
$35 \leqslant x < 40$	3
$40 \leqslant x < 45$	6
$45 \leqslant x < 50$	7
$50 \leqslant x < 55$	11
$55 \leqslant x < 60$	2

  b

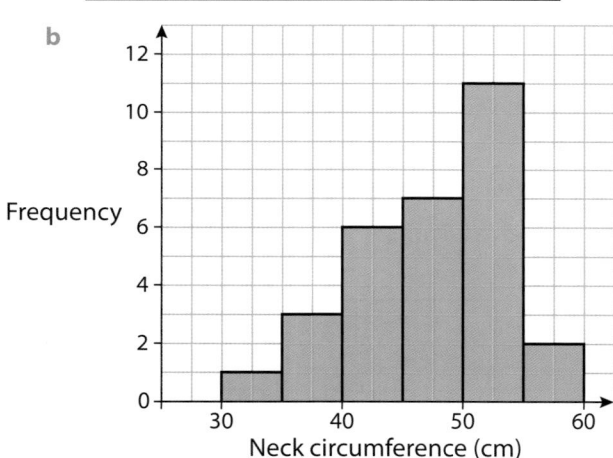

2   75.5

3   a   £30   b   Between 4 and 5 years old

G4.4 Constructions

1

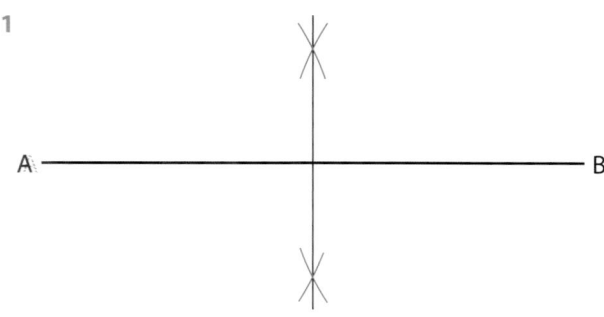

2

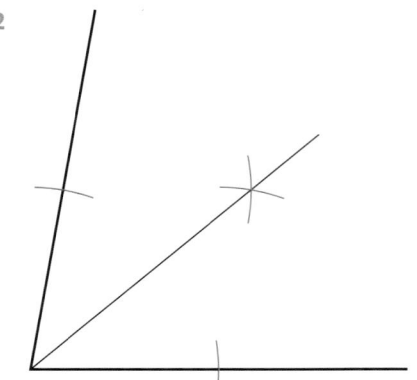

3

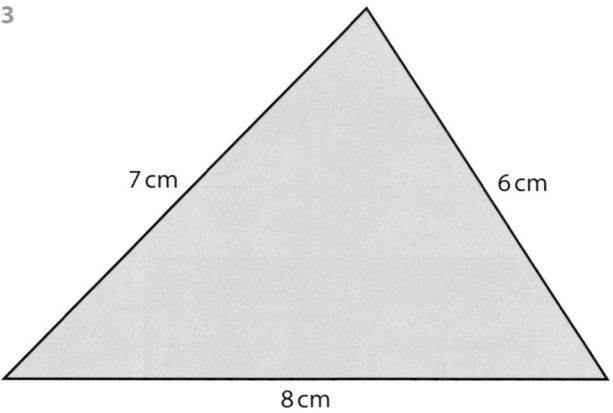

4

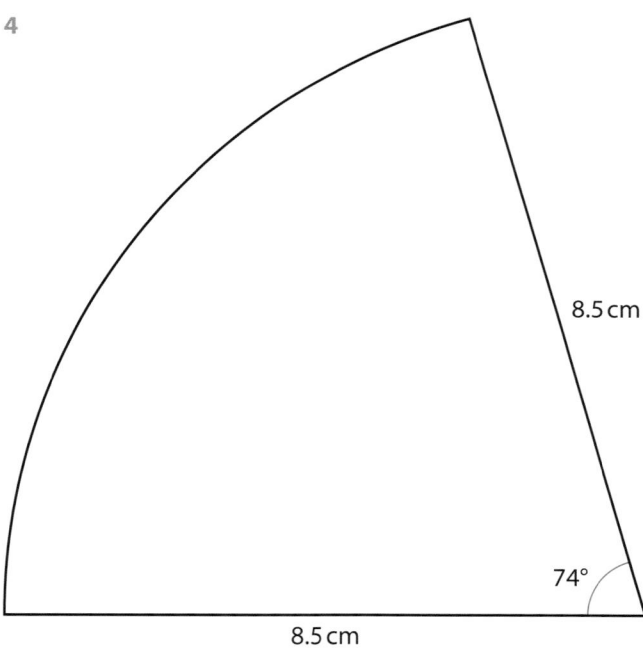

5   a, b

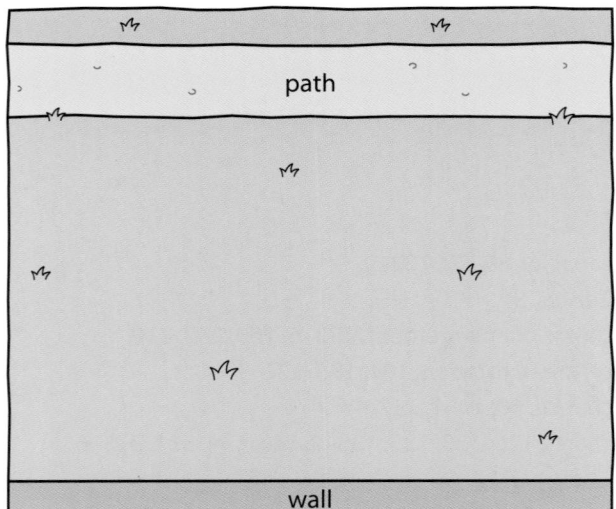

6   a   FORWARD 10
        TURN RIGHT 120°
        FORWARD 10
        TURN RIGHT 120°
        FORWARD 10
    b   FORWARD 8
        TURN RIGHT 45°
        FORWARD 6
        TURN RIGHT 135°
        FORWARD 8
        TURN RIGHT 45°
        FORWARD 6
7   a   20 metres   b   18 centimetres
8   a   5.5 cm   b   110 km
    c   050°   d   230°

A4.5 Using algebra

1   $3(3x - 8)$
2   $8x + 31$
3   $n = 0.5$
4   $y = 6.5$
5   11
6   $m = 50°$
7   a $x = 8$ b $y = x + 7$
    c $y = x - 1$
8   a   Company A:
        The first **3** hours used every month are free,
        then they charge £2 for every hour.
        Company B:
        They charge £10 each month, with an extra
        charge of **25**p for each hour used.
    b   Company C:
        They charge a flat rate of £10 each month.

N4.5 Solving problems

1   2, 4, 6, 8
2   a $120 \times 16 = 1920$ b $1200 \times 16 = 19\,200$
    c $120 \times 160 = 19\,200$ d $12 \times 1.6 = 19.2$
    e $1.2 \times 1.6 = 1.92$ f $12 \times 17 = 204$
3   6
4   a   e.g. $1164 = 521 + 643$
        $750 = 214 + 536$
    b   e.g. $115 = 356 - 241$
5   203
6   a 28×9
        $= (20 \times 9) + (8 \times 9)$
        $= 180 + 72 = 252$
    b $27 \times 28 = 3 \times (9 \times 28)$
        $= 3 \times 252 = 756$
7   $54 \times 3 = 162$

Index